Lecture Notes of the Institute for Computer Sciences, Social Informatics and Telecommunications Engineering 250

More information about this series at http://www.springer.com/series/8197

Victor Odumuyiwa · Ojo Adegboyega
Charles Uwadia (Eds.)

e-Infrastructure
and e-Services
for Developing Countries

9th International Conference, AFRICOMM 2017
Lagos, Nigeria, December 11–12, 2017
Proceedings

 Springer

Editors
Victor Odumuyiwa
Department of Computer Science
University of Lagos
Lagos
Nigeria

Charles Uwadia
University of Lagos
Lagos
Nigeria

Ojo Adegboyega
National University of Ireland, Galway
Galway
Ireland

ISSN 1867-8211   ISSN 1867-822X (electronic)
Lecture Notes of the Institute for Computer Sciences, Social Informatics
and Telecommunications Engineering
ISBN 978-3-319-98826-9   ISBN 978-3-319-98827-6 (eBook)
https://doi.org/10.1007/978-3-319-98827-6

Library of Congress Control Number: 2018950846

This Springer imprint is published by the registered company Springer Nature Switzerland AG
The registered company address is: Gewerbestrasse 11, 6330 Cham, Switzerland

Preface

We are delighted to introduce the proceedings of the 9th European Alliance for Innovation (EAI) International Conference on e-Infrastructure and e-Services for Developing Countries (AFRICOMM 2017) held in Lagos, Nigeria, during December 11–12, 2017. AFRICOMM 2017 provided a unique opportunity for researchers, policy makers, and practitioners in ICT to engage in intellectual discourse and showcase their research output, work, innovations, and on-the-field experiences in advancing ICT deployment and usage in developing countries with emphasis on e-Governance, e-Infrastructure, and e-Business.

The AFRICOMM 2017 technical program, which included 19 full papers, 12 short papers, and 5 workshop papers, was carefully put together to create a formidable experience for the participants. The technical papers were presented in eight sessions: e-Government; Network and Load Management; Digital Inclusion; Knowledge Extraction, Representation and Sharing; Networks and Communications; ICT Applications for Development, Decision Support; and e-Business and e-Services. Aside from the high-quality technical presentations, AFRICOMM 2017 also featured a very enlightening and thought-provoking keynote speech delivered by Dr. Ekwow Spio-Garbrah (Ghana's former Minister for Communications) and a roundtable session involving ICT experts and policy makers from the industry, government, and academia. An international workshop on Internet Measurements Research in Africa (IMRA) was also organized to facilitate discussions on mechanisms and challenges of measuring Africa's Internet topology.

AFRICOMM 2017 would not have been made possible if not for the volunteering efforts of the various committee members who worked tirelessly to ensure the success of the conference. We are greatly indebted to the Technical Program Committee co-chairs, Dr. Victor Odumuyiwa, Dr. Gboyega Ojo, and Prof. Amos David, for their great effort in ensuring a high-quality technical program. Special thanks to the conference manager, Alzbeta Mackova, for striving earnestly to ensure the conference succeeded and for providing great administrative assistance whenever needed. We are also grateful to all authors who submitted their papers to the AFRICOMM 2017 conference and workshop.

AFRICOMM 2017 indeed provided a platform for the cross-fertilization of ideas from participants cutting across Africa and Europe and specifically from over 16 countries including Germany, Ghana, Finland, Italy, Ireland, Kenya, Luxembourg, Malawi, Namibia, Nigeria, Norway, Portugal, Republic of Benin, Rwanda, South Africa, and Uganda.

July 2018   Victor Odumuyiwa
                                                                  Charles Uwadia

Organization

Steering Committee

Imrich Chlamtac (Co-chair)	Create-Net, Italy
Roch Glitho (Co-chair)	Concordia University, Canada and IMSP/ University of Abomey Calavi, Republic of Benin
Karl Jonas	Bonn-Rhein-Sieg University of Applied Science, Germany
David Johnson	Meraka, CSIR and University of Cape Town, South Africa
Yacine Ghamri-Doudane	Université de la Rochelle, France
Bjorn Pehrson	KTH, Sweden

Organizing Committee

General Chair

Charles Uwadia — University of Lagos, Nigeria

General Co-chairs

Florence Oladeji	University of Lagos, Nigeria
Victor Odumuyiwa	University of Lagos, Nigeria

TPC Co-chairs

Amos David	Lorraine University, France
Adegboyega Ojo	Insight Centre for Data Analytics, National University of Ireland, Galway (NUIG)
Victor Odumuyiwa	University of Lagos, Nigeria

Local Chair

Victor Odumuyiwa — University of Lagos, Nigeria

Web Chair

Olusoji Okunoye — University of Lagos, Nigeria

Publicity and Social Media Co-chairs

Chika Yinka-Banjo	University of Lagos, Nigeria
Rossi Kamal	University of Asia Pacific, Kyung Hee University, IEEE Computer Society, Seoul Chapter, South Korea

Workshop Chair

Titi Akinlade   University of Lagos, Nigeria

Sponsorship and Exhibits Chair

Oladipupo Sennaike   University of Lagos, Nigeria

Publications Co-chairs

Victor Odumuyiwa   University of Lagos, Nigeria
Adegboyega Ojo   Insight Centre for Data Analytics, National University
                                        of Ireland, Galway (NUIG)

Panels Chair

Philip Adewole   University of Lagos, Nigeria

Tutorials Chair

Toyin Popoola   University of Lagos, Nigeria

Demos Chair

Babatunde Sawyerr   University of Lagos, Nigeria

Posters and PhD Track Chair

Williams Onifade   University of Ibadan, Nigeria

Industry Forum Co-chairs

Funke Opeke   Mainone
Ifeloju Alakija   Mainone

Conference Manager

Alzbeta Mackova   EAI (European Alliance for Innovation)

Technical Program Committee

Ahmed Kora   ESMT, Dakar, Senegal
Hatem Ben Sta   .
Patrick Chikumba   .
Malo Sadouanouan   Ecole Polytechnique de Bobo-Dioulasso, Burkina Faso
Amos Nugu   DIT
Osianoh Glenn Aliu   Fraunhofer FIT, Germany
Maganizo Monawe   University of Malawi, Malawi
Clement Khalika Banda   University of Malawi, Malawi
Ernesto Damiani   University of Milan, Italy
Idris A. Rai   Makerere University, Uganda

Nizar Bouguila	Concordia University, Montreal, Canada
Thomas Olwal	CSIR
Mesmin Dandjinou	Université Polytechnique de Bobo-Dioulasso, Burkina Faso
Harry Gombachika	University of Malawi, The Polytechnic, Malawi
Max Agueh	LACSC-ECE Paris, France
Pasteur Poda	Université Polytechnique de Bobo-Dioulasso, Burkina Faso
Vincent Oria	NJIT, USA
Isaac Osunmakinde	School of Computing, UNISA, South Africa
Gertjan van Stam	SIRDC
Desire Banse	Prometheus Computing
Oladeji Florence Alaba	University of Lagos, Nigeria
Tiguiane Yélémou	Université polytechnique de Bobo-Dioulasso, Burkina Faso
Boubakar Barry	WACREN
Olufade F. Williams Onifade	University of Ibadan, Nigeria
Tounwendyam Frederic Ouedraogo	Université de Koudougou, Burkina Faso
Marc Lobelle	UCL, Belgium
Iman Abdelrahman	University of Kharthoum, Sudan
Koffi Fabrice	Djossou ARC, South Africa
Karl Jonas	.
Laurence Capus	Université Laval, Canada
Chipo Kanjo	University of Malawi, Chancellor College, Malawi
Kokou Yetongnon	University of Bourgogne, France
Roch Glitho	Concordia University, Canada
Adam Ouorou	Orange Labs, France
Ezin C. Eugene	University of Abomey-Calavi, Republic of Benin
Oladipupo Sennaike	University of Lagos, Nigeria
Adewole Rufai	University of Lagos, Nigeria
Olusoji Okunoye	University of Lagos, Nigeria
Akinlade Titi	University of Lagos, Nigeria
Ebun Fasina	University of Lagos, Nigeria
Porwol Lukasz	Insight Centre, Ireland
Ahmadizeleti Fatemeh	Insight Centre, Ireland
Kretschmer Mathias	Fraunhofer FIT, Germany
Onireti Oluwakayode	.
Yinka-Banjo Chika	University of Lagos, Nigeria
Charles Robert	University of Ibadan, Nigeria

Contents

Knowledge Extraction, Representation and Sharing

Networks and Communications

ICT Applications for Development

Decision Support

e-Business and e-Services

e-Government

A Model for Designing, Implementing and Evaluating Citizen-Centric e-Government in Namibia

Karin Fröhlich$^{(\boxtimes)}$ and Anicia Peters

Department of Informatics, Namibia University of Science and Technology,
Windhoek, Namibia
nangula2013@gmail.com, apeters@nust.na

Abstract. There is a shortage of e-Government research from a citizen-centric perspective within the African continent. Focus has been on how governments can improve service delivery by being efficient and effective. Arguably, the focus of e-Government research appears inspired by the New Public Management theory that aims to import private sector operations into the public sector. While benefits can be drawn from this approach, governments appear to fail to completely play their role of generating public value among citizens. The focus on government's view on e-Government often short charge the citizens who are expected to adopt and use e-Government. This paper adds to the body of knowledge by proposing a model for citizen centric e-Government that is suitable for Namibia.

Keywords: e-Government · Citizen-centric · ICT · Public value

1 Introduction

Despite the plethora of research on electronic government (e-Government) the success of e-Government remains low [1]. The failure rate is even higher within the African continent as reflected by a low electronic participation [2]. African researchers have proposed different models showing factors that could contribute to successful e-Government [2–4]. Of concern is little focus on citizen-centric e-Government. The literature suggests that e-Government constitutes of different stakeholders with different needs [5]. Of all the stakeholders, it is the users who play a critical role that determines the success of e-Government hence the need for citizen-centric e-Government [6]. At international level, research appears to shift towards the proposition of citizen-centric e-Government [5, 7, 8]. Authors have focused on factors for improving electronic service (e-Service) delivery while some have focused on user satisfaction [8]. Some authors focused on factors of designing, implementing and evaluating citizen-centric e-Government [10] while another growing research base has focused on the principles of public value as a determiner for citizen-centric e-Government [7, 9].

The literature presents different models and frameworks that can be adopted to promote citizen-centric e-Government. There seems to be a lack of consensus and conclusion on the subject as researchers suggest similar and different factors. Hence,

© ICST Institute for Computer Sciences, Social Informatics and Telecommunications Engineering 2018
V. Odumuyiwa et al. (Eds.): AFRICOMM 2017, LNICST 250, pp. 3–15, 2018.
https://doi.org/10.1007/978-3-319-98827-6_1

these different models may pose a challenge to under resourced African countries as they look at adopt frameworks or models for implementing citizen-centred e-Government. Besides, contextual factors have shown to play a critical role in shaping the success of e-Government. As such, this study aims to propose a model for citizen-centric e-Government suitable for Namibia. Namibia is one of the countries in Southern Africa that has shown interest in e-Government as reflected by the publication of an e-Government strategic action plan for 2014 to 2018. To meet its objectives, the paper uses public reform theories to justify its view of citizen-centric e-Government. The paper makes use of a literature review to argue for a suitable model of citizen-centric e-Government for Namibia.

1.1   Citizen-Centric e-Government

e-Government has many stakeholders with different interests and objectives. This is clearly shown in the literature were the conceptualisation of e-Government has been mainly from one particular stakeholder, that is the government's point of view with topics of improving public service delivery, accountability, efficiency and transparency taking the centre stage [10, 11]. This focus on government centred e-Government can be attributed to the dominant public sector reform theory a government can adopt. However, the popularity of government centred e-Government has created a shortage of holistic models and theoretical frameworks for evaluating e-Government from other stakeholders' perspective with citizens in particular. This is important given that these stakeholders face unique challenges in relation to their adoption and use of e-Government. [12], in reference to the Obama administration, pointed out that a government's commitment towards transparency through e-Government does not translate to increased citizen engagement or participation. More so, citizens constitute the most significant stakeholders of e-Government services hence their involvement is key to the success of e-Government [5, 6]. By focusing on the interests, aspirations and the ICTs used by the citizens, resultant e-Government platforms are expected to create public value that is widely regarded and expected by the citizens [10, 11]. The next section uses public sector reform theories to explain how investments in e-Government can end up being government centred or citizen-centric.

1.2   Theories on Public Sector Reform

Theories or paradigms that define the way governments operate can be divided according to New Public Management (NPM), joint-up government and public value [10]. According to [10], these public sector reform theories determine the way a government invests and conceptualise e-Government.

NPM and Joint-Up Government. The principles that underlines the NPM theory were copied from the private sector and adopted in government with the idea of making governments efficient, effective and accountable [13]. According to [10], each government is therefore expected to streamline its operations into 'silos' with citizens viewed like customers just like in the private sector. In addition to NPM, the introduction of joined-up government saw a slight shift from NPM public sector reform theory that had more focus on "structural devolution, disaggregation, and single-purpose organizations, to propose a joined-up approach, which treats government as an integrated" unit [10]. The joined-up government public reform focuses on reducing challenges associated with fragmented government structures. However, both the NPM and joined-up government remain closely related with a focus on effectiveness and efficiency though joined-up government advocate for coordination among different government units. As such, technology investments under NPM would see the government focusing on meeting these goals of being more responsive, accountable, transparent, and results-driven, as well as decentralized, efficient, and customer-oriented. This implies that if Namibia assumes a NPM and joined-up government, the government's adoption and use of e-Government would focus on improving service delivery.

Public Value Public Sector Reform. Moore introduced the concept of public value in 1995 [7, 14]. Researchers pointed out that there is no universal definition of what public value is given that it is driven by contextual factors [7, 14]. Different forms of public value can be identified as the government create value for citizens that included operating public organisations effectively and efficiently, promoting "equity, democracy, openness, transparency, confidentiality, responsiveness, environmental sustainability, citizen's self-development, user orientation, quality services" [10]. The public value concept argues that governments do not operate like private companies as assumed by NPM. As such, the public value paradigm suggests that public managers and citizens have a role to play in a society [12]. It is believed that "citizens derive value from the consumption of public services" (Kelly et al. 2002 in [7]) hence the state should be guided by principles of public value in its delivery of public service [11]. This implies that the use of ICTs is not meant to derive benefits to the state alone as suggested by NPM and joined-up government theories but rather help the state create and deliver value to the citizens. This could be reflected by a government's focus on citizen-centric e-Government. For instance, Namibia's e-Government strategic action plan for 2014 to 2018 shows a shift towards citizen-centric e-Government through implementation of these reforms remain behind.

2 Literature Review

Shift towards the emphasis on citizen-centric e-Government has shown a growth in publications aligned to the subject. For instance, [5] used a literature review to propose seven strategies for developing and implementing citizen-centred e-Government. The proposed strategies included comprehensive planning for citizen-centred design; citizen information needs assessments; ICTs availability, expertise and preference; citizen engagement; iterative evaluation for continual improvement; community based partnerships and Politically Based Content and Design [5]. [7] proposed a framework for evaluating public value in e-Government. Their framework was evaluated through a data collection and analysis in Sri Lanka. Their framework concedes that e-Government can create public value through the "delivery of public services (DPS), the efficiency of public organizations (EPO), and achievement of socially desirable outcomes (ASO)" [7]. Three factors determine DPS from a citizen's point of view namely the quality of information, the quality of e-Government service (two way communications) and the extent to which the e-Government platform is user-oriented. EPO is determined by the efficiency of the public office through e-Government and its openness as determined by transparency. Lastly, factors contributing to ASO include equity, self-development, trust in the government and environment sustainability. [7] conceded that the e-Government's compatibility to disabled citizens, use of native language and its available in rural areas promote the equity of e-Government.

[2] did a study aimed at sustainability of electronic participation (e-Participation) in South Africa. Their study looked into reducing the digital divide by engaging mobile technology in extending e-Government. In a way, their study is citizen centric as it focused on exploiting technologies that are popular among citizens in promoting e-Participation. Access to ICTs, ICT skills and attitude were evaluated using data collection and analysis to establish their influence on e-Participation using mobile technology. Their study found that socially excluded citizens are open to the idea of using mobile phones for accessing e-Government service despite a lack of formal structures and policies supporting mobile government (m-Government). Further to that, it was found that citizens' ICT skills and attitude play a critical role in promoting the acceptance of m-Government.

A recent study by Sigwej and Pather [11] evaluated the effectiveness of citizen centric e-Government in Tanzania. The study aimed at proposing a framework for assessing citizen centric e-Government. Sigwej and Pather [11] noted that current frameworks and models for e-Government are not suitable for the African continent hence the need of a "more African-appropriate e-Government metrics" that are shaped by the "African environmental, cultural and contextual factors". A framework proposed by Sigwej and Pather [11] divided e-Government citizen satisfaction into two namely citizen expectations and facilitating conditions. Together, citizen expectations and facilitating conditions influence a citizen's intent to use e-Government service that prompts the use of e-Government services from which citizens derive satisfaction. It should be noted that citizen expectations of e-Government are shaped by the functionality of service and motivation to use service. The functionality of service is determined by performance, service and interoperability. Motivation to use service is determined by trust, ease of use, perceived benefits and internet skills. Facilitating conditions are shaped by an enabling infrastructure and government's preparedness. Factors contributing to enabling infrastructure include internet penetration, accessibility and multichannel. In addition, government preparedness is determined by coordination, commitments from top management, awareness, funding, government process change, towards a citizen-centric mode and legal issues.

3   Namibia's e-Government Initiatives

Namibia has documented a number of policy frameworks and various initiatives towards promoting e-Government. Among them include the Information Technology (IT) policy, the e-Government Policy, Web design standards and guidelines and the e-Government Strategic Action Plan (eGSAP) that is guiding e-Government initiatives since the year 2014 to 2018. Namibia introduced its first e-Government Policy in 2005 at the auspices of the Millennium Declaration that seeks to address some socio-economic challenges faced by countries world over. Namibia's e-Government policy of 2005 focused on four areas namely "service delivery, citizen empowerment, marketing enhancement and development, and exposure and outreach" (Republic of Namibia [15, p. 16]).

Table 1. Strategic goals of e-GSAP for the Public Service [15, p. IV].

Strategic thrust area	Description and goals
Impact and visibility	Aims to achieve streamline and efficient Government operations, as well as improved online services by 2018
Collaboration and networking	Aims to achieve networked OMAs sharing Government resources (data, infrastructure, services and solutions) through a collaborative approach by 2018
Consistency and standardisation	Aims to achieve a homogeneous, standardised and consistent approach, interfaces and interactions for developing and implementing solutions and rendering of services by Government by 2016
Training, education and research	Aims to have: • A skilled and able workforce to render public services, and • Skilled and able citizens, communities and business participation in e-Government services
Foundational support	Aims to have well-founded laws, policies and institutions in place by 2015 to drive e-Government reform

An improved eGSAP that aims to guide e-Government initiatives from the year 2014 to 2018 was introduced and it brought in new changes on the 2005 e-Government policy. The current eGSAP policy is guided by a vision: *"To be a Leading Networked Government, providing Client-centred, Transparent, Affordable and Efficient Services to All."* Table 1 shows a summary of the key thrust areas that guide the eGSAP for 2014 to2018.

Despite the notable progressing on coming up with a policy for e-Government, Namibia is considered one of the countries that need to make progress in the designing and implementation of e-Government. The Republic of Namibia [15] report that, in terms of e-Government electronic readiness (e-readiness), Namibia is rated 2.2 out of 4. Namibia has e-Government supporting policies (rated 2.11 out of 4); with e-Government accessibility by different stakeholders rated 2.71 out of 4. However, Namibia does not seem to exploit different ICTs for e-Government purposes (rated 1.95 out of 4) and have a shortage of ICT skills (rated 2.21 out of 4) with a low willingness to use e-Government, rated 2.05. The United Nations' [16] e-Government Development Index (EGDI) rated Namibia 117th world-over after looking at the provision of online services, telecommunication connectivity and human capacity. However, Namibia is among the top ten in Africa in terms of e-Government readiness.

Findings by the United Nations [16] shows that Namibia's e-Government services are mainly (69%) focused on the provision of information to citizens with a few (32%) the government's websites making provisions for two-way communication such as downloading and submitting forms online. Tomlinson [17] made similar observations as he concluded that Namibia's government agencies websites are informational, interactive and rarely does one come across transaction-oriented websites. In particular to telecommunication connectivity, Namibia has few people with fixed broadband with only 2.91 per 100 inhabitants having broadband [16]. The majority of citizens have access to mobile phone communication with 107.79 having access per 100 inhabitants [16].

4 Methodology

The paper uses a literature review to argue for a citizen-centric model suitable for the Namibian government. The paper combines and renames some of factors of citizen centric e-Government that were proposed in the literature. The paper is therefore guided by the literature in identifying factors of citizen-centric. Table 2 shows a summary of studies that were considered to identify factors of citizen-centric e-Government. It should be noted that there is quite a few studies research in Africa that have focused on citizen centric e-Government [11].

Table 2. The identified factors of citizen-centric.

Factor	Category of factor	Source
Planning for citizen-centred design		[5]
Citizen information needs assessments		
ICTs availability, expertise and preference		
Citizen engagement		
Iterative evaluation for continual improvement		
Community based partnerships		
Politically based content and design		
Quality of information	Delivery of public services	[7]
e-Government service		
User-orientation		
Efficiency	Efficiency of public organizations	
Openness		
Equity	Achievement of socially desirable outcomes	
Self-development		
Trust		
Environment sustainability		

(*continued*)

Table 2. (continued)

Factor	Category of factor	Source
Access to ICTs		[2]
ICT skills		
Attitude		
Citizen expectations factors		[11]
Performance	Functionality of service	
Service		
Interoperability		
Trust	Motivation	
Ease of use		
Perceived benefits		
Internet skills		
Facilitating conditions		
Internet penetration	Enabling infrastructure	
Accessibility		
Multichannel		
Coordination	Government preparedness	
Commitments from top management		
Awareness		
Funding		
Government process change		
Towards a citizen-centric mode		
Legal issues		

5 The Proposed Model for Citizen-Centric e-Government

This study proposes a citizen-centric e-Government model that encompasses the e-Government design and implementation, and evaluation component. The study adopts an empirically evaluated public value driven citizen-centric e-Government evaluation framework proposed by Karunasena and Deng [7]. Karunasena and Deng's [7] framework is based on a thoroughly tested public value in e-Government model by Kearns that has since been applied in different countries and sectors of the economy such as the United Kingdom's electronic health initiatives. However, this study is of the view that a model that focuses on evaluating e-Government may not be adequate to address challenges faced by developing countries in Africa given that the majority of the countries' e-Government presence remains low. This occurrence is common in Namibia were there has been good e-Government frameworks with little progress when it comes to implementation. As such, this study incorporates the e-Government design and implementation component that could guide governments on the design factors that should be in place and create a platform for generating public value through e-Government. These design and implementation, and evaluation components are considered from a citizen-centric perspective.

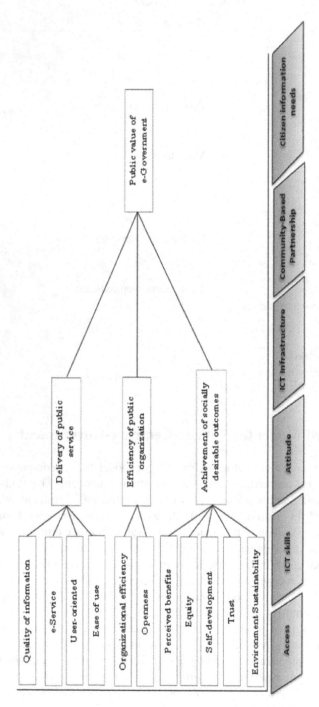

Fig. 1. The proposed model for citizen-centric e-Government for Namibia

5.1   The e-Government Design and Implementation Component

Figure 1 gives a summary of a model of e-Government design, implementation and evaluation suitable for Namibia. The model emphasises the fact that, if Namibia's e-Government is to be a success, it is important that the government centres the design and implementation of its e-Government around the accessibility of ICTs, technologies used by citizens and preferred languages; citizens' ICT skill development; look into partnering e-Government with community based partnerships like schools; ICT infrastructure and taking into account citizen's information needs. In addition, the resultant e-Government should be able to create public value in three ways namely delivery of public services, efficiency of public organizations and achievement of socially desirable outcomes.

Factors of e-Government Design and Implementation

Access to ICTs. Jaeger and Bertot [5] noted that governments should understand technology access capabilities of citizens if they are to develop systems that meet their needs. The Namibian e-Government platforms are mainly informational and not mobile phone compatible something that can limit their accessibility [15, 16]. This is a factor of great concern given that few (2.91 per 100 inhabitants) Namibians have fixed broadband connection compared to those who have access to mobile phones (107.79 per 100 inhabitants) [16]. Interestingly, the majority of citizens are now using mobile phones to access ICT services with 80% Namibians accessing the internet via mobile phones [18]. Further to that, issues pertaining to language and access to electricity are also critical factors that define the accessibility of e-Government services [19]. The study agrees with [19] who states that "policy design issues for e-Government need to consider measures or modes available for accessing information from e-Government systems, especially through the national information infrastructure." Similarly, [20] supports this idea by indicating that governments should look for ways to promote the access of e-Government through mobile phones given their wide acceptance even in countries with low internet penetration rates.

ICT Skills. A literature review by [2] noted that a shortage of ICT skills is one of the factors contributing to the digital divide. With Namibia moving towards a knowledge based economy in 2030, it is expected that ICT skills will play an important role. Van Deursen and Van Dijk (2010) in [5] found that such internet skills can include: "Operational Skills: The skills to operate computer and network hardware and software; Information Skills: The skills to search, select and process information in computer and network sources; and Strategic Skills: The capacities to use these sources as the means for specific goals and for the general goal of improving one's position in society". To affirm the importance of skills, the Republic of Namibia's [15] e-GSAP for the Public Service assets that Namibia aims to have a "skilled and able citizens, communities and business participation in e-Government services." However, one of the limitations of the e-GSAP in this regard is that the government's focus on training, education and research on ICTs is limited to civil servants with e-Government awareness programs being extended to citizens [15].

Community-Based Partnership. Making reference to the United States of America, [5] recommended that citizen centric e-Government has to integrate into community-based partnerships such as public libraries to increase its acceptance. On the other hand, [19] suggest that e-Government need to be understood within the African context and explore ways to make it relevant. This can be achieved by building social structures at community level that support ICTs for e-Government use. In Namibia, this could be facilitated through schools distributed across the country. Such an approach limits the practice of "the government 'off-loading' e-Government services, instructions and support to community organizations without coordinating, training, and involvement" something that is less likely to promote citizen-oriented services [5]. Training, education and research is one of the five key strategic areas as highlighted in the e-GSAP for the Public Service [15]. Through its Science, Technology, Engineering and Mathematics (STEM) programme, Namibia is promoting the growth of science and technology skills across the nation with primary and secondary schools expected to play a key role. Hence, the study suggests it would increase the acceptance of e-Government services if they are distributed through these educational institutions.

Citizen Information Needs. This study agrees with [5] that if e-Government is to be citizen centric, it is important that the designers of e-Government understand the citizens' information needs. Jaeger and Bertot [5] went on to state that "governments need to understand how citizens:

- Seek information on a particular topic or issues (strategy)
- Acquire information on a topic or issue (acquisition)
- Solicit expertise (source)
- Use of that information (application)"
- In addition, a study by [21] reports of changes in the way citizens search and consume information. She noted that a sizable amount of USA citizens no longer rely on accessing information from the government website, rather they make use of the social media. Thus, there seems to be a growing trust in information received via a friendship network such as Facebook [21]. Further to that the use of social media has gained popularity across different age groups, income groups, culture groups, gender and geographic location. Accordingly, the Namibian government need to design e-Government services that reach out to technologies used by its citizens for accessing and sharing information. A study by [18] found that Namibian internet users access internet over the phone for purposes of engaging on social media sites like Facebook.

ICT Infrastructure. This paper suggests that Namibia should look into the provision of an ICT infrastructure. This can include the provision ICT supporting infrastructure like electricity. Further to that, findings of few Namibians who have access to fixed broadband suggest a need to widen internet access to other regions. [11] note that for a successful citizen centric e-Government, there is a need for improving internet penetration, accessibility and increasing the use of multichannel. This is critical to Namibia given a low internet penetration in the rural areas that is further complicated by the lack of electricity in other sections [15]. It has already been noted that most rural residences are excluded from access and participation in e-Government due to a lack of telecommunication connectivity for broadband despite the high numbers of mobile phone and mobile phone users [22].

Attitude. There is a growing belief that attitude is slowly becoming one of the important factors that determines ICT use [2]. Studies on e-Government have shown that attitude can be one of the determining factors of e-Government use. For example, [15] note that the willingness among various stakeholders to use ICTs can play an important role in the use of e-Government. Therefore, attitude is considered one of the factors that could influence the design and implementation of citizen centric e-Government. The study suggests that the government need to understand the attitude towards technology in its designing and implementation of e-Government. Such information can be critical in influence the citizens' attitude towards the use of ICTs in government.

5.2 Factors of e-Government Evaluation

The previous section discussed factors that could play a critical role in informing e-Government services designers and implementers on how to structure and distribute the respective e-Services. As indicated earlier, the study argues that maintaining an e-Government presence will not guarantee its success. Hence there is a need for e-Government citizen centric evaluation that could inform the extent of use as determined by the value e-Government creates to citizens. The study adopts and uses Karunasena and Deng's [7] criterion of e-Government public value creation. The next section discusses factors of e-Government evaluation.

Delivery of Public Services (DPS). Three factors play an important role in determining DPS. These include the quality of information, e-Services and user-orientation of e-Government [7]. For instance, studies have shown that citizens expect to find accurate information that is timely disseminated, expect to be able to perform two way transaction using simple e-Services and expect to use e-Government websites that are easy to remember [7, 20]. Shea and Garson (2010) in [21] even noted the need for "one-stop shopping or transaction-oriented websites". Mergel [21] went on to recommend real-time two way information communication between government and citizens via e-Government. As indicated earlier, Namibia's current e-Government is characterised with static information that need to be revamped if they are to deliver public service to the citizens. The Republic of Namibia's [15] impact and visibility, one of the strategic objectives in the e-GSAP complement the need for citizen-centric service delivery. Issues cited include one-stop shop portals, delivery of timely and accurate information. Further to that, a user's perception on the e-Government's ease of use can play a critical role in evaluating the extent to which they are citizen-centred.

The Efficiency of Public Organizations (EPO). [7] found that improving the access of ICT infrastructure that focuses on enhancing public operations a key element to the generation of public value. It was also noted that equipping public organisation employees with ICT skills and re-engineering public organisation business processes around principles of citizen centric adding to public value. However, it is important to realise that government's initiatives of using ICTs to save money by cutting employees is not considered as creating public value [7]. Hence, it can be suggested that Namibia look into these critical factors and improve its service delivery using e-Government. For instance, the government can align its e-Government programs with grassroots level social activities like the traditional approaches to governance participation such as the regularly held indaba, "a council or conference for deliberations" [4].

Achievement of Socially Desirable Outcomes (ASO). Research findings by [7] suggest that the government can use e-Government and create public value to citizens by meeting their social desirable outcomes. Social desirable can differ in respect to the country in question. In reference to Sri Lanka, it was noted that citizens value education such as electronic content with "children education low cost ICT training, applications that help to develop social and network skills, and availability of resources to develop the ICT skills of citizens" [7]. In addition, citizens show to value government trust, privacy of their sensitive information in e-Government systems and the respect of law. Similarly, Namibia can use e-Government to advance social desirable goals such as those in training, education and research, and other major government reform programs such as the Harambe Prosperity Plan. Research findings by [11] suggest the perceived benefits to be derived from using e-Government can also play an influential role among Namibians.

6   Conclusion

The study motivates for citizen-centric e-Government. It uses public reform theories to justify its view for generating public value through e-Government. A literature review on citizen-centric e-Government was conducted. Using the literature, the study proposed a model of citizen-centric e-Government that could be suitable for Namibia. The study argues that, while it is important to evaluate the extent or effectiveness of e-Government's citizen-centric, it is also important to give government guidance on important factors that need to be looked into when designing and implementing e-Government. A literature review has shown that governments' e-Government implementations are often not tailor made to align with technologies used by citizens. Accordingly, the proposed model gives an outline for factors that are critical in e-Government designing and implementation, and evaluation. The study agrees with the current state of literature that suggests a need to evaluate the extent to which an e-Government platform is citizen-centric.

References

1. Larsson, H., Grönlund, A.: Future-oriented eGovernance: the sustainability concept in eGov research, and ways forward. Gov. Inf. Q. **31**(2014), 137–149 (2014)
2. Ochara, N.M., Mawela, T.: Enabling social sustainability of e-participation through mobile technology. Inf. Technol. Dev. **21**(2), 205–228 (2013)
3. Bwalya, K.J., Healy, M.: Harnessing e-government adoption in the SADC region: a conceptual underppining. Electron. J. e-Gov. **8**(1), 23–32 (2010)

4. Ochara, N.M.: Grass roots community participation as a key to e-governance sustainability in Africa. Afr. J. Inf. Commun. **12**(2012), 26–47 (2012)
5. Jaeger, P.T., Bertot, J.C.: Designing, implementing, and evaluating user-centered and citizen-centered e-government. Int. J. Electron. Gov. Res. **6**(2), 1–17 (2010)
6. Sorn-in, K., Tuamsuk, K., Chaopanon, W.: Factors affecting the development of e-government using a citizen-centric approach. J. Sci. Technol. Policy Manag. **6**(3), 206–222 (2015)
7. Karunasena, K., Deng, H.: A revised framework for evaluating the public value of e-Government. In: 15th Pacific Asia Conference on Information Systems (PACIS 2011), pp. 1–12. AIS (2011)
8. Osman, I.H., et al.: COBRA framework to evaluate e-government services: a citizen-centric perspective. Gov. Inf. Q. **31**(2), 243–256 (2014)
9. Bai, W.: A public value based framework for evaluating the performance of e-Government in China. iBusiness **5**, 26–29 (2013)
10. Karunasena, K., Deng, H.: A citizen-oriented approach for evaluating the performance of e-Government in Sri Lanka. Int. J. Electron. Gov. Res. (IJEGR) **8**(1), 43–63 (2012)
11. Sigwejo, A., Pather, S.: A citizen-centric framework for assessing e-Government effectiveness. Electron. J. Inf. Syst. Dev. Ctries. **74**, 1–27 (2016)
12. Jaeger, P.T., Bertot, J.C.: Transparency and technological change: ensuring equal and sustained public access to government information. Gov. Inf. Q. **27**(4), 371–376 (2010)
13. Chadwick, A., May, C.: Interaction between states and citizens in the age of the internet: "e-Government" in the United States, Britain, and the European Union. Governance **16**(2), 271–300 (2003)
14. Cordella, A., Bonina, C.M.: A public value perspective for ICT enabled public sector reforms: a theoretical reflection. Gov. Inf. Q. **29**(2012), 512–520 (2012)
15. Republic of Namibia: e-Government Strategic Action Plan for the Republic of Namibia (2014). http://bit.ly/1Ehgl3N
16. United Nations: United Nations e-Government Survey 2014. e-Government for the Future We Want. Economic and Social Affairs. United Nations (2014)
17. Tomlinson, J.: e-Government in Namibia. Unpublished document. LIS 619/Debbie Rabina (2011)
18. Stork, C., Calandro, E., Gillwald, A.: Internet going mobile: internet access and use in 11 African countries. info **15**(5), 34–51 (2013)
19. Ochara, N.M.: Emergence of the e-Government artifact in an environment of social exclusion in Kenya. Afr. J. Inf. Syst. **1**(1), 18–43 (2008)
20. Criado, J.G., Gil-García, J.R.: Electronic government and public policy current status and future trends in Latin America. Gestión y Política Pública **22**(2), 3A–3A (2013)
21. Mergel, I.: Social Media in the Public Sector: A Guide to Participation, Collaboration and Transparency in the Networked World. Wiley, Hoboken (2012)
22. Ministry of Information and Technology: 2nd National ICT Summit: Bridging the Digital Divide, Windhoek, Namibia (2015)

Towards an Interoperability
e-Government Framework for Uganda

Benjamin Kanagwa(✉), Joyce Nakatumba-Nabende, Raymond Mugwanya,
Evelyn Kigozi Kahiigi, and Silas Ngabirano

Makerere University, Kampala, Uganda
{bkanagwa,jnakatumba,rmugwanya,ekahiigi}@cis.mak.ac.ug
ngabirano.silas@gmail.com

Abstract. In the absence of a single entity that develops all systems
for government, there is need to support a common understanding of the
development environments such that new products can easily be integrated within existing services. Owing to the size of governments, different departments tend to conceive and develop services independently
and yet they serve the same citizens. These services should be consistent
regardless of which entity is providing the service. This paper proposes a
National Enterprise Architecture (NEA) to support the implementation
of an e-government interoperability framework (e-GIF). The architecture is driven by a Service Oriented Architecture (SOA) model and uses
ontologies to provide semantic interoperability.

Keywords: Interoperability · e-government · Enterprise architecture

1 Introduction

Most government services are being delivered through the use of Information
and Communication Technology (ICT). The Government of Uganda through the
National IT Authority Uganda (NITA-U)[1] is supporting several e-government
systems which include: systems for registration of persons (e.g. national identity cards, passport and driving permit), business registration systems, Integrated Financial Management System, Integrated Personnel and Payroll System (IPPS), e-Tax System, and the e-Visa Application System. However, most
of these systems are decentralized and interoperability between them is not
achieved.

As a result, there are numerous failed initiatives of adoption of e-government
frameworks especially in developing countries. This can be attributed to the fact
that the development process is mainly inclined to technology while eliminating
the non-technical issues which affect the main goal of interoperability [16]. As
[12] asserts, an important step in achieving seamless delivery of public services
across government entities is ensuring that the systems used are compatible and

---

[1] http://www.nita.go.ug.

© ICST Institute for Computer Sciences, Social Informatics and Telecommunications Engineering 2018
V. Odumuyiwa et al. (Eds.): AFRICOMM 2017, LNICST 250, pp. 16–28, 2018.
https://doi.org/10.1007/978-3-319-98827-6_2

interface coherently. This requires a holistic approach that defines standards and structures for any e-government system to be able to share information and processes.

In this paper, we propose an e-government interoperability framework (e-GIF) that is based on an ontology enabled National Enterprise Architecture (NEA) driven by a Service Oriented Architecture (SOA) model and interoperability standards developed for use as a reference for implementing e-government systems in Uganda. The developed e-GIF was evaluated by users, application developers and public service officials who used their knowledge of software engineering and public service delivery to validate the framework for appropriateness, completeness and accuracy.

The rest of this paper is organized as follows. First, we provide an overview of related work in Sect. 2. Section 3 discusses the methodology used in this paper. Section 4 discusses the interoperability framework introduced in this paper. We discuss the evaluation carried out based on the framework in Sect. 5. Finally, Sect. 6 concludes the paper.

2   Related Work

E-government interoperability is the ability for government agencies to use ICTs to meaningfully and seamlessly exchange and use information [23]. As stated in [16], interoperability can be defined at three levels of operation: organizational, semantic and technical [1,13]. These dimensions also form the capabilities of an e-GIF required to improve interoperability [13]. Interoperability improvement can be achieved through the right mix of policy, structure, standards, process, management and technology across all these three constructs. Consequently improving the ability of government organizations to deliver coordinated public services [13,16].

Review of Existing e-GIFs: There have been several initiatives to develop e-GIFs and here we analyze some existing e-GIFs drawn from different countries at different levels of economic development and e-government maturity. This analysis was based on their scope, design principles and conceptual frameworks.

Scope of the Framework: This covers the interoperability dimensions and categories of the e-services offered. The e-GIF's in Estonia [8], Nepal [21] and Mozambique [19] provided detailed organizational interoperability. All these e-GIF's offered the common e-government services. The UK [22] and Estonia e-GIFs provide for Government to other Government e-services, while Estonia also provided for the private sector to implement the e-GIF in their own Business to Business services.

Design Principles: This parameter covers the guiding principles on which the e-GIFs are based. All the e-GIFs recommended the e-government applications to be Internet based and the use of open standards. Other common design principles included resource sharing and reuse, collaboration, scalability and confidentiality.

For example, Estonia and Australia [3] use federated identity management where the users can use various identities for authentication and authorization to access the e-government systems.

Conceptual Framework: This identifies which components of the e-GIFs that semantic and technical interoperability used. The European Interoperability Framework (EIF) [14] provides conceptual guidance for the creation of an European Interoperability Reference Architecture (EIRA). In general, all the e-GIFs identify interoperability standards for implementing (i) interconnection; (ii) data integration; (iii) content management and metadata; (iv) information access and presentation; and (v) security. All the e-GIFs recommend the use of SOA and XML standards. With the exception of Nepal and Estonia who used ontologies. All the e-GIFs recommend and adopt metadata standards for semantic interoperability.

Review of Enterprise Architecture Development Frameworks: Numerous authors have carried out a comprehensive survey to provide comparisons between the leading enterprise architecture frameworks and modeling tools [2,4,9,10,20,24]. The work carried out in [2] affirms that a large number of organizations apply one of these three enterprise architecture frameworks because of their level of maturity: the Zachman framework [25], the Open Group Architecture Framework (TOGAF) [11], and the Federal Enterprise Architecture (FEA) [6]. The Zachman's Framework focuses on constructing views of an enterprise rather than on providing a process for the creation of an architectural description [4,25].

The TOGAF has an Architecture Development Method which is used as a process to describe how to create an enterprise architecture [4,11]. The Federal Enterprise Architecture Framework (FEAF) extends the Zachman Architecture Framework. It comprises a set of models, principles, and methods that are used to implement an enterprise architecture. The framework provides a means to communicate information about architectural artifacts, their relationships to each other, and to their stakeholders using a common vocabulary [4,20]. Another prominent framework is the new European Interoperability Framework [14] that provides specific guidance on how to improve governance of interoperability activities, establish cross-organizational relationships, streamline processes supporting end-to-end digital services, and ensure that both existing and new legislation do not compromise interoperability efforts. Although, these are the most popular frameworks, there is not a single framework that addresses all the needs of a particular organization. This is one of the leading reasons as to why organizations are taking a hybrid framework approach in developing an Enterprise Architecture Framework [9,24].

In this paper we extend the TOGAF framework as it provides a holistic and systemic view of all Enterprise Architecture components, and their business, organizational and environmental contexts. We further adopt a Service Oriented Architecture and an e-government ontology which provides for a classification methodology that can be used by a government to create a common understanding of concepts based on the country's laws policies and procedures

[15]. The uniqueness of this approach is that the interoperability requirements are elicited from the actual practitioners and are analyzed to derive the design principles and specifications the proposed e-GIF.

3   Methodology

The requirements elicitation phase commenced with the selection of the repondents. A purposive sample selection method was used where 20 Ministries and 10 Agencies were selected. A questionnaire guide was designed for eliciting the interoperability requirements from officials in the selected Ministries and Agencies. Data collection was carried out using interviews and observations. Interviews were held with the key informants using the questionnaire guide. The key informants for this study were domain experts who included heads of IT departments, heads of user departments and industry experts such as Application Developers.

In order to acclimatize ourselves with the finer intricacies of the existing systems in use, we carried out observations of some of these systems while in use and also got to interview some of the actual users. Our interactions with the users focused on analyzing the systems' interfaces in relation to (i) the application boundaries; (ii) stakeholder satisfaction; and (iii) inputs/outputs processing. Lastly, we also studied some of the systems' manuals so as to understand further the interoperability requirements in relation to the existing systems.

3.1   Analysis and Design Phase

During this phase, the requirements collected from the field were edited and categorized into main themes and sub themes for analysis. The major themes were namely (i) current state, (ii) desired state and (iii) adoption factors for interoperability. The responses under each theme were further sub-divided into sub-missions according to the earlier identified dimensions of interoperability. Lastly, the categorization of the findings and the subsequent data analysis were aligned to the research objective. The results from this analysis were then used to develop the interoperability Framework design principles and the aggregated interoperability requirements.

3.2   Framework Design and Evaluation

Overall, the development of the e-GIF was guided by the interoperability design principles and the aggregated interoperability requirements developed from the analysis and design phase. Two comparative studies, one on existing e-GIFs and the other on Enterprise Architectures were carried. Some of the lessons learned from these studies were later adopted into the proposed interoperability framework. In addition, we propose standards guidelines that are based on industry best practice and the interoperability design principles and aggregated requirements developed from the analysis and design phase. A case study on the registration of a natural person was also carried out to demonstration e-government interoperability. The interoperability Framework thus developed was presented to a focus group for validation and the feedback obtained was then used to fine tune the e-GIF. The evaluation employed the Enterprise Architecture (EA) Scorecard [18] which provides a qualitative measure of EA quality and completeness.

4   The Framework

Our architectural framework follows the TOGAF version 9 architecture development methodology [11]. Unlike TOGAF which has four major domains, the proposed architecture has five major domains namely (i) the services architecture; (ii) the business processes architecture, (iii) the data architecture; (iv) the organizational architecture; and (v) the technology architecture as illustrated in Fig. 1.

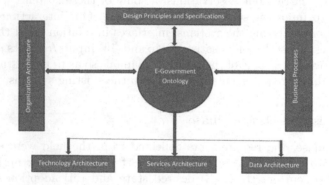

Fig. 1. Enterprise Architecture of the framework that consists of organizational architecture, technology architecture, services architecture, business process architecture and the data architecture.

A central aspect to this architectural framework is an e-Government ontology which is the main engine for driving interoperability. The interactions between architectural components are guided by the concepts, relationships and rules defined in the e-government ontology. Overall, the architecture is premised on a SOA model [24] that is realized using Web Services [17]. The section that follows briefly explains the different architecture components.

4.1   e-Government Ontology

The e-Government ontology concepts, attributes, relationships and axioms form the basis upon which the XML Schemas of the exchanged messages are built. All the messages exchanged by the Web services must comply with the terminology, semantics, business rules, data structures, coding and naming schemes agreed upon in the ontology in order for such messages to be processed and exchanged in a meaningful manner. The e-government ontology is decomposed into modules that form the e-government domain. The modules are based on the major government services.

Typical modules include the Registration, Financial, Health Services and Support Service Modules. Each module contains the following artifacts: (i) Concepts which are the objects under each module (ii) Properties: for each concept, e.g. a concept Person may have attributes such as identification number, surname, etc. (iii) Relationships: identify and define the relationships between concepts and properties, e.g., the relationship between the concepts Person and Voter may be depicted as Voter *is-a* Person and (iv) Constraints - determine the rules that bind the concepts, attributes and the relations, e.g., a person must have only one national identification number.

Figure 2 shows an example of ontological relationships between the various registration documents for registration of persons. Due to space limitations we include only small part of the ontology. Under the Uganda Registration of Persons Act of 2015, all persons resident in Uganda should be registered except for refugees and visitors whose stay in the country does not exceed a period of 90 days. The officially recognized registration documents

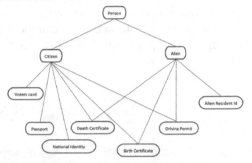

Fig. 2. Part of ontology for Registration of Persons.

include: (i) birth certificate; (ii) baptism card; (iii) immunization card; (iv) voters identification card; (v) immigration document; (vi) National identity card; (vii) valid Ugandan or foreign Passport; (viii) valid driving permit; (ix) valid residence permit; (x) certificate of acquired citizenship.

4.2   Services Architecture

In order to achieve high levels of interoperability, the e-Government services must be defined from a global perspective and not separately for each entity. The choice is to use web services implementation of SOA. The individual services provided by Government entities are loosely coupled with little dependence. Due to the scalability requirements of National Enterprise Architecture, the services are provided over the Internet using web services. The following characteristics are provided by web services: (i) communicate via open Internet protocols (such as HTTP, SMTP); (ii) process XML messages framed using SOAP; (iii) use XML schemas to describe messages; (iv) WSDL [5] will be used to provide an endpoint description of the web service; (v) web services can be discovered by use of the UDDI registry [7]. The web services metadata must be stored in a globally accessible services repository. Further, these services should be loosely coupled such that it is easy to add or modify the services so as to enable the building of new business processes thus supporting the evolution and sustainable maintenance of the systems which is one of the core design principles for the overall proposed architecture framework.

4.3   Business Process Architecture

The business process architecture is a segmentation of logically related tasks performed to achieve a defined business outcome. As shown in Fig. 3 the business process architecture is comprised of sub-components namely: process categories, activities and tasks. *Major Process Categories* are based on the purpose and outcome of the business process, e.g., registration. The *Sub-categories* are complete sets of related activities which transform inputs into outputs under a given major category, e.g., Human Resources Management System. The *Activities* are sets of actions carried out in each sub category, e.g., under the Human Resources Management System the activities can include recruitment, leave roster management, and staff deployment. The *Tasks* are the individual actions that are carried out under each activity.

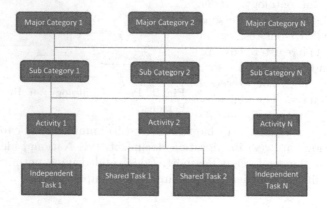

Fig. 3. Business Process Architecture comprises of the major process categories based on the purpose and outcome of the business process.

The business process architecture identifies the relationships between the tasks. This information provides key input for the development of the both atomic and compound services. Functionality for reusable tasks are built into common Web services. In our running example, the personal registration and verification is a common task that is shared across different services.

4.4   Data Architecture

The data architecture promotes the common identification, use and sharing of data across the Government entities through the standardization of the data. As illustrated in Fig. 4, the major components of the data architecture include: (i) metadata standards, (ii) data integration standards, and (iii) information access and presentation standards.

Fig. 4. Data Architecture that consists of three major components: metadata standards, data integration standards, and information access and presentation standards.

The aim of the metadata standards is to provide a means to uniformly describe data, thereby supporting its discoverability and shareability. The metadata standards are comprised of two sub-elements namely: (a) Naming and addressing data standards: which follow a predefined set of rules for choosing the character sequences to be used for identifiers. They denote objects such as variables, types, web services in the source code and documentation; and (b) Database of databases: this is a repository of metadata and statistics about all databases used by the e-government applications.

4.5   Organization Architecture

This provides mechanisms for implementing and managing the entities while facilitating inter-agency collaboration. The processes carried out while implementing the organizational architecture include: (i) Aligning the business goals and organizational resources with the e-government infrastructure; (ii) Implementing business process re-engineering; (iii) Planning and executing migration plans from the legacy systems to the new e-government applications; (iv) Carrying out quality assurance of the e-government applications and products; and (v) Ensuring compliance to the interoperability framework. Due to scope constraints, the organizational architecture was not developed further in this study.

The main benefits to be derived from the use of the developed architecture include: (a) Alignment of the business goals to the IT infrastructure through the various architecture artifacts, like the Business Process Architecture, the Technology architecture, the data architecture and the services architecture; (b) Development of the e-government ontology which provides a common vocabulary for sharing information across multiple software agents; (c) Provision of a governance mechanism to conform compliance with the interoperability requirements; (d) Provision of a mechanism through which entities can collaborate while managing changes to facilitate manageable growth of large scale government systems; (e) Provision of a database of databases which functions as a central control registry of e-government databases where no database will be allowed to operate without being registered in this central database. This helps to address the problem of data redundancy where entities re-register information already registered in the databases of other institutions.

5   Framework Evaluation

In this section, we present an evaluation of the e-GIF framework in order to determine its suitability for implementing interoperability of e-government services. The analysis of the evaluation results was done for each of the six levels of abstraction: contextual, environmental, conceptual, logical, physical and transformational levels. At each level the analysis was done with respect to each aspect area: *business, information, information systems* and *technical infrastructure*.

In accordance with the EA Scorecard methodology, a score of two was awarded for each clear rating, one for each partially clear rating and zero for each unclear rating. The detailed scores for each evaluator were aggregated for each abstract level and aspect area. Given that a question that produced a clear response was awarded two (2) points, then the possible maximum points per level were equivalent to 2 points * total number of questions in that level. The individual points at each level and aspect area where then summed up using Microsoft Visual Fox Pro database management software.

5.1   Results from the Evaluation

Table 1 provides a summary of the results from the evaluation of the architecture. The results shown here are presented based on the Enterprise Architecture Scorecard [18] which summarizes the rating for each aspect areas and abstract level. In the following, we discuss the results shown in Table 1 in more detail.

Table 1. Summary of the evaluation framework scores (%) based on the Enterprise Architecture scorecard which highlights the different abstract levels and aspect areas of the framework.

Abstract Levels	Aspect areas			
	Business	Information	Information systems	Technical infrastructure
Contextual	75	68.8	56.3	54.7
Environmental	62.5	45	55	67.5
Conceptual	50	42.5	50	62.5
Logical	54.2	43.8	58.3	64.6
Physical	54.2	58.3	70.8	68.8
Transformational	35	22.5	52.5	47.5

In provide a summary of the aspect areas that were scored well and the ones that were scored poorly under each abstract level as shown in Table 1.

Contextual Level: Was used to measure the extent to which the architecture meet the scope, mission and vision of the organization. The *Business* aspect area had an average score of 75% which indicates that the proposed architecture satisfies the business goals of the client who is the Government of Uganda (GOU) and that the architecture is based on appropriate business drivers and concepts. The technical infrastructure aspect area had an average score of 54.7% which implies that the architecture satisfies the technical infrastructure requirements in respect to the technical goals, drivers and concepts.

Environmental Level: Measured the business relationships and information flows. The *Business* aspect area had an average score of 62.5% which implied that the architecture meets the requirements for business collaborations between the various MDAs. The *Information* aspect area had a low score of 45% and the framework does not model all the possible information exchanges that are required in a fully automated e-government environment.

Conceptual Level: Explored the architectural functional and non-functional requirements, goals and objectives. The *Information* aspect area had an average score of 42.5% which implied that the architecture does not sufficiently meet the required level of information interaction. This result is attributed to the lack of enough detailed functional requirements for the GOU since the proposed solution put more emphasis on specifying requirements for a few selected priority areas. The *Technical infrastructure* aspect area had an average score of 62.5% which implies that the provision for inter-connection at the conceptual level is sufficiently high.

Logical Level: Measured the logical solutions and sub-functions within each aspect area. The *Information* aspect area had an average score of 43.8% which implies that the architecture did not sufficiently provide for all the possible types of information interaction since the focus here was on only a few subfunctions that the architecture performs. The *Technical infrastructure* aspect area had an average score of 64.6% which showed that the type of interconnection proposed in the architecture has sufficient interconnection layers.

Physical Level: Was concerned with assessing the physical solutions, concrete products and techniques proposed in the architecture. The *Business* aspect area had an average score of 54.2% which indicated that the proposed architecture has sufficient business solutions for the MDAs to collaborate at the physical business level. The *Information systems* aspect area had an average score of 70.8% which implied that the proposed architecture has excellent provisions for interoperability at the physical level.

Transformational Level: Was concerned with assessing the impact of the architecture on the enterprise after its implementation. The *Information* aspect had an average score of 22.5% which showed that the proposed architecture does not have adequate provisions for changes in information interaction. The focus was not on all the possible information exchanges that are required in a fully automated e-government environment. The *Information systems* aspect area had an average score of 52.5% which indicated that the provisions for change in the information systems are adequate.

5.2 Discussion

It is pertinent to note that four aspect areas do not have an equal impact on the enterprise architecture. However, in this study all the aspect areas were considered to be of equal importance. The results show that the information aspect area received the least scores compared to all the other aspect areas across four of the five abstract levels. This could be attributed to the fact that not all the possible information exchanges are mot modeled and the architecture focused on few priority areas.

Furthermore, the transformational abstract areas has received the least scores across the four aspect areas. This could be due to the fact that the abstract level focused on good design, cost savings and organizational change yet these were not mainly highlighted in the implementation of the architecture, for example, the cost sequences and all the possible information exchanges that are required in a fully automated e-government environment. Overall, the results indicate that the proposed architecture is acceptable as presented.

6 Conclusion

This paper presents an e-government interoperability framework that is driven by a Service Oriented Architecture (SOA) model and interoperability standards developed for use as a reference for implementing e-government systems in Uganda. The interoperability is achieved through a set of related ontologies. Lessons from the study of existing country e-GIFs and enterprise architectures were enjoined to complement the proposed architecture.

The developed e-GIF was evaluated by a focus group comprised of users, application developers and public service officials who used their knowledge of software engineering and public service delivery to validate the framework for appropriateness, completeness and accuracy. It is therefore, our conviction therefore, that the proposed architectural Framework and interoperability standards selection procedures are best suited for resolving the e-government interoperability challenge in Uganda. Future studies will consider further development of the organizational architecture and prototype implementation in partnership with the Government of Uganda and NITA-U.

References

1. Al-Khanjari, Z., Al-Hosni, N., Kraiem, N.: Developing a service oriented E-government architecture towards achieving E-government interoperability. Int. J. Softw. Eng. Appl. **8**(5), 29–42 (2014)
2. Ahlemann, F., Stettiner, E., Messerschmidt, M., Legner, C., Basten, D., Brons, D.: EA frameworks, modelling and tools. In: Ahlemann, F., Stettiner, E., Messerschmidt, M., Legner, C. (eds.) Strategic Enterprise Architecture Management. Management for Professionals, pp. 201–227. Springer, Heidelberg (2012). https://doi.org/10.1007/978-3-642-24223-6_8
3. Australia Electronic Government Interoperability Framework. http://www.egov.wa.gov.au/index.cfm?event=policiesEgif
4. Cameron, B.H., McMillan, E.: Analyzing the current trends in enterprise architecture frameworks. J. Enterp. Archit. **9**(1), 60–71 (2013)
5. Christensen, E., Curbera, F., Greg, M., Weerawarana, S.: Web services description language (WSDL) 1.1 (2001)
6. Chief Information Officers Council: Federal Enterprise Architecture Framework version 1.1. Retrieved from 80, pp. 3–1 (1999)
7. Curbera, F., Duftler, M., Khalaf, R., Nagy, W., Mukhi, N., Weerawarana, S.: Unraveling the web services web: an introduction to SOAP WSDL, and UDDI. EEE Internet Comput. **6**(2), 86–93 (2002)
8. Ministry of Economic Affairs and Communications Department of State Information Systems, Estonian IT Interoperability Framework. http://www.riso.ee/en/files/framework2005.pdf
9. Goethals, F.: An overview of enterprise architecture framework deliverables (2005)
10. Guijarro, L.: Interoperability frameworks and enterprise architectures in e-government initiatives in Europe and the United States. Gov. Inf. Q. **24**(1), 89–101 (2007)
11. Harrison, R.: TOGAF 9 Foundation Study Guide. Van Haren, Zaltbommel (2013)
12. Heeks, R.: Implementing and Managing eGovernment: An International Text. Sage, Thousand Oaks (2005)
13. Lallana, C.E.: E-government interoperability (2008). http://unpan1.un.org/intradoc/groups/public/documents/UN-OTHER/UNPAN032094
14. The new European Interoperability Framework (2017). https://ec.europa.eu/isa2/publications/new-european-interoperability-framework_en
15. Mustafa, J., Deik, A., Farraj, B.: Ontology-based data and process governance framework-the case of e-government interoperability in Palestine (2011)
16. Novakouski, M., Lewis, G.A.: Interoperability in the e-Government Context. Technical Report CMUP (2012)
17. Paik, H., Lemos, A.L., Barukh, M.C., Benatallah, B., Natarajan, A.: Web services – REST or restful services. Web Service Implementation and Composition Techniques, pp. 67–91. Springer, Cham (2017). https://doi.org/10.1007/978-3-319-55542-3_3
18. Schekkerman, J.: Extended enterprise architecture framework essentials guide. Institute for Enterprise Architecture Developments (2004)
19. Shvaiko, P., Villafiorita, A., Zorer, A., Chemane, L., Fumo, T.: E-government interoperability framework: a case study in a developing country. In: Reddick, C. (ed.) Comparative E-Government. Integrated Series in Information Systems, vol. 25, pp. 639–662. Springer, Heidelberg (2010)

20. Tang, A., Han, J., Chen, P.: A comparative analysis of architecture frameworks. In: 11th Asia-Pacific Software Engineering Conference, pp. 640–647. IEEE (2004)
21. Kharel, P., Shakya, S.: e-Government implementation in Nepal: a challenges. Int. J. Adv. Res. Comput. Sci. Softw. Eng. **2**(1) (2012)
22. United kingdom e-government interoperability framework version 6.1 (2005). http://www.govtalk.gov.uk/documents/eGIF%20v6_1%281%29.pdf
23. UNDP e-Government Interoperability: Overview. United Nations Development Programme (2007)
24. Urbaczewski, L., Mrdalj, S.: A comparison of enterprise architecture frameworks. Issues Inf. Syst. **7**(2), 18–23 (2006)
25. Zachman, J.A.: A framework for information systems architecture. IBM Syst. J. **26**, 276–292 (1987)

The State of e-Government Security in South Africa: Analysing the National Information Security Policy

Bukelwa Ngoqo[✉] and Kennedy Njenga

University of Johannesburg, Johannesburg, South Africa
bukelwa.ngoqo@gmail.com, knjenga@uj.ac.za

Abstract. As a result of the growing reliance by public sector organisations on technological resources for capturing and processing information, protection of information in the public sector has become an issue of national concern. While considering the South African national strategy for protecting this state asset ('information') this paper contrasts existing local, provincial or national e-Government information security policies against the adopted national guidelines. The paper postulates that with sound policies and guidelines in place 'interpretation and application' remain as two barriers that pose a threat to state information. The main question addressed in this paper is whether e-Government information security policies adequately address prescribed key security components. To achieve a comprehensive understanding of the pillars underpinning the protection of national information security in South Africa, the authors followed systematic procedures for reviewing and evaluating existing e-Government information security policies. The objective of this paper is to investigate whether existing government information security policies are aligned to national policy or guidelines. This paper will contribute empirical evidence which supports the notion observed by the South African Auditor General that (Auditor-General 2012) security weaknesses in government departments and state entities are attributed to the lack of formally designed and implemented information security policies and standards. The results of this preliminary investigation indicate that although information security policies exist in the majority of state entities, there is no consistency in the application of the 'security controls', as outlined in the national guidelines.

Keywords: National information security · Information security policy
e-Government · Information security legislation · Security controls

1 Introduction

E-Government has transformed the traditional views of 'service delivery' by government institutions. Mutula and Mostert [12] refer to an 'inextricably intertwined' relationship between e-Government and service delivery. This suggests that the role government plays in meeting the needs of its citizens cannot be separated from its application of e-Government. According to Crous [5] this role would encompass the implementation of laws and the actual provision of services and products by

© ICST Institute for Computer Sciences, Social Informatics and Telecommunications Engineering 2018
V. Odumuyiwa et al. (Eds.): AFRICOMM 2017, LNICST 250, pp. 29–46, 2018.
https://doi.org/10.1007/978-3-319-98827-6_3

government. The topic of e-Government has been discussed by researchers since the mid-1990s, thus e-Government research is still maturing in terms of theory development and empirical research [22]. The definition of e-Government adopted for purposes of this study is the World Bank [21] defining e-Government as; "The use by government agencies of information technologies (such as Wide Area Networks, the Internet, and mobile computing) that have the ability to transform relations with citizens, businesses, and other arms of government. These technologies can serve a variety of different ends: better delivery of government services to citizens, improved interactions with business and industry, citizen empowerment through access to information, or more efficient government management. The resulting benefits can be less corruption, increased transparency, greater convenience, revenue growth, and/or cost reductions."

South Africa is recognised by Cloete [4] as one of the early adopters of e-Government with policy change recommendations made as early as 1998 by the Presidential Commission on the Transformation of the Public Service (PRC 1998, Sect. 6.9). While there are possible benefits of e-Government as highlighted in the World Bank definition quoted above, [14] caution that an inherent threat to information security persists and attacks will continue as long as technologies continue to develop. This threat is further accentuated for state entities where information is captured, processed, stored and retrieved electronically. This study adopts the definition of information security as the set of processes, procedures, personnel, and technology charged with protecting an organization's information assets [20]. The information security policy is prescribed by researchers as a formal document that details acceptable and unacceptable behaviour of users in relation to dealing with information assets in a secure manner [2].

Information security is recognised as being an important aspect of IT governance [2]; however, government entities still struggle to design and implement effective controls that are aimed at optimising such security. This challenge is echoed in a report by the Auditor-General [3], in which security weaknesses in government departments and state entities are attributed to the lack of formally designed and implemented information security policies and standards. Shava and Van Greunen [16] suggest that despite security policies being in place in most organisations, there are concerns relating to the lack of user awareness on the meaning and implications of such policy implementation. This stance is echoed in the reference to 'two barriers that pose a threat to state information' (interpretation and application) mentioned earlier in this paper. This paper suggests that in cases where information security policies are in place as prescribed by government and government entities still face information security challenges, investigation into the cause must go beyond user awareness and include an analysis into the contents of the information security policy. The problem addressed by this paper is that even in cases where the relevant policies exist, if they fail to address key security concerns then they cannot be used as a benchmark for assessing any measure of information security effectiveness (e.g. user awareness). National security and service delivery can be negatively affected in cases where the operational integrity of the state is compromised by a lack of effective IT controls [3].

To gain a better understanding of the current South African information security landscape, this paper initially examines existing literature relating to South African e-Government research, the national information security landscape, information security linked legislation and the prescribed national information security constructs. This is followed by a discussion of the research methodology and the study findings, and some concluding remarks.

2 e-Government Research

Cloete [4] further raises concern about how South Africa has gradually lagged behind in e-Government implementation despite its early start. While research efforts continue in the field of e-Government in South Africa, some areas of global e-Government interest still remained marginally explored in the South African case. Zhao *et al.* [22] mention six critical topics of e-Government research: e-Government technology; infrastructure and resources; socio-economic issues such as access issues and digital divide; policies and strategies; user behaviour and intentions; and cultural issues. Table 1 below identifies the themes in South African e-Government research and aligns them to the key topics of e-Government research as outlined by [22].

Table 1. South African e-Government research focus (1).

Topic	Title	Year	Author(s)
Technology	*Smart card initiative for South African e-governance - a study*	2006	Nkomo, Terzoli, Muyingi and Rao
	Semantic-driven e-government: A case study of normal representation of government domain ontology	2011	Dombeu and Huisman
	The use of focus groups to improve and e-Government website	2011	Pretorius and Calitz
	A study of some e-Government activities in South Africa	2012	Thakur and Singh
	Next generation citizen centric e-Services	2014	Sharma, Guttoo and Ogra
	Towards a "Smart Society" through connected and smart citizenry in South Africa: A review of the National Broadband strategy and policy	2016	Manda and Backhouse
Infrastructure & resources	*Case study: Assessing and evaluating the readiness of the ICT infrastructure to provide e-government services at a local government level in South Africa*	2012	Monyepao and Weeks
Socio-economic issues	*Challenges and opportunities for e-government in South Africa*	2010	Mutula and Mostert
	The e-Government evaluation challenge: A South African Batho Pele-aligned service quality approach	2011	Kaisara and Pather
	e-Government development in Sub-Saharan Africa (SSA): Relationships with macro level indices and possible implications	2016	Verkijika and De Wet

(*continued*)

Table 1. (*continued*)

Topic	Title	Year	Author(s)
Policies and strategies	*South African e-Government policy and practises: A framework to close the gap*	2003	Trusler
	Questioning the pace and pathway of e-government development in Africa: A case study South Africa's Cape Gateway project	2008	Maumbe, Owei and Alexander
	Comparison of Sub-Saharan Africa's e-government status with development and transitional nations	2008	Mutula
	Are e-Government investments delivering against expected payoffs? Evidence from the United Kingdom and South Africa	2010	Naidoo and Palk
	Measuring the public value of e-government: Methodology of a South African case study	2010	Friedland and Gross
	A conceptual ontology for e-government monitoring of development projects in Sub Saharan Africa	2010	Dombeu
	South Africa's e-development still a futuristic task	2011	Abrahams
	Innovation in monitoring and evaluation for e-development and transformational government	2012	Abrahams and Burke
	Strategic planning for transformational government: A South African perspective	2012	Mawela
	e-Government implementations in developing countries: Success and failure, two case studies	2012	Rajapakse, Van Der Vyver and Hommes
	e-Government lessons from South Africa 2001–2011: Institutions, state of progress and measurement	2012	Cloete
	An exploration of critical success factors for e-Governance Project Initiation: A preliminary framework	2015	Hatsu and Ngasaam
User behaviour and intentions	*Use of e-government services: the role of trust*	2015	Mpinganjira
Cultural issues	*Diffusing the Ubuntu philosophy into e-Government: A South African perspective*	2010	Twinomurinzi, Pahlamohlaka and Byrne
	Global survey on culture differences and context in using e-Government systems: A pilot study	2011	Herselman and Van Greunen

South African researchers investigated a wide variety of related topics aligned to the six key e-Government research areas. These research efforts have concentrated mainly in topics related to *Technology* as well as e-Governance *Policies and strategies*. The progression of South African e-Government research has gradually evolved with researchers progressively exploring the following research areas:

2003–2015: The initial focus of South African researchers was on Policies and strategies. This early e-Government research addressed pertinent questions such as: *Do we have the policies in place? Are we implementing e-Government quickly enough compared to other developing nations? Are we getting value from e-Government investments? How can we monitor and evaluate e-Government implementation? What are the critical success factors for e-Government investments?* While areas of focus have changed over time the topic of e-Government Policies and strategies continues to be a relevant one. This paper further adds to the Policy and strategies debate but drawing specific attention to the area of e-Government information security policies.

2006–2016: Applicable technologies were subsequently discussed by South African researchers. The focus of research was on the following technologies/technology related topics: *Smart cards, semantic-driven e-Government, e-Government websites, e-Services and Smart societies.*

2010–2016: South African is referred to as a 'rainbow nation' due to the number of diverse cultures that form part of the national social fabric. This is evidenced in the staggering number of official languages in the country which currently stands at eleven. The resultant socio-economic and cultural issues also filter through to the e-Government research sphere. Linked to the socio-economic issue e-Government researcher explored: *e-Government challenges/opportunities, Batho Pele-aligned e-services, and e-Government relationships with macro level indices.* Researchers focusing on cultural issues discussed principles such as: *Ubuntu philosophy in e-Government, Culture differences and context in using of e-Government systems.*

2012: The topic of infrastructure & resources appears in later e-Government researcher where the important question of '*Do we have the infrastructure to support e-Government services?* is examined.

2015: Initially the focus of e-Government research was on policies and technology, the focus eventually shifted to the e-Government user. The role of trust is discussed user behaviour and intentions *(The role of Trust).*

The least researched topics in the case of South African e-Government research are *Infrastructure & resources* and *User behaviour & intentions.* South African research in the field of e-Government can be deemed as sporadic two additional e-Government areas have been explored by South African researchers (*2010–2014*): *Security* and *m-Government* (see Table 2).

Table 2. South African e-Government research focus (2).

Topic	Title	Year	Author(s)
Security	*South African eGov: Secure e-services*	2010	Dlamini, Ngobeni and Mutanga
	Secure e-government services: Towards a framework for integrating it security services into e-government maturity models	2011	Karakola, Kowalski and Yongstrom
m-Government	*Mobile government for improved public service provision in South Africa*	2010	Nkosi and Mekuria
	Mobi4D: A next generation service delivery platform for mobile government services: An African perspective	2011	Ogunleye, Makitla, Botha, Tomay, Fogwill, Seetharan and Geldenhuys
	Exploring the success, failure and factors influencing m-Government implementation in developing countries	2014	Ogunleye and Van Belle

The literature shows that most research has been concentrated on e-Government Policy and strategy. This observation further accentuates the problem identified in this paper where information security is deemed as an inherent policy issue that has been overlooked in previous e-Government research. This paper links two of the topics mentioned above namely: Policies and strategy and Security. It also adds clarity to these two broad topics by specifically focusing on the information security as it relates to the information Security Policy. The next section outlines the background to the South African national information security landscape.

3 National Information Security

In South Africa, the Department of Public Service and Administration (DPSA) is responsible for the development and coordination of the government's overall e-Government strategy [17]. The Department of Communications [17] also mentions two complementary statutory bodies established to coordinate the implementation of e-Government projects, namely, the State Information Technology Agency (SITA), which is responsible for the acquisition, installation, implementation and maintenance of public sector IT assets, and the Government Information Technology Officers (GITO) council, which is responsible for consolidating and coordinating IT initiatives in government to facilitate service delivery.

Information security management is one of the IT governance processes [3] identified in the framework presented below (Fig. 1), which is endorsed by the DPSA and the GITO council.

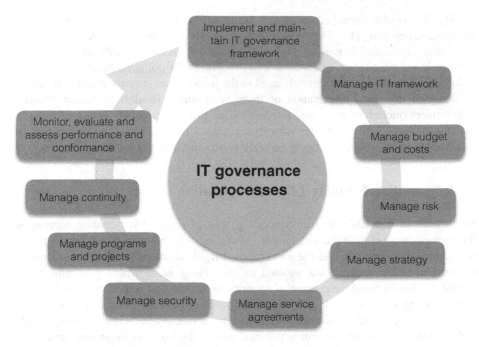

Fig. 1. Information technology governance process [3]

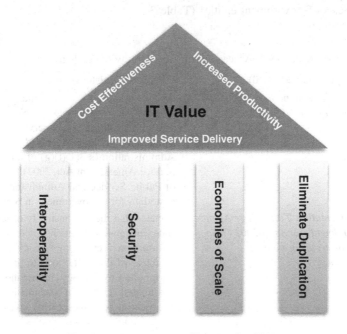

Fig. 2. e-Government Pillars (DPSA 2011)

Security is also identified as one of the four pillars (Fig. 2) of e-Government in South Africa cited by [17]. For the purposes of this study, information security refers to the measures adopted to prevent the unauthorised use, misuse, modification, or denial of knowledge, facts, data or capabilities [10]. Although policies, standards and procedures are terms that are commonly used in the information security domain, it cannot be assumed that the interpretation of these is common to all information security stakeholders (including end users, information security practitioners, management and external parties). Existing South African legislation that informs the construction of e-Government information security policies is presented in the following section.

4   Information Security Linked Legislation

South African legislation that influences the area of national information security is fragmented across multiple disciplines, including communication, cyber security, protection of information and the constitutional rights of citizens. Existing research in the area of cyber security has assisted in identifying areas where government has lagged behind in the development of security protocols and standards, as well as in implementing such protocols and standards [9]. Based on the areas of concern identified by [18], government has adopted a more proactive stance to information security with "adequate information security policies" being viewed as an important contributor to the security and wellbeing of government information resources. The DPSA [18] highlights eight pieces of South African legislation that are relevant to the information security policies of government entities (Table 3):

Table 3. South African information security linked legislation.

Legislation (Question addressed)	Purpose of legislation
The Public Service Amendment Act of 2007 *(Who is responsible for the policies?)*	Assigns responsibility for policies relating to information management and electronic government in the public service to the Minister of Public Service and Administration (s 3(1)(f)(g) of the Public Service Amendment Act, 2007). The Minister of Public Service and Administration is the custodian for e-Government in South Africa
The State Information Technology Agency (SITA) Amendment Act 38 of 2002 (Who is responsible for securing national information assets?)	Dictates that the responsibility of securing state information assets lies with the State Information Technology Agency (SITA). The objective of this Act "(a) is to provide information technology, information systems and related services in a maintained information systems security environment to departments and public bodies".

(continued)

Table 3. (*continued*)

Legislation (Question addressed)	Purpose of legislation
	The objective of the principal SITA Act 88 of 1998 was revised to in the SITA Amendment Act 38 of 2002 to firstly change the wording of the objective to make SITA relevant to all departments and public bodies, versus the initial proclamation which referred to '… participating departments and organs of state…'. The amendment (SITA Amendment Act, 2002) subsequently include a key sub-section (b) which states: "(b) to promote the efficiency of departments and public bodies through the use of information technology." This revision to the SITA Act is indicative of the evolving stages of e-Government implementation, hence confirming the importance of e-Government to National Government
The Minimum Information Security Standards (MISS) (Preventative measures)	Set out a range of measures to protect classified information, including the classification and reclassification of documents, handling of classified documents, access to classified information, storage of classified document and removal of classified documents from premises. The MISS also provides for the security vetting of personnel. The MISS sets out security measures to protect classified information, including physical security, access control, computer security and communication security (Protection of Information Bill 6, of 2010)
National Strategic Intelligence Act 39 of 1994 (What happens if the threats are realised?)	This Act describes the counterintelligence role of the National Intelligence Agency in measuring and undertaking activities to neutralise threats and protect classified information from hostile or foreign intelligence operations
National Archives of South Africa Act 43 of 1996 (Records management & preservation)	"Aims to provide for a National Archives, the proper management and care of the records of governmental bodies and the preservation and use of a national archival heritage." This Act covers details on topics such as the "classification of records", the "management of electronic records" and the "electronic reproduction of records"

(continued)

Table 3. *(continued)*

Legislation (Question addressed)	Purpose of legislation
Protection of Information Act 84 of 1982 *(Protection of public information)*	Provides for the protection from disclosure of certain information. Some of the offences/prohibitions mentioned in the Act include prohibited places and the obtaining or disclosure of certain information. The Protection of Information Act stipulates regulations, permissions and prohibitions on how public information can be obtained, used and when or how it can be disclosed
Electronics Communications and Transactions Act of 2002 (Critical data)	In this act the Minister of Communications is given the power to deem information to be "critical data" and discretion in guiding the way critical databases are managed. In the Act, critical data is defined as "data that are of critical importance to the national security of the Republic, and/or the economic and social well-being of its citizens"
Interception and Monitoring Bill 50 of 2001 (The 'Big Brother' role of the state)	With the South African government embracing "the use of information and communication technologies in the public service to improve its internal functioning and to render services to the public" (Public Service Amendment Act, 2007) e-Government as a necessary part of service delivery. Securing information that is transmitted through telecommunications services should also be a national information security concern. The Interception and Monitoring Bill 50 of 2001 regulates the following areas of certain communication (postal or telecommunications) or matters connected therewith: *"…the interception and monitoring of certain communications"* *"…to provide for the interception of postal articles and communications and for the monitoring of communications in the case of a serious offence or if the security or other compelling national interests of the Republic are threatened"* *"to prohibit the provision of certain telecommunication services which do not have the capacity to be monitored"* *"to regulate authorised telecommunications monitoring"*

State entities' information security policies are crafted based on the legislation mentioned above as well as guidelines that can be obtained from national government structures. These guidelines are based on existing information security frameworks. For example, the DPSA used the ISO 17799 framework as a basis for establishing its information security policies. The next section introduces the ISO 17799 constructs.

5 National Information Security Policy Constructs

Da Veiga [6] relies on the ISO/IEC/ 27001 (2013) description of the role of the information security policy as a document which outlines the organisation's approach to information security that provides a framework for setting control objectives and controls. The South African Department of Public Service and Administration [18] adopts the ISO 17799 framework in conceptualising security management controls for public entities. In examining the contents of various e-Government information security policies this paper uses the DPSA's (ISO 17799 adapted) security controls (securing hardware, peripherals and equipment; controlling access to information; processing information documents; purchasing and maintaining commercial software; developing and maintaining in-house software; combating cybercrime; complying with legal and policy requirements, planning for business continuity; addressing personnel issues relating to security; controlling e-transaction information security; delivering training and staff awareness; dealing with premises related considerations; detecting and responding to information security incidents; and classifying information and data) to contextualise key information security policy components.

Having clearly defined the fifteen key constructs of an e-Government information security policy, as recommended by the DPSA guidelines, this paper suggests that possible weaknesses in e-Governance information security can be attributed to poorly constructed (designed) information security policies that do not adequately address all the necessary information security controls. In the next section, the methodology used for collecting the data during the first phase of this study is described.

6 Methodology

This study employed content analysis as an approach to study the web presence of Information Security Policies of various South African state entities. Qualitative content analysis was used to analyse the contents of existing information security policies for 56 government department and municipalities sourced on the web. Content analysis describes a family of analytic approaches ranging from impressionistic, intuitive, interpretive analyses to systematic, strict textual analyses [15]. In this research, the qualitative content analysis is applied through the interpretation (subjective) of the content of text data through and subsequently the systematic classification process of coding and identifying themes or patterns [8]. Based on this approach to gathering data this study systematically analysed published e-Government information security policies.

There are currently 278 metropolitan, district and local municipalities in South Africa. The sample taken during this preliminary data collection stage of the study represented 20% of the total population. The secondary data collected during this stage by collecting South African (e-Government) Information Security Policies through conducting online searches. The policies were accessed by using conventional search engines, which provided links to the policies, and then the researchers traced them to the respective government department or municipality website. Considering that there are various types of government entity, including parastatals and government agencies, the first criterion for choosing a policy as a potential candidate was that it should belong to a national/provincial government department or a metropolitan/district/local municipality. A second criterion was that candidate policies should specifically address information security concerns. After refining our search results according to these criteria, we ended up with 56 information security policies for our content analysis.

While the literature phase of this paper provided insight into the South African e-Government landscape, second phase to addresses the following sub-research questions:

- Is there an existing information security policy?
- Do these policies contain information exclusively related to information security?
- To what extent does the policy address the key security controls stipulated in the DPSA guidelines?

In answering these sub-research questions the main question in this paper (*Do e-Government information security policies adequately address prescribed key security components?*) will be addressed. The findings presented in the next section include an objective analysis that compares the DPSA set "standard" against the actual contents of e-Government information security policies of various South African state entities.

7 Findings

Analysis of Textual Data: Existing Policies Within Municipalities

Is There an Existing Information Security Policy?

Based on the data collected online at least 56 South African government entities had policies that addressed information security concerns. The data collected thus disputes the Auditor General's (2015) assumption of non-existent information security policies and standards within state entities as this was found not to be applicable to the departments or state entities in this study sample.

The findings above (Fig. 3) indicate that in the case of the sample taken in this study, only five percent of the entities considered did not have information security policies in place. The 'No policy' finding was applied in cases where on closer analysis the policies found online were deemed not to be information security policies. However, the majority of the sample had policies in place. While the information security linked policies are found for this study population the next section interrogates the contents 'design' of these policies. Discounting the first part of the Auditor General's concerns, the ensuing question becomes: *"Do these information security policies provide clear guidance on critical information security controls?"*

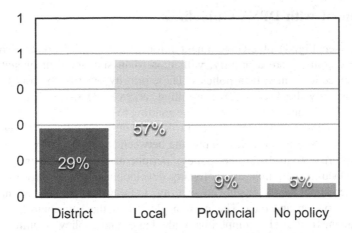

Fig. 3. Is there an existing information security policy?

Do Policies Contain Information Exclusively Related to Information Security?

The findings (see Table 4) further show that just over fifty percent of the policies analysed contained information that was exclusively related to information security. Various names were used to describe these policies, and this is also an indication that ambiguity may exist within state entities regarding the intended use of these information security policies. The use of different names hints at the ambiguity that possibly exists around the interpretation and/or implementation of these policies. Further insights on how the stakeholders perceive the information security policy is beyond the scope of this paper. The DPSA [18] proposes a clear structure for what should be included in an e-Government information security policy. The structure of the 56 policies examined was compared to the 15 key controls (see Fig. 4) provided in the DPSA guidelines. The findings discussed below answer the following question: *"In cases where the information security policy is in place, to what extent does it address the key security controls stipulated in the DPSA guidelines?"*

Table 4. Does the policy contain information exclusively related to information security?

Total number	Name of document
Yes (28)	Information and Communication Technology Security Policy, IT Data and System Security Policy, Information Security Policy, Information Security Management Policy, Security Policy, Information Security Policy, Policy on ICT Security, Information Security Controls Policy, Information Technology and Security Policy, User Security Policy, Information Technology Security Management Policy, Information Systems Security Policy, IT and Information Management Security Policy
No (25)	Security Policy & Standard Operating Procedures, Security Policy, ICT & Information Security Policy, Information and Communication Technology Security Policy, Information Technology Policy, ICT Acceptable Use Policy

8 Alignment with DPSA Guidelines

An analysis (see Fig. 4) of e-Government information security policies shows that some security controls are a priority, with more than sixty percent of state entities making reference to them in their policies. These priority security controls seem to me to be (1) security hardware, (2) controlling access, (3) combating cybercrime, (4) premise-related considerations and (5) responding to information security incidents. However, the majority of the security controls were only partially addressed by most state entities, with scores for inclusion ranging between twenty and fifty percent for the following security controls in the policy: peripherals and equipment, processing information documents, purchasing software, developing in-house software, business continuity, personnel issues relating to security, training and awareness and classification of information and data. The most neglected of the key controls (as per the DPSA guidelines) are (1) complying with legal and policy requirements and (2) e-transaction security, with both scoring below ten percent.

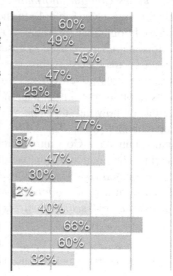

Fig. 4. Alignment with DPSA guidelines

9 Discussion of Findings

Making reference to the initial question raised in this paper 'Do e-Government information security policies adequately address prescribed key security components?' The findings show that in the case of South African e-Government information security policies department and/or entities observed in this study do have information security related policies in place. However, there is misalignment between the prescribed DPSA guidelines (key security controls) and the controls actually put in place through these policies. Of particular concern are the two controls (*controlling e-transaction information security* and *complying with legal and policy requirements*) which both we mentioned in the information security policy by less than ten percent of the departments or entities considered in this study. An additional observation based on these findings is that the people who draft these policies (IT Department representatives) put more of an emphasis on the 'Technology related/Infrastructure' aspects of information security with controls like: *include security hardware, controlling access, combating cyber-crime, premise-related considerations* and *reporting to information security incidents* scoring sixty percent and above for inclusion in the information security policies of the study population. While the majority of stakeholder related security controls were only partially addressed: *personnel issues relating to security, training & awareness, classification of information & data* and *processing of information documents*.

This paper suggests the use of the overall classification scale, 'low priority', 'medium priority' and 'critical', as a tool for analysing the findings. The ratings used in this scale are based on the coverage (i.e. number of key security controls) of 15 key information security controls in each department or state entity policy from the 56 analysed in this study. This scale (Table 5 below) has been used in this study to give an indication of areas that have been insufficiently covered by the information security policies of a group of state entities.

Table 5. Analysis scale

	Scale	Score (information security controls)
Low priority	50–100%	8–15
Medium priority	20–49%	4–7
Critical	0–20%	1–3

Applying this scale to the data (Table 6 below), the following inferences can be drawn. Based on the number of security controls that were addressed in the information security policies of the state entities in the sample, only seventeen percent fits the 'critical' category in that less than twenty percent of the information security controls are mentioned in their policies. The 'medium priority' category includes those state entities that have scored above twenty percent but less than fifty percent in their coverage of the key security controls in their information security policies. Forty per cent of the sample fell into the medium priority category.

Table 6. Application of findings to analysis scale

	Critical	Medium priority	Low priority
District municipality	2	9	13
Local municipality	7	11	5
Provincial department		1	4
Metropolitan municipality			1

Forty-three per cent of the sampled state entities scored above fifty percent, meeting the minimum criteria for the 'low priority' category. The evidence confirms that most (57%) of the state entities sampled have information security policies that fail to address even half of the security controls delineated in the DPSA guidelines.

This analysis provides a good summary of key information security control 'coverage' in existing e-Government information security policies. This paper proposes that in the e-Government environment, an information security policy that does not adequately address key security controls is as effective as no policy at all. These findings give a good indication of inherent (within state entities) security policy weaknesses that could potentially result in the weaknesses identified by the Auditor-General.

10   Implications for Practice

South African researchers have explored the topic of information security policy from various angles: *policy development* [13, 19] *conceptual threat assessment framework development* [11] and *legal implications* [7]. Limited research exists in South Africa that explores the links between the development of policy, and its the application in the e-Government environment.

This paper presented an environmental overview on the way the information security policy should be structured, as well as the underlying legislation that influences its development. The paper concludes by highlighting the gaps that exists in the information security policies of various government entities. The contribution made by this paper should stimulate further research on the application of information security policies in the e-Government environment.

11   Conclusion

The information security policy is an instrumental document that guides the process of effective information security management in the e-Government environment. While guidelines have been provided by the DPSA, as the state entity responsible for the development and coordination of government's overall e-Government strategy, including e-Government information security, responsibility for selecting the controls that are most suitable for consideration in their respective environments rests with the state entities themselves. This paper presented an analysis of existing South African e-Government information security policies. The analysis highlighted the areas in which key security controls had been overlooked in the majority of the information security policies of state entities examined. This paper argues that these weaknesses are not necessarily limited to the lack of formally designed and implemented information security policies, but that the contents of these information security policies should scrutinised to ensure that key security controls have been addressed.

The progress that has been made in this research thus far and the findings of this particular study are encouraging and the intention is to proceed with a follow-up study aimed at measuring e-Government information security policy awareness focusing on the areas referred to in this study as the 'two barriers that pose a threat to state information' (interpretation and application). Specific goals of the follow-up study are to (1) conduct an in-depth study into the factors that influence information security policy awareness within the e-Government context; and (2) develop e-Government information security behaviour profiles based on empirical data collected. The broader objectives of the study outside the scope of this paper include measuring the information security policy awareness levels of government employees and identifying possible vulnerabilities based on user information security behaviour profiles.

References

1. Ajzen, I.: The theory of planned behavior. Organ. Behav. Hum. Decis. Process. **50**, 179–211 (1991)
2. Alotaibi, M., Furnell, S., Clarke, N.: Information security policies: a review of challenges and influencing factors. In: Proceedings of the 11th International Conference for Internet Technology and Secured Transactions (ICITS-2016), 5–7 December 2016, Barcelona, Spain (2016). ISBN 978-1-908320-73-5
3. Auditor-General South Africa: The Drivers of Internal Control: Information Technology Management as a Driver of Audit Outcomes. Consolidated General report on the 2011–12 national and provincial audit outcomes (2012). https://www.agsa.co.za/Portals/0/MFMA2011-12Extracts/MFMA_2011-12_consolidated_reports/AGSA_MFMA_CONSOLIDATED_REPORT_2011_12.pdf. Accessed 12 July 2016
4. Cloete, F.: E-government lessons from South Africa 2001–2011: institutions, state of progress and measurement. Afr. J. Inf. Commun. **12**, 128–142 (2012)
5. Crous, M.: Service delivery in the South African public service: implementation of the Batho Pele principles by statistics South Africa. J. Publ. Adm. **39**(4.1) (2004)
6. Da Veiga, A.: Comparing the information security culture of employees who had read the information security policy and those who had not Illustrated through an empirical study. Inf. Comput. Secur. **24**(2), 139–151 (2016)
7. Etsebeth, V.: Information security policies - the legal risk of uninformed personnel. In: Proceedings of the ISSA 2006 from Insight to Foresight Conference, 5–7 July 2006, Sandton, South Africa (2006). ISBN 1-86854-636-5
8. Hsieh, H., Shannon, S.E.: Three approaches to qualitative content analysis. Qual. Health Res. **15**(9), 1277–1288 (2005)
9. Kortjan, N., Von Solms, R.: A conceptual framework for cyber-security awareness and education in SA. South Afr. Comput. J. (SACJ) **52**, 29–41 (2014)
10. Maiwald, E.: Fundamentals of Network Security. McGraw-Hill Education, New York (2004)
11. Mbowe, J.E., Zlotnikova, I., Msanjila, S.S., Oreku, G.S.: A conceptual framework for threat assessment based on organization's information security policy. J. Inf. Secur. **5**, 166–177 (2014)
12. Mutula, S.M., Mostert, J.: Challenges and opportunities of E-Government in South Africa. Electron. Libr. **28**(1), 38–53 (2010)
13. Ngobeni, S.J., Grobler, M.M.: Information security policies for governmental organisations: the minimum criteria. In: Proceedings of ISSA, 6–8 July 2009, Johannesburg, South Africa, pp. 455–466 (2009)
14. Njotini, M.N.: Protecting critical databases: towards risk based assessment of Critical Information Infrastructures (CIIS) in South Africa. Potchefstroomse Elektroniese Regsblad (PER) **16**(1), 451–481 (2013)

15. Rosengren, K.E.: Advances in Content Analysis. Sage Publications, Beverly Hills (1981)
16. Shava, F.B., Van Greunen, D.: Designing user security metrics for security awareness at higher and tertiary institutions. In: Proceedings of the 8th International Development Informatics Association Conference, 3–4 November 2014, Port Elizabeth, South Africa, pp. 280–296 (2014)
17. South Africa. Department of Communications: National Integrated ICT Policy. Government Gazette, No. 37261, 24 January 2014
18. South Africa. Department of Public Service and Administration: Draft position Paper on Information Security. Version 0.3 (2015)
19. Tuyikeze, T., Pottas, D.: An information security policy development life cycle. In: Proceedings of the South African Information Security Multi-Conference (SAISMC), Port Elizabeth, South Africa, pp. 165–176, 17–18 May 2010. ISBN 978-1-84102-256-7
20. Whitman, M.E., Mattord, H.J.: Principles of Information Security. Course Technology, Boston (2003)
21. World Bank: New-Economy Sector Study: Electronic Government and Governance: Lessons for Argentina (2002). http://documents.worldbank.org/curated/en/527061468769894044/pdf/266390WP0E1Gov1gentina1Final1Report.pdf. Accessed 17 Feb 2017
22. Zhao, F., Scavarda, A.J., Waxin, M.: Key issues and challenges in e-Government development: an integrative case study of the number one eCity in the Arab world. Inf. Technol. People 25(4), 395–422 (2012)

Network and Load Management

A Priority Load-Aware Scheduling Algorithm for Wireless Broadband Networks

Aminu Mohammed[1], Ibrahim Saidu[2], and Abdulhakeem Abdulazeez[1(✉)]

[1] Department of Mathematics, Computer Science Unit,
Usmanu Danfodiyo University, P.M.B 2346, Sokoto, Nigeria
{mohammed.aminu, abdulhakeem.abdulazeez}@udusok.edu.ng
[2] Department of Information and Communications Technology,
Usmanu Danfodiyo University, P.M.B 2346, Sokoto, Nigeria
ibrahim.saidu@udusok.edu.ng

Abstract. Wireless broadband networks are emerging as reliable internet access alternatives for delivery of high speed multimedia services. WiMAX is one of such networks, designed to provide quality of service (QoS) support for different service classes with varying QoS requirements. Scheduling algorithms are required to provide such support. The existing scheduling algorithm uses dynamic weight to allocate resources based on traffic loads. However, it increases delay of real time traffics due to failure of the weight to prioritize traffics. This paper proposes a priority load aware scheduling (PLAS) algorithm to reduce delay in real time traffics. The PLAS algorithm introduces a priority value to prioritize real time traffics over non-real time traffics. The algorithm was evaluated using extensive simulations. The results show that the PLAS outperforms the existing algorithm in terms of delay.

Keywords: WRR · Scheduling algorithm · WiMAX · QoS

1 Introduction

Wireless broadband networks have become reliable means to meet the increasing demand for internet connections and integrated multimedia services. WiMAX being one of such networks provides last mile internet access to both residential and enterprise users. It defines the physical (PHY) layer and media access control (MAC) layer. Apart from its ease and cheap cost of deployment as well as maintenance, it also supports multiple QoS classes [1]. The QoS classes are as follows:

I. Unsolicited Grant Service (UGS) is designed for real-time services like Voice over Internet Protocol (VoIP)) that require constant bit rate flows. UGS is given higher priority because of its low tolerant for delay and requirement for maximum latency.
II. real time Polling Service (rtPS) is designed for real-time services such as MPEG that generates variable data size periodically. It is more delay tolerant than the UGS.

© ICST Institute for Computer Sciences, Social Informatics and Telecommunications Engineering 2018
V. Odumuyiwa et al. (Eds.): AFRICOMM 2017, LNICST 250, pp. 49–59, 2018.
https://doi.org/10.1007/978-3-319-98827-6_4

III. non-real time Polling Service (nrtPS) is designed for non real-time services like file transfer protocol (FTP) which also generates variable data size periodically. This class is delay tolerant and has minimum bandwidth requirement.

IV. Best Effort (BE) is intended for services that do not require QoS guarantee such as Hyper Text Transfer Protocol (HTTP).

The MAC layer is responsible for scheduling these classes with varying QoS requirements such as bandwidth, delay, jitter and packet loss. To satisfy these requirements, an efficient scheduling algorithm is needed.

Several scheduling algorithms have been proposed for resource allocation [2–9]. Recently, Load Aware Weighted Round Robin (LAWRR) has been proposed to mitigate the weakness of Weighted Round Robin (WRR). The LAWRR separates packets into different QoS classes and allocates a dynamic weight to each queue based on its traffic load characteristics. The algorithm employs the dynamic weight to determine the number of packets to be served in each queue. It reduces not only delay and packet loss but also improves average throughput for non-real time traffics. However, it increases delay due to its failure to prioritize real time traffics.

In this paper, a priority load aware scheduling (PLAS) algorithm is proposed to reduce delay in real time traffics. The PLAS introduces a priority weight to increase the service rate of the real time traffics. The algorithm is evaluated using simulations. The result demonstrates that the PLAS achieves superior performance compared to the existing scheme.

The rest of this paper is organized as follows: Sect. 2 presents related works. In Sect. 3, the proposed PLAS is prescribed; Sect. 4 presents performance evaluation while Sect. 5 concludes the paper.

2 Related Works

In this section, some of the scheduling algorithms proposed for WiMAX networks are reviewed as follows:

[1], proposed a priority weighted round robin (PWRR) scheduling algorithm to minimize delay. The PWRR employs a classifier that separate packets based on their priorities. The algorithm employs the priority scheduling (PS) and the weighted round robin (WRR) disciplines to determine packets to transmit. The PS schedule packets from the high priority classes while WRR from low priority classes. The PWRR reduces delay and increases throughput of high priority traffics but starves the low priority classes.

In [9], a modified weighted round-robin (MWRR) scheduling algorithm is proposed to avoid starvation of lower priority classes. The MWRR algorithm assigns weight to each active queue based on its priority. The algorithm multiplies the static WRR and a constant multiplier value to increase the number of packets to be serviced from each queue. The multiplier is an integer value obtained base on a network size; the larger the network the smaller the multiplier value and vice versa. The MWRR reduces delay and increases throughput but may lead to an increase in average delay and decrease in average throughput if the multiplier is wrongly selected.

In [4], a variant of WRR known as adaptive weighted round-robin (AWRR) scheduling algorithm is also proposed to reduce starvation of lower service classes. The AWRR uses input and output schedulers to adjust service classes' weights. The input scheduler gives priorities to high priority traffic over low priority traffic based on their bandwidth and latency requirements. On the other hand, the output scheduler controls data flows and manage the service classes. The algorithm also employs a threshold for each class which when exceeded triggers dynamic weight adjustment. It reduces delay as well as improves throughput. However, the algorithm increases average delay and packet loss as well as decrease in throughput if the threshold value is inappropriately set.

[5], proposed a low latency weighted round robin (LLWRR) scheduling algorithm to improve latency and fairness in high priority traffics. The LLWRR computes varying weights by multiplying a coefficient value and the static WRR weight at the beginning of each service round. The coefficient value is a function of number of queues, which decreases as the number of queues increases. LLWRR adjusts the weight values based on number of queues. The algorithm improves not only fairness and average throughput but also decreases latency. However, it may lead to an increase in average delay and packet lost under busty input traffics with large number of queues.

[3], proposed a load-aware weighted round-robin (LAWRR) algorithm to address the WRR performance degradation problem under busty traffic condition. The LAWRR algorithm dynamically computes weight of a queue according to its current loads characteristics. The weight of each queue is computed as the product of the dynamic coefficient of a queue and the static WRR weight at the beginning of each base station (BS) round. The dynamic coefficient is obtained by computing the root mean square error from the load variance of the queues. The algorithm reduces not only average delay and packet loss but also improves average throughput for non real- time traffics. However, it increases delay due to starvation of real time traffics.

In addition to the scheduling algorithms reviewed above, other resource management schemes are proposed in [10, 11]. However, to the best of our knowledge, none of the existing algorithms is capable of decreasing delay of real time traffics by prioritization using dynamic weight.

3   The Proposed PLAS Algorithm

This section describes the proposed scheduling algorithm named PLAS. The PLAS is a variant of the LAWRR. However, first, the weakness of LAWRR is described. The LAWRR separates packets into different service classes considering their QoS requirements. It uses a dynamic weight to service each class. The weight is computed in Eqs. (1)–(4) as follows:

First, the root mean square error is computed as:

$$R_{r=\sqrt{v_r}}.$$ (1)

Where v_r is the load variance of the queues.

Then the dynamic coefficient of queue i at round r is derived as:

$$w_{i,r} = \left\lceil \frac{L_{i,r}}{R_r + 1} \right\rceil. \tag{2}$$

Where $L_{i,r}$ is the load of queue i at round r.
Next, the static WRR weight is computed as:

$$Sw_i = \frac{MRTR_i}{\sum_{i=1}^{n} MRTR_i}. \tag{3}$$

Where $MRTR_i$ is the minimum reserve traffic rate of queue i and n is the total number of queues in a class.
Finally, a dynamic weight of queue i at round r is obtained as:

$$dw_{i,r} = w_{i,r}Sw_i. \tag{4}$$

The algorithm employs Eq. (4) to determine number of packets to be served in each queue. It assigns a weight counter to all non-empty queues. At the beginning of every counter reset, a dynamic weight is assigned to each weight counter. If a packet is sent from a queue, the weight counter value of that queue is decremented by 1. Every queue is served once in every round in a round robin (RR) fashion. The scheduler moves to next round when all queues are served in the current round. The scheduler continues in this fashion until the weight counter of each queue is zero or all queues are empty. To demonstrate the algorithm, Fig. 1 is used.

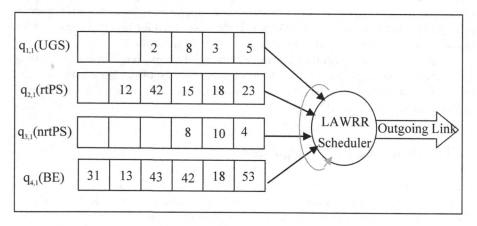

Fig. 1. Shows the state of a LAWRR scheduler before weights assignment.

From Fig. 1, the dynamic weights are computed using Eq. (4) and shown in Table 1. The dynamic weights are assigned to the weight counters of the queues shown in Fig. 2. The queues in this Fig. are served starting from $q_{1,r}$ to $q_{4,r}$ in every service round and the counter weight of each queue is decremented by 1 when a packet is served. By the end of second round in first counter reset, the counter values of $q_{1,2}$ and

$q_{3,2}$ become zero each while that of $q_{2,2}$ and $q_{4,2}$ become 2 and 4, respectively as shown in Fig. 3. That means, no queue will be served from $q_{1,2}$ and $q_{3,2}$ until after the next four rounds when all counter weights become zero and the counter values are reset. By the end of first counter reset, a total of 3 packets remain in $q_{1,6}$ (UGS) and $q_{2,6}$(rtPS) as shown in Fig. 4. This example shows that packets waiting in UGS and rtPS classes are delayed at the end of every counter reset until subsequent counter reset. However, the delay incurred in these queues may cause packet drop and decrease in average throughput in real time traffics. Therefore, LAWRR is only suitable for nrtPS and BE but not for real time traffics.

Table 1. Computation of dynamic weight for LAWRR

$q_{i,1}$	$L_{i,1}$	$L_{i,1} - L_1$	$dw_{i,1}$
$q_{1,1}$	18	4,830.25	2
$q_{2,1}$	110	506.25	4
$q_{3,1}$	22	4,290.25	2
$q_{4,1}$	200	12,656.25	6
Total	**350**	**22,283**	
Stat.	**L1 = 87.5**	**v1 = 5,570.75,** **R1 = 74.6375**	

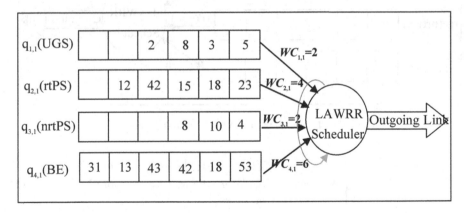

Fig. 2. Shows the state of a LAWRR after weights assignment

To address the shortcomings of the LAWRR, a PLAS algorithm is proposed to increase the service rate of real time traffics. First, the scheme modifies the LAWRR weight in Eq. (4) by introducing a priority value derived as follows:

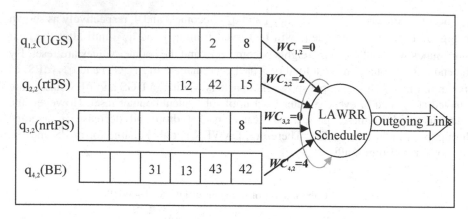

Fig. 3. Shows the LAWRR after second round.

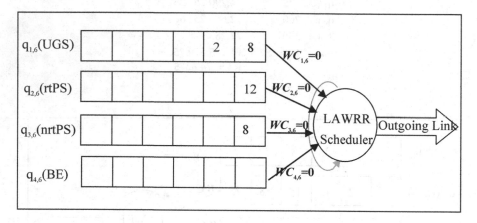

Fig. 4. Shows the LAWRR after last round

$$Pv_{i,r} = \begin{cases} 2 & \text{if UGS or rtPS \& } Nq_i \leq Bf/2 \\ Nq_i/dw_{i,r} & \text{if UGS or rtPS \& } Nq_i > Bf/2 \\ 1 & \text{Otherwise} \end{cases} \quad (5)$$

Where $dw_{i,r}$ is the LAWRR dynamic weight of queue i at round r, Bf is the size of buffer and Nq_i is the number of packets in queue i.

Then, the modified weight of queue i at round r is computed as:

$$Mw_{i,r} = Pv_{i,r} \cdot dw_{i,r}. \quad (6)$$

Also, Fig. 1 is used to demonstrate the effect of the proposed PLAS. The Fig. and Eq. (6) are used to compute the modified weights as shown in Table 2. The table shows that the modified weights are computed and represented as: $Mw_{1,1} = 4$, $Mw_{2,1} = 4$,

$Mw_{3,1} = 2$, and $Mw_{4,1} = 6$. These weights are assigned to respective weight counters as: $WC_{1,1} = 4$, $WC_{2,1} = 4$, $WC_{3,1} = 2$, and $WC_{4,1} = 6$ as shown in Fig. 5. This Fig. schedules packet as:

$q_{1,1} \rightarrow q_{2,1} \rightarrow q_{3,1} \rightarrow q_{4,1} \rightarrow q_{1,2} \rightarrow q_{2,2} \rightarrow q_{3,2} \rightarrow q_{4,2} \rightarrow q_{1,3} \rightarrow q_{2,3} \rightarrow q_{4,3} \rightarrow$
$q_{1,4} \rightarrow q_{2,5} \rightarrow q_{4,4} \rightarrow q_{2,5} \rightarrow q_{4,5} \rightarrow q_{4,6}$

Table 2. Modified weight computation

$q_{i,1}$	$Nq_{i,1}$	$dw_{i,1}$	$Pv_{i,1}$	$Mw_{i,1}$
$q_{1,1}$	4	2	2	4
$q_{2,1}$	5	4	5/4	5
$q_{3,1}$	3	2	1	2
$q_{4,1}$	6	6	1	6

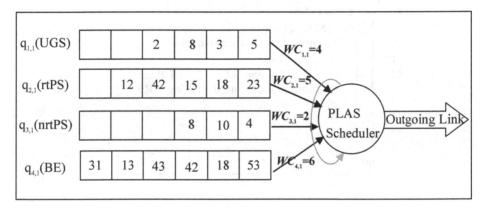

Fig. 5. Shows the state of a PLAS after weights are assigned

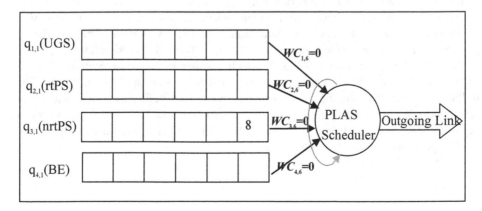

Fig. 6. Shows the PLAS after weights have been exhausted

After packets are scheduled from Fig. 5, only one packet is queued before the next counter reset as shown in Fig. 6. In this Fig., as compared with the LAWRR scheduler in Fig. 4, the PLAS scheduler reduced the total number of delayed packets from four to one. Hence, the number of delay sensitive packets ($q_{1,6}$ and $q_{2,6}$) that were delayed have been reduced from three to zero.

The Pseudo Code for the algorithm is shown in Algorithm 1.

Algorithm 1. PLAS Algorithm

```
1    n    ← number of connected queues
2    qi,r ← queue I at round r
3    Mwi,r ← modified weight of queue i at round r
4    WCi,r ← weight counter value of queue I at round r
5    r ← current RR round
6    WCi,r ← 0(i=1,2...n-1)
7    r ← 0
8    for i ←0 to n-1 do
9        if qi,r ≠ NULL, then
10           Compute Mwi,r using Equation 6
11           WCi,r ← Mwi,r
12           if qi,r ≠NULL and WCi,r ≠ NULL then
13               Transmit packet from qi,r using WRR
14           else
15               r ← r +1
16       else
17           Next i
18   end
```

---

4 Performance Evaluation

In this section, we compare the performance of LAWRR [3] with the proposed PLAS scheduling algorithm in terms of average delay. A discrete-event simulator was developed and used to conduct simulations for the evaluation. The simulation parameters used were adopted from [3] as shown in Table 3. The simulation topology in [3] was adopted as shown in Fig. 7, which consists of one Base Station (BS), 35 Subscriber Stations (SS) distributed around the BS, and an application server. The traffics are generated from the server, which provides four traffics each from a different application. We assume that each user traffic is carried by one SS and that each user can only use one type of traffic in a given time. The traffics are prioritized according to their QoS requirements in the following order:

UGS → rtPS → nrtPS → BE.

Figure 8 shows the average delay on SSs for LAWRR and PLAS for the rtPS class. The figure demonstrates that the PLAS achieves better result compared to the other scheme. This is as a result of the increase in the service rate that allow majority of packets to be sent and hence lead to a smaller number of packets being delayed in each around.

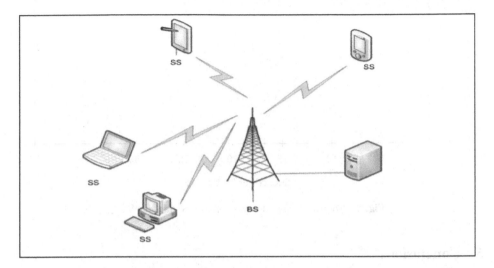

Fig. 7. Shows simulation network topology

Table 3. Simulation parameters

Parameter	Value
Base station Freq.	2.5 GHz
Duplexing mode	TDD
Bandwidth	5 Mbps
Frame length	5 ms
Cyclic prefix duration	11.43 μs
Basic symbol	91.43 μs
FFT	1,024
PHY	OFDM
DL permutation zone	PUSC
MAC PDU length	Variable
Fragmentation	Enable
ARQ and packing	Disable
DL-UL MAPS	Variable

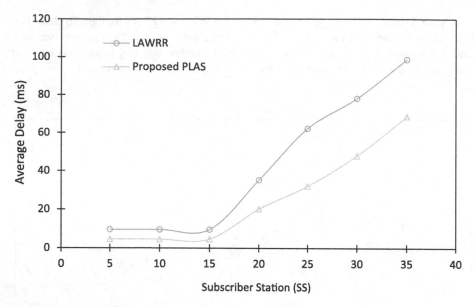

Fig. 8. Shows average delay for the rtPS class on SS

5 Conclusions

In this paper, a PLAS is proposed to increase the service rate of real time traffics in WiMAX networks. The algorithm introduces a mechanism that prioritizes real time over non-real time traffics. Simulation experiments were carried out to evaluate the performance of the proposed PLAS and the LAWRR algorithms. The results demonstrated that PLAS yields better performance than LAWRR in terms of average delay.

Acknowledgement. The authors would like to appreciate the Tertiary Education Trust Fund (TETFund) Nigeria for supporting this research work through the National Research Fund (NRF) Grant No: CC – STI.

References

1. Chakchai, S., Raj, J., Adel-Karim, T.: Scheduling in IEEE 802.16e mobile WiMAX networks: key issues and a survey. IEEE J. Sel. Areas Commun. **27**, 156–171 (2009)
2. Audace, M., Saadi. B., Lami, C.F.: A priority-weighted round robin scheduling strategy for a WBAN based healthcare monitoring system. In: 13th IEEE Consumer Communications & Networking Conference (CCNC), pp. 224–229 (2016)
3. Ibrahim, S., Shamala, S., Azmin, J., Zuriati, Z.: A load-aware weighted round-robin algorithm for IEEE 802.16 networks. EURASIP J. Wirel. Commun. Netw. **2014**, 1–12 (2014)

4. Mohamed-el-Amine, B., Abdelhafid, A., Lorenz, P.: Adaptive scheduling mechanism for IPTV over WiMAX IEEE 802.16j networks. Int. J. Commun. Syst. (2012) **27**, 1009–1019 (2014)
5. Zuber, P., Uperia, D.: Design and implementation of low latency weighted round robin (LLWRR) scheduling for high speed networks. Int. J. Wirel. Mob. Netw. (IJWMN) **6**, 59–71 (2014)
6. Claudio, C., Luciano, L., Enzo, M.: Quality of service support in IEEE 802.16 networks. IEEE Netw. Mag **20**, 50–55 (2006)
7. Alexander, S., Olli, A., Timo, H.: Scheduling solution for IEEE 802.16 base station. Int. J. Comput. Telecommun. Netw. **52**, 96–115 (2008)
8. Chih-Peng, L., Jenhui, C., Hsing-Lung, C.: An efficient bandwidth allocation algorithm for real-time VBR stream transmission under IEEE 802.16 wireless networks. J. Netw. Comput. Appl. **33**, 467–476 (2010)
9. Mardini, W., Abu Alfoul, M.M.: Modified WRR scheduling algorithm for WiMAX networks. Netw. Protoc. Algorithms J. **3**, 24–53 (2011)
10. Saha, D., Mukherjee, S., Tripathi, S.: Carry-over round robin: a simple cell scheduling mechanism for ATM networks. IEEE/ACM Trans. Netw. **6**, 779–796 (1996)
11. Manoli, K., Stefanos, S., Costas, C.: IEEE J. Sel. Areas Commun. **9**, 1265–1279 (1991)

Scheduling Cloud Workloads Using Carry-On Weighted Round Robin

Olasupo Ajayi(⊠), Florence Oladeji, Charles Uwadia,
and Afolorunsho Omosowun

Department of Computer Sciences, University of Lagos, Lagos, Nigeria
{olaajayi, foladeji, couwadia}@unilag.edu.ng,
afolorunshoi5l@gmail.com

Abstract. Cloud Computing represents a paradigm shift in computing. It advocates the use of computing resources as a service rather than as a product. The numerous advantages which the Cloud offers has led to many users adopting it at a phenomenal rate. Providing service to this ever growing number of users in a fast and effective manner is a major challenge. Numerous researchers have proposed various approaches to scheduling user workloads, notable among which are the First-Come-First-Serve and Weight Round Robin (WRR), and have obtained varied levels of successes. Unfairness and excess allocation delay are some of the shortcomings of these approach. There is also the assumption that all Cloud users' workloads belong to a single class of requirement. This work proposes an efficient and fair Cloud workload scheduling algorithm called Adaptive Carry-On Weighted Round Robin (ACWRR), and also takes into consideration multiple workloads classes. Experimental simulations were conducted with ACWRR benchmarked against WRR. Results show that ACWRR performs better than WRR by at least 13% in terms of system latency and 38% for makespan.

Keywords: Cloud computing · Multi-queues · Queuing · Scheduling
Weighted Round Robin

1 Introduction

Cloud Computing is a model for enabling ubiquitous and on-demand access to shared pool of computing resource [1]. These resources are made available to customers on a pay-per-use model, similar to utilities such as electricity and water supply. Cloud data centres are building where a large number of inter-connected servers are operated. Each server hosts a number of virtual servers on which user requests are deployed. Cloud computing is being adapted at a phenomenal rate, as recent reports have shown that there are over 140 million active Cloud users [2] and are growing at a rate of about 17% annually [3]. With this huge number of users allocation of requests to Cloud servers must be done efficiently. In [4], the authors grouped Cloud users into three group – Gold, Silver and Bronze and prioritized allocation of their requests to Cloud servers. The Gold class enjoyed highest priority and least delay however the Silver and particularly the Bronze class users were not treated fairly and suffered long delays.

© ICST Institute for Computer Sciences, Social Informatics and Telecommunications Engineering 2018
V. Odumuyiwa et al. (Eds.): AFRICOMM 2017, LNICST 250, pp. 60–71, 2018.
https://doi.org/10.1007/978-3-319-98827-6_5

This work therefore proposes a user request allocation scheme that takes into consideration multiple user classes and allocated requests to servers in a fair manner. In the remaining sections of this paper, the terms Cloud servers and Physical Machines (PMs) are used interchangeably as well as the terms user request and user workload. The rest of this paper is organized as follows: related works on workload allocation in Cloud computing are discussed in Sect. 2. A detailed description of the proposed approach is given in Sect. 3. Experimental setup and performance analysis are done in Sect. 4. Sections 5 and 6 respectively presents the contributions and conclusion of this paper.

2 Related Works

Round Robin [5] though mostly suited for static environments has been proposed by numerous authors as a technique for workload allocation in Cloud Computing. It is a circular variant of First-Come-First-Serve (FCFS) allocation scheme, wherein workloads are allocated resources in time sharing manner. However, being a static approach, it does not take into consideration the status or current workload of the PMs into consideration when allocating workloads.

Round Robin with Server Affinity (RRSA) was proposed by [6]. The work introduced a variant of round-robin, which allocates workloads to PMs with a view of keeping a workload balance amongst the PMs. RRSA distributes workloads using the conventional round robin algorithm but introduces hash map and PM state list which store information about the last PM allocations and the current state of PMs respectively. Experimental results showed that when compared to the classic Round Robin, the response time improved as the number of data centres increased however processing time was only marginally better. There is also the high possibility of dip in performance during the process of searching the hash map.

In [7] an efficient version of the throttled allocation scheme was presented. Throttled allocation is a scheme that allocated workload to VMs with a view of keeping a balanced workload distribution amongst VMs. Prior to workload allocation, the scheduler checks its index-table for the status of all VMs. If a suitable VM is found for the workload, it is immediately allocated to the VM, otherwise it is enqueued. In the work, the proposed Efficient Throttled Algorithm (ETA) addressed the long execution time experienced by workloads when the using the classic throttled algorithm. The authors compared the performance of ETA with Round Robin, classic throttled and Equal Spread Current Execution algorithms and reported improvements in average processing time and overall response time. However the proposed approach was only minutely better than the classic throttled and at par with the two other algorithms on all metrics. The Round Robin and throttled algorithms are two of the default algorithms included in CloudAnalyst [8] - a popular Cloud research and simulation toolkit based on CloudSim.

Join Idle Queue was proposed in [9] as an approach that combines distributed dispatcher with Idle Queues (IQ). Each dispatcher has an IQ onto which idle PMs queue. On arrival of a task, the dispatcher checks its IQ for idle PM(s). If found, it dispatches the task to the first PM on the IQ else it is randomly dispatched to any PM. Idle PMs also enqueue themselves onto a dispatcher's IQ randomly or based on the shortest IQ. Though effective, the approach does not take workload imbalanced between busy PMs into consideration. In [10], the author analysed the performance of JIQ [9] using fluid limit approach and showed that it is advantageous for a PM to enqueue itself on a dispatchers IQ, while still actively servicing user requests. The use of early threshold was also recommended.

In [11, 12], a linear workload allocation scheme called based on Best Fit Descending (BFD) was proposed. The scheme, sorts all PMs in descending order of available resources then searches through the list of PMs for one which best matches the user workload requirements (VM). Though an efficient allocation scheme in terms of resource utilization, the linear search process used can increase allocation time especially in data centres with large number of PMs and user workloads with multiple resource requirements.

All the above reviewed works considered single user workload queue, implying that it is assumed that all user workloads belong to a single class of requirement. This is not true in reality, as factors such as users' purchasing power and socio-economic status play a significant role in daily lives and can therefore not be ignored. The authors in [4] therefore considered user workload classes and used these classes for workload allocation. The introduction of the Double-Depth Half Interval Scheduling (2DHIS) as a replacement to the BD scheme used in [11, 12], allowed the proposed algorithm finds suitable PMs for user workloads faster thus reducing allocation delay time. However, similar to [11, 12], a First-Come-First-Serve (FCFS) approach was also used for workload scheduling. Also the authors primarily focused on workloads within the Gold class with highest priority, thereby resulting in increased delay times for workloads of lower priority classes.

The authors in [13] introduced a modified Weighted Round Robin (WRR) [14], called Carry-on Weighted Round Robin (cWRR). It is a multi-queue scheduling algorithm like WRR but unlike WRR, in this work whenever a queue has less packets than its allocated service quantum, the excess quantum is carried over to the next active queue rather than being ignored as in the case of WRR. Unlike Deficit Round Robin (DRR) [15], the extra quantum is used in the current round, and not in the subsequent round. This in effect allows cWRR to better utilize the available bandwidth per round. Also the fact that cWRR refreshes each queues' service quantum ever round makes it a fair scheduling algorithm.

This paper adapts the cWRR by applying it as a workload scheduling algorithm for Cloud environments with multiple workload classes. The new scheme, simply called adapted-cWRR or ACWRR improves on the work of [4] with the introduction of cWRR which is able to schedule multiple user workload classes in an efficient and fair manner to all classes.

3   Proposed Approach

In this section, the Adapted-Carry-On Weighted Round Robin (ACWRR) is presented. ACWRR groups users' workloads into three (3) classes of Gold, Silver and Bronze, similar to [4]. However, rather than the first-come-first-serve used, a cWRR based scheduler is used to allocate user workloads to VMs/PMs in the Cloud Data centre (DC).

The ACWRR model shown in Fig. 1 can be broken into the following steps below, while a logical flow is depicted in Fig. 2.

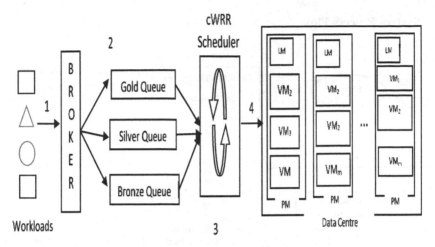

Fig. 1. The Adapted-Carry-On Weighted Round Robin (ACWRR) model

1. Workloads are submitted by users.
2. The workloads are grouped into three classes.
3. CWRR is used to select workload to schedule, this is shown in Algorithm 1.
4. Selected work are allocated to resources within the DC for processing.

3.1 Algorithm 1: CWRR

```
1. Initialization:
      a. ActiveList = NULL
      b. Bonus = 0      ,
      c. Enqueuing module: on arrival of queue o
      d. InsertWorkload(Qᵢ)
      e. i= ExtractFlow(p)
2. If(ExistsinActiveList(i) = = FALSE) then
      a. AppendToActiveList(i) // Create scheduler
         queue for flow i
      b. SetWeight(i)
3. Dequeuing module:
      a. While (TRUE){
      b. If NotEmpty(ActiveList) q = getqueueindex ()
      c. if(ExistinActiveList(q))        i = getQueue(q)
      d. Qq =Qq+Bonus   }
4. While ((Qq > 0) and Not Empty(i)){ // Process a
   workload from queue i
      a. p = Dequeue(q)
      b. Qq = Qq - 1                             }
5. If(Qq >= 0 And Empty(i)){
      a. RemoveinActiveList(i)
      b. Bonus=Qi
      c. Qi=0     }
6. If (Qi= 0 and Empty(i))     AppendToActiveList(q)
            }
```

3.2 System Process Flow

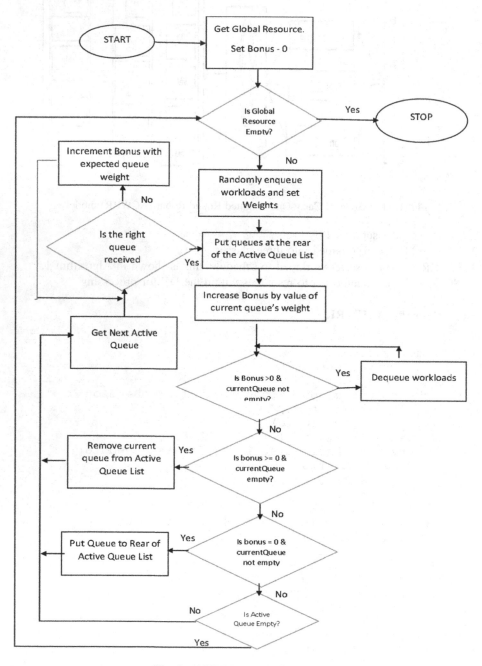

Fig. 2. ACWRR system flow chart

4   Performance Evaluation

In evaluating the efficacy of the proposed ACWRR model, simulated experiments were conducted using CloudSim [16]. The experimental setup used consist of a DC with 800 host machines of with two different processing powers in Millions of Instructions Per Second (MIPS) - 1,860 MIPS and 2,660 MIPS. Real workload traces from PlanetLab day 3 [17] were used, and consisted of 1078 workloads. The ACWRR model was benchmarked against the conventional WRR using the following metrics:

1. Average workload delay per queue – which is a measure of the time spent by a user workload on any given queue waiting to be scheduled; and given in (1).

$$\frac{\sum_i^n (D_i - A_i)}{n}. \tag{1}$$

   Where D_i is departure time of a workload i, A_i is arrival time of a workload i, and n is number of workloads on a queue.

2. Makespan per queue – a measure of the time it takes to schedule the last workload on a queue.

$$D_l - D_o. \tag{2}$$

   In (2), D_l is the departure time of the last workload on a queue, and D_o is the departure time of the first workload on the queue.

3. Average overall workload delay – average time spent by a workload across all queues. It is given in (3)

$$m * \sum_k^m \frac{\sum_i^n (D_{i,k} - A_{i,k})}{n}. \tag{3}$$

   Where $D_{i,k}$ is departure time of a workload i on a queue k, $A_{i,k}$ is arrival time of a workload i on a queue k, n is number of workloads on queue k, and m is the number of queues.

4. Latency per queue – inverse of the number of workloads scheduled on a queue per unit time and given in (4)

$$\left\{ \frac{\sum w_q}{T_q} \right\}^{-1}. \tag{4}$$

   Where w is number of workloads on a queue q and T is time taken to schedule all workloads on q.

5. Average system throughput – inverse of the average number of workloads scheduled per unit time across all queues.

$$\left\{ Q * \sum_q^Q \frac{\sum w_q}{T_q} \right\}^{-1}. \tag{5}$$

In (5), Q is the total number of queues, w_q and T_q are the workloads and allocation time on queue q.

5   Results

Implementation was in two phases. At the first phase, workloads were enqueued onto the three queues, while in the second phase, the enqueued workloads were selected/dequeued for allocation using one of three arrival schemes viz. random, equal and double. Using the random scheme, workloads were enqueued onto randomly selected queues. With the equal scheme, an even proportion of workloads to be dequeued were enqueued, such that at each iteration the arrival rate of workloads equal the departure rate. Finally with the double, departure rate is twice the arrival rate. For each of these schemes, a dequeueing ratio of 5:3:2 was maintained for all queues.

In Fig. 3, the latency (inverse of throughput) of ACWRR and WRR are depicted. In this graph, for all queues, ACWRR outperformed WRR by at least 13.8% and implies that ACWRR is able to schedule at least 38.7% more workloads on the average than WRR.

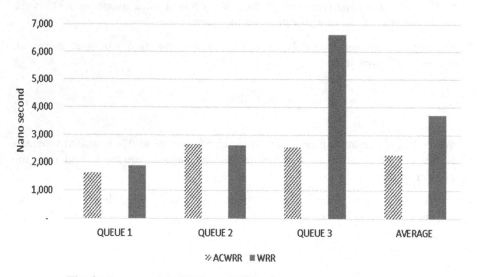

Fig. 3. Latency of ACWRR vs. WRR using random enqueue scheme

A comparison of the makepan is shown in Fig. 4 and though WRR is shown to have lower makespan for all three queues versus ACWRR, the values vary across these queues. For queue 1, WRR results in 30,420 ns, while ACWRR gave 37,030 ns. For queue 2, makespans of 33,058 ns and 36,839 ns were recorded for WRR and ACWRR

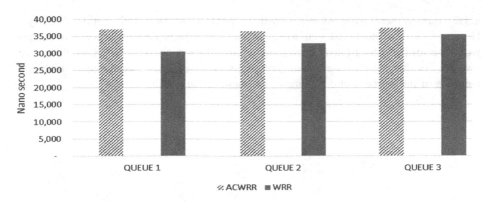

Fig. 4. Makespan of ACWRR vs. WRR using random enqueue scheme

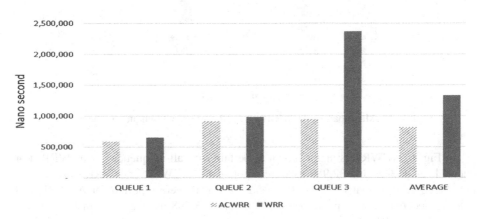

Fig. 5. Scheduling delay of ACWRR vs. WRR using random enqueue scheme

respectively. While for queue 3, WRR resulted in 35,672 ns versus ACWRR at 37,563 ns. These results show that the dequeuing ratio largely influences the makespan when WRR is used, resulting in queue 1 (with highest the dequeue ratio) having shortest makespan and queue 3 (with lowest dequeue ratio) having the longest makespan. However, when ACWRR is used, despite the dequeuing ratio (5:3:2), all queues experiences similar makespans, thus making ACWRR fairer to all its queues versus WRR.

Figure 5 shows the waiting time or delay of workloads in a queue. For queue 1, which has the highest dequeue ratio, workloads experience 10.5% less delay with ACWRR versus WRR. For the second queue, workload delays improved by 6.8% when ACWRR is used, while for the last queue, ACWRR resulted in significantly less waiting time with an improvement of 150.9% versus WRR. On the average, ACWRR resulted in 38.7% lower workload delay time than WRR.

Due to the unpredictability of the random allocation scheme and to have a fair benchmarking assessment, the equal and double schemes were also used. When using the equal scheme (equal arrival and departure times), WRR resulted in an average of

4.5% improvement over ACWRR with respect to latency and workload delays. However, it must be noted that when arrival rate equals departure rate, no queues would be formed hence queue management algorithms such as ACWRR would not be needed. For this reasons, these results are not shown, except for Makespan which is a measure of the fairness of a scheme to its queues. This is shown in Fig. 6.

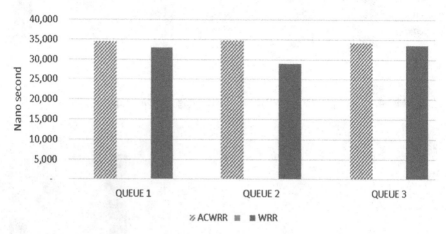

Fig. 6. Makespan of ACWRR vs. WRR using equal enqueue scheme

In Fig. 6, ACWRR is again shown to be fairer on all its queues versus WRR. For queue 1, 34,453 ns and 32,989 ns were reported for ACWRR and WRR respectively. For queue 2, makespans of 34,790 ns and 29,014 ns were reported for ACWRR and WRR respectively. For queue 3, 34,202 ns and 33,588 ns, were the makespans for ACWRR and WRR. As with the random enqueuing scheme, ACWRR is fairer to all its queues versus WRR.

In order to further ascertain the results, a last test was conducted using the double enqueue scheme, wherein, arrival rate is half the departure rate. In Fig. 7, the latency of ACWRR and WRR when using the double enqueue scheme are compared. The results show that under the same circumstances (enqueuing rate), ACWRR has significantly better latency (inverse of throughput) than WRR. On the average, ACWRR has a latency of 91 versus WRR's 1977.

Figure 8, shows the makespan of ACWRR versus WRR. For all measurements, lower values are desirable. Across all queues, and consistent with the other enqueuing schemes, ACWRR results in an even makespan across all queues. ACWRR results in makespans of 73,755 ns, 73,466 ns and 71,400 ns for queues 1, 2 and 3 respectively. Similarly WRR also results in an even spread of makespan across all queues at 353,479 ns, 353,322 ns and 352,875 ns.

Finally, and in tandem with the latency and makespan, Fig. 9, shows that ACWRR schedules workloads significantly faster than WRR across all queues, with an average delay of 66,968 ns versus 1,449,857 ns for ACWRR and WRR respectively. This implies that using ACWRR, workloads experience shorted delays than with WRR.

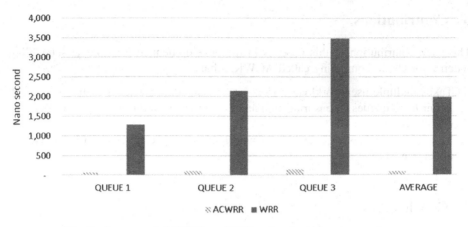

Fig. 7. Latency of ACWRR vs. WRR using double enqueue scheme

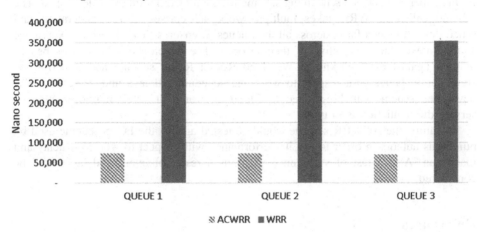

Fig. 8. Makespan of ACWRR vs. WRR using double enqueue scheme

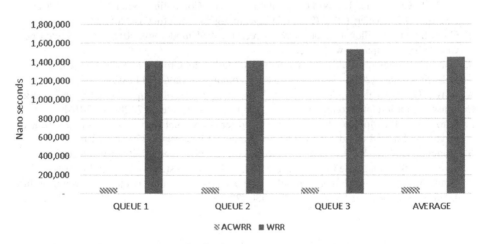

Fig. 9. Scheduling delay of ACWRR vs. WRR using double enqueue scheme

6 Contributions

The main contribution of this paper is in the development of a workload scheduling scheme for Cloud computing called ACWRR that:

a. Takes multiple user workload classes into consideration when scheduling.
b. Is fair to all queues by ensuring all queues experience similar makespan irrespective of their priority.
c. Reduces the delays experienced by workload waiting on queues to be scheduled allocation.

7 Conclusion

In this paper, a workload scheduling scheme for Cloud Computing was developed. The scheme called ACWRR takes multiple workload classes into consideration and schedules workloads fairly across all the queues. It ensures that all queues experience similar makespan irrespective of their priority. The developed scheme was benchmarked against the well-known Weighted Round Robin scheme and it performed significantly better with respect to workload scheduling delays and makespan. The developed scheme can be applied to Cloud environment wherein prioritization or service differentiation is in use.

In future, the ACWRR scheme would be tested against the FCFS scheme used by numerous authors in order to test its performance with respect to workload delay and makespan. Also a test of violation of SLA as a result of queuing delay would be considered.

References

1. Mell, P., Grance, T.: The NIST Definition of Cloud Computing. NIST Special Publication 800-145. Whitepaper, NIST (2011). http://acm.org/citation.cfm?id=2206223
2. Cisco Inc.: Cisco Global Cloud Index: Forecast and Methodology, 2015–2020. Whitepaper, Cisco (2016). http://www.cisco.com
3. Gartner: Worldwide Public Cloud Services Market to Grow 17 Percent in 2016, Press Release, Gartner (2016). http://www.gartner.com/newsroom/id/3443517
4. Ajayi, O., Oladeji, F., Uwadia, C.: Multi-class load balancing for QoS and energy conservation in cloud computing. West Afr. J. Ind. Acad. Res. 17, 28–36 (2016)
5. Sotomayor, B., Montero, R., Llorente, I., Foster, I.: Virtual infrastructure management in private and hybrid clouds. IEEE Internet Comput. 13(5), 14–22 (2009). IEEE
6. Mahajan, K., Makroo, A., Dahiya, D.: Round robin with server affinity: a VM load balancing algorithm for cloud based infrastructure. J. Inf. Process Syst. 9(3), 379–394 (2013)
7. Patel, D., Rajawat, A.: Efficient throttled load balancing algorithm in cloud environment. Int. J. Modern Trends Eng. Res. 2(3), 463–480 (2015)

8. Wickremasinghe, B., Calheiros, R., Buyya, R.: Cloudanalyst: a cloudsim-based visual modeller for analysing cloud computing environments and applications. In: 2010 24th IEEE International Conference on Advanced Information Networking and Applications (AINA), pp. 446–452. IEEE (2010)
9. Lu, Y., Xie, G., Kliot, G., Geller, A., Larus, J., Greenberg, A.: Join-Idle-Queue: a novel load balancing algorithm for dynamically scalable web services. Perform. Eval. **68**(11), 1056–1071 (2011)
10. Mitzenmacher, M.: Analyzing distributed Join-Idle-Queue: a fluid limit approach. In: 2016 54th Annual Allerton Conference on Communication, Control and Computing (Allerton), pp. 312–318. IEEE (2016)
11. Beloglazov, A., Buyya, R.: Optimal online deterministic algorithms and adaptive heuristics for energy and performance efficient dynamic consolidation of virtual machines in Cloud data centers. Concurrency Comput.: Pract. Experience **24**(13), 1397–1420 (2012)
12. Farahnakian, F., Pahikkala, T., Liljeberg, P., Plosila, J., Hieu, N., Tenhunen, H.: Energy-aware VM consolidation in cloud data centers using utilization prediction model. IEEE Trans. Cloud Comput. 13 (2016). http://ieeexplore.ieee.org/document/7593250/
13. Oladeji, F., Oyetunji, M., Okunoye, O.: CWRR: a scheduling algorithm for maximizing performance of quality of service network router. Int. J. Comput. Appl. **41**(2), 30–34 (2012)
14. Shimonishi, H., Yoshida, M., Fan, R., Suzuki, H.: An improvement of weighted round robin cell scheduling in ATM networks. In: Global Telecommunications Conference, GLOBE-COM 1997, vol. 2, pp. 1119–1123. IEEE (1997)
15. Shreedar, M., Varghese, G.: Efficient fair queuing using deficit round robin. IEEE/ACM Trans. Netw. **4**(3), 375–385 (1996). ACM
16. Beloglazov, A., Buyya, R.: Optimal online deterministic algorithms and adaptive heuristics for energy and performance efficient dynamic consolidation of virtual machines in cloud data centers. Concurrency Comput.: Pract. Experience (CCPE) **24**(13), 1397–1420 (2012)
17. Park, K., Pai, V.: CoMon: a mostly-scalable monitoring system for PlanetLab. ACM SIGOPS Oper. Syst. Rev. **40**(1), 65–74 (2006). ACM

Performance Analysis of a Collaborative DSA-Based Network with Malicious Nodes

Augustine Takyi[1(✉)], Melissa Densmore[1], Senka Hadzic[1], and David Johnson[1,2]

[1] Department of Computer Science, University of Cape Town, Rondebosch 7701,
South Africa
{atakyi,mdensmore,shadzic}@cs.uct.ac.za

[2] Center for Scientific and Industrial Research, Meiring Naudé Road Brummeria,
Pretoria, South Africa
djohnson@csir.co.za

Abstract. This work analyses the performance of a Dynamic Spectrum Access (DSA) network with secondary nodes to provide Internet services, and studies the impact of malicious nodes and cooperative secondary nodes on the performance of the network and spectrum utilization. The work mathematically models the throughput, latency, and spectrum utilization with varying numbers of malicious nodes, secondary nodes, miss probabilities, and false alarm probabilities, and studies their effect on performance of the network. The results point to rapid spectrum starvation as the number of malicious nodes increase, as well as the negative impact of too many secondary nodes crowding out available spectrum with resultant degradation of throughput and latency.

Keywords: Spectrum utilization · Secondary node · Backhaul
Malicious node · Throughput · Latency · Primary user

1 Introduction

Estimates have confirmed availability of white spaces (unused licensed bands) and similar observation of under-utilization of the allocated spectrum have been reported by Spectrum Policy Task Force appointed by Federal Communication Commission in the United States and others [1,4]. Spectrum efficiency can be increased significantly by giving opportunistic access of these frequency bands to a group of potential users (unlicensed users) for whom the band has not officially been allocated to use [4]. The users in these networks are expected to be opportunistic. The users refer to the nodes on the network. Therefore granting access to such users in the spectrum may create room for malicious nodes (secondary nodes which do not follow spectrum etiquette and cause harm to other spectrum users). There is the need for all the opportunistic nodes within a specified location to collaborate or cooperate to ensure fairness in the spectrum. Recently, there has been much research in the areas of nodes collaboration or cooperation

© ICST Institute for Computer Sciences, Social Informatics and Telecommunications Engineering 2018
V. Odumuyiwa et al. (Eds.): AFRICOMM 2017, LNICST 250, pp. 72–82, 2018.
https://doi.org/10.1007/978-3-319-98827-6_6

and the effects of malicious nodes presence in the DSA-based (dynamic spectrum access based) networks [1–3,5–10]. The rationale for the collaboration is to help detect secondary nodes present in the network or to help report system abuse to the decision centers to identify malicious nodes in the network.

Neighbour collaborative monitoring was demonstrated in [5] where nodes monitor neighbours by measuring their RSSI (received signal strength indicator) values to estimate the distance of the neighbour nodes, which effectively help to detect sybil nodes. Sybil (replicated nodes produced by a secondary node) Nodes Detection is a neighbour monitoring approach used to detect sybil attacks on a network. It uses localization verification technique based on received signal strength, which allows a node to verify the authenticity of another node by estimating its future geographic location and comparing them to its evaluated position. However, the sybil detection failed to prove the validity of the RSS (received signal strength) in estimating the distance to determine the future distance. It was observed in [5] that communication cost was too high which will have a severe negative effect on the performance metrics (throughput and delay) of the network.

Again, neighbour nodes discovery was proposed in [6]. This approach considers a single seed node (with all the parameters known) to locate other nodes by broadcasting a message to all neighbour nodes within its range. The most distant node from the seed node becomes the next seed node, using the above process, all the nodes coordinates are estimated [6]. The proposed protocol seems promising, but it may unnecessarily increase network communication overhead when implemented in the real world: which can be a major problem for opportunistic networks that have limited channels to use for communication.

Moreover, the presence of malicious nodes in a DSA-based network was proposed by Jin et al. [8]. In their work, it was observed that the closer the malicious nodes to the secondary node, the higher the values of miss and false alarm probabilities obtained. The higher probabilities also affected the detection of the presence of the primary user by the honest secondary node (the unlicensed user in the spectrum that does not work against the spectrum etiquette).

Furthermore, Pinifolo et al. [11] considered interference of neighbour nodes in the secondary devices that operate on UHF (Ultra high frequency) band. It discovered that neighbour nodes within a distance range of 7 km apart could have neighbour nodes interference in the UHF band. However, it failed to consider neighbour monitoring in the cooperative network to know the impact on the performance of the density of the secondary nodes in the network.

The main contribution of this paper is three folds. Firstly, we model dynamic spectrum access network that uses neighbour monitoring in cooperative secondary nodes and analyses how malicious nodes present in the network may downgrade performance indicators such as throughput and delay and also affect spectrum utilization. Secondly, It also assesses the impact on performance by increasing the number of collaborative secondary nodes in backhaul nodes of a DSA-based network. Thirdly, The study developed mathematical models to measure throughput, latency and spectrum utilization taking into consideration all possible interferences. We demonstrate this work through simulations. The paper is organized as follows; Sect. 1 considers introduction, Sect. 2 considers general system model and the performance metrics, Sect. 3 results and discussion and finally Sect. 4 conclusion and future work.

2   System Model

In our model, we positioned fixed secondary nodes (the unlicensed users within the spectrum) connected to the fusion center. The secondary nodes are positioned within a square area of $(d * d)\,km$. The ith device, with position coordinates $P_i = (x_i, y_j)$ where, $i = 1, 2, 3, ..., N$ and $j = 1, 2, 3, ..., N$ the positions of n nodes are assumed to be independent of each other. Each of the secondary nodes has a transmission range R within the area. Primary user (license user within the spectrum) is located at a minimum distance of $\sqrt{(x_i^2 + y_i^2)}$, from the secondary node. The fusion center is empowered with the responsibility of making spectrum decisions for the secondary nodes. Secondary and malicious nodes sensed the spectrum using energy detection, as shown in Fig. 1. Secondary nodes are also embedded with spectrum analyzers to capture the received signal strength from the neighbours, which is forwarded to the fusion center. We make the following assumptions to perform the analysis.

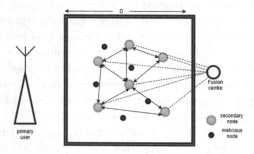

Fig. 1. Network with TV white space devices as back haul controlled by FC

2.1   Assumptions

    I. There are N secondary nodes and M malicious nodes in the system.
   II. Each secondary node, shall communicate to the fusion center using control channel.
 III. Secondary nodes are static and do not change position.
 IV. Secondary nodes are used as backhaul nodes to provide access network to rural communities
  V. The primary user (transmitter) is at a minimum distance of $\sqrt{(x_q^2 + y_q^2)}$, where $q = 1, 2, 3, ..., \infty$, Such that x_q and y_q are position coordinates of a secondary node.

VI. The primary user transmits at the power of P_t, the secondary node at P_s and the malicious node at a P_m.

VII. The positions of the secondary nodes and the malicious nodes are uniformly distributed in the square of a side length of $(d)km$. They are statistically independent of each other.

VIII. Malicious nodes are randomly distributed.

IX. The received signal strength indicator values received by the fusion center are normally distributed random variables with mean μ and variance σ^2.

X. There is cooperation between the secondary nodes. Therefore a malicious node attack is analyzed collaboratively.

XI. Two access networks are connected to the backhaul network via access point device.

XII. The fusion center has Internet connectivity through a gateway node and therefore provides access to broadband internet through the backhaul secondary nodes to the users.

XIII. Each secondary node has an adaptive modulation scheme which offers the capability to increase the radio's receiver sensitivity.

2.2 Performance Metrics

We shall consider how malicious nodes affect throughput, latency and spectrum utilization of the network shown in Fig. 1. In computing the latency and the Throughput we assume that the transmitter is fully able to utilize the entire channel capacity. Also channel coefficient values are dependent on the transmission environment parameters such as, distance, antenna height, etc. But, The channel coefficients are independent on the Bandwidth. Coefficients were derived from the Hata propagation model.

Throughput is defined as the amount of data that can be transmitted through a given channel or link per second. It is measured in bits per second (bps) Given the bandwidth of the channel in the backhaul network as B. We arbitrary considered a bandwidth value of $100\,MHz$, this is because of the scenario of the backhaul nodes we considered. We assume that there are m secondary nodes in the network. The throughput can therefore be estimated as follows,

$$Throughput(TP) = Blog_2 \left(\frac{|h_t|P_t}{|h_{int}|P_{int}+p_{miss}\sum_{m=0}^{M}|h_m|P_m+\sigma^2} \right), \quad (1)$$

where
h_t = transmitter coefficient
P_t = transmitter power
h_{int} = interference coefficient
P_{int} = interference power
h_m = malicious node interference coefficient
P_m = malicious node power

p_{miss} = miss detection probability
σ = additive white Gaussian noise.

Also, including the factor of the secondary nodes collaborating in the network, throughput will be given by:

$$Throughput(TP) = Blog_2\left(\frac{|h_t|P_t}{|h_{int}|P_{int}+p_{miss}\sum_{m=0}^{M}|h_m|P_m+\sum_{S=0}^{S}|h_s|P_s+\sigma^2}\right), \quad (2)$$

where

h_s = secondary node coefficient
P_s = secondary node power
σ = .additive white Gaussian noise

Latency is the time it takes for data transmitted by a sender to reach the intended receiver (destination). Considering Fig. 1, when user 1 sends message to user 4 on the other network with data size of (D)Mbps.

$$Latency = D\left[\frac{1}{TP_1} + \frac{1}{TP_2} + \frac{1}{TP_3} + ... + \frac{1}{TP_q}\right], \quad (3)$$

where,
TP_q = Throughput for the link between the transmitter and the receiver, $\forall q, q = 1, 2, 3, 4, ..., n$. The latency is the sum of all the individual links delay because, the backhual nodes operate mesh routing protocol which may route packet through any of the links available and optimal at all times. We therefore assumed that packets travel through all the q links.

Spectrum utilization in simple terms is the usage of the spectrum. Both the secondary and malicious nodes sense the spectrum with a given probability of detection, miss-detection (Miss detection probability is when the transmission is made by the primary transmitter, but the secondary node assumes the transmission is made by the malicious node [8]) or false alarm (is when the actual transmission is made by the malicious node but the secondary node assumes the transmission is from the primary transmitter [8]) probabilities.

Let N be the set of secondary nodes that provide backhaul to the access point.

$$N = \{n_1, n_2, n_1, ..., n_\alpha\} \quad (4)$$

In addition, let C be the set of channels that can be used by the backhaul secondary nodes:

$$C = \begin{bmatrix} c_{n_1}^1 & c_{n_1}^2, ..., & c_{n_1}^\beta \\ c_{n_2}^1 & c_{n_2}^2, ..., & c_{n_2}^\beta \\ . & . & . \\ . & . & . \\ . & . & . \\ c_{n_\alpha}^1 & c_{n_\alpha}^2, ..., & c_{n_\alpha}^\beta \end{bmatrix}, \quad (5)$$

where $c_{n_x}^y$; $n_x \in N, y \in \beta$ is the yth channel of secondary backhaul node n_x. Furthermore, let $p_{fa}(c_{n_x}^y)$ be the false alarm probability of y in n_x. The spectrum utilization, S_1 derived as,

$$S_1 = \frac{\sum_{x=1}^{\alpha} \sum_{y=1}^{\beta} (1 - p_{fa}(c_{n_x}^y)) B(c_{n_x}^y)}{\sum_{x=1}^{\alpha} \sum_{y=1}^{\beta} B(c_{n_x}^y)} \qquad (6)$$

Considering presence of malicious node in spectrum utilization, let γ_{n_x} be the set of malicious nodes around secondary node in the backhaul n_x

$$\gamma_{n_x} = \{\gamma_{n_x}^1, \gamma_{n_x}^2, ..., \gamma_{n_x}^\Phi\} \qquad (7)$$

Hence, with the malicious nodes present, spectrum utilization S_2 is given by (8)

$$S_2 = \frac{\sum_{x=1}^{\alpha} \sum_{y=1}^{\beta} (1 - p_{fa}(c_{n_x}^y)) B(c_{n_x}^y) - |\gamma_{n_x}| p_{fa}(c_{n_x}^y) B(\gamma_{n_x})}{\sum_{x=1}^{\alpha} \sum_{y=1}^{\beta} B(c_{n_x}^y)} \qquad (8)$$

3   Results and Discussions

The values of the numerical parameters we considered for our simulation test are listed in Table 1. Also, miss detection and false alarm probability values were adopted from Jin et al. [8]. Statistically, we validated our simulation results by running about thirty different simulations tests by randomly varying various parameters within fixed ranges. The results presented by all the tests did not show any significant variation.

In Fig. 2, the throughput was obtained by varying miss probability values. Again, in Fig. 3 throughput depended on the variation in the number of malicious nodes present in the network. Also, In both Figs. 4 and 5, latency and spectrum utilization depended on the number of malicious nodes found in the network. Figure 6 we varied the number of secondary node nodes and kept some malicious nodes constant and plotted against the simulated throughput values obtained. And, in Fig. 7 we simulated the latency as we kept fixed the number of malicious nodes and varied the number of secondary nodes in the backhaul and lastly, Fig. 8 presents throughput against number of malicious nodes present in the network. We again simulated the network throughput by varying the number of secondary nodes with fixed number of secondary nodes in the backhaul nodes.

Figure 2 measures channel throughput against miss detection probabilities. Looking closely at the simulation results it shows that when miss detection rate was zero, two things were considered, that is, the malicious nodes may be present but do not cause any miss detection attacks, or there may be no malicious node found in the network. The throughput obtained by the simulation at zero miss detection rate was 0.136 Mbps. Also, at miss detection probability rate of 0.01, the throughput dropped to 0.082 Mbps which represents a percentage decrease of about 39% from when there was zero recording of miss detection, which shows

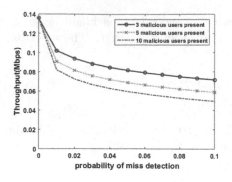

Fig. 2. Throughput versus miss detection rate

Table 1. Simulation parameters

Parameter	Value
Secondary power	(35–41) dBm
Malicious power	(33–38) dBm
Frequency	(470–790) MHz
Nodes density	1 to 10
Interference power	(4–11) dBm
Coefficient values	0.1 t0 2
Bandwidth	100 MHz
Data Size	100 MB

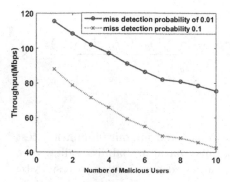

Fig. 3. Throughput versus number of malicious nodes present around the backhaul secondary nodes

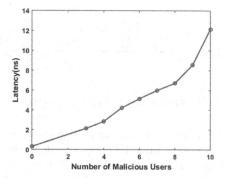

Fig. 4. Latency versus number of malicious nodes present around the backhaul secondary nodes

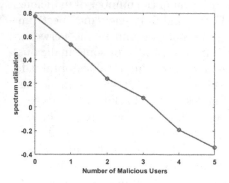

Fig. 5. Utilization versus number of malicious nodes around the backhaul secondary nodes

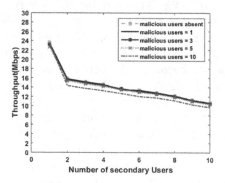

Fig. 6. Throughput versus density of secondary nodes around the backhaul secondary nodes

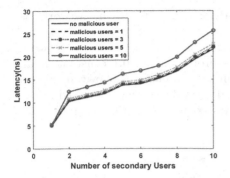
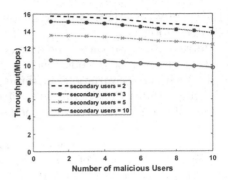

Fig. 7. Latency versus density of secondary nodes around the backhaul secondary nodes

Fig. 8. Throughput versus number of malicious nodes present around the backhaul nodes

that at 99% detection the maximum quality of service can not be guaranteed. The same decrease trend was observed in the throughput with the number of malicious nodes of 3, 5 and 10 with varying miss detection rates. But there was a significant difference in the drop in throughput when the number of malicious nodes increases as shown in Fig. 2. Inversely, from Fig. 2 the result indicates that increased in miss detection probability directly decreased the value of the throughput.

In Fig. 3 throughput was also found to decrease with the increase in the number of malicious nodes in the network with constant miss detection rate. But the higher the miss detection probability value, the greater the drop in throughput as shown in Fig. 3. The miss detection probability of 0.1 recorded much decrease in throughput as compared to miss probability value of 0.01 as shown in Fig. 3.

We also considered an end-to-end effect of latency by the presence of malicious nodes on the network. End-to-end here refers to a user on a different network connected to our backhaul network, which is supposed to serve one community and another user on a different network connected to our backhaul network serving another community. We assume that user 1 on the network connected to secondary node say D sends a message to user 4 on the network connected to secondary node say C. The simulation result shows that when there was no malicious node present in the network, the delay recorded was 0.30 ns but once malicious nodes were introduced into the network, the latency increased as the number of malicious nodes also increased as shown in Fig. 4.

We further modeled and simulated spectrum utilization using different false alarm probability rate on various channels and using four fixed secondary nodes as backhaul nodes. We kept the false alarm probabilities constant for each channel and varied the number of malicious nodes. It was observed that it is not possible for the spectrum to hold more than three malicious nodes at a time if the quality of service is to be guaranteed for the users on the network, as indicated in Fig. 5.

Moreover, we also varied the density of the secondary nodes in the network and kept the malicious nodes and the miss probability of 0.1 constant at all cases. We observed variations in throughput and latency, as shown in Figs. 6 and 7 respectfully. Considering Fig. 6 it could be deduced that increased in the number of cooperative secondary nodes reduced the throughput significantly from one secondary node present to two secondary nodes present. But, as the number of cooperative secondary nodes increased the variation in the throughput as against fixed number of malicious nodes present did not significantly affect the throughput (from two to ten cooperative secondary node). However, there was a significant increase in the latency as data traveled from one network to another network. For fixed ten malicious nodes as against no malicious node present among the backhaul nodes (the cooperative secondary nodes) recorded high increase. We also inferred that as the cooperative sensing nodes increase, malicious nodes combined effect on latency also reduced, as demonstrated in Fig. 7.

Again, Fig. 8 shows that when cooperative nodes of a size of 2, 3 *or* 5 secondary nodes considerably work better than 10 cooperative nodes, which indicates when the cooperative or collaborative nodes increase it affects the throughput of the network. We inferred that when the number of cooperative nodes increased, it introduced a lot of interference signals to the network. So, therefore, the lower the cooperative nodes, the lesser the network interference. Also, the lower the number of cooperative nodes are, the greater the performance (throughput) of the network. But the performance deteriorated when the number of cooperative nodes grew up to a size of 10 as shown in Fig. 8.

Our system model above is closest to the model adopted by Jin et al. [8], however, it failed to measure the performance metrics and utilization of the network. Again, their model considered only one secondary node with multiple malicious nodes. Also, their model was used to detect primary user emulation attack. However, In our model, we considered various numbers of secondary nodes as against multiple numbers of malicious nodes. Also, we varied the distances from all the secondary nodes to the primary transmitter based on their coordinate points (X and Y). Again, our work confirmed the research findings of Pinifolo et al. [11], that neighbour nodes within a distance range of 7 km produces interference to the neighbour nodes. However, we further showed that secondary nodes might be able to collaborate well by monitoring each node if malicious nodes are not existing in the network.

4   Conclusion

In conclusion, we have demonstrated through simulations that, the presence of malicious nodes in dynamic spectrum access networks downgrades the performance of the network. We further showed that densely collaborated nodes in DSA network might affect the performance of the network, as interferences are introduced into the spectrum. Again, we demonstrated that, if malicious users are absent in the DSA network, neighbour monitoring collaborative network may be feasible to implement with fewer legitimate secondary nodes at a time. The malicious nodes present can significantly affect the authorized users, as the spectrum may occasionally appear to be fully utilized. The major limitation of this study is that, the interference factors used in the performance and the utilization models may not be realistic in real world application. In future, we shall undertake real world measurements to get actual impact of the malicious nodes on the performance of a DSA-based network. Again, we shall consider developing detection algorithm to identify the malicious nodes to reduce their impact on the performance of DSA-based collaborative networks.

References

1. Kaligineedi, P., Khabbazian, M., Bhargava, V.K.: Secure cooperative sensing techniques for cognitive radio systems. In: 2008 IEEE International Conference on Communications, pp. 3406–3410 (2008)
2. Yu, F.R., et al.: Defense against spectrum sensing data falsification attacks in mobile ad hoc networks with cognitive radios. In: 2009 Military Communications Conference, MILCOM 2009. IEEE (2009)
3. Chen, R., Park, J.-M., Bian, K.: Robust distributed spectrum sensing in cognitive radio networks. In: INFOCOM 2008, The 27th Conference on Computer Communications. IEEE (2008)
4. Mfupe, L., Mekuria, F., Montsi, L., Mzyece, M.: Geo-location white space spectrum databases: review of models and design of a dynamic spectrum access coexistence planner and manager. In: Mishra, A., Johnson, D. (eds.) White Space Communication, pp. 153–194. Springer, Cham (2015). https://doi.org/10.1007/978-3-319-08747-4_6
5. Bouassida, M.S., et al.: Sybil nodes detection based on received signal strength variations within VANET. Int. J. Netw. Secur. 9(1), 22–33 (2009)
6. Othman, A.K., Adams, A.E., Tsimenidis, C.C.: Node discovery protocol and localization for distributed underwater acoustic networks. In: 2006 International Conference on Internet and Web Applications and Services/Advanced International Conference on Telecommunications, AICT-ICIW 2006. IEEE (2006)
7. Takyi, A., Densmore, M., Johnson, D.: Collaborative neighbour monitoring in TV white space network. In: Proceedings Southern Africa Telecommunication Networks and Applications Conference (SATNAC 2016), George, South Africa (2016)
8. Jin, Z., Anand, S., Subbalakshmi, K.P.: Detecting primary user emulation attacks in dynamic spectrum access networks. In: 2009 IEEE International Conference on Communications, ICC 2009. IEEE (2009)
9. Sharma, S.K., Chatzinotas, S., Ottersten, B.: Cooperative spectrum sensing for heterogeneous sensor networks using multiple decision statistics. In: Weichold, M., Hamdi, M., Shakir, M.Z., Abdallah, M., Karagiannidis, G.K., Ismail, M. (eds.) CrownCom 2015. LNICST, vol. 156, pp. 321–333. Springer, Cham (2015). https://doi.org/10.1007/978-3-319-24540-9_26
10. Jain, M., Kumar, V., Gangopadhyay, R., Debnath, S.: Cooperative spectrum sensing using improved p-norm detector in generalized κ-μ fading channel. In: Weichold, M., Hamdi, M., Shakir, M., Abdallah, M., Karagiannidis, G., Ismail, M.

(eds.) CrownCom 2015. Lecture Notes of the Institute for Computer Sciences, Social Informatics and Telecommunications Engineering, vol. 156, pp. 225–234. Springer, Cham (2015). https://doi.org/10.1007/978-3-319-24540-9_18

11. Pinifolo, J., et al.: Successful deployment and key applications of television white space networks (TVWS) in Malawi. In: Proceedings and Report of the 7th UbuntuNet Alliance Annual Conference, pp. 347–354 (2014)

Digital Inclusion

Digital Inclusion: A Model for e-Infrastructure and e-Services in Developing Countries

Alfredo Terzoli[1]([⊠]), Ingrid Siebörger[1], Mosiuoa Tsietsi[1], and Sibukele Gumbo[2]

[1] Computer Science Department, Rhodes University,
Grahamstown, South Africa
{a.terzoli,i.sieborger,m.tsietsi}@ru.ac.za
[2] Computer Science Department, University of Fort Hare,
Alice campus, Alice, South Africa
sgumbo@ufh.ac.za

Abstract. A large portion of the South African population is still not connected in a productive manner to the Internet, despite the existence of a government plan for public broadband, 'SA Connect'. One reason for this could be the lack of an appropriate model, through which connectivity can be diffused in a meaningful way through all areas of South Africa. This paper presents the model developed over more than a decade of experimentation in real life settings in the Siyakhula Living Lab, a joint venture between the universities of Rhodes and Fort Hare, South Africa. The model proposes the 'Broadband Island' as basic e-infrastructure unit, which clusters nearby points-of-presence hosted in schools. In each Broadband Island is located an applications integration platform, TeleWeaver, which monetizes channels of access to the local community, to support the e-infrastructure while providing useful services to the population and the Government.

Keywords: e-Infrastructure · e-Services · e-Government · ICT4D
Networks · Teleweaver · Broadband island

1 Introduction

For citizens of the Global North, Information and Communication Technologies (ICTs) have diffused into almost every area of human life. On the back of the successful rollout of mobile and fixed broadband technologies such as LTE and optical fibre networks, urban cities are becoming virtual playgrounds for technologists to develop and deploy 'smart' applications that can enhance the lives of city dwellers. With calls on the increase for municipal, regional and national frameworks to be developed that can help realise the goals of evolving paradigms such as 'smart cities' and the 'Internet of Things' (IoT), this trend will only continue to expand and take on more diverse forms [1].

While most countries in the Global South possess nowhere near the same level of the proliferation of ICTs, many governments have nonetheless affirmed their commitment to drive the penetration of technology in their home countries. For instance, in

© ICST Institute for Computer Sciences, Social Informatics and Telecommunications Engineering 2018
V. Odumuyiwa et al. (Eds.): AFRICOMM 2017, LNICST 250, pp. 85–98, 2018.
https://doi.org/10.1007/978-3-319-98827-6_7

2013 the Department of Communications in South Africa outlined its plan to launch an ambitious project under the code-name 'South Africa Connect' as part of its national broadband policy; the implementation of which was officially launched at the beginning of 2015, in the 'State of the Nation' address by the South Africa President [2]. The policy articulates the government's aims to provide broadband access to 50% of the population by 2016, 90% by 2020 and 100% by 2030, with a universal average download speed of 100 Mbps by 2030 [3]. There are two key aspects of this policy that are important. Firstly, it prioritises the closing of the digital divide by ensuring that communities in marginalised areas are duly connected. Secondly, it emphasises the goal to create a strong skills base in the technology sector that can contribute to the production of content and applications, especially those that are contextually relevant. Initially, Telkom, the former telecommunications incumbent in South Africa, was named the lead implementer of SA Connect, hinting at a centralized point of control. No specific model was proposed, but implicitly the assumption was that each implementing entity would be connected directly to the Internet by the lead implementer. This model was not the most efficient, or viable, in rural and poor peri-urban areas, where the plan was supposed to bring the most significant changes. In fact, more than two years after the presidential announcement, very little progress had been made, and the government accepted that other models should be explored [4]. While the implementation is delayed, an abundant yet critical resource in many Africa countries, the youth, is getting wasted through learning in environments that are not conductive to prepare anybody for the transformation of the economy that is already underway.

A more efficient (and detailed) model has been under development for more than a decade in the Siyakhula Living Lab (SLL). SLL is a test site in the rural Eastern Cape province of South Africa where researchers and industry partners have been involved in setting up computing infrastructure since 2005 [5]. The site covers a geographic area of approximately 15,254 hectares and has approximately 15,000 people living in villages in the area. Computers and network infrastructure have been set up at 17 schools across the region, where thin-client computers are available for use by the community and Internet connectivity is provided through a WiMAX local loop with a very small aperture terminal (VSAT) backhaul [6]. An important inclusion to the SLL (which hearkens to the goals of 'South Africa Connect') that has serious implications for the overall sustainability of the infrastructure project is the development of highly contextualised, relevant software applications for the community. As such, a single consistent platform for use as a docking station for all applications, allowing developers to share common software resources and benefit from a standard service environment was developed. TeleWeaver is a service platform that is based on the Java 2 Enterprise Edition (J2EE) application server known as Wildfly [7] and works in conjunction with various other open source components that add value to the platform. The goal of the platform is to host various Java (and non-Java) applications and provide the underlying functionality needed for these applications to run reliably.

This paper describes the holistic model of Information Communication Technology for Development (ICT4D) implementation within the SLL focusing on e-infrastructure and e-services in an effort to bring marginalized communities of South Africa into the digital fold. The paper draws on and brings together a number of papers that give partial perspectives authored by us on the model and it is organised as follows: Sect. 1

provides the relevant literature required in order to understand the model implemented in the SLL, while Sect. 2 provides a description of the SLL initiative. Section 3 describes the e-infrastructure and Sect. 4 the e-services components of the model, with reasons for the design and implementation choices. Finally Sect. 6 concludes the paper.

2 The Siyakhula Living Lab

The SLL is a long term experiment in connecting the unconnected and its team has been conducting research into providing sustainable, off-the-shelf and appropriate computing infrastructure in rural communities in South Africa, locating the infrastructure in schools. The SLL is structured such that it is a quadruple helix partnership of academia, industry, government and the community. It was initiated in 2005 to conduct applied ICT4D postgraduate research work in the two departments of Computer Science at Rhodes University and the University of Fort Hare, through the support of the Telkom Centres of Excellence (CoEs) programme located in those departments. This work then expanded into the SLL project which is a multidisciplinary initiative which also incorporates researchers from Information Systems, Education, African Languages, Communication, Anthropology and Sociology. The SLL believes that ICTs in low income and marginalised areas (of which rural communities are an example) can facilitate:

- Poverty alleviation;
- Development of local economies;
- The achievement of basic standards of health, education, access to governmental services and other developmental infrastructure and services;
- The encouragement of people (though empowering them) to invest in themselves and their communities; and
- Cultural regeneration, including the development and integration of indigenous knowledge systems into a community's "ways of doing and learning".

In order to ground the research properly in the local context, the SLL employs the 'living lab methodology', that is "an approach that deals with user driven innovation of products and services that are introduced, tested and validated in real life environments" [8].

The SLL is located in several villages in the Mbhashe Municipality of the Eastern Cape province of South Africa (located within the former Transkei Homeland), adjacent to the Dwesa-Cwebe nature reserves. The natural environment of the area (the reserve and the unspoiled coastline) are assets for the community and have the potential to promote eco-tourism in the region. In addition, the rich soil and high levels of rainfall make the region lucrative for controlled agricultural intensification and commercial forestry [9]. However, despite these natural assets, the municipality and the region is plagued with remnants of the past. The former Transkei was classified as a Homeland within the South African borders during Apartheid and systematically denied infrastructure and development. As such the region, like many rural areas (and particularly former Homelands) in South Africa is characterised by a lack of electricity, telecommunication infrastructure, and poor road networks. Furthermore, service delivery in the area is poor and limited to basic education and health care. Seventeen local schools have been targeted in the SLL and house the computers and IT infrastructure of the SLL within their grounds. Facilities are available to teachers and learners during school operating hours and to the rest of the community after school, in order to support local education and rural life. For more about the SLL please see the following papers [6, 10, 11].

3   The Model: e-Infrastructure

3.1   The Network: The Broadband Island

The fundamental constraint that any e-infrastructure in rural and marginalized areas have to fulfill is efficiency. A second one is the ability, from the very beginning (i.e. from the moment in which the infrastructure is being deployed, not only after deployment), to activate grassroot activity in the target community. A third one is that it offers a path to digital activities to the youngest segment of the population, the most inclined to embrace innovation. A fourth one is that it is easy to maintain as well as expand. We will see that these constraints are fulfilled by the model developed in the SLL.

Communal infrastructure is inherently efficient, as many examples in a variety of sectors attest. Because of that, our model is built on community owned, shared e-infrastructure, accessible in appropriate communal spaces, at least for what we define 'large ICTs'. In this context, 'large ICTs' are ICT installations that provide user terminals that resemble personal computers and easily allow work related to digital content, especially the production of software or the administration of software and hardware systems. This contrasts with 'small ICTs', which are installations that only support access to user terminals such as mobile phones or hand-held tablets. Often, mobile phones and tablets are individual instruments, though the most important characteristic from the point of view of this discussion is that they are not easily used for development of real life software systems or the professional processing of digital content, at least in their current form. (Naturally, such instruments are easily integrated in the e-infrastructure we propose, via the co-location of WiFi hotspots with the 'large ICTs' installations.) One should note that while crucial for first deployment, the communal nature of the e-infrastructure we propose is transient: the very deployment of such e-infrastructure should put the target communities on a better economic trajectory and therefore move them organically to 'large ICTs' owned and used privately, like it has happened or is happening in other segments of society right now.

What would be appropriate, (relatively) open spaces that are easily reachable in most communities and do not need to be purpose-built (which would make them inefficient from an economic point of view)? The answer in rural and township areas is schools, certainly in South Africa. Reachability, which is crucial for actual use, is due to the schools number, more than one order of magnitude higher than the next possible location, the Post Office outlets for the public [12]. Schools have other important characteristics that make them a good choice for hosting communal e-infrastructure. First of all, they are a focus point in the community, because their educational core activity involves a large section of the community, directly and indirectly. Then, they are formally connected with the community through their School Boards. Finally, schools are places that directly expose e-infrastructure to the segment of society for which the benefits are expected to be the strongest and most obvious: the youth. Underexposure or, often, lack of exposure to 'large ICTs', prevents the youth to imagine themselves in and prepare in time for professions in the fast emerging digital economy. This is a critical problem at the moment in South Africa and has strong negative repercussions on the future of the economy of the country. Interestingly, the South African Department of Education saw the possibility (and importance, even in terms of sustainability) of opening ICT school infrastructure to the surrounding communities already in 2004, as can be seen in points 5.52–54 of the Draft White Paper on e-Education: "Government will support community access to e-schools. The objective will be to increase the opportunities for communities to use e-school resources, develop their computer and Internet skills, and take advantages of services offered through ICTs. In return the community will support the sustainability of ICTs in the e-schools" [13].

Having decided to host the infrastructure in schools, how should schools be connected? In our model, schools should be aggregated in clusters, with high speed connectivity among schools in the cluster and then one or, ideally, two paths from the cluster to the Internet. We call such a cluster a 'Broadband Island' as shown in Fig. 1 [14]. This respects the efficiency constraint set above and has other benefits. Firstly, it allows the deployment of general local services (such as an Internet cache or a Tele-Weaver server, as explained later) as single instances for the entire cluster. Secondly, it allows high-bandwidth streams with very little latency to be routed between schools in the cluster, supporting rich, high speed communication such as video communication for shared lecture or distributed community meetings. From a topological point of view, the Broadband Island uses the classical LAN/WAN distinction, with the LAN represented by the high speed connectivity among the schools in the cluster and the WAN the connection(s) to the Internet. A LAN/WAN topology originated historically from the difference in cost of local and wide area connections. While such a difference is fading in other context (making the 'cloud' more and more viable in the process), it remains strong in the context of interest here, marginalized areas. Again, as discussed about communal vs private availability of 'large ICTs', one has to expect that the difference in cost between LAN and WAN connections will reduce and then disappear in marginalized context too. At that point, the topology in the model will change and the Broadband Island might disappear.

The LAN part of the network, i.e. the Broadband Island, is implemented through fixed wireless links. Wireless is the obvious choice, given the total absence of telephone lines in large part of the poor rural areas of South Africa and its very sparse presence and low quality in poor peri-urban areas ('townships' in South African terminology). Fixed wireless is obvious too, because of the advantages of fixed over mobile wireless for the scenarios on hand. Operating with specified and non-mutable geometries, fixed wireless make possible to achieve higher speed at lower costs than mobile wireless. As reported in [14] the technology used in the SLL, is fixed WiMAX, which proved to be very good and inexpensive. A very important aspect of fixed WiMAX was the simplicity of basic deployment, very close to the simplicity of WiFi. The WiMAX hardware we happened to use required a licence for the frequency at which it was operating, so we need to associate with a small network operator, Unfortunately, the market did not support WiMAX, for a series of non-technical reasons that we will not discuss here, so the specific technology will not be viable in the future and had to be replaced in our model. Among the various possible candidates, a realistic choice at the time of writing this paper is outdoor WiFi, for which good, inexpensive hardware is available. An important advantage of WiFi compared to other possible fixed wireless technology is its simplicity, both technical and regulatory, which allows the network to be deployed by small, 'grassroot' organizations, as opposed to large network providers, as it would be the case with LTE, for example.

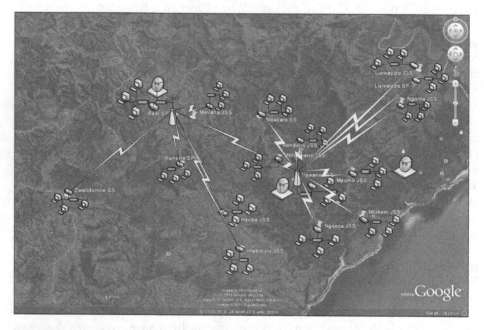

Fig. 1. The Siyakhula Living Lab Broadband Island [14]

3.2   The 'Large ICT' Installation: The Digital Access Node

Once the Broadband Island has been deployed, 'large' computing infrastructure need to be put into the schools (now community access points and called Digital Access Nodes (DANs) within the island). While the computing infrastructure will have to server at a minimum a dual purpose (support teaching in the schools and allow access to services by the broader community), a general architecture to maximize efficiency was needed. So, a thin client topology was chosen, with the possible variation of 'thin/thick' clients as explained later [13]. Centralized computing topologies such as thin client (and their variations) have advantages, from an efficiency point of view, compared to classical fat clients (independent PCs) found often in schools installation. Firstly, they support statistical multiplexing, making the computing resource better utilized. Secondly, they allow much easier administration of the installation, both in terms of initial deployment and ongoing maintenance. Finally, they make the theft of the end-user station less attractive to thieves, for its inability to work as standalone station. Even in the thin/thick implementation, where the end-user terminal has more power than a thin client and is actually executing the application code served by the central server, the end user terminal cannot be used as stand alone.

The main disadvantage of the thin client model and its variations is the single point of failure introduced by the central server. We explored a number of ways to mitigate for this, the best being realizing the central server as a cluster of small, easily replaceable servers. This solution allows to use cheaper, possibly refurbished hardware for the central server, but does have some complexity in the daily management of the installation on the part of the users, at least until a fully automated, hot pluggable cluster server solution is available. In the meantime, a low-tech solution is to have one or two spare servers available in the Broadband Island, ready to be deployed if one node experiences a server failure [13].

It is important to note that the decision of using a thin client architecture or its variations does not bring any constraint on the physical location where the various user stations are deployed, within a DAN. They can be clustered as in a classic school lab or Internet Café, or located each one in a classroom as support for teaching, for example.

To complete the installation of the computing infrastructure in our model, we locate a WiFi hotspot in the DAN and immediately surrounding area. This allows the use of the Internet, as well as authorized other e-services using personal devices when they are available, during as well as outside the opening hours of the DAN.

Unsurprisingly, the software run on the computing infrastructure is Free/Libre Open Source (FLOSS). The operating system is Linux, in the Ubuntu distribution. Besides the obvious cost reduction at the time of installation and upgrades, the philosophy of FLOSS is naturally aligned to the spirit of sharing, transparency and grassroot, distributed involvement which underlies the model described in this paper. FLOSS has another important advantage: it might help orienting the younger segment of the target communities towards careers in the digital economy, especially software development.

Access to the infrastructure is naturally regulated and requires users to authenticate themselves after registering in any DAN belonging to a specific Broadband Island. (Registration typically starts with the users directly associated to the schools hosting the DAN, pupils and teachers.) User information for authentications are kept in a Lightweight Directory Access Protocol (LDAP) directory. We will see in the next session on e-services how this can be leveraged by the application layer by our main applications integrator, TeleWeaver.

4 The Model: e-Services

4.1 TeleWeaver: The Business Model

The deployment of e-services on top of the e-infrastructure described in the previous section has been a focus of the SLL from the start, because without applications the infrastructure is useless and so unable to sustain itself. Obvious initial applications were office productivity suites [14] as well as Voice and Video communication over IP [15] through customization of standard software. It was clear, however that real income streams were necessary, both to support the e-infrastructure and to make it work for the hosting community, and these revenue streams had to be provided by the application layer. Initial work in that direction produced an e-commerce website for local artists and artisans to advertise their work and sell it online [15]. To this end, support for micro-tourism could be added easily. While this has clearly potential, it is predicated on the existence of valuable production of artifacts or tourist attraction, or the presence of activities that make viable, for example, the selling of accommodation. This is gen-erally seldom true for the communities of interest. Even when it is true (or partially true, as it was in the case for micro-tourism in the area of the SLL, which happens to be in a magnificent natural area, if rather hard to reach), the stream would be rather small.

So, a more general revenue model was necessary, independent from the presence of specific, sellable products or services in the community and able to bring in revenue streams of the size needed to support ICTs. As noted above, however, the work done by us and other trying to diffuse ICTs in poor communities, rural and not, has the hope of starting a virtuous cycle that will make possible to have products and services present in those communities. But this is a longer term perspective, which is unhelpful with the initial sustainability of the e-infrastructure. As described in [16], we adapted a now well established Internet business model, where the resource to be monetized.

Naturally, we needed to find who the 'advertisers' were in our context, that is who was interested and was actually already spending money trying to reach members of the communities in which we deploy e-infrastructure. Government departments, their units and subunits all do, and actually the spend is already or will be important, especially if one includes the 'brick & mortar' investment in front-end offices as well as mobile units for hard to reach areas, and related personnel. An initial illustration is offered by the 'information dissemination' function of the Department of Health, where the nature of the interaction with the communities of interest in this context is directly advertising [17]. Such function will run information campaigns using a variety of channels, including travelling personnel. The most common channels will be newspapers, street posters, radio and television. In a sense, this function within the Department of Health does run advertising campaigns, with the costs of an advertising campaign as well as the difficulty of reaching the correct target. If a channel is made available to deliver the message, possibly in a targeted manner, the Department of Health could divert the money spent over other channels to the new channel.

A more general model, and how the various parts fit together and how the cash is generated, is illustrated in Fig. 2.

In Fig. 2, the Broadband Island is represented by a single DAN. The 'owner' of the Broadband Island, in the sense of the entity that started it, injecting the cash for the e-infrastructure and the procurement of the TeleWeaver platform, is a Municipality, for the sake of illustration. (It could any other entity such as an NGO, the local Department of Education district, a cooperative or a private investor when the model has proven to be viable.) The software house building and maintaining the core of TeleWeaver and part of its ecosystem of services is called Reed House Systems (RHS) (historically, a software house project within the two Universities behind the SLL). Finally, the three entities at the bottom of Fig. 2 are examples of a very small set of public or private

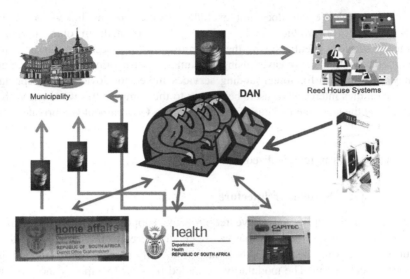

Fig. 2. The TeleWeaver business model

institutions with an interest of interacting with the users of the Broadband Island: the Department of Home Affairs, the Department of Health and Capitec, a South African bank catering especially for segments of society with lower financial power. The arrows with money overlapping them represent payments (with cash flowing to the entity at the tip of the arrow), the others represent interactions about specific services or products offered by the entities connected by the arrow.

After establishing a Broadband Island, the Municipality pays for a license of TeleWeaver, which gets deployed in the Broadband Island and activates bidirectional channels of communication with the three entities at the bottom. For example, the Department of Health will be able to use a healthMessenger application to run information campaigns on HIV/Aids, or to collect information about the health status of the individuals making use of the Broadband Island [17]. Each applications hosted in TeleWeaver have a pre-approved contract with the entity gaining benefit from the application, which get activated on installation, with the details of the specific Broadband Island and its 'owner'. This contract specifies how the channel is paid for: maybe for each recorded interaction (an info message clicked by a user in the Broadband Island, the reporting of a birth etc.), or maybe on a fixed, monthly base, independent of the number of transactions. The payment is done to the owner of the Broadband Island, making the installation viable, provided that a minimum number of services get activated. In fact, because the income from a Broadband Island will depend on the number of services, the interest of the owner will be to devise and promote more and more services over time. The better and better viability of the installations within this model will make the model more and more interesting to the entities using its channels, in a virtuous circle. (As an aside, the 'weaving' of the monetized access channels, to support the financial viability of the e-infrastructure described in the previous section, is the reason for the name of the integration platform, TeleWeaver.)

Of course, TeleWeaver does not exclude income streams linked to channels through which local products and services get distributed: in other terms, the e-commerce services mentioned at the beginning of this sections can be simply re-implemented within TeleWeaver, using the same infrastructure (and so offering good efficiency). The reason for foregrounding services linked to Government (especially) and private entities interested in users belonging to the communities we target with our work is that, at the start, the revenues from channels to Government and private entities can be expected to be much bigger and have a realistic chance to support the e-infrastructure. In other words, they are better channels for 'bootstrapping' the diffusion of large ICTs in marginalized areas.

4.2   TeleWeaver: System Architecture

The business model illustrated above requires the support of a highly distributed, highly modular software platform that has open interfaces to the outside world. The distribution is necessary because DANs could potentially be deployed in several areas in a geographical region. The modularity is needed in order to simplify the process of incorporating diverse applications into the platform, by providing the basic enablers that most applications would need in order to function. Finally, the openness is crucial to the value proposition of the platform since external entities such as those depicted in Fig. 2 above would need to reliably push and pull data to deployed nodes in a region, preferably using their own existing systems, assuming these systems are capable of standard communication mechanisms that are prevalent in industry [15].

These broad overarching goals would take an exorbitant amount of time to develop, test and maintain through custom software. In addition, while the business model is novel, many of the technical challenges implicit in its realisation have largely been solved in various 'middleware' platforms that have emerged over the years. Middleware is a classical architectural model which permits the development of modular applications that rely on pre-provisioned service enablers that abstract away the details of the underlying operating system and networks upon which those applications are executed.

While there are several middleware solutions to choose from, the Java language, and in particular, the Java Enterprise Edition (J2EE) has a long history in these contexts, with several popular and well supported solutions available. A notable example is JBoss Application Server, now re-branded as Wildfly, which is fully J2EE compatible and enjoys wide support by virtue of the backing it receives from the parent company RedHat, as well as its adoption by the open source community. Regular and incremental release cycles make Wildfly an attractive platform and a solid basis to build from.

TeleWeaver makes extensive use of Wildfly's services in the development of two levels of services and applications [15]. Core services are those that TeleWeaver ships with, and are recognised as services that all applications that reside inside the platform make use of. The most critical core service is the user profile which sits at the heart of the value proposition of the platform. Rich user data that profiles community members is what makes TeleWeaver attractive to partners such as those depicted in the business model diagram above. The richer the data, the more targeted services can be delivered to communities. In its current state, the user profile is a combination of both static and dynamic data and a service module implemented as an enterprise Java application. The static data is implemented using LDAP while the dynamic data is stored within a relational database. The goal of this construction is to partition user information into data that does not change frequently (such as personal details) which are stored in LDAP, while data that pertains to an individual's use of specific applications would be stored in a relational database. The enterprise application then maintains the association between these two, managing updates and coordinating the linking of these two sets of data.

The second core service is the web service adapter which sits between the platform and external services that need to communicate with TeleWeaver [15]. The adapter itself was not developed from scratch, as Wildfly ships with a Java restful web service stack called RESTEasy, but the adapter needs to be configured to work with applications, in particular in the authorisation of ingress requests.

The deployment model that Wildfly supports also makes it ideal for the context because it inherently supports a distributed approach. Wildfly can run in either standalone or domain mode, the latter of which allows Wildfly nodes to run as domain controllers, while others run as host controllers under the control of a domain controller. This distributed architectural model allows Wildfly hosts to work in concert, sharing information and syncing data in order to realise a super-network of TeleWeaver entities. This feature makes TeleWeaver appropriate for its context, given the distributed nature of DAN nodes.

A diagram summarizing the architecture of TeleWeaver is presented in Fig. 3.

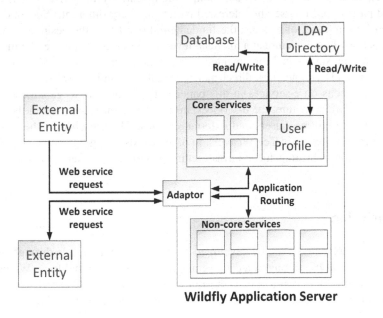

Fig. 3. An architectural view of TeleWeaver

5 Discussion

One fundamental aspect of the model for e-infrastructure presented in this paper is that everything, from the Broadband Island, to the computing infrastructure in the schools, except possibly the WAN technology, can be easily built and operated by small companies or community organizations, maybe with some initial technical support) [14]. This is fundamental for at least three reasons. Firstly, it would trigger local economic development, which remains a major challenge. Secondly, it would make the e-infrastructure (and then the services on top of it) accepted as part of the assets of the community, which will trigger protection from vandalism and meaningful utilization, starting a virtuous cycle with a real transformative power. This was seen quite clearly on the SLL main site in the Mbhashe Municipality, if in an initial form - as it should be expected in socio-economic environments that have been static and dominated by lack of hope in change for a long time. Thirdly, but equally importantly, it will break the 'bottleneck effect' created by centralizing the control of the deployment of e-infrastructure. Of course, as discussed in [14], lack of centralization might have disadvantages, but they are in our opinion manageable and less important than the block of the operations on the ground.

The reader will also have noted that the revenue streams depicted in Fig. 2 accrue to the owner of the Broadband Island from which the interactions with the external interested entities originate, and not, say, to the software house creating the actual software channels, RHS in Fig. 2. This is an important way in which the model of e-services presented in this paper differs from the model used by mainstream Internet companies, such as Google and Faccbook, which similarly monetize user access to interested parties. (Of course, the interested parties are very different.) Such a decision was taken for a number of reasons, the fundamental one being the desire to reflect the general distributed architecture at a financial level too. As a consequence, the model we are proposing can start being implemented without the need of large financial means, is more resilient and activates in a direct manner local economic growth.

While the focus on e-services in this paper is their potential to guarantee sustainability to the e-infrastructure, the e-services are of course of importance in themselves to the interacting parties - users and external entities. The presence of the e-services (not only the ones hosted in TeleWeaver), in other words, bring a positive contribution to the communities hosting the e-infrastructure, becoming in themselves a transformative force.

6 Conclusion

The paper has presented a model developed over more than a decade through work at the SLL, in the real life setting of a deep rural community of South Africa. We feel that the model has the potential to break the impasse in which SA Connect, the national public broadband plan, seems to find itself, at least in poor provinces like the Eastern Cape.

If the model is rolled out on a large scale, in our opinion it has the further potential of fostering a local ICT industry for local content and might help usher in South Africa economy a more modern, knowledge based economy.

References

1. Bonino, D., Alizo, A., Alapetite, A., Gilbert, T.: ALMANAC: Internet of Things for smart cities. In: FiCloud 2015: 3rd International Conference on Future Internet of Things and Cloud, Rome, Italy, pp. 309–316 (2015)
2. South African Government, President Jacob Zuma: State of the Nation Address 2015. http://www.gov.za/president-jacob-zuma-state-nation-address-2015. Accessed 06 Feb 2018
3. Department of Communications, South Africa Connect: Creating opportunities, ensuring inclusion – South Africa's Broadband Policy, National Gazette No. 37119 (2013)
4. Mzekandaba, S.: Govt looks to other means to implement broadband project. http://www.itweb.co.za/index.php?option=com_content&view=article&id=158906. Accessed 06 Feb 2017
5. Gumbo, S., Thinyane, H., Thinyane, M., Terzoli, A., Hansen, S.: Living lab methodology as an approach to innovation in ICT4D: the Siyakhula Living Lab experience. In: Proceedings of the IST-Africa 2012 Conference, Tanzania (2012)
6. Pade-Khene, C., Sieborger, I., Thinyane, H., Dalvit, L.: The Siyakhula Living Lab: a holistic approach to rural development through ICT in rural South Africa. In: Steyn, J., van Belle, J., Villeneuva, E.M. (eds.) ICTs and Sustainable Solutions for the Digital Divide: Practical Approaches - Development Informatics and Regional Information Technologies: Theory, Practice and the Digital Divide, vol. 2, pp. 42–77. IGI Global (2010)
7. RedHat Wildfly. http://wildfly.org/
8. Mulder, I., Bohle, W., Boshomane, S., Morris, C., Tempelman, H., Velthausz, D.: Real world innovation in rural South Africa. Electron. J. Virtual Org. Netw. **10**, 8–20 (2008)
9. Palmer, R., Timmermans, H., Fay, D.: From Conflict to Negotiation Nature-Based Development on the South African Wild Coast. HSRC Press, Pretoria (2002)
10. Dalvit, L., Siebörger, I., Thinyane, H.: The expansion of the Siyakhula Living Lab: a holistic perspective. In: Popescu-Zeletin, R., Jonas, K., Rai, I.A., Glitho, R., Villafiorita, A. (eds.) AFRICOMM 2011. LNICSSITE, vol. 92, pp. 228–238. Springer, Heidelberg (2012). https://doi.org/10.1007/978-3-642-29093-0_22
11. Dalvit, L., Thinyane, M., Terzoli, A., Muyingi, H.: The deployment of an e-commerce platform and related projects in a rural area in South Africa. In: 3rd Annual International Conference on Computing and ICT Research - SREC07, Kampala, Uganda (2007)
12. Parlimentary Monitoring Group, South African Post Office on its 2015 strategic plan and current position. https://pmg.org.za/committee-meeting/20963/. Accessed 25 Aug 2017
13. Sieborger, I.: Evolving an efficient and effective off-the-shelf computing infrastructure for schools in rural areas of South Africa. Doctoral thesis, Rhodes University, Grahamstown, South Africa (2017)
14. Terzoli, A., Sieborger, I., Gumbo, S.: Community broadband islands' for digital government access in rural South Africa. In: Proceeding of the 17th European Conference on Digital Government, Lisbon, Portugal (2017)
15. Tsietsi, M., Terzoli, A., Gumbo, S.: TeleWeaver: an architectural overview of a customised application server for rurality. In: Proceedings of the IST-Africa 2016 Conference Durban, South Africa (2016)

16. Gumbo, S., Terzoli, A., Tsietsi, M.: e-Government as a means to support communal large ICT infrastructure. In: Proceedings of the European Conference on e-Government. Ljubljana, Slovenia (2016)
17. Gremu, C., Terzoli, A., Tsietsi, M.: HealthMessenger: an e-Health service to support ICT deployments in poor areas. In: Proceedings of the IST-Africa 2016 Conference, Durban, South Africa (2016)

SV4D Architecture: Building Sustainable Villages for Developing Countries

André Pereira, Pedro Madureira, Carlos Resende, Pedro Almeida,
and Waldir Moreira$^{(\boxtimes)}$

Fraunhofer Portugal AICOS,
Rua Alfredo Allen, 455/461, 4200-135 Porto, Portugal
{andre.pereira, pedro.madureira, carlos.resende,
pedro.almeida, waldir.junior}@fraunhofer.pt

Abstract. The introduction of Information and Communication Technologies (ICT) in a society is known to influence its gross domestic product and human development index. Still, access to ICT is not universal, with the problem being further aggravated in developing countries. In order to fill in this digital divide gap, we present our Sustainable Villages for Development (SV4D) architecture, which is a collection of hardware and software conceived to promote digital inclusion and consequently improve the quality of life of citizens of these underserved communities. We also present a set of preliminary performance evaluation tests carried out in the SV4D testbed deployed in Porto, Portugal, that shows the potential of our proposed architecture for deployment in developing countries.

Keywords: Sustainable Villages · Developing countries · Digital inclusion
Intermittent connectivity · Communication for development

1 Introduction

Despite of the evolution on Information and Communication Technology (ICT), the International Telecommunication Union has estimated that still 53% of the world's population remain without Internet access. This problem is even more evident in developing countries (e.g., approximately 75% of the citizens in African countries have no Internet access) [1].

The reason for low-populated, isolated regions not to be covered by operators relates to the high costs per user: the efforts in deploying fibre infrastructure and/or broadband cells do not justify the investment in such regions. Moreover, these regions spread over a large geographical areas, meaning that, once in these communities, citizens may be completely disconnected, with occasional periods of connectivity (i.e., user may access online contents when in a town with connectivity or in a region with cellular coverage).

The lack of infrastructure and disruptive connectivity characterize a rather challenging scenario when compared to a scenario in which a user regularly accesses in large and developed urban areas. Intermittent connectivity, high latency, limited number of equipment, and the non-existence of end-to-end paths between

© ICST Institute for Computer Sciences, Social Informatics and Telecommunications Engineering 2018
V. Odumuyiwa et al. (Eds.): AFRICOMM 2017, LNICST 250, pp. 99–108, 2018.
https://doi.org/10.1007/978-3-319-98827-6_8

communicating parties are just few examples of the challenges to overcome [2]. Furthermore, this reduced and/or non-existent access to ICT (along with poor education and health systems) negatively impact the human development index of a society [3], and contributes to the digital divide that we observe nowadays.

With this in mind, we present our SV4D architecture, which is built based on low-cost, off-the-shelf hardware to provide these underserved communities with a communication for development (Comm4Dev) infrastructure. Additionally, our service framework is intended to cope with this occasional connectivity characteristic, allowing the development of easy-to-use applications destined to citizens with little or complete lack of digital knowledge, focusing on improving their quality of life.

The paper is structured as follows. Section 2 introduces our proposed SV4D architecture, detailing its hardware and software. Section 3 presents preliminary performance evaluation testes carried out on our testbed in Porto, Portugal, to understand the capability of the used technology and to assess the potential of the SV4D architecture for deployment in developing countries. And finally Sect. 4 concludes the paper.

2 SV4D Architecture

Figure 1 presents our SV4D architecture, which focuses on:

Fig. 1. The SV4D architecture.

Promoting the digital inclusion of citizens in isolated and poor communities of developing countries, offering them access to an infrastructure for broadband Internet.

Being far away from urban centres and having low population density make such communities unattractive for operators from a profit perspective, thus contributing to their isolation and increasing digital divide. The SV4D architecture adapts existing technology to connect citizens, filling in this digital gap.

Improving the quality of life of these underserved communities by employing a service framework that provides support to services such as health (e.g., in-situ malaria diagnosis [4]); education (e.g., literacy and access to reading [5]). This framework simulates the notion of permanent connectivity (based on the concept of Delay/Disruption Tolerant Networks [6]), allowing the exchange of data (i.e., emails, documents, e-books, diagnosis) between mobile devices until the information reaches a connected area, and then being forwarded to the desired destination (i.e., citizen, government agencies, schools, doctors).

Reducing deployment costs by allowing flexible and interoperable integration into existing networks, extending their capillarity towards remote communities and refraining from costly investments on infrastructure (i.e., optical fibre).

2.1   Communication for Development (Comm4Dev) Infrastructure

The Comm4Dev infrastructure is based on the WiBACK[1] technology, developed by Fraunhofer FIT/DeFuTech which aims to provide carrier-grade service quality for voice and data transmission over a large area with low-cost wireless technology.

In the context of the Comm4Dev infrastructure, the WiBACK QoS-provisioning, auto-configuration, self-management, self-healing and "Plug & Play" characteristics are an added value, as they allow the network to be setup and maintained by non-technical individuals as long as some basic training on the WiBACK is performed, i.e., expensive and often unavailable technical expertise is not needed.

(a)   (b)

Fig. 2.   WiBACK (a) controller and (b) node.

The Comm4Dev infrastructure has two main components, namely the WiBACK controller and the nodes. The controller is responsible for managing and controlling the Comm4Dev network (cf., Fig. 2a).

The node (cf., Fig. 2b) is the two-radio element used to propagate the radio signal through directional antennas from one node to other neighbouring nodes. It is an outdoor and low power device, so it can be deployed off-grid and power supplied by

---

[1] http://www.defutech.de/en/wiback-technology/.

renewable energy sources. In non-off-grid installations, the WiBACK node can be powered through Power over Ethernet (PoE) (IEEE 802.3 at).

WiBACK nodes can be used as a relay to propagate radio signal. At an intermediate location, or at an "endpoint" installation (e.g., hotspot) it serves as a bridge to equipment that might be connected to it by Ethernet (IEEE 802.3) and/or Wi-Fi (IEEE 802.11a/b/g/n).

2.2 Framework for Occasional Connectivity – Postbox Sync

Our SV4D architecture also considers the Postbox Web software [7], later dubbed Postbox Sync, which has been improved to provide support to services that promote digital inclusion in the underserved communities.

Usually, in these communities, readily available data connections are limited. Thus, Postbox Sync provides means for a user to request and receive content (e.g., email) even when connectivity is not available. This is done by means of the Store-Carry-Forward (SCF) data exchange paradigm observed in Delay/Disruption-Tolerant Networking (DTN) [6]. Users temporarily store requests for data or the data itself on behalf of others for later forwarding to the target destinations.

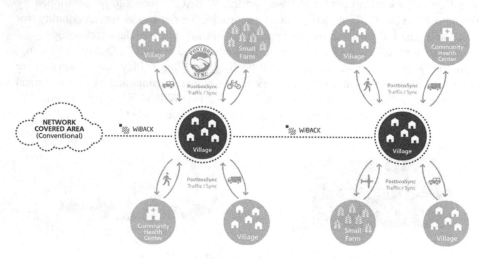

Fig. 3. Postbox Sync and Comm4Dev ecosystem.

This allows the development of services that are able to work offline without disruption, performing whatever tasks when connected in a transparent manner for the user, and that would be otherwise impossible to happen given the lack of continuous connectivity. The Postbox Sync framework considers two main types of users: one living in a partially or entirely disconnected area; and an intermediate one who often travels between connected and disconnected areas, called the Postman[2].

---

[2] The framework and the intermediate make reference to the postal service in which a box is used to store incoming and outgoing mails (i.e., data), and a postman bringing such mails to destinations.

The main idea is that users create data (e.g., email) on their mobile devices, and later synchronize this data with the Postman's device. When a Postman reaches a connected area, data is sent to the correct destination over the Web.

Figure 3 shows the Comm4Dev and Postbox Sync ecosystem, where the former extends connectivity from a conventional network-covered area to villages that were once offline, and Postbox Sync provides offline network access to smaller villages and localities, where it would be expensive or unnecessary to use additional hardware.

This way, we can effectively build a growing network that expands the existing infrastructure without interfering with it, and ensure that every user is able to send and receive data through the Internet.

3   SV4D Testbed Preliminary Performance Evaluation

The SV4D testbed, deployed in the city of Porto, Portugal, is geographically distributed in the buildings of Fraunhofer Portugal (FhP) and Engineering Faculty of University of Porto (FEUP), and comprises three sites (FhP North, FEUP, and FhP South) as depicted in Fig. 4.

Fig. 4. SV4D testbed installation in Porto, Portugal.

The setup is as follows. The FhP North site is directly connected to the FhP test network by Ethernet, and extends the SV4D network and cellular services to the FEUP site through the Comm4Dev infrastructure based on the WiBACK technology. The FEUP site serves as relay, and extends the Internet and cellular services to FhP South. Finally, the FhP South site is the last hop of the testbed, and it counts with a commercial NanoStation 2 Wi-Fi Access Point (AP) and a GSM Base Transceiver Station (BTS) serving users at the 2nd floor of the office.

The services provided to users located at FhP South site include access to the SV4D network, GSM voice calls, and Short Message Service (SMS). Thus, besides the WiBACK technology that serves the purpose of backhaul and the commercial Wi-Fi AP that allows access to the SV4D network, our testbed comprises (cf., Fig. 5): an OpenEPC++ [8], responsible for managing and controlling the GSM network; and a nanoBTS [9], the GSM BTS allowing user access to our emulated cellular network.

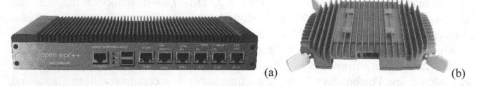

(a)   (b)

Fig. 5. (a) OpenEPC ++ and (b) nanoBTS hardware for cellular services.

The goals of this preliminary performance evaluation are to (i) understand the capabilities of the links of the Comm4Dev infrastructure; (ii) test the compliance of the Comm4Dev infrastructure with different access technologies (i.e., Wi-Fi and cellular); and (iii) guarantee that the SV4D architecture is able to provide services that can cope with online and offline connectivity.

For the tests carried out during the performance evaluation we used different smartphones (Samsung Galaxy S2, Samsung Galaxy Nexus, LG Nexus 4, and Motorola Moto G) with Android flavours ranging from version 4.1 to 5.1, and a laptop computer.

Regarding the network signal and bandwidth measurement tools we have considered the Network Signal Info and Signal Widget, and iPerf[3].

The tests comprised: iPerf sessions between the smartphones (placed at different distances from the Wi-Fi AP) and the laptop, as well as the users placing calls and sending SMSs to one another at different distances from the nanoBTS. Users could be inside as well as outside the office.

3.1 Testing Link Capability

The testbed was subject to several tests, and generated several iterations on the network configuration. This happened because the first bandwidth results were not in line with the ones claimed by the equipment manufacturer. In fact, the link between FEUP and FhP South was unstable, with intermittent connectivity.

Adjustments on the WiBACK antenna height, tilt, and WiBACK node software version were performed in the Porto testbed. Such optimizations stabilized the WiBACK links and improved the network bandwidth to around 1/6, for upload and download, of what it is specified by the manufacturer (up to 180 Mbps [10]).

By closely troubleshooting, we were able to identify two issues: (i) a misalignment of the emitting and receiving antennas; and (ii) the short distance between the two antennas at FEUP.

Once corrected these installation issues, and updated the software of the WiBACK radios, the links became very stable and the available bandwidth was improved. Only one issue remained, the partial obstruction of the Fresnel zone between the antennas of FhP North and FEUP. As this is not entirely clear of obstacles, the network bandwidth was not performing at its best.

---

[3] https://iperf.fr/.

To overcome such issue, the antennas height should have been increased, but such intervention was not possible since the mast was not long enough. To minimize this issue, the radios at FEUP and FhP North were replaced by a newer hardware version N2C2, which is more resilient to this situations, and helped to improve the network bandwidth but still not as expected.

As these new nodes were running an old version of the WiBACK software, only after updating them '*in loco*' the links capacity as well as the available bandwidth achieved values in accordance to the ones claimed by the manufacturer, approximately 90 Mbps on uplink and downlink.

3.2   Supporting Different Access Technologies

Regarding the cellular service, the maximum distance at which the GSM signal and the GSM services (calls and SMS) are available is at around 200 m. The GSM signal reaches approximately 300 m, but at this distance, even with clear line of sight, the services are not available. This is mainly due to indoor antennas being used on the nanoBTS. By replacing these with outdoor ones, which have higher sensibility, we believe that the range covered by the cells can increase.

To summarize, we could observe that: at distances below 120 m, the lack of clear line of sight is not crucial, but it needs to be taken into consideration, because if there are too many obstacles along the way, the services might not be available at all; at distances between 120 m and 240 m, clear line of sight is imperative for the suitable provision of the services, but it is possible to have signal and services in the presence of some trees; and at distances between 240 m and 360 m only points with clear line of sight can receive the GSM signal. However, most of the time no services are available. In the case when they are available, the observed quality is not as good as with locations closer to the nanoBTS.

As for the access to the SV4D network, the Wi-Fi is usable only in a range of 35 m from the AP, and even in this range the maximum bandwidth achieved was 2.97 Mb/s. Beyond this distance and below 70 m the Wi-Fi signal is available, but the bandwidth is much lower - always below 1 Mb/s.

We could also observe that the quality of the Wi-Fi signal varies with the device being used to connect to it. The Moto G is the device that presents the best results, since it is the most stable of the 3 phones studied and the one that presents the highest bandwidth result - 2.97 Mb/s. On the other hand, the Samsung Galaxy Nexus is the one that presents the lowest results - its bandwidth never reaches 1 Mb/s. This behaviour can be related to the wireless card used in each phone, its antenna sensibility, the number of hosts in the vicinity and so forth.

3.3   Dealing with Intermittent Connectivity

To validate the application in an intermittent connectivity environment, periods of online and offline connectivity were simulated, with three smartphones distributed to different users which were asked to mimic a potential usage scenario of sending Emails (online and offline) to each other.

At each time, one of the users specifically created an Email offline and later paired his device with one of the other users to emulate the scenario where an intermediate user (e.g., Postman, as mentioned in Sect. 2.2) goes to an offline village to gather the villagers' requests.

At a first phase of testing, the users reported an issue related to the time needed to send/receive an Email. In cases when a user tried to open his Email inbox and the Emails had attachments of considerable size, the time to access the information grew exponentially.

The situation was carefully analysed and the problem was identified as an issue with the parsing of Emails inside the Postbox Sync package. After the improvements, the time needed to open the inbox grows linearly (and not exponentially) with the amount of information in the inbox (limited with the available bandwidth), and the time needed to fetch each email decreased in average approximately 50% resulting in a much more pleasant experience to the end user.

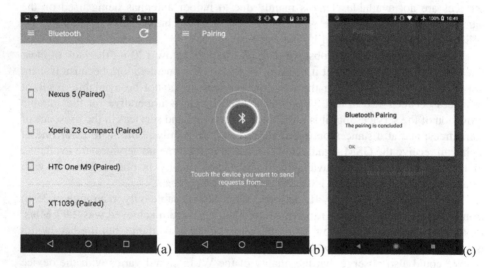

Fig. 6. (a) Device selection screen, (b) Start of data exchange, and (c) Data exchange concluded.

In a second phase of testing, we identified a possible issue with the communication pairing[4] mechanism, which is an important aspect of Postbox Sync since it allows users to opportunistically exchange data requests with intermediate nodes until these requests reach an area with connectivity.

The identified issue related to a scenario where a Postman had more than one Postbox Sync user waiting to pair its requests.

---

[4] Postbox Sync pairing refers to the process of establishing the communication link between devices and the exchange of Postbox Sync packages. In this case such process is done over Bluetooth technology.

After receiving the requests from the first user, the user acting as Postman remained on the screen showing that the communication pairing process had finished. In the case another user tried to connect to it (via Bluetooth), the device of the Postman understood this as a reconnect tentative from the former user and tried to re-establish the connection. As the MAC address of the client is different (e.g., a new user is now requesting communication pairing), the process of pairing for this new user would fail.

As this is a particularity of the envisioned scenario, we added a dialog informing the user that the communication pairing (i.e., data exchange) process is finished. Moreover, a button was included to redirect the user to the device selection screen in the case the user wants to initiate a new data exchange, avoiding the reported issue. Thus, after selecting the device for data exchange (Fig. 6a), the user who wants to send/receive data requests must confirm that by touching the screen (Fig. 6b). Once data exchange is concluded, a dialog (Fig. 6b) informs the user that the communication pairing is concluded, and after the user presses the "OK" button, the user is brought back to the device selection screen as shown in Fig. 6a.

4   Conclusions and Future Work

This paper presents our SV4D architecture that aims to promote digital inclusion and improve the quality of life of citizens in underserved communities of developing countries. The SV4D architecture is a collection of hardware and software tailored to answer the needs of such communities, which still lack access to broadband Internet today.

The hardware is based on WiBACK technology that considers off-the-shelf components turning it into a cost-effective alternative since it (i) allows the extension of the capillarity of existing infrastructure towards isolated areas; and (ii) requires little maintenance efforts given its auto-configuration, self-management, and self-healing features.

In regards to the software, the Postbox Sync framework allows the implementation of services to cope with an inherent characteristics of these communities, that is, the occasional connectivity. Thus, users can send and receive data even being offline, with content being forwarded either directly to the Internet once the user is connected, or to an intermediate user (i.e., Postman) who takes the content to a connected area.

The SV4D architecture has been tested and presents a level of maturity that allows for its deployment in real-world scenarios.

By looking at the preliminary performance evaluation tests carried out over the SV4D testbed, we could observer that:

1. Link capability is a product of proper antenna alignment, clear line of sight, and updated WiBACK software, and currently we are fine-tuning our testbed to reach the capability as per manufacturer specification;
2. The Comm4Dev infrastructure does support different access technologies, and coverage and data rates are solely connected to capabilities of the hardware considered and user devices;

3. The Postbox Sync allows users to produce content (i.e., emails) independently of connectivity availability, and may exploit contact opportunities with others to relay the produced content to the desired destination.

These observations show great potential of the SV4D architecture for deployment in underserved communities to allow mitigating the effect of digital divide, consequently improving the quality of life of citizens of such communities in developing countries.

As next steps, we are currently preparing the SV4D architecture for deployment of its first pilot in the Zambézia province in Mozambique. The first phase of this pilot comprises the installation of the Comm4Dev infrastructure, which will provide Internet access to the citizens while they are in schools, formation institutes, hospitals, and administration offices. Once deployed, we will be monitoring the utilization of the SV4D network with the intention to fine-tune it as to allow the best experience for users. In a later phase, applications running on the top of the Postbox Sync framework will be used to offer different services (e.g., education, health, and e-government) for these communities.

Acknowledgments. The authors would like to acknowledge the financial support obtained from North Portugal Region Operational Programme (NORTE 2020), Portugal 2020 and the European Regional Development Fund (ERDF) from European Union through the project Symbiotic technology for societal efficiency gains: Deus ex Machina (DEM), NORTE-01-0145-FEDER-000026, and project Collective Transfer FhP, NORTE-01-0246-FEDER-000029.

References

1. International Telecommunication Union – ITU: ICT Facts and Figures 2016 (2016)
2. Moreira, W.: Sustainable villages for development: promoting digital inclusion. In: Proceedings of 8° Congresso Luso-Moçambicano de Engenharia, pp. 1109–1110 (2017)
3. Ngwenyama, O., Andoh-Baidoo, F.K., Bollou, F., Morawczynski, O.: Is there a relationship between ICT, health, education and development? An empirical analysis of five West African countries from 1997–2003. Electron. J. Inf. Syst. Dev. Ctries. **23**, 1–11 (2006)
4. Devezas, T., Domingos, L., Vasconcelos, A., Carreira, C., Giesteira, B.: MalariaScope's user interface usability tests: results comparison between European and African users. In: Nungu, A., Pehrson, B., Sansa-Otim, J. (eds.) AFRICOMM 2014. LNICSSITE, vol. 147, pp. 241–250. Springer, Cham (2015). https://doi.org/10.1007/978-3-319-16886-9_25
5. Almeida, P., Teixeira, V., Oliveira, R., Elias, D.: Innovation in digital street libraries to enhance social development and cultural cooperation. In: Proceedings of 7° Congresso Luso-Moçambicano de Engenharia, pp. 473–474 (2014)
6. Burleigh, S., et al.: RFC4838-Delay-Tolerant Networking Architecture (2007)
7. Oliveira, R., Teixeira, V., Elias, D.: Framework for offline mobile data communications. In: Proceedings of Tech4Dev International Conference (2014)
8. Core Network Dynamics: OpenEPC by CND. http://www.openepc.com/
9. ip.access: Enterprise and Public Access - small cells for complex coverage. http://www.ipaccess.com/en/public-access
10. DeFuTech: FAQ. http://www.defutech.de/en/use-cases/wiback-faq/

Design and Implementation of a Smart Meter

Florien Gumyusenge$^{(\boxtimes)}$, Jeannette Mukamana, Robert Mugisha,
Aminata A. Garba, and Martin Saint

Carnegie Mellon University, Kigali, Rwanda
{fgumyuse, jmukaman, rmugisha, aminata,
msaint}@andrew.cmu.edu

Abstract. This paper presents the design and the implementation of a smart meter for prepaid electricity using an Arduino microcontroller, a global system for mobile communication (GSM) module, and a liquid crystal display (LCD). The smart meter allows users to remotely recharge their meter after purchasing prepaid electricity using a mobile phone. It also allows the meter owner to receive notifications about the level of prepaid credit available in the meter, the meter status, and a threshold for recharge notifications. This paper also discusses the advantages of the proposed system to customers, and the utility company, as well as some of the challenges encountered, and provides recommendations to various stakeholders.

Keywords: Smart meter · GSM module · Arduino microcontroller

1 Introduction

Smart electric meters are more capable, more reliable, and more accurate than traditional electric meters, driving the replacement of traditional meters with smart meters. Smart electricity meters track energy consumption, automatically recharge prepaid electrical credit, and provide feedback to users about the energy consumption of household appliances or business equipment. Smart electricity meters fall under the domain of Internet of Things (IoT) devices because they can communicate with other existing systems without human interaction [1].

Many projects have been carried out to enhance the capabilities of smart electricity meters [2]. These projects include providing feedback to users and semi-automatically recharging the meter credit using either wired or wireless communications. These systems typically recharge the meter using messages sent by mobile phone to interact with the utility company. However, this approach is not entirely automated because the user must load a code or token into the meter manually. The system explained in this paper completely automates the process. Tokens from the utility company are sent directly to a wireless GSM communication module that communicates with a microcontroller, and the microcontroller is used to recharge the meter credit automatically.

© ICST Institute for Computer Sciences, Social Informatics and Telecommunications Engineering 2018
V. Odumuyiwa et al. (Eds.): AFRICOMM 2017, LNICST 250, pp. 109–120, 2018.
https://doi.org/10.1007/978-3-319-98827-6_9

1.1 Problem Statement

Prepaid electric meters are in everyday use in many parts of the world, and the majority of electricity meters are conventional in type, with metal discs and electric motors that rotate at a speed that is proportional to the amount of power supplied during electricity consumption. These meters are inexpensive and are less vulnerable to lightning strikes than electronic meters. In a traditional prepaid electricity system, a meter is recharged using a token provided to the users when they have purchased electricity. The token number obtained from the vendor is then manually typed in the meter to update the new electricity balance. This process is time-consuming and is vulnerable to human error. When the meter cuts power to the user due to expired credit, there is no warning, and the process of recharging the meter credit is inconvenient and may involve lengthy delays during reconnection. For instance, it may be necessary to travel to a vendor authorized to sell electricity tokens, purchase the desired amount of credit, and travel back to recharge the meter. These factors, combined with the lack of communication between the users and the utility company, resulting in inconveniences to the user. To solve this, we designed and implemented a smart electricity meter that is user-friendly and reduces most of the errors and inconveniences faced when using conventional meters. This smart electricity meter is automated and requires few user interventions. It can remotely load power tokens, alert the user when electricity reaches a minimum threshold, and send a notification when the meter credit is recharged. Moreover, our proposed metering system is programmed to keep track of power usage and communicates directly with the utility company through the GSM infrastructure of a telecommunication company. This data facilitates further analysis by the power company.

1.2 Objectives

- Automatic recharge of smart electricity meters using wireless communications.
- Provide real-time updates to the user and the utility company.
- Allow domestic power consumption management.

2 Related Work and Background

The prepaid metering system eliminates disadvantages of postpaid billing system, such as the need for meter reading, bill calculations and bill delivery. The prepaid system can be implemented in any country and is beneficial to both consumers and power distribution companies [1].

Smart meter systems can collect power consumption data in real time, and can display price information, enabling variable market pricing based on supply and demand, and demand-side management of connected loads. Wired and wireless communications facilitate this exchange of data between the user and the utility company [2]. A survey on the use of smart electricity meters provided economic, social, and environmental benefits for multiple stakeholders. One of the critical factors that will determine the success of smart meters is smart meter data analytics, covering data acquisition, transmission, processing, and interpretation [3].

A smart electricity meter is a type of IoT device that can be programmed to control the electricity consumption of home appliances and uses two-way communication to give and transmit real-time electricity prices [4]. Weiss et al. developed an application that can send information about the power consumption of each device connected to the circuit and relay it to the consumer. This application aims to address the complexity of other methods of monitoring individual loads and to address a lack of feedback on the power consumption of individual devices in existing systems [4]. It stores this information in a microcontroller, making utility and price information accessible in real time, and summarizes user's consumption data [2].

The smart meter system consists of metering equipment connected to the electrical circuit that measures total electric consumption. It has a software-based application that manages collected data and serves as a lightweight communications gateway. The gateway has a mobile user interface to provide real-time data from a database [5]. Several communications technologies typically exist in each meter and can be selected based on data rates, distance, type of data, and protocols. Communications and data exchange help to quantify demand habits so that utilities and consumers can better predict their base and peak load, enable demand-side management, and provide rapid automatic outage detection and restoration. The life expectancy of smart meters is about 20 years [6].

2.1 Conventional Electricity Meter Design

Conventional meters have a minimal user interface. Their design does not allow the integration of other platform modules like protocols and functions. The portability of one coding language to another is platform-dependent. Currently, 8-bit microcontrollers are used and have limited memory and performance capabilities. The software architecture of a conventional electricity meter is shown in Fig. 1. It consists of six components: an energy measurement and calculation unit, a processing module, a load survey tamper detection and processing module, a power management and real-time clock (RTC) module, a display and key module, and a universal asynchronous receiver-transmitter (UART) interface and communication Modbus.

2.2 Smart Electricity Meter Design

A smart electricity meter is integrated into a 32-bit microprocessor implemented on a shared peripheral and memory interface bus, which makes the system flexible and scalable [6]. Smart meters are optimized for resource-handling reliability and scheduling management. This design helps in scheduling policies, inter-process communication, and resource sharing. The meter architecture provides interrupt handlers, task priority assignments, synchronizes concurrent processes and threads, and manages measurements and billings as shown in Fig. 2 [6].

A smart electricity meter has two main components: communications and processing. The communications component manages the internal communications and information-sharing between the meter and the user. The processing component uses an analog-to-digital converter to convert the voltage and current of a load into digital a form representation, and stores data in an internal memory. These data are used to

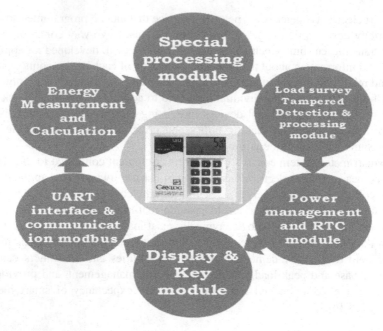

Fig. 1. Software architecture of a conventional electricity meter, showing communications with other meter components [4].

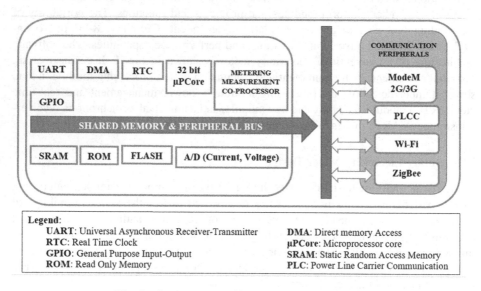

Fig. 2. Smart meter architecture adapted from [5].

calculate power consumption and record outage events. The most common topologies used in smart electricity meter communications are star, tree, and mesh [7]. Figure 2 shows the hardware architecture of a silicon-and-chip-based smart electricity meter. Its main components are a shared memory and peripheral bus, a metering measurement co-processor, an analog-to-digital converter, and common peripherals.

2.3   Requirements and Challenges in the Design and Implementation of Smart Meters

There are a number of requirements and challenges in the design and implementation of smart electricity meters. These include:

- Communication security: Secure communications may require regular security upgrades.
- Interoperability: Communications and command sets should be interoperable with existing advanced metering infrastructure.
- Communication ports: Port specifications should be based on a common standard to enable longevity, upgradeability, and interoperability.
- Input/output capability: A sufficient number of interfaces should be available for current and future connections [6].
- Limitations on network coverage, data capacity, and propagation can be problematic for the utility company.
- Network maintenance is difficult in large, widely-distributed systems, particularly if physical access is required [5].

3   Design of the Proposed System

The main objective of this project work is to design and implement a smart meter system that interacts with the utility companies and meter users. We focus on prepaid electricity where a meter is charged/recharged after the owner has purchased electricity. Traditionally, this is done manually where a token number obtained from the vendor is manually typed in the meter to update the new electricity balance. We replace this manual transaction by a transaction where the token is sent directly to update meter by the utility company or the user using their phones. We also aim to programming the meter to keep track of the remaining power and communicates directly with the utility company through the GSM infrastructure of a telecommunication company.

The system requires human intervention in the recharging process only. It facilitates power management by prioritizing the use of home appliances and providing the data necessary for upcoming plans.

The proposed system is designed by putting together electronic devices composed of a microcontroller, GSM module, push button circuit and a physically-connected LCD. These components communicate using an electric current. The control and communication mechanisms are aided by a software component that was developed by programming the microcontroller. The communication processes of this smart electricity meter are based on flowchart and block diagram in Fig. 3 that explain the working principles of the system and shows the physical interconnection of the different parts.

Our smart meter has four main systems: the control and management system, the display system, the communication and database system.

3.1   Control and Management System

This is comprised of the microcontroller and push button. The microcontroller is designed to perform management and control while the push button is used to emulate the load. These are explained below:

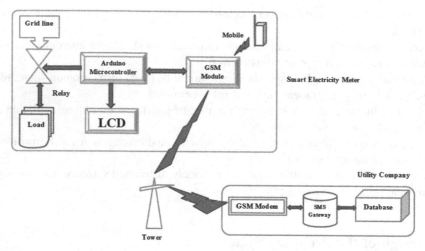

Fig. 3. System block diagram of a smart electricity meter showing all the parts of the metering system.

As shown in Fig. 3, the circuit design has a programmed microcontroller which controls the overall system operations. It reads the input signal in the form of a current and uses the installed software to provide the necessary output. The output action connects or disconnects the loads to/from the grid and, switches on or off certain appliances. It also instructs the GSM module to send the message to the user when the power is low, when any amount of electricity has been recharged or when a system error has occurred. This microcontroller is able to communicate with the GSM module and LCD.

3.2   Display System

Our metering system uses a 16 × 2 LCD which serves as an output device for displaying the electrical energy balance. This system can receive and display the remaining power balance from the microcontroller. It can also respond to all microcontroller signals and perform the display actions as requested.

3.3   Communication System

The communication system consists of wired and wireless systems. Apart from the internal communication of devices inside the meter, the external communication is based on the interface between the SIM900A GSM module and the Arduino micro-controller. The GSM module acts as a link between the user and the smart meter circuit. It receives the powering message from the utility company and sends it to the microcontroller. It also receives the signals from the microcontroller and communicates them to the user via a wireless channel. The owner of the meter, herein termed "the user", receives the information from the meter as an SMS with the help of this GSM module. On the server side, a token generated by the utility database will be sent to the GMS module on the client side via a MODEM and telephone line.

3.4   Database System

The database system will be owned by the utility company. It will hold a status of valid tokens so that those which have been used cannot be reused. It will also generate random token numbers whenever a user buys electricity, and send them to Ozeki SMS gateway to the GSM module at the client's home. It will be designed and implemented through the Xamp open platform and MYSQL database. The Ozeki SMS Gateway will be used to send electricity token number from the utility company to home GSM module in the form of an SMS. The communication between all of the above systems is illustrated on the flowchart in Fig. 4 below:

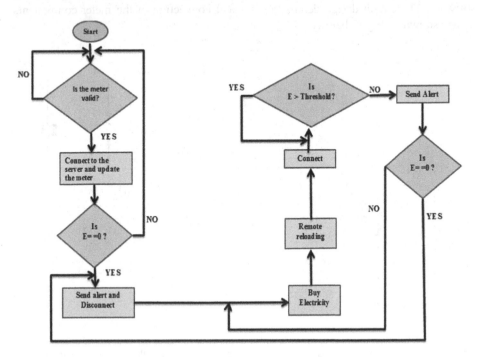

Fig. 4. System flowchart showing the information flow during communication from the different parts of the meter.

As shown on the flowchart in Fig. 4, whenever the meter is connected for the first time, the system will check whether the meter is valid and allow it to be used for further operations. Whenever the meter is connected, the system continuously checks the electricity level to determine whether it is equal to zero or not, and sends an alert message to the user or home owner's phone when the balance reaches the threshold. When the electricity balance reaches zero, the system sends an alert message and disconnects the meter. By the time a user buys electricity, the meter is reconnected and goes in a state of electricity level tracking so as to alert the user whenever it reaches the threshold value or zero.

4   Implementation and Demonstration

The implementation is structured in three steps: circuit design and implementation, software implementation, and database design and implementation. The system testing is structured in such a way that each part is first tested individually and then again after interconnecting it with other parts. However, the database has not been implemented. The implementation of the system uses open source hardware like Arduino boards and software.

4.1   Circuit Design and Implementation

The design of the smart electricity circuit was based on the block diagram of the smart electricity meter. The circuit design and simulation were conducted using Fritzing software. The circuit design details the physical connection of the meter components and is shown in Fig. 5 below:

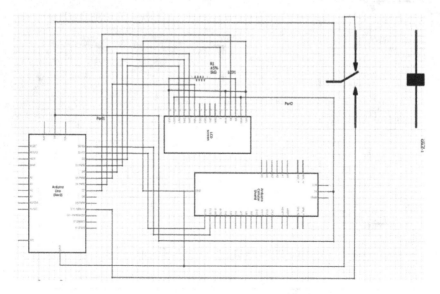

Fig. 5. Circuit design of a smart electricity meter showing all internal connections of components of the meter.

4.2   Circuit Software Implementation

We have implemented a software which allows the user visualize the amount of electricity remaining in the meter using an Arduino integrated development environment (IDE) platform. This is made by activating an LCD display which displays the amount of initial or pre-configured of electricity units on the meter. The current system accepts the message from the utility company for loading the meter (Fig. 6).

Fig. 6. Display on the screen of a smart electricity meter is shown as the number of units.

The GSM module can communicate to the external mobile device with the help of an embedded SIM card. Since this SIM card belongs to the telecommunication company, there should be the agreement between the telecom and the utility company so that it can freely send SMS to the user and remain in service without requiring airtime.

The message on the Fig. 7 should begin with # and end with * for the software to decode it and save it as units. The units loaded in the meter decrease as the load is connected and increase whenever the user recharges it with new credits. In case the load is not connected, the amount of electricity in the meter stays constant.

4.3   Database Implementation

The database component of the meter has not been implemented in this paper. The format of the required database tables is shown on table in Figs. 8 and 9. Nonetheless, the working mechanism of the smart electricity meter will involve the use of the database that will store the information about the meter and its working history. This meter will be based, owned and monitored by the utility company. It will contain two tables: one for the meter information and the other for the used and unused token

Fig. 7. Message as sent by the mobile phone to the meter.

numbers. The information in the table below will be responsible for keeping the ID of the meter, the meter number, the name of its user, the phone number of the meter embedded SIM card, the user's phone number, the address, the used the token number and the number of units. The meter number, its phone number, and the name and contact addresses of the user will be installed at the time the user collects the meter from the utility company. However, the token number and the units will be automatically loaded as the user recharges meter. The token table will contain the token number and its status (i.e. used or unused).

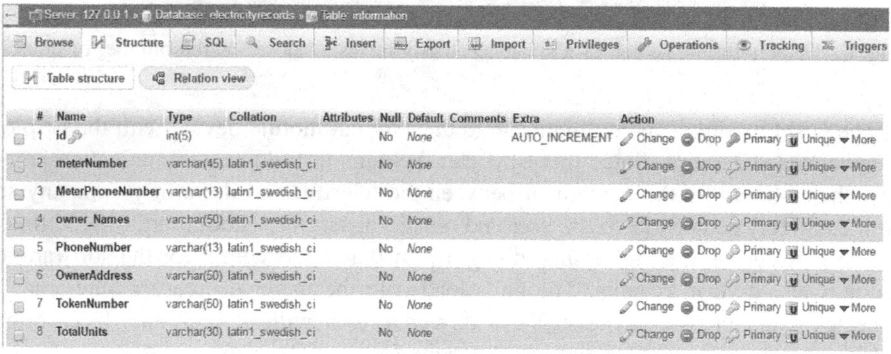

#	Name	Type	Collation	Attributes	Null	Default	Comments	Extra	Action
1	id	int(5)			No	None		AUTO_INCREMENT	Change Drop Primary Unique More
2	meterNumber	varchar(45) latin1_swedish_ci			No	None			Change Drop Primary Unique More
3	MeterPhoneNumber	varchar(13) latin1_swedish_ci			No	None			Change Drop Primary Unique More
4	owner_Names	varchar(50) latin1_swedish_ci			No	None			Change Drop Primary Unique More
5	PhoneNumber	varchar(13) latin1_swedish_ci			No	None			Change Drop Primary Unique More
6	OwnerAddress	varchar(50) latin1_swedish_ci			No	None			Change Drop Primary Unique More
7	TokenNumber	varchar(50) latin1_swedish_ci			No	None			Change Drop Primary Unique More
8	TotalUnits	varchar(30) latin1_swedish_ci			No	None			Change Drop Primary Unique More

Fig. 8. Information table database of a smart electricity meter detailing all the necessary information of the meter and the owner.

4.4 Case Study

The meter prototype was tested by loading electricity using a cell phone. The meter was recharged by dialing # Electricity units* on a cell phone and automatically loads itself. The load that was supposed to consume electricity was emulated using a push button.

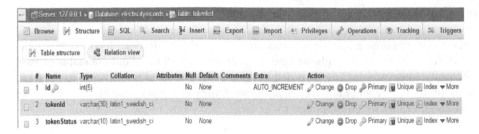

Fig. 9. Token table database of a smart electricity meter containing tokens and their status.

Whenever the push button was pressed, the electricity level in the meter was reducing. By recharging new electricity units, the meter calculates the current balance by adding it to the initial balance. The meter sends notifications to the user when electricity has been consumed up to a certain threshold so that he can recharge.

5 Discussion

In the design of this smart electricity meter, we used a push button to replace the load which can consume the full units of electricity as you press it. This meter is designed in such a way that it can receive and decode the message sent to it and display the units. However, not all messages can be decoded into units; only those with some specifications can be decoded.

Furthermore, users may face various challenges with the adoption and use of this electricity meter. Most of these are cost and policy-related. Smart electricity meters are more expensive than conventional meters. Another challenge is that this meter is using GSM technology; it may require a final agreement between telecommunications operators and utility companies. However, the most important challenge that has to be addressed with the advent of smart meters is cyber security. Since smart meters are becoming digitized and automatic, they face security attacks like data hacking and the introduction of malware.

In designing this meter, we planned the functionality of sending a message alert to the user when the units balance reaches a certain threshold. However, due to time limitations, this feature is not yet implemented. We aim to implement it in our future work.

For the use and adoption of smart electricity meters, we offer the following recommendations to; governments and other stakeholders: governments should give some incentives and grants to utilities so that customers can afford the smart electricity meters; utilities should cooperate with telecommunications operators for the use of the communication and billing systems; utilities are also recommended to invest in security to ensure the security and privacy of users and their devices.

6 Conclusion

This paper proposes a smart electricity meter that allows users to load prepaid electricity remotely using their phones and to receive notifications about the status of their electricity consumption. The proposed meter provides updated information to the users about their use of energy and its management. Utility companies can also use real-time data about electricity consumption to set tariffs according to the load status.

References

1. Valluru, S.: Design and assembly of low cost prepaid smart card energy meter – a novel design. Int. J. Electr. Eng. Inform. 6(1), 65–73 (2014)
2. Xie, H., Huang, P., Li, Y., Zhao, L., Wang, F.: Design of real-time electricity prices and wireless communication smart meter. Energy Power Eng. 05(04), 1357–1361 (2013)
3. Alahakoon, D., Yu, X.: Smart electricity meter data intelligence for future energy systems: a survey. IEEE Trans. Industr. Inf. 12(1), 425–436 (2016)
4. Rastogi, S., Sharma, M., Varshney, P.: Internet of Things based smart electricity meters. Int. J. Comput. Appl. (0975 – 8887) 8, 13–16 (2016)
5. Weiss, M., Mattern, F., Graml, T., Staake, T., Fleisch, E.: Handy feedback: connecting smart meters with mobile phones, pp. 22–25 (2009)
6. Jaganmohan, M.S., Manikandan, K.: Challenges in Smart Meter Design. Easun Reyrolle Ltd (2010)
7. Shang-Wen, L., Jen-Hao, T., Shun-Yu, C., Lain-Chyr, H.: Development of a smart power meter for AMI based on ZigBee communication. In: PEDS 2009, pp. 661–665 (2009)

Towards a Persuasive Technology
for Electricity Theft Reduction in Uganda

Ruth Mbabazi Mutebi[1(✉)], Julianne Sansa Otim[1], and Ben Sebitosi[2]

[1] Makerere University, Kampala, Uganda
{rmbabazi, sansa}@cit.ac.ug
[2] StellenBosch University, Stellenbosch, South Africa
sebitosi@sun.ac.za

Abstract. Technology for changing attitude and behaviour, known as persuasive technology, has been applied to solve many challenges, ranging from personal health and finance, to environmental sustainability. In this paper, an application to persuade electricity consumers in Kampala, Uganda, to partner with the electricity utility company in fighting electricity theft is proposed. The persuasive application will implement a number of persuasive techniques including tailoring, reduction, notifications and suggestion. These techniques, along with the choice of technology, were derived basing on Fogg's process of persuasive systems development.

Keywords: Persuasive technology · Electricity theft · Non-technical losses
Fogg's eight steps

1 Introduction

Electricity theft is a complex socio-economic technical problem in Uganda leading to loss of lives, property and at least $10 million in financial losses annually [1]. In attempts to curb this crime, the electricity utility company has implemented deterrent measures like prepaid metering, aerial bundle conductors and automatic metering. In addition, for sustainable results [2], honest consumers are encouraged to actively participate in fighting this vice through mass media campaigns.

However a study to understand electricity theft among consumers in Kampala [3] revealed that, (i) despite a recently concluded mass media campaign and the risk of possible fines or imprisonment, people are still not willing to engage in electricity theft reduction efforts; and (ii) people are not aware (and/or perhaps do not care) that electricity theft negatively affects even honest consumers. We argue that persuasive technologies may be better at convincing consumers to fight against electricity theft.

Persuasive systems are interactive computing systems designed to change people's attitudes or behavior [4]. Behaviour change support systems (BCSS), a class of persuasive technologies, are defined as "socio-technical information systems with psychological and behavioural outcomes designed to form, alter or reinforce attitudes and behaviours without using coercion or deception" [5]. Persuasive technologies have been used in a number of sectors including energy [6], health [7], aviation safety [8], and to shape social beliefs among rural Indian women [9]. Depending on the

© ICST Institute for Computer Sciences, Social Informatics and Telecommunications Engineering 2018
V. Odumuyiwa et al. (Eds.): AFRICOMM 2017, LNICST 250, pp. 121–130, 2018.
https://doi.org/10.1007/978-3-319-98827-6_10

technology used, persuasive technologies are better than public campaigns for achieving attitude and behavior change because they can be tailored [7], are ubiquitous, offer anonymity [10] and make it possible to have feedback.

Persuasive design frameworks include Fogg's eight steps [11], Persuasive system design (PSD) [12], unified-framework for analysing, designing and evaluating persuasion systems (U-FADE) [13]. Each has strengths and weaknesses. We selected Fogg's eight step process as we deemed it most suited for our challenge. In this paper we discuss how we adapted Fogg's process to design a persuasive technology for increased willingness to fight electricity theft.

The rest of this paper is organized as follows: we offer a brief discussion of persuasive techniques in Sect. 2, and persuasive design frameworks and why we adapted Fogg's design steps in Sect. 3. In Sect. 4 we discuss how the adapted framework was used to develop a persuasive mobile application. We discuss and conclude in Sects. 5 and 6 respectively.

2 Persuasive Techniques

Fogg [4] proposed a functional triad that shows three perspectives of how computers can be used; as tools, media and social actors of persuasion. Computers can act as tools of persuasion through; *reduction*-making a certain task easier to do; *tunneling*-guiding a user through information; *tailoring*-providing user appropriate information; *self-monitoring*-allowing users to monitor themselves and providing real time feedback; *surveillance*-monitoring others in order to modify their behaviour; and *conditioning*-use of operant conditioning to change behaviour. Torning and Oinas-Kukkonen [12] proposed additional techniques which they classified into four persuasion dimensions; primary task support, dialogue support, social support and system credibility support.

3 Design of Persuasion Technologies

There are basically three frameworks for designing persuasion technologies; Fogg's eight step process [11], persuasive systems design (PSD) [12] and U-FADE [13].

3.1 Fogg's Eight Steps

Fogg's eight step process, shown in Fig. 1:A [11] begins by selecting an appropriate behaviour to target for change. The second step is to select an appropriate audience for the technology. Thirdly the team should find out why people are not performing the target behaviour. Reasons may be a lack of motivation, ability, or a trigger for behaviour or any combination of the three reasons. The team should then select the technology to use that favours both the audience and target behaviour. It will make it easier for the audience to adapt the technology. Steps 5 and 6 are identifying successful projects and imitating them. He then proposes that the team tests and iterates quickly (step 7). If the project is successful then it can be expanded (step 8).

3.2   Persuasive System Design (PSD)

Oinas-Kukkonen and Harjumaa [12] defined a generic 3 step process for Persuasive system design. The first step is to analyse the persuasion context and select persuasive design principles, secondly to define the requirements and lastly to implement the software. Persuasion context is made up of the intent, the event and the strategy. The intent includes the persuader and the deliberate target behaviour that the system is to cause in the user [12]. The event contains the use, user, and technology sub-contexts. The use sub-context refers to the problem domain-dependent features in the form of well-known problems in the domain; user sub-context includes traits of the application user, and technology sub-context refers to the features of the technological platform. Lastly strategy includes the message and the route/form. While message refers to content, route is the form in which the content selected is delivered for intended transformation [12].

3.3   Unified-Framework for Analysing, Designing and Evaluating Persuasion Systems

Wiafe [13] proposed the unified-framework for analysing and designing and evaluating (U-FADE) persuasion technologies. Building on PSD, it starts with event analysis that is made up of user and use analysis. User analysis evaluates the users level of cognitive dissonance [14] using the 3-dimensional relationship between attitude and behaviour (3D-RAB) model and use analysis is done basing on the persuasive technologies organisation (PTO) model. Then persuasion strategies are selected using the persuasive pathway model (PPM). These strategies are summarized in transitions description cards (TDC). After development, the system is evaluated basing on the 3D-RAB model.

3.4   Selecting the Persuasive Design Method

Persuasive technology development, like any typical software, follows software engineering practices, with the water fall model as a guide. However persuasive design is about achieving one requirement-system persuasiveness [12]. Thus the presented design methods can also be seen as a software engineering process that mainly elaborates requirements engineering, with some aspects of design and development. For example, PSD is mainly requirements engineering, while UFADE is both requirements engineering and usability testing. Fogg's eight steps, however, cover all software engineering stages.

Secondly, PSD and U-FADE are suitable for developing behaviour change support systems. Therefore they focus on understanding the user and use case, and proposing persuasive features based on individual users. This study targets changing attitude and behaviour of a society rather than an individual. We need a method with a broader focus than both PSD and U-FADE. Fogg's eight steps fit this criterion. Thirdly, Fogg's process is open (beginning with a selection of target behaviour and audience) and closely follows a typical software engineering water fall model with iterations within design, development and testing. Indeed Yamakami [15] described it as a "good guidance not only for creating persuasion, but also for introducing innovation". For these reasons, we based our persuasive technology on Fogg's process. It has been used by Da Silva *et al.* [16] to design a role playing game for stretching, while Pereira *et al.* [17] used it to develop a mobile application to change eating habits.

4   Adaptation of Fogg's Eight Steps

We designed a persuasive system to improve attitudes towards electricity theft reduction by adapting Foggs's eight steps as shown in Fig. 1:B.

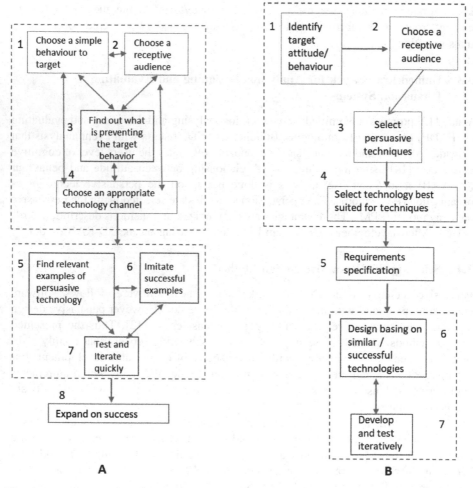

Fig. 1. A: Fogg's eight steps for design of the system [11], B: Our adaption of Fogg's process.

4.1   Step 1: Identify Target Behaviour/Attitude

We modified this from choosing a behaviour to identification of behavior/attitude. In reducing electricity theft, there are a number of behaviours and attitudes to change. There are; attitudes and behaviours associated with the actual event of using electricity illegally (basically attitudes and behaviours of the culprits), and the attitudes and behaviours of those that do not use electricity illegally but in one way or another encourage those engaging in the crime [2]. We decided to focus on the latter. This is because culprits were not easy to identify and they would not be a willing audience to engage.

Since the earlier mentioned study (in introduction) revealed that people are not willing to engage in electricity theft reduction [3], we focused on changing the attitude that "*electricity theft is not my problem*", to "*electricity theft is my problem. let me deal with it*". Hopefully if that attitude is changed then individuals would engage in electricity theft reduction efforts.

4.2   Step 2: Choose Audience

This step remained unchanged. It is very crucial in developing this application because the general population is very heterogeneous; a mixture of illiterate, semiliterate and highly literate. Their technology skills levels, as well as attitude to electricity theft, vary. We design an application for the educated population that is technology savvy and uses the various technologies, including smart mobile phones.

4.3   Step 3: Selecting Persuasion Techniques

We reasoned that the basis for Fogg's third step, "understand why people are not performing the desired behaviour" is to select persuasive techniques, thus our third step. Part of the earlier mentioned survey (refer to Sect. 1), respondents were asked: "What would you do if you found your neighbour stealing electricity?" [3]. Responses of those who said they would not take any action to reduce electricity theft were classified under the following themes:

- Individualism: People do not want to be bothered.
- Utility: They feel it is the utility's job to fight electricity theft.
- Financial sympathy: These said they would do nothing because they appreciated the other person's economic struggles.
- Safety first: These are respondents who said that as long as the illegal electricity was being used in a way that did not endanger anyone then there was no need to bother.
- Ignorance: These are people who did not know where to report, or what to do, or the reward for reporting.
- Relationship: These valued their relationship with those around so they did not want to make enemies.
- Self-preservation: These felt that if they reported others, they too would be reported.
- No reward: These felt there was no benefit from reducing electricity theft.
- Hopeless: These felt it was useless to take any action.

We match these reasons to appropriate persuasion techniques basing on PSD [18] as shown in Table 1 below:

Table 1. Appropriate persuasive techniques

Reason	Corresponding technique	PSD dimension
Individualism, safety first, financial empathy	Tailoring of information- through localisation and visualisation	Primary task support
Relationship, self-preservation, hopeless	Notification	Dialogue support, social support
Ignorance	Reduction	Primary task support
No reward, utility	Rewards	Dialogue support
Ignorance	Suggestion	Dialogue support
Hopeless	Praise	Dialogue support

Tailoring

Information about the economic impact of electricity theft is normally provided in Newspaper publications and television media as the total non-technical losses (NTLs) and financial loss incurred by the company. This information can be localized, such that electricity users in the same area are periodically provided with figures of NTLs within their area. In this way it would appeal to the consumers.

Additionally information of deaths, fires, and other electricity theft related accidents is reported once in a while in newspapers and eventually forgotten. This information can be represented on a map, showing the locality of user.

Lastly, through mass media campaigns, electricity consumers are informed that they bear the financial burden of for electricity theft through the tariff. However this information is not clearly quantified and presented to consumers. Data visualization can be used to communicate the economic burden of electricity theft to consumers.

Notification

Consumers ought to receive a notification whenever someone in their neighborhood participates in fighting electricity theft. This would increase willingness to participate since according to the social proof theory, "individuals are more likely to engage in behaviours which they perceive others are also engage in" [19].

Reduction

People normally report electricity theft by calling on a toll free line and they are asked for details. The process could be made simpler by providing a template or form on a website or mobile application. This template would guide a person reporting on what information to provide, as well, as provide an option for uploading a picture of the case so that one does not have to input a lot of information.

Suggestion

Suggestion should be used to remind people to report electricity theft. This could be done when electricity theft in an area increases or when an accident occurs due to electricity theft.

Praise and Rewards
When a user reports any case, they could be praised by the technology. IT should also provide a mechanism for rewarding users when they provide information.

4.4 Step 4: Selection of Technology

We propose to use a mobile phone application because mobile phones enable citizen participation in governance and are useful in awareness campaigns [20]. We specifically recommend smart phones because they provide the necessary platform for display of graphics. They also make it possible to personalize features. Data visualization can easily be achieved on a mobile application. For example, after a user purchases prepaid electricity on their mobile application, then a bar chart can be used to show how much money paid is for power and what that for power theft. Lastly, the mobile application would also make reporting electricity theft anonymous such that people are not bothered about being found out by the community as snitches.

4.5 Step 5: Requirements Specification

Documenting requirements as a formal requirements specification is part of requirements engineering [21]. It is important for requirements management. It should take place after requirements analysis and modeling. While this step is missing in Fogg's original process, we include it in this modified process to ensure quality and traceability of requirements.

4.6 Step 6: Design Basing on Similar/Successful Technologies

Fogg's process does not explicitly have a design step, however steps 5 and 6 provide guidelines on how to design. We combined them into our sixth step. If relevant design patterns for corresponding technology and features are available they may be used.

In this study the process of design is ongoing. So far we are basing on the utility's mobile application for communicating to users to design the look and feel of the interface.

Steps 7 and 8 remain the same as in original process.

5 Discussion

Different people respond differently to differing persuasion techniques. If an inappropriate technique is used, the technology may be counterproductive [22]. Methods of how to select persuasive techniques from the available ones proposed by Fogg and PSD are scanty [23]. We relied on results from the previously mentioned study [3]. This empirical approach to proposing persuasive techniques is common in persuasive technologies development. For example, Kulyk et al. [24] used focus group discussions to propose persuasion strategies for an application for young adults used, while Mubin [25] used a survey to propose persuasion techniques to design of an electronic health book for Sri Lankan children.

The selected persuasive features basing on primary support, social support and dialogue support dimensions. Dialogue and social support are critical features for Ugandans being a largely collective culture [26].

Information concerning the impact of electricity theft to electricity consumers in Kampala is broadcasted on radio and Television once in a while. People do not appreciate the impact of electricity theft to their day-to-day lives and with time forget about it. This we overcome by information tailoring. Tailoring is a highly used technique in persuasive system design [18]. Tailoring ensures that information meets the "potential needs, interests, personality, usage context, of users" [12]. It can be achieved through various techniques including, data visualisation, localisation and contextualisation. Data visualisation makes it easier to process information and to make decisions [27]. Foth *et al.* [28] used Google maps to achieve real time visualisation of blood donations to motivate youth to donate blood, while [29] developed an application that visualises crime on a map. Our aim is to do the same for electricity theft reduction.

Lastly, ethical considerations are crucial in persuasive technology design. We followed Berdichevsky and Neuenschwander's "golden rule": "creators of a persuasive technology should never seek to persuade anyone of something they themselves would not consent to be persuaded of" [30]. To the best of our comprehension the intended outcome of this technology is ethical. However, the actual outcome can only be validated after users interact with it.

6 Conclusion

In this paper we have proposed persuasive features of a persuasive technology to change the negative attitude electricity consumers in Kampala have towards curbing electricity theft. These features, namely; tailoring, reduction, notification, rewards, praise and suggestion, were proposed basing on a modification of Fogg's eight steps of persuasion technology design. A mobile application is the selected technology as it is suitable for implementing these features. As further work we will design, develop, and evaluate the proposed mobile application.

Acknowledgements. The researchers are grateful for the funding provided by the Makerere University-SIDA bi-lateral partnership 2010–2014, through the Gender Main steaming directorate.

References

1. Umeme addresses impacts of power theft. https://www.esi-africa.com/news/umeme-addresses-impacts-of-power-theft/
2. Winther, T.: Electricity theft as a relational issue: a comparative look at Zanzibar, Tanzania, and the Sunderban Islands India. Energy Sustain. Dev. **16**(1), 111–119 (2012)
3. Mutebi, R.M., Otim, J.S., Okou, R., Sebitosi, B.: Electricity theft in kampala and potential ICT solutions. In: Nungu, A., Pehrson, B., Sansa-Otim, J. (eds.) AFRICOMM 2014. LNICST, vol. 147, pp. 198–206. Springer, Cham (2015). https://doi.org/10.1007/978-3-319-16886-9_21

4. Fogg, B.: Persuasive Technology: Using Computers to Change What We Think and Do. Morgan Kaufmann, San Francisco (2003)
5. Oinas-Kukkonen, H.: A foundation for the study of behavior change support systems. Pers. Ubiquit. Comput. **17**(6), 1223–1235 (2013)
6. McCalley, T., Kaiser, F., Midden, C., Keser, M., Teunissen, M.: Persuasive appliances: goal priming and behavioral response to product-integrated energy feedback. In: IJsselsteijn, W. A., de Kort, Y.A.W., Midden, C., Eggen, B., van den Hoven, E. (eds.) PERSUASIVE 2006. LNCS, vol. 3962, pp. 45–49. Springer, Heidelberg (2006). https://doi.org/10.1007/11755494_7
7. Kaptein, M., De Ruyter, B., Markopoulos, P., Aarts, E.: Adaptive persuasive systems: a study of tailored persuasive text messages to reduce snacking. ACM Trans. Interact. Intell. Syst. **2**(2), 1–25 (2012)
8. Chittaro, L., Corbett, C.L., McLean, G.A., Zangrando, N.: Mobile persuasive apps for changing passengers' attitudes towards aviation safety. In: 11th International Conference on Persuasive Technologies, pp. 55–58 (2016)
9. Parmar, V., Keyson, D., deBont, C.: Persuasive technology for shaping social beliefs of rural women in India: an approach based on the theory of planned behaviour. In: Oinas-Kukkonen, H., Hasle, P., Harjumaa, M., Segerståhl, K., Øhrstrøm, P. (eds.) PERSUASIVE 2008. LNCS, vol. 5033, pp. 104–115. Springer, Heidelberg (2008). https://doi.org/10.1007/978-3-540-68504-3_10
10. Oduor, M., Alahäivälä, T., Oinas-Kukkonen, H.: Persuasive software design patterns for social influence. Pers. Ubiquit. Comput. **18**(7), 1689–1704 (2014)
11. Fogg, B.F.: Creating persuasive technologies: an eight-step design process. In: Technology, vol. 91, pp. 1–6 (2009)
12. Oinas-kukkonen, H., Harjumaa, M.: Persuasive systems design: key issues, process model, and system features. Commun. Assoc. Inf. Syst. **24**(1), 485–500 (2009)
13. Wiafe, I., Frempong, D.A.: Enhancing persuasive features of behaviour change support systems: the role of U-FADE. In: BCSS, pp. 17–27 (2015)
14. Wiafe, I., Nakata, K., Gulliver, S.: Categorizing users in behavior change support systems based on cognitive dissonance. Pers. Ubiquit. Comput. **18**(7), 1677–1687 (2014)
15. Yamakami, T.: Mobile social game design from the perspective of persuasive technology. In: 15th International Conference on Network-Based Information Systems, pp. 221–225 (2012)
16. Da Silva, J.P.S., Schneider, D., De Souza, J., Da Silva, M.A.: A role-playing-game approach to accomplishing daily tasks to improve health. In: IEEE 17th International Conference on Computer Supported Cooperative Work in Design, pp. 350–356 (2013)
17. Pereira, C.V., Figueiredo, G, Esteves, M.G.P., De Souza, J.M.: We4Fit: a game with a purpose for behavior change. In: 18th International Conference on Computer Supported Cooperative Work in Design, pp. 83–88 (2014)
18. Torning, K., Oinas-Kukkonen, H.: Persuasive system design: state of the art and future directions. In: Persuasive, pp. 1–8 (2009)
19. Cialdini, R.B.: Harnessing the science of persuasion. Harv. Bus. Rev. **79**, 72–79 (2001)
20. Hellström, J: Mobile phones for good governance – challenges and way forward, pp. 1–13 (2007)
21. Nuseibeh, B., Easterbrook, S.: Requirements engineering: a roadmap. In: Conference on the Future of Software Engineering, pp. 35–46 (2000)
22. Orji, R.: Persuasion and culture: individualism–collectivism and susceptibility to influence strategies. In: Workshop Personalization in Persuasive Technology (2016)
23. Wiafe, I., Nakata, K.: Bibliographic analysis of persuasive systems: techniques, methods and domains of application, pp. 61–64

24. Kulyk, O., Den Daas, C., David, S., Van Gemert-Pijnen, L.: How persuasive are serious games, social media and mHealth technologies for vulnerable young adults? Design factors for health behavior and lifestyle change support: sexual health case. In: International Workshop on Behavior Change Support Systems (2015)
25. Mubin, O., Ahmad, M., Jarzabek, S.: Towards the design of an electronic health book for Sri Lankan children: a survey-based approach
26. Hofstede, G., Hofstede, G.J.: Cultures and Organizations: Software of the Mind. McGraw-Hill, New York (2005)
27. Hong, S.: Information Visualization: How Information Visualization Aids Human Cognition. Sarahjanehong.Github.Io (2014)
28. Foth, M., Stchell, C., Seeburger, J., Russell-Bennett, R.: Social and mobile interaction design to increase the loyalty rates of young blood donors. In: International Conference on Communities and Technologies, pp. 64–73 (2013)
29. Kadar, C., Cvijikj, I.P.: CityWatch: the personalized crime prevention assistant. In: 13th International Conference on Mobile and Ubiquitous Multimedia, pp. 260–261 (2014)
30. Berdichevsky, D., Neuenschwander, B.: Toward an ethics of persuasive technology. Commun. ACM 42(5), 51–58 (1999)

The Role of Culture in the Design of Effective Cybersecurity Training and Awareness Programmes. A Case Study of the United Arab Emirates (UAE)

Abdulla Al Neaimi[(⊠)] and Philip Lutaaya

SecureTech, LLC, Abu Dhabi, UAE
alneaimi@gmail.com, lutaphilo@gmail.com

Abstract. The question whether culture of a society needs to be considered when designing cybersecurity training and awareness programs has recently risen in literature. While some programs may be effective in the west, they may not apply in the Middle East or Africa. Since cybersecurity has overtaken terrorism as the leading security concern globally, criticality of user training and awareness programmes cannot be overemphasized. This paper demonstrates that a cybersecurity training or awareness program that considers cultures of the people is more effective than generic one. Staff in a midsized organization were randomly divided into two groups. Group one consisting of Indians was treated to a culturally sensitive training programme in Hindi while group two consisting of Ugandans, Nepalese, Pakistanis and the Philippines undertook a generic one in English. A survey was conducted subsequent to the treatments. Results revealed that group one demonstrated better understanding of cybersecurity issues after one month.

Keywords: Training and awareness · Culture · Cybersecurity
United Arab Emirates (UAE)
Information and Communication Technology (ICT) · Internet of Things (IoT)

1 Introduction

The worldwide increase in ICT security threats has primarily been due to recent rapid increase in volumes of electronic data, increased number of mobile terminals and other digital electronic devices like digital watches and Smart TVs among others interconnected via the internet as IoT devices.

Well organized attacking groups with sophisticated profiles and meagre cybersecurity awareness amongst employees has deepened the gap in most organization's cybersecurity systems [1]. Many countries globally including the United States, Africa and the Middle East have introduced cyber laws with strict punishment against cybercrime. Unfortunately, cyber threats still succeed because people lack appropriate training and awareness. More still, authors in [1] argue that while organizations continue to train their professionals in technology very little effort has been put into

© ICST Institute for Computer Sciences, Social Informatics and Telecommunications Engineering 2018
V. Odumuyiwa et al. (Eds.): AFRICOMM 2017, LNICST 250, pp. 131–139, 2018.
https://doi.org/10.1007/978-3-319-98827-6_11

cybersecurity awareness and training programmes which possess a major risk to the employees in case of cyber-attacks.

Employees are the weakest link to information security of any organization, those who undergo awareness sessions and comply with rules and procedures for information security assist in strengthening the organization's overall security and attitude to prevent cyberattacks [2]. It is revealed that information security awareness and education is very important in improving organization's overall security [3]. Additionally, cybersecurity training is looked at as a key influence to behavior of users on security issues by reducing the knowing-doing gap amongst organization's employees [4]. Cybersecurity can be defined as the protection of systems, networks and data in cyberspace from any form of unauthorized access or attacks. Among these attacks include viruses erasing an entire system, someone breaking into network system and altering files, someone using computers to attack others on the same or different networks, or someone stealing credit card information and making unauthorized purchases. Unfortunately, there's no 100% guarantee that even with the best technological precautions in place these attacks won't happen.

Organizations need to establish cultural sensitive cybersecurity training and awareness programs to disseminate information regarding the identification, protection, detection, response and recovery from cybercrime [5]. Available empirical evidence reveals that the human factor has become the major ambiguity in the implementation of information security programmes in different organizations since employees are usually careless and unaware of most information security practices, policies and procedures [6]. Our hope is that the findings of this paper bring out the role of designing cultural sensitive cyber and information security training and awareness programs in different entities across the UAE, Africa and Globally. The rest of the paper is divided into five sections, Sect. 2 provides a critical review of related literature and the research strategy, Sect. 3 presents results from the pre and post awareness training assessment given to two distinct groups and describes the case study used, Sect. 4 provides a brief discussion from the survey, and finally Sect. 5 concludes the study.

2   Study Background

Information security training and awareness programmes explain the role of employees towards information security of their organizations by showing what they need or can do to protect their organization's critical data in case of cyber-attacks [7]. User behaviors and attitudes need to change if cyber and information security incidents are to be reduced in any organization. In addition, cultural aspects of the people also need to be considered to ensure quick information dissemination and understanding. This notion has been discussed by several authors in literature, for instance Garett [8] looks at culture as the totality of socially transmitted behavior patterns, arts, beliefs and all other products of human work.

It represents a shared set of traditions and behaviors shaped by history, religion, ethnic identity, language and nationality that provides a lens through which people can see and understand the world. Governments and employers need to play a leadership role towards instituting a cyber-security culture amongst nationals through multi-disciplinary and multi-stakeholder approaches that includes training and awareness, cultural sensitive cybersecurity policies and Education [8].

Awareness programs explain an employee's role in information security by showing the users what they can do to protect their organization's critical data and instilling a sense of responsibility and purpose into the employees who manage critical information. Additionally, people's mistakes cannot be solved by mere addition of technology but through a joint effort and partnerships between the IT community of interest, the business community, the nationals through training and awareness along with critical government and top management support [9].

In [10] Seibert et al., looks at culture as an organized group of learned responses with readily made solutions to problems faced by people through interactions with others in the society. It is revealed that culture shapes responses to illness and treatment of people in society. Further, over 85% of the UAE population is from foreign labour which implies that several cultures, cultural norms and religious practices have been imported in the region from different continents like Asia, Africa, Europe, and the Gulf Cooperation Council (GCC) among others. This has created a multi-cultural society speaking different languages.

In this paper, we believe that cultural sensitive cybersecurity training and awareness programmes would close the communication gap and improve employee awareness and knowledge of cyber threats. Meanwhile, different cultures of people have different training and awareness needs implying the need to design appropriate training and awareness programmes and requires planning with clearly defined roles and responsibilities. Furthermore, awareness programs need to teach people information security issues like confidentiality, integrity and availability of information with emphasis on what needs to be protected, against who, when and how [11]. Business success depends upon continuity of operations and information provided to the business processes by information systems. Awareness programs help in sensitizing users on how to behave and benefit from information without jeopardizing its confidentiality, integrity and availability. Lack of awareness and mishandling of information could expose it to competitors or attackers. Therefore, the only thing which can change the behavior and thinking of the staff is awareness and training, since people join organizations with different beliefs, values, culture and principles in line with the aim of this paper [12].

It is patent that solely technological solutions are unlikely to prevent security cracks within organizations [2, 13]. Therefore, security functions need to organize employee training and awareness programmes in addition to the existing technological defenses by acknowledging the influence of individual cultural differences, personality traits and cognitive abilities. Meanwhile, an online survey about information security threats was conducted for a period of one month on a group of two hundred (200) users who volunteered to answer the survey questions. Survey results showed that users who had ever attended information security training programmes before demonstrated more knowledge in the understanding of information security issues. However, this survey did not consider the cultural context of the people online [14].

Authors in [15] argue that cultural factors impact the security knowledge and behavior of different people. The authors used an information security vocabulary test to assess the level of awareness, knowledge and behaviors amongst students in two selected Universities in South Africa. Their main objective was to identify whether cultural differences would affect students' understanding of security issues. The findings revealed that cultural factors such as a person's mother tongue and place of origin showed a significant impact on awareness levels of security issues among selected students. Therefore, the issue of culture cannot be under estimated when designing cyber and information security training and awareness programmes.

Meanwhile, Kruger and Dhillon [16, 17], claims that informal behavior forms a fundamental role in describing characteristics of people and acts of communication that form information. It is stated that the process of communication forms a central hub in information systems and that patterns of learning, culture as well as norms are form constituent elements of informal behavior. Therefore, complete management of information security can only be ensured if the behavioral aspects of individuals and groups have been well understood. This necessitates a study to prove validity of these findings especially in a multi-cultural environment like the United Arab Emirates. In this study a randomly selected group of 50 employees from a mid-sized organization were divided into two groups based on country of origin, culture and common language examining them before and after a cybersecurity training and awareness programme as detailed in the next section;

3 Case Study

A total of fifty (50) employees were randomly selected from a midsized organization in Abu Dhabi and divided into two groups. Group one, involving employees from a similar cultural background and language (Indians only) while Group two considered members from different cultural backgrounds (Ugandans, Nepalese and Philippines). A survey consisting questionnaire items concerning cyber and information security issues pertaining their organization was administered to members before a cybersecurity awareness training programme, the aim was to assess if they understood cyber and information security vulnerabilities affecting their organizations. Pre training assessment results from the two groups were kept and an information security awareness training programme was organized.

Group one went through a *culturally sensitive* cybersecurity awareness programme conducted in HINDI while Group two was given a generic one conducted in English. The survey involved provision of a post training assessment after a period of one month with help of scored questionnaires tailored towards cybersecurity awareness and information security administered to the two groups. The responses from the respondents in the two cases were later coded into IBM SPSS 21, a statistical application for analysis of data and generation of results. The results of the survey following the above treatments were as seen in Tables 1 and 2 below;

Table 1. Pre training assessment results for group one and group two

Variable (questionnaire item)	Available Options	(Group one) (100%) Hindi session	(Group two) (100%) English session
I know What to do If a security breach occurs	Yes (1)	15.4	51
	No (5)	84.6	49
Valuable Information is stored in	Private Email (3)	57.7	27.3
	Company Email (5)	38.5	0
	Different Location (1)	3.8	72.7
Information in email won't be changed by virus	Yes (5)	73.1	63.6
	No (1)	3.8	18.2
	I don't know (3)	23.1	18.2
I have Undergone Cybersecurity Training before	Yes (1)	11.1	16
	No (5)	88.5	84
I understand Cybersecurity Concept	Yes (5)	26.9	37
	No (1)	73.1	73
	Yes	53.8	45.5
	No	3.8	45.5
My organization has a cyber-Security Plan	Not Sure	42.3	9.1
I understand different forms of Cyber attacks	Yes (1)	23.1	59.2
	No (5)	73.1	90.9
I know Email Scam	Yes	50	40.8
	No	42.3	90.9
	Yes (1)	11.5	45.5
I know my responsibility in Cybersecurity	No (5)	38.5	15
	Not Sure (4)	42.3	39.5
I Share documents with staff	Yes	54.5	15.4
	No	45.5	84.6
	Yes	19.2	0
My company has a Cybersecurity Team	No	0	9.1
	I don't know	76.9	90.1
I have ever found a Computer Virus	Yes	34.6	100
	No	3.8	0
	I don't know	53.8	0
Password Sharing is good	Yes	0	0
	No	100	100
Security of my Computer	Very secure	0	7.7
	Not secure	18.2	15.4
	Am not sure	81.8	76.9
	Yes	0	15.4
Firewall is enabled on my Computer	No	0	23.1
	I don't know	100	50
	Yes (1)	0	3.85
I know Phishing attack	No (5)	100	92.31
Download and Install software	Yes (5)	38.5	0
	No (1)	61.5	100
	Yes	0	18.2
Use same Password for different accounts	No	100	81.8

Table 2. Post training assessment results for group one and group two

Variable (questionnaire item)	Available Options	(Group one) (100%) Hindi session	(Group two) (100%) English session
I know who to contact if a security threat occurs	Yes	95.5	83.3
	No	4.5	16.7
I know phishing attack	Yes	75	68.2
	No	25	31.8
The Best Place for storage of critical data	Private Email	33.3	40.9
	Company Email	9.1	31.3
	Personal Computer	18.2	32.2
	External Location	48.5	27.8
Undergone Cybersecurity Training before	Yes	100	100
	No	0	0
I understand my Role in Cybersecurity	Yes	86.4	91.7
	No	9.1	8.3
Not a sign of cyber Attack	Persistent popups	0	27.3
	Missing Data	0	27.7
	System behavior change	8.7	27.3
	Computer makes Noise	91.3	13.6
I understand different forms of Cyber attacks	Yes	72.7	50
	No	18.2	50
I understand Email Scam	Yes	81.8	85
	No	13.6	15
I know my responsibility in Cybersecurity	Yes	91.3	69
	No	3	27
	Not Sure	5.7	2
I open email attachment only when….	I know the person or company it comes from	54.5	50
	As long as it's a person	36.4	41.7
	There is nothing wrong	0	-
I share Passwords with others	Yes	0	0
	No	100	100
Why people fail to Understand security issues	Nothing important	59.1	41.7
	Technology working	13.6	25.0
	All the above	18.2	33.3
Why do we need security?	Privacy concerns	91.7	27.3
	To kill attackers	0	0
	Protect managers	8.3	63.6
	Yes	63.6	66.7
I know signs when my PC is Hacked	No	31.8	16.7
I use personal device to transfer data	Yes	8.3	36.4
	No	87	45.5
	I don't know	4.7	16.7
My computer has no value to hackers	Yes	18.2	0
	No	72.7	100

4 Discussions

Figure 1 below extracts results concerning the respondent's understanding of "*Phishing attacks*" as detailed in Tables 1 and 2 above before and after the culturally sensitive cybersecurity awareness training session;

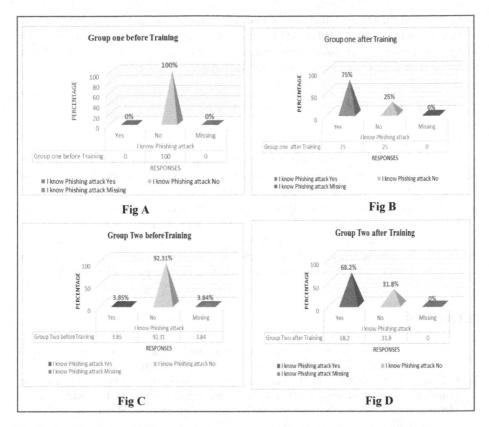

Fig. 1. Results from phishing attacks assessment before and after cybersecurity awareness training sessions

Generally, after comparing employee responses to information security question-naire items in Tables 1 and 2, we observe a considerable improvement in the under-standing of cyber and information security issues by the two groups (group one and group two) after the cybersecurity awareness training session. The post awareness training assessment conducted a month later showed that participants who undertook a culturally sensitive awareness training programme exhibited better understanding of the Cyber and information security issues including phishing attacks as compared to the generic group. For instance, results in Fig. 1A shows that participants from the cul-turally sensitive group (group one) had no idea of phishing attacks before the aware-ness session, while 3.85% from the generic group (group two, Fig. 1C) understood phishing attacks before the awareness session.

After the awareness session, post training assessment results show that 75% of the participants from the culturally sensitive group one understood Phishing attacks as indicated by the post assessment results (Fig. 1B). This was higher than the 68.2% from the generic group two (Fig. 1D). This trend clearly confirms that when people are trained cybersecurity concepts in their local languages considering their cultural background and languages, they understand the concepts better than generic training programs conducted in secondary languages. This approach is very critical for developing countries and the UAE where most of the expatriates come from different countries with different cultural beliefs and languages.

5   Conclusion

In this paper, the question of whether the culture of a society needs to be taken into account when designing cybersecurity training and awareness programs has been clearly discussed and critically evaluated by using the survey results. Culturally sensitive cybersecurity training programs will provide a good avenue for the local and international people to fully participate and embrace security issues of critical importance to their organizations and the government at large. Our results can be used as a stepping stone in the design of appropriate training and awareness programs for combating the cybersecurity problem that emerged recently as one of the key security issue in the United Arab Emirates and other multi-cultural regions like Africa.

References

1. Aloul, F.A.: The need for effective information security awareness. J. Adv. Inf. Technol. **3** (3), 176–183 (2012). Academy Publisher, https://doi.org/10.4304/jait.3.3.176-183
2. Bulgurcu, B., Cavusoglu, H., Benbasat, I.: Information security policy compliance: an empirical study of rationality-based beliefs and information security awareness. In: Management Information Systems Research Centre, University of Minnesota, USA, vol. 34, no. 3 (2010)
3. Siponen, M.T.: A conceptual foundation for organizational information security awareness. Inf. Manag. Comput. Secur. **8**(1), 31–41 (2000)
4. Horcher, A.-M., Tejay, G.P.: Building a better password: the role of cognitive load in information security training. In: IEEE, Richardson, TX, USA (2009)
5. Wunderle, W.D.: Through the Lens of Cultural Awareness: A Primer for US Armed Forces Deploying to Arab and Middle Eastern Countries, Combat Studies Institute Press Fort Leavenworth, KS 66027 (2006)
6. Lim, J.S., Ahmad, A., Chang, S., Maynard, S.B.: Embedding information security culture emerging concerns and challenges. In: PACIS 2010 Proceedings, Brisbane, Australia, pp. 463–474 (2010)
7. McCrohan, K., et al.: Influence of awareness and training on cyber-security. J. Internet Commer. **9**, 23–41 (2010). Method Approaches, pp. 3–23. Sage/Media, Inc., London/Hingham
8. Garret, C.: Developing a Security-Awareness Culture - Improving Security Decision Making. SANs Institute (2005)
9. Hight, S.D.: The importance of a security, education, training and awareness program (2005). http://www.infosecwriters.com/Papers/SHight_SETA.pdf. Accessed 25 Oct 2017
10. Seibert, P.S., Stridh-lgo, P., Zimmerman, C.G.: A checklist to facilitate cultural awareness and sensitivity. J. Med. Ethics **28**, 143–146 (2002)

11. Whitmer, M.G.: IT security awareness and training, changing the culture of state government (2007). https://www.nascio.org/Portals/0/Publications/Documents/NASCIO-ITSecurityAwarenessAndTraining.pdf. Accessed 15 Oct 2017
12. Ashraf, S.: Organization Need and Everyone's Responsibility Information Security Awareness. SANS Institute (2005)
13. Kritzinger, E., Von Solms, S.H.: Cyber-security for home users: a new way of protection through awareness enforcement. Comput. Secur. **29**(8), 840–847 (2010)
14. Parsons, K., McCormac, A., Butavicius, M., Ferguson, L.: Human factors and information security: individual, culture and security environment. Australian Government, Department of Defence (2010)
15. Al Shehri, Y.: Information security awareness and culture. Br. J. Arts Soc. Sci. (2012). ISSN: 2046-9578. British Journal Publishing
16. Kruger, H.A., Flowerday, S., Drevin, L., Steyn, T.: An assessment of the role of cultural factors in Information Security awareness. ISSA, IEEE Xplore Digital Library (2011). www.researchgate.net
17. Dhillon, G.: Principles of Information Systems Security, Text and Cases. Wiley, New Jersey (2007)

Knowledge Extraction, Representation and Sharing

Development of Collaborative Customer Service Officer Knowledge Sharing System (CCSOKSS)

Bolanle F. Oladejo$^{(\boxtimes)}$ and Oyinlola Odetoye

Computer Science Department, University of Ibadan, Ibadan, Nigeria
oladejobola2002@gmail.com, smile4oyin2005@yahoo.co.uk

Abstract. In recent years, the banking industry across the nation have been undergoing swift economic revolution due to the surge created by the Central Bank of Nigeria's (CBN) restructuring and policies on Commercial Banks Capitalization. As a result of more competitive environments and struggling economies, these banks are trying to survive the economic recession and depression in the marketplace through mergers and acquisitions to improve capital bases. This mergers/acquisitions come with the challenge of streamlining technical information between/among staff members who have come together from different bank cultures and backgrounds. Thus, this paper aimed at the development of a Knowledge Sharing System for Customer Service Officers (CSOs) which exploits knowledge resident in them for competitive advantage after such mergers and acquisitions to ensure a seamless and quick integration process. Online SMS, chat rooms are collaboration techniques used in the system. Resolutions are stored for reuse in the Knowledge Repository.

Keywords: Knowledge sharing · Banking · Merger · Acquisition
Customer service officer

1 Introduction

In a highly demanding business world today, an organization's competitive edge depends almost entirely on how well it can manage and deploy its corporate assets. These assets can be categorized into tangible and intangible assets. Traditionally, tangible assets like plant, equipment, inventory and financial capital are considered the most fundamental corporate assets. Intangible assets play a very little or marginal role in an organization regardless from which industry it comes from [1]. Generally, many organizations till date still downplay the importance of their intangible assets. However, despite managing and giving prime focus to all their tangible assets, these organizations still find it very hard to gain the advantage to beat their competitors. Hence, it is getting greater attention of the managers that organizations require a much broader range of resources to be able to compete and succeed in the current competitive market. This is evident by an increasing number of organizations giving more emphasis to their intangible assets, previously left idle, unexplored and unmanaged [1].

© ICST Institute for Computer Sciences, Social Informatics and Telecommunications Engineering 2018
V. Odumuyiwa et al. (Eds.): AFRICOMM 2017, LNICST 250, pp. 143–156, 2018.
https://doi.org/10.1007/978-3-319-98827-6_12

The purpose of this paper is to affirm the above claim and provide a knowledge sharing framework for customer service officers in the Nigerian Banking industry. The paper is organized as follows: Sect. 2 briefly discusses theoretical background to the study and also reviews existing knowledge management systems. Section 3 focuses on the methodology used in this work. Section 4 discusses result findings and practical implications of the developed knowledge sharing system. Section 5 concludes the paper and offers recommendations.

2   Knowledge

Knowledge is an intangible intellectual asset of invaluable potentials. It has been the subject of intensive research in almost every area of organizational inquiry [2]. It has been a fashionable subject in recent years, with significant attention focused on areas such as the key role of knowledge workers, the need to generate and share knowledge, the creation of knowledge and intensive organizations and societies [3].

However, there is no generally acceptable definition of knowledge. Different perspectives of knowledge ranges from philosophical (epistemology), data processing, artificial intelligence - knowledge representation, to theoretical point of views. This work asserts according to [4], that knowledge could be referred to as the cognizance of facts or events by individual(s) from an observation, learning, experience, and understanding of a reality in a particular context at a specific period of time as illustrated in Fig. 1.

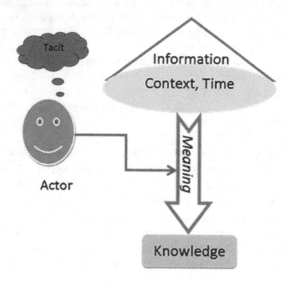

Fig. 1. Concept of knowledge [5]

Knowledge is attributed to individuals, that is, a stakeholder (Actor) who possesses experience, expertise, skill and competence. Albeit, two major type of knowledge exist, namely, Explicit (know) and Tacit (know-hows) knowledge. The features of each type is analyzed in Table 1.

Table 1. Types of knowledge [6].

Explicit	Tacit
Formal and systematic	Insights, intuitions, and hunches
Knowledge of rationality (mind)	Knowledge of experience (body)
Can be expressed in words and numbers	Not easily visible and expressible: it resides in people's heads
Easily communicated and shared in form of data, formula, graphs, manuals, books, documents, or theories etc.	Highly personal, hard to formalize, difficult to communicate or share with others
Can be expressed in computer code, databases, simulations, sets of general principles etc.	Rooted in individual's actions and experiences: in form of rules of thumb, ideals, values, or emotions

2.1 Knowledge Management

Knowledge Management (KM) is based on the premise that, just as human beings are unable to draw on the full potential of their brains, organizations are generally not able to fully utilize the knowledge that they possess. Through KM, organizations seek to acquire or create potentially useful knowledge and to make it available to those who can use it at a time and place that is appropriate for them to achieve maximum effective usage in order to positively influence organizational performance. It is generally believed that if an organization can increase its effective knowledge utilization by only a small percentage, great benefits will result [7]. Thus KM is pivotal to organizational success.

In [8] from [9], KM is described as "a discipline that promotes an integrated approach to identifying, capturing, evaluating, retrieving and sharing all of an enterprise information assets". In other words, KM "is fundamentally about making the right knowledge or the right knowledge sources (including people) available to the right people at the right time" [10]. Also, KM is the process of conscious coordination of knowledge - skills, operation procedures, databases, etc.; in an organization, in order to organize, store and re-use the knowledge for achieving organizational goals and innovation [11].

Certain factors drive successful adoption of KM initiatives in organizations. Thus, KM initiatives to thrive, it should be aligned with KM spectrum which "entails people of common socio-cultural group who have common goals geared towards organizational productivity and application of technological tools for creation and use of knowledge" [12]. Therefore, KM processes span across identification and acquisition of people's experience and expertise (who knows what?) in a domain; evaluation and storage of knowledge (retain *knows and know-hows*); externalization and exploitation *(share to reuse)* through communication and collaboration; and evolution of knowledge *(discover know-hows)*. Figure 2 depicts a set of KM processes in which *codification* of knowledge process is meant for knowledge representation and storage in a Repository (otherwise called *Corporate Memory*). In reality, each process does not link with subsequent process linearly, rather, it is an iterative process for validation purpose.

The outcome of technological impact on KM processes yields a KM system (KMS). A KMS should address four broad objectives namely, management of knowledge as an asset, enhancement of knowledge environment, improvement of the asset and creation of knowledge repository [13]. However, successful adoption of KM initiatives should not solely rely on technology, rather organizational goals and culture should be given preference for value or knowledge creation.

2.2 Knowledge Sharing

Organizations where knowledge transfer and/or sharing is a commonplace thrive and gain competitive advantage. Knowledge sharing (KS) allows exchange of information, skill or expertise among personnel throughout an organization to avoid redundancy, recurrent mistakes and loss of vital knowledge asset. KS may occur among people, friends, or members of a family, a community or an organization [14].

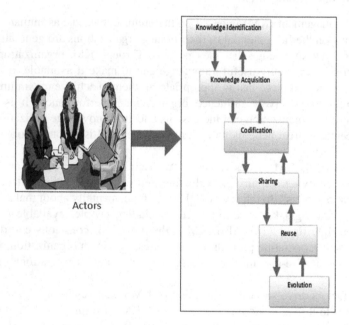

Fig. 2. Knowledge management processes [10]

Organizations need to consider the type of knowledge assets to be shared in order to determine the appropriate KM processes to be applied to sharing of such assets. Table 2 summarizes KM processes as well as the role of technology in the sharing of explicit and tacit knowledge respectively.

Knowledge sharing is significant as knowledge held by individuals cannot become organizational knowledge until it is shared throughout the organization. Figure 3 depicts the process of KS which starts with the involvement of individuals to create, locate and disseminate idea or information in an organization. KS is essential in the

Table 2. Features of knowledge sharing [15].

Characteristics of knowledge sharing	Explicit knowledge	Tacit knowledge
Characteristics	Codified knowledge found in documents, databases, etc. Easy to share, modify, and copy	Intuitive, knowledge rooted in context & practice. Difficult to articulate, share, modify, and copy
Management	Organize, categorize, refine, & share	Common practice, mentoring, apprenticeships, project teams, informal networks, chaos, etc.
Use of IT	Very useful for storage, transfer, and combination	Moderate – with careful implementation

implementation of any KM initiative. It should not be a one-directional transfer but rather between individuals (e.g. employees and their co-workers) and units within an organization [16]. The success of KS depends on willingness of individuals to encourage and share their organizational knowledge through internal organizational social exchanges applying the knowledge sharing model [14].

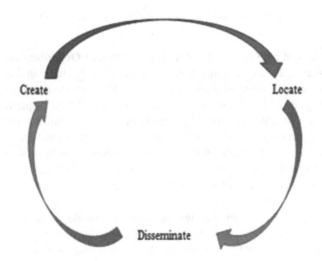

Fig. 3. Knowledge sharing model [14]

2.3   Review of Existing Knowledge Management in Organizations

An overview of a KM model and comparison of related works are subsequently considered in Sects. 2.3.1 and 2.3.2 respectively.

2.3.1   Banking Knowledge Management Model (BKMM)

A Knowledge Management Process in banking sector is depicted by Fig. 4. The environment forces such as, the importance for an organization to maintain its competitive advantage by managing knowledge well, the requirement of the organization to distribute its knowledge among its geographically dispersed human resources, may compel the organization to initiate a KM programme. Through a combination of people and technology, information and energy are transformed into knowledge progress and structures that produce products and services [17]. There are mainly three components in the knowledge progress, namely, knowledge creation, knowledge retention and knowledge sharing.

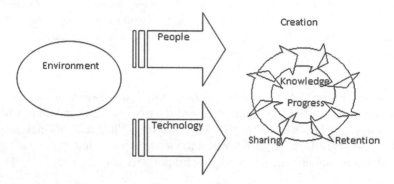

Fig. 4. Banking knowledge management model [17]

2.3.2   Comparison of Knowledge Sharing Systems in Organizations

Knowledge sharing among organization's personnel, especially in banking sectors were reviewed in the light of organizational goals, knowledge sharing approach according to Fig. 3, and techniques with the outcomes of KM implementation. The review deduced that collaborative and social interaction platforms including storytelling played significant role in sharing and transfer of personnel and organizational knowledge. Consequently, competitive advantage in terms of both economic (financial) and knowledge retention was gained by organizations. Table 3 presents the summary of the comparative evaluation of some related works.

2.3.3   Overview of Customer Service in the Nigerian Banking Industry

In Nigeria, the customer service unit is more effective in the banks than in all other organizations of the economy. Yet, the banks have a long way to go in achieving standardization.

In most banks, the knowledge platform is operated by their central IT department which keeps track of all record concerning customer complaint. The banking business today has gone beyond armchair banking era where the customers had to look for the banker to transact business. It is now the era of highly competitive business among banks. The financial institutions, including banks engage in aggressive search of customer to patronize their products and services. For effective customer service, the relationship between customer satisfaction and business performance should be taken into consideration.

Table 3. Comparative evaluation of some related works.

Authors	Methodology	Technique	Strength	Limitation
Hafizi and Hayati [17]	Data collection (environment and people), framework building, knowledge management	Electronic forum, online libraries and e-mails	Well designed and organized framework with emphasis on knowledge creation, retention and sharing	Small sample size i.e. case studies which makes the extent of KM integration little
Voelpel and Han [18]	Data Collection – in-depth case and direct observation of executives and line managers in Siemens. Internal documents, project manual, annual reports, etc.	Sharenet – knowledge library and forums e.g. live chat rooms, discussion groups	Online real time – had urgent request section for urgent resolution of time-bound challenges	Lack of attention on non-monetary incentives and cultural impact
Puterman [19]	Data collection – employee engagement survey called heartbeat	Blue connection – staff social networking site similar to the following platforms: Facebook, Twitter and Linkedin	Strictly business platform, all communications are made public to ensure strict official interaction	Communication on the networking site is not vetted before posting to the public
Rozwell [20]	Customer relationship management and knowledge management system	Knowledge base and story telling	Ability to capture, document and disseminate tacit and explicit knowledge. Decrease in their training costs all due to the implementation of the CRM/KM system	Little focus on individuals or team and the implementation of the customer self-service interface

Bad quality of service often has negative effects on the bank's image by limiting the number of prospective customers who patronize banking services. This is because a customer who has once been disappointed by a bank's services decides to tell others not to use that same service.

A company seeking to win through superior customer service constantly has to create new and different ways of enabling customers to realize value. Customers complain that banks do not handle their problems accurately or quickly. They are made to feel at fault regardless of where the problem actually lies. A customer- focused bank that is customer service oriented recognizes these wants and needs of the customer and takes steps to accommodate them.

3 Methodology

The focus of this work is to provide a robust solution whereby customer service officers collaborate on customer complaints in order to meet individual customer's needs, hence, the need for the development of a Collaborative Customer Service Officer Knowledge Sharing System, (CCSOKSS). The following sections analyzes the approach, technique, and implementation of Knowledge sharing system for Bank CSO in this work.

3.1 Knowledge Acquisition from Existing Officers After Mergers/Acquisitions

The approach employed for information gathering of this work includes interview, observation, working document review and online survey to the intent of acquiring relevant knowledge. The target of the Interactive sessions focused on the following areas:

The use of Knowledge Management system with emphasis on knowledge sharing by the bank personnel during mergers and acquisitions and how it impacts on their throughput.

How could knowledge sharing and collaboration affect the overall business strategy of the banks considering the different organizational structures and ethical cultures of the corresponding banks?

Handling customers' queries and resolutions by categorizing knowledge in terms of importance and relevance of the query in question.

Customer service officers' learning curve and response time to customers' queries.

3.2 Architecture of Collaborative Customer Service Officer Knowledge Sharing System (CCSOKSS)

The KM processes that facilitate knowledge sharing formed the basic phases of CCSOKSS as depicted in the system architecture of Fig. 5. It illustrates the integration of database, data warehouse, and knowledge based system to support an information rich and knowledge sharing platform for resolving customers' complaints in an automated banking system.

CCSOKSS incorporates an innovative technology in the area of knowledge sharing and customer management directly related to the banking system. The CCSOKSS architecture is a framework which incorporates technologies like knowledge repository, OLAP, Intelligent miner and other reporting applications, integrated upon a web based bootstrapped interface. The system also combines specific methodologies needed to acquire the right information necessary for the business of knowledge sharing and decision making with the overall purpose of enhancing the Customer Service Officer training curve at a very low cost. Tacit knowledge which has been externalized is shared during collaboration, rated and filtered based on user experience as well as comment's usefulness before storage in a repository. Stored knowledge is reused by the end user to achieve the goal of the system. The documentation of the architecture is discussed as follows.

3.2.1   User Access
Easy and comfortable information access is mandatory for any KM system. CCSOKSS presents CSO an access to knowledge capture and exploitation through usable interfaces.

3.2.2   Creation
The user interaction channel contains typical customer service information system which serves as a temporary area in the banking operational environment. This layer contains three different components which are designed to meet the CCSOKSS objectives of eliciting knowledge from customers to meet the customer care knowledge needs and the business process of the bank.

Create New Complaint: this component allows the user to create a new complaint if such complaint does not already exist in the database of the system. This ensures that the knowledge in the database of the system is always novel.

Edit Previous Complaint: this component provides a platform for the user to edit previous knowledge in the database, thereby creating room for error correction and management.

Complaint Resolution System: this component ensures that the knowledge in the repository is relevant and important to resolving customer complaint. It serves as a point for searching knowledge in the repository.

3.2.3   Filtering
All data stored in the operational database is being parsed to the filtering platform for ranking, categorization and mapping. Since the operational database is the source of knowledge for the repository, this layer ensures that the knowledge parsed to the repository is considered by the users of the system as relevant and useful to the needs of the bank. This is a very important stage because it represents the whole point of the system, which is to arm the bank personnel with the necessary information or knowledge to resolve customer query with little or no training at all.

3.2.4   Sharing
All business knowledge stored in the operational database needs to be managed and shared effectively for all users to utilize. New complaints posted on the forum are broadcasted to all users that are logged on for the business day; officers are alerted on the dashboard like a star network topology that routes data from a single to multiple nodes. A user posts to groups created in the forum: branch location-based e.g. market branches, university branches, to mention a few. Comments made on new complaints in the forum are sorted and rated in order of importance using the length of years of a user's experience on the job function as well as employee rating of comment's usefulness.

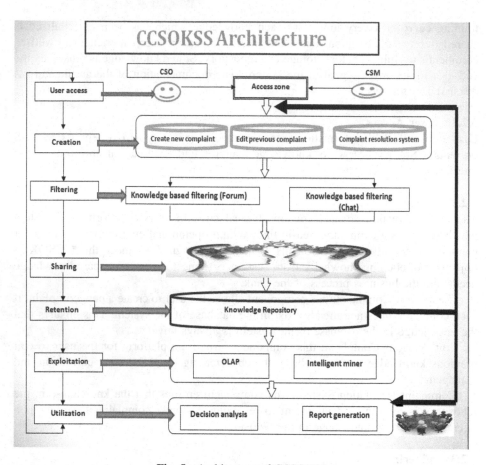

Fig. 5. Architecture of CCSOKSS

3.2.5 Retention

Knowledge Repository acts as a repository for current and historical operational data, where it is organized and validated so that it could serve decision-making objectives. The banking industry has a high volume of record in terms of information system, so data are widely used (and misused) in an ad hoc manner. The knowledge repository allows information to be presented in several formats and to be distributed in a more widely manner. The various stores of the business data are extracted, transformed and loaded from the transactional systems into the knowledge repository. It is also responsible for collecting, converting, cleaning, aggregating, and indexing customers' complaint resolution.

3.2.6 Exploitation

The Query layer contains collective intelligence components which includes intelligent miner, OLAP, and decision analysis. Each component is implemented through a series of operations.

The Intelligent Miner: The Intelligent miner is among the tools used by the bank employee to gain access to the Knowledge Repository. These tools provide the means for business intelligence through ad hoc and managed query environment and knowledge mining. These tools improve the decision-making process by providing new information that otherwise users would not have been able to access on a timely basis. The Intelligent Miner is a data mining tools for determining patterns, generalizations, regularities and rules in data resources as it relates to customer care complaints.

Online Analytic Processing: At the same time, OLAP functionality is used to gain a deeper understanding of specific customer service operational issues. The system takes advantage of OLAP flexible and timely manipulation of data. It enables the user to extract data quickly and easily and translate them into information in several ways.

3.2.7   Utilization

The system users need the utilization layer to access the system's various types of resource.

The customer service officers' key in to the platform to extract knowledge necessary for making decisions that resolves customers' complaints. The Officer accesses the suggested solutions in the complaint resolution system and makes a feedback to the system. The system also generates Reports. The reporting platform is generated with queries based on customer information and solutions recommended.

4   Discussion of Findings

Knowledge is retained in the repository for re-use after they are rated and filtered according to usefulness and CSO years of experience. It contains different topics as it relates to the experience of users of the system. It allows users to ask questions and comment on topics. Figure 6 illustrates a snap-shot of the knowledge acquisition to resolve customers' complaints through inline SMS in CCSOKSS.

The Collaborative Customer Service Officers' Knowledge Sharing System (CCSOKSS) was put to use by selected CSOs (two from each of ten branches of a selected Bank in Ibadan, Nigeria totaling twenty participants). A feedback form was designed for this purpose, and the outcome of filled forms was analyzed to determine the functionality (organizational goal), usability (culture), and socialization impact (organizational learning). Figure 7 presents the analysis of users' feedback.

With CCSOKSS, officers learn without physical barriers (online real time) and at the least cost possible, eliminating the need for classroom training sessions which could not go round all officers and are time consuming. Usually, most things learned in the classroom are usually not reviewed until the need for it arises. It also limits massive redeployment which is costly to the bank (redeployment allowances payment) and inconvenience for staff members who have to be away from their families as a result of mergers/acquisitions.

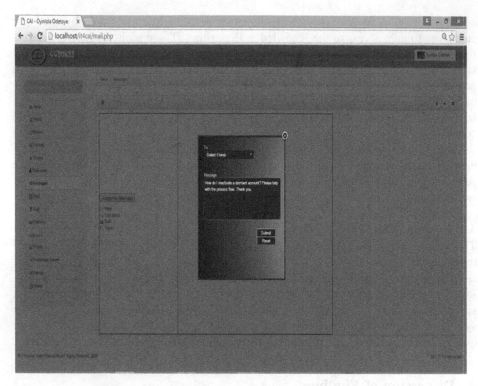

Fig. 6. CCSOKSS knowledge acquisition via online SMS

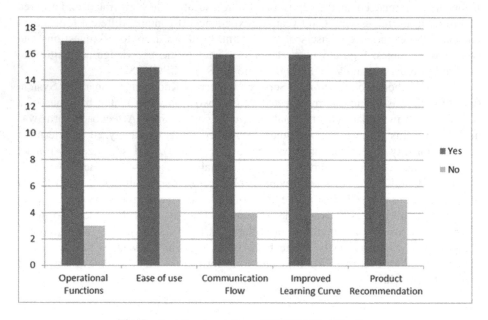

Fig. 7. Result presentation of CCSOKSS utilization

5 Conclusion and Recommendation

Mergers and acquisition are processes that continue through-out the life time of banks as new policies come into play which necessitates them. The process should be concluded in the least amount of time, cost and lay-off as can be managed. Customers expect every interaction with bank employees to be as enjoyable and stress free as there can be irrespective of mergers and acquisition. Employee knowledge should be incorporated in the corporate strategy of banks and should permeate the entire organization irrespective of branch location. The CCSOKSS delivers the ideal solution for ensuring a seamless merger process as regards the Customer Service desk which is the soul of a Bank.

When adopted, the CCSOKSS will create a customer-centric culture that encourages knowledge dissemination to flourish within the banking industry with the global aim of giving customers a uniform feel at each and every branch location they visit irrespective of bank mergers and acquisition. It also helps Customer Service Officers develop an in-depth understanding of the required job function with a view to rendering excellent service at all times and keeping a competitive edge in the industry.

Thus, Banks should deploy Knowledge Sharing System for tracking down undocumented knowledge embedded in employees that will help prevent loss that may arise from employee exit as well as mergers and acquisition.

References

1. Vorbeck, J., Heisig, P., Martin, A., Schutt, P.: Knowledge management in a global company – IBM global services. In: Mertins, K., Heisig, P., Vorbeck, J. (eds.) Knowledge management, pp. 174–185. Springer, Heidelberg (2001). https://doi.org/10.1007/978-3-662-04466-7_12
2. Tzokas, N., Saren, M.: Competitive advantage, knowledge and relationship marketing: where, what and how? J. Bus. Ind. Mark. **19**(2), 124–135 (2004)
3. Walsham, G.: Knowledge management: the benefits and limitations of computer systems. Eur. Manag. J. **19**(6), 599–608 (2001)
4. Oladejo, B., Osofisan, A.: A conceptual framework for knowledge integration in the context of decision making progress. Afr. J. Comput. ICT **4**(2), 25–32 (2011)
5. Oladejo, F.B.: User-centered capitalization of knowledge in the context of economic intelligence systems. Doctoral thesis, Lorraine University, LORIA, France, December 2011
6. Oladejo, B., David, A., Osofisan, A.: Representation of knowledge resource in the context of economic intelligence systems. In: Proceedings of IX Congress ISKO Spanish Chapter, Valencia, Spain, pp. 75–90 (2009). http://hal.inria.fr/inria-00431200/
7. William, R.K.: Knowledge management and organizational learning. Ann. Inf. Syst. **4**(1), 2–5 (2009)
8. Michael, E.D.K.: Knowledge Management Explained. Knowledge Management World Magazine (2012). www.kmworld.com
9. Oladejo, B.F., Ojutalayo, O.M.: Knowledge management as a tool for mitigating software crisis. Eur. J. Comput. Sci. Inf. Technol. **5**(3), 14–27 (2017)
10. Frost A.: Knowledge Management (2017). http://www.knowledge-management-tools.net/knowledge-management.html

11. Oladejo, B., Osofisan, A.O., Odumuyiwa, V.: Dynamic knowledge management in economic intelligence with reasoning on temporal attributes. In: Proceedings of International Seminar of Veille Strategique Scientifique et Technologique (VSST), Toulouse, France, October 2009

12. Oladejo, B.: Facilitating decision making through knowledge capitalization of maintenance projects management with KDD technique. In: David, A., Uwadia, C. (eds.) Transition from Observation to Knowledge to Intelligence, pp. 37–57. ISKO-France, Houdemont (2014)

13. Davenport, T., Prusak, L.: Working Knowledge, How Organizations Manage What They Know, p. 240. Harvard Business School Press, Boston (2000). ISBN 1-57851-301-4

14. Hussain, H., Shamsuar, N.: Concept map in knowledge sharing model. Int. J. Inf. Educ. Technol. 3(3), 398 (2013)

15. Frost, A.: Knowledge Sharing (2017). http://www.knowledge-sharing-tools.net/knowledge-sharing.html

16. Riege, A.: Actions to overcome knowledge transfer barriers. J. Knowl. Manag. 11(1), 48–67 (2007)

17. Hafizi, A., Hayati, N.: Knowledge management in malaysian banks: a new paradigm. J. Knowl. Manag. Pract. 7(3), 1–13 (2006)

18. Voelpel, J., Han, Z.: Managing knowledge sharing in China: the case of Siemens ShareNet. J. Knowl. Manag. 9(3), 51–63 (2005)

19. Puterman, S.: Standard Bank 'moving forward' launches staff social network (2009). http://www.bizcomminity.com/Article/196/82/38010.html

20. Rozwell, C.: Case study: 3M uses storytelling to uncover tacit knowledge. United Kingdom, Gartner research (2009)

Towards Building a Knowledge Graph with Open Data – A Roadmap

Farouk Musa Aliyu[1]([⊠]) and Adegboyega Ojo[2]

[1] Federal University Birnin Kebbi, Birnin Kebbi, Kebbi, Nigeria
musa.farouk@fubk.edu.ng
[2] Insight Centre for Data Analytics, National University of Ireland,
Galway (NUIG), Galway, Ireland
adegboyega.ojo@insight-centre.org

Abstract. With the increasing interest in knowledge graph over the years, several approaches have been proposed for building knowledge graphs. Most of the recent approaches involve using semi-structured sources such as Wikipedia or information crawled from the web using a combination of extraction methods and Natural Language Processing (NLP) techniques. In most cases, these approaches tend to make a compromise between accuracy and completeness. In our ongoing work, we examine a technique for building a knowledge graph over the increasing volume of open data published on the web. The rationale for this is two-fold. First, we intend to provide a foundation for making existing open datasets searchable through keywords similar to how information is sought on the web. The second reason is to generate logically consistent facts from usually inaccurate and inconsistent open datasets. Our approach to knowledge graph development will compute the confidence score of every relationship elicited from underpinning open data in the knowledge graph. Our method will also provide a scheme for extending coverage of a knowledge graph by predicting new relationships that are not in the knowledge graph. In our opinion, our work has major implications for truly opening up access to the hitherto untapped value in open datasets not directly accessible on the World Wide Web today.

Keywords: Knowledge graph · Open data

1 Introduction

In this section, we briefly introduced knowledge graph and open data.

1.1 Open Data

According to open definition [7] open data refers to data that "anyone can freely access, use, modify, and share for any purpose (subject, at most, to requirements that preserve provenance and openness)." From this definition, open data includes any kind of data that can be freely accessed, modified and share on the web. Open data exist in different formats including text documents, spreadsheet, structured documents in RDF or JSON format, pictures, geographic files formats, etc. Popular examples of common open data sets include those published in government portals such as data.gov.* (e.g. uk, i.e., and

© ICST Institute for Computer Sciences, Social Informatics and Telecommunications Engineering 2018
V. Odumuyiwa et al. (Eds.): AFRICOMM 2017, LNICST 250, pp. 157–162, 2018.
https://doi.org/10.1007/978-3-319-98827-6_13

es). Examples of open data portals in Africa include http://data.edostate.gov.ng of the Edo State Government in Nigeria, http://www.opendata.go.ke/ of the Kenyan Government and http://dataportal.opendataforafrica.org/ maintained by the African Development Bank. See Fig. 1 for example of an open data portal. Related to open data are also public data and resource such as DBpedia [14], YAGO [3], Geonames[1], Wikipedia, word-Net[2], dbtune.org, New York Times dataset[3], opendatacommunities. org datasets, etc. Open data covers a wide range of domains which are heterogeneous in nature and noisy. Open data, therefore, reveal a large variation in quality. Applications consuming this data need to therefore, engage in other processing steps to deal with the inconsistencies and misleading information. The issues with open data include: accuracy, representation, integration and linking. One way to address this problem is by integrating islands of non-consistent open datasets to build a more consistent global dataset in the form of knowledge graph.

Fig. 1. Example of an open data portal (http://dataportal.opendataforafrica.org/)

1.2   Knowledge Graph

There is no generally agreed definition of what a knowledge graph is. The term knowledge graph was originally used by Google when introducing their knowledge graph [5] in 2012. Ever since, researchers have often used the term to refer to semantic

---

[1] www.geonames.org/.

[2] https://wordnet.princeton.edu/.

[3] www.nytimes.com/.

web repositories such as DBpedia [14] and YAGO [3]. [4] Defines knowledge graph by given its characteristics: *"A knowledge graph*

1. *Mainly describes real world entities and their interrelations, organized in a graph*
2. *Defines possible classes and relations of entities in a schema*
3. *Allows for potentially interrelating arbitrary entities with each other*
4. *Covers various topical domains."*

Another study [6] titled "Towards a Definition of Knowledge Graphs" conducted a study on the term knowledge graph and define Knowledge Graph as:

"A knowledge graph acquires and integrates information into an ontology and applies a reasoner to derive new knowledge."

Knowledge graphs are often differentiated based on their architecture, operational purposes, data sources, coverage and the technologies used in building them. Knowledge graphs are a key driving force for the future of artificial intelligence systems and a lot of other applications that consume and reason with structured data including search engines, enterprise and business systems, recommender systems etc.

2 Related Work

Building a Knowledge Graph is a very difficult task due to the heterogeneity of the data sources on the internet, volume or size of the data and veracity or noise in the data [1]. Knowledge graphs or knowledge base systems have been in used for some period of time. In [8], the authors show that the theory and practice of knowledge graph date back to 1982. The recent years has witnessed the evolvement of several Knowledge graphs including: Wikidata [9], YAGO [3], Freebase [13], NELL [2] PROSPERA [10] Knowledge Vault (KV) [11], Google Knowledge Graph [5], Microsoft Bing Satori [17] etc. These knowledge graphs can be classified based on their information source, scope and operational purpose. In the case of information source for example, some of the knowledge graph systems surf the internet to extract information from unstructured data sources, example of such systems include KV, NELL and PROSPERA. Other knowledge graph system may rely on human annotation and structured sources such as Freebase, or may combine the two scenarios e.g. YAGO2 [12]. In the case of scope or coverage, some focused on gathering information about a specific domain (domain specific knowledge graphs) examples include [1, 11, 15]. While others gather every information or facts across wide domains (Domain independent knowledge graphs) examples are [5, 13, 14, 17]. In the case of purpose, some of the knowledge graphs were built to be used independently such as [3, 14], while others were used as part of other systems to enhance their productivity and efficiency as it is in the case of Google Knowledge Graph and Microsoft Bing Satori.

Knowledge graphs have been built and used in other research and projects. For example in [1], a generic approach for building domain-specific knowledge graphs was proposed and this approach was employed to build a knowledge graph to combat human trafficking.

Another study [18], which complements the traditional approach of building knowledge graphs like Google's Knowledge graph focused on building event centric knowledge graph. They try to capture the dynamic state of the world by extracting information about events reported in news using state-of-the-art natural language processing and semantic web techniques. Their study also provides a method and tools to automatically build knowledge graphs from news article.

While our approach may intersect with previous methods based on information source, scope and purpose, the previous methods did not use refinement methods that improve both coverage and accuracy of knowledge graph. In addition, our proposed method will compute the correctness score for every relationship in the graph and based on that, the system can determine whether to store the newly generated knowledge after judiciously setting an accuracy threshold.

3 Proposed Architecture of the Knowledge Graph System

The architecture of the proposed system for building the knowledge graph is as shown in Fig. 2. The stages for building the knowledge graph are briefly explained below.

Data Extraction Module: This sub-system is responsible for gathering information from different sources available in open data portals through the underlying platforms application programing interfaces.

Data Analysis Module: in this stage, the information is interpreted using NLP techniques. Specifically, attempts are made to discover entities of interest from the open datasets.

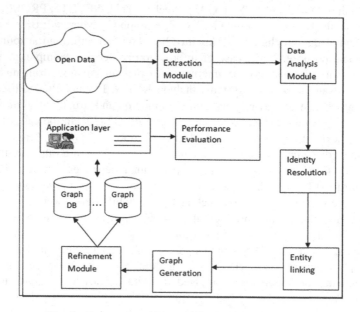

Fig. 2. Proposed architecture for the knowledge graph

Identity/Entity Resolution: in this section, we employ entity resolution methods such as Silk Link Discovery Framework [16] to resolve common entities.
Refinement Module: In this module, we improve on the quality as well as the coverage of the knowledge graph.
Performance Evaluation: This module evaluates the overall performance of the system based on some well-known gold standard graph evaluation resource.

4 Conclusions

In this work, we have considered the problem of building knowledge graph using open data. Our research agenda has the potentials to open up access to open data that are currently only accessible to a very few technical users of open data portals. Opening up access to open data as knowledge graphs will make contents of open datasets searchable using keywords or natural language phrases on existing search engines like Google. So far, only large multinational search engine providers such as Google and Microsoft provide knowledge graphs (on entities that are core to their interests) to support more intelligent search on the web. In addition our work will also significantly impact the continuous efforts of the W3C in publishing more Linked Open Data (semantically rich, open and machine readable data) on the web. Our knowledge graph approach will exploit the state of the art approach with focus on accuracy of graph relations, reasoning to discover more relations and seeking ways to increase the confidence score of relationship in the knowledge graph over time.

References

1. Szekely, P., et al.: Building and using a knowledge graph to combat human trafficking. In: Arenas, M., et al. (eds.) ISWC 2015. LNCS, vol. 9367, pp. 205–221. Springer, Cham (2015). https://doi.org/10.1007/978-3-319-25010-6_12
2. Carlson, A., Betteridge, J., Kisiel, B., Settles, B., Hruschka, Jr. E.R., Mitchell, T.M.: Toward an architecture for never-ending language learning. In: AAAI 2010, vol. 5, p. 3, July 11 2010
3. Suchanek, F.M., Kasneci, G., Weikum, G.: Yago: a core of semantic knowledge. In: Proceedings of the 16th International Conference on World Wide Web 2007, pp. 697–706. ACM, 8 May 2007
4. Paulheim, H.: Knowledge graph refinement: a survey of approaches and evaluation methods. In: Semantic Web Preprint, pp. 1–20 (2016)
5. Singhal, A.: Introducing the knowledge graph: things, not strings. Official Google Blog (2012)
6. Ehrlinger, L., Wöß, W.: Towards a definition of knowledge graphs. In: SEMANTiCS (Posters, Demos, SuCCESS) (2016)
7. http://opendefinition.org/. Accessed 15 Jan 2017
8. Nurdiati, S., Hoede, C.: 25 years development of knowledge graph theory: the results and the challenge (2008)
9. Vrandečić, D., Krötzsch, M.: Wikidata: a free collaborative knowledgebase. Commun. ACM **57**(10), 78–85 (2014)

10. Nakashole, N., Theobald, M., Weikum, G.: Scalable knowledge harvesting with high precision and high recall. In: Proceedings of the Fourth ACM International Conference on Web Search and Data Mining. ACM (2011)
11. Dong, X., et al.: Knowledge vault: a web-scale approach to probabilistic knowledge fusion. In: Proceedings of the 20th ACM SIGKDD International Conference on Knowledge Discovery and Data Mining. ACM (2014)
12. Hoffart, J., Suchanek, F.M., Berberich, K., Weikum, G.: YAGO2: a spatially and temporally enhanced knowledge base from Wikipedia. Artif. Intell. J. (2012)
13. Bollacker, K., Evans, C., Paritosh, P., Sturge, T., Taylor, J.: Freebase: a collaboratively created graph database for structuring human knowledge. In: SIGMOD, pp. 1247–1250. ACM (2008)
14. Auer, S., Bizer, C., Kobilarov, G., Lehmann, J., Cyganiak, R., Ives, Z.: DBpedia: a nucleus for a web of open data. In: Aberer, K., et al. (eds.) ASWC/ISWC -2007. LNCS, vol. 4825, pp. 722–735. Springer, Heidelberg (2007). https://doi.org/10.1007/978-3-540-76298-0_52
15. Schultz, A., et al.: LDIF-linked data integration framework. In: Proceedings of the Second International Conference on Consuming Linked Data, vol. 782. CEUR-WS.org (2011)
16. Isele, R., Jentzsch, A., Bizer, B.: Silk server – adding missing links while consuming linked data. In: 1st International Workshop on Consuming Linked Data (COLD 2010), Shanghai, November 2010
17. Qian, R.: Understand Your World with Bing, 21 March 2013. http://blogs.bing.com/search/2013/03/21/understand-your-world-with-bing/. Accessed 15 Jan 2017
18. Rospocher, M., et al.: Building event-centric knowledge graphs from news. Web Semant.: Sci. Serv. Agents World Wide Web 37, 132–151 (2016)

A Secured Preposition-Enabled Natural Language Parser for Extracting Spatial Context from Unstructured Data

Patience U. Usip$^{(\boxtimes)}$, Moses E. Ekpenyong, and James Nwachukwu

Computer Science Department, University of Uyo, Uyo, Nigeria
{patiencebassey, mosesekpenyong}@uniuyo.edu.ng,
nwachukwujames7@gmail.com

Abstract. Acquiring data within the health domain is generally intractable due to privacy or confidentiality concerns. Given the spatial nature of health information, and coupled with the accompanying large and unstructured dataset, research in this area is yet to flourish. Further, obtaining spatial information from unstructured data is very challenging and requires spatial reasoning. Hence, this paper proposes a secure Preposition-enabled Natural Language Parser (PeNLP), sufficient for mining unstructured data to extract suitable spatial reference with geographic locations. The proposed PeNLP is a subcomponent of a larger framework: the Preposition-enabled Spatial ONTology (PeSONT) – an ongoing project. The short term impact of PeNLP is its availability as a reliable information extractor for spatial data analysis of health records. In the long run, PeSONT shall aid quality decision making and drive robust policy enactment that will greatly impact the health sector and the populace.

Keywords: Knowledge representation · Ontology · Spatial reasoning
Unstructured data

1 Introduction

The emergence of massive patient databases of electronic health records has provided new opportunities to test clinical hypotheses, inform clinical decision making, and optimize healthcare services. Improved medical decision making requires accurate predictive models, but the spatial nature of observational health data presents unique challenges, and requires an understanding of the impact of data representation on prediction. In [1], a sparse coding representation of medical records was implemented, and interfaced with the Observational Health Data Sciences and Informatics (OHDSI) software tools for predictive modeling. An empirical evaluation of the performance of traditional predictive models with and without sparse coding was also demonstrated to prove the importance of data representation as a step in building predictive models.

Traditional analytic methods are often ill-suited to the evolving world of healthcare big data usually characterized by massive volume, complexity, and velocity [2]. Numerous machine learning methods have effectively addressed such limitations, but they are still subject to the usual sources of bias that commonly arise in observational

© ICST Institute for Computer Sciences, Social Informatics and Telecommunications Engineering 2018
V. Odumuyiwa et al. (Eds.): AFRICOMM 2017, LNICST 250, pp. 163–168, 2018.
https://doi.org/10.1007/978-3-319-98827-6_14

studies. Consequently, novel methods for developing good model estimates to efficiently represent, predict, and evaluate datasets containing healthcare utilization, clinical, personal devices, and many other sources, are required. The Spatial ontology is therefore concerned with the application of human intelligence to spatial reasoning, hence, simplifying the complexities involved in scanning through numerous pages of textual data or listening to a multimedia files in search of spatial (location-based) concepts, which are necessary requirements for decision making. Decision making towards the formulation of strong public health policies in support of good health and well-being [3] (for instance) depends on real-time location-based data. These data are sometimes unavailable and unstructured and may lead to inconsistent data manipulation because of their geographic spread.

Health data requires ethical approval and hence are intractable to obtain due privacy or confidentiality concerns. The ability to link data in a manner that protects patient privacy has improved dramatically through the use of salting and hashing methodologies [2]. The sparse health data including spatial or location-based information has generally hindered research progress owing to the volume of data, alongside their characteristics (such as the unevenness of data completeness), which raises questions about the potential for using new methods to analyze areas such as treatment effectiveness, health care value, strengths and weaknesses of alternative care organization models, and policy interventions. Although statistical methods are mostly used to provide answers to these questions, they are either too generic or insufficient to handle spatial data analysis [4]. The categorization of locational data (place terms) using Linguistic and Logical perception [5] plays a key role in the classification and engineering in PeSONT.

The focus of this paper is limited to public health, with an attempt to answer basic research questions posed as follows:

(i)   Can spatial concepts be obtained from a poll of unstructured public health data?
(ii) Are the extracted data, spatial?
(iii) Is the confidentiality of health data compromised?
(iv) Do resulting decisions share equal accuracy with all spatial data?
(v)   If research progress in public health is hindered, how can researchers, decision makers and the public, enjoy a strong public health policy?

To answer the above research questions, a spatial tool that accepts unstructured data such as health data (as input) to produce geographic context-aware reference in spatial form (as output), for decision making and policy enactment, is proposed. The extracted spatial information shall be evaluated using three metrics namely, Precision, Recall and F-measure. The resulting locational concepts and attributes shall be linked to the GIS tool, and identified geographic locations ported to Google Maps.

2   Formal Theory/Concept

Within the medical domain, spatial ontology should integrate the principles of mereology (the study of parts and the wholes they form) and spatial reasoning [6]. Whereas mereology has been explored in various ways as applications of predicate logic to formal ontology, spatial reasoning on the other hand forms a central component of medical research and practice, and must be incorporated into any successful medical informatics programme. The spatial concepts most often utilized in this field are not the quantitative, point-based concepts of classical geometry, but rather qualitative relations among extended objects. Hence, this paper pursues formalism for qualitative spatial relations – patients/healthcare services and location relations. The proposed PeNLP is a location based parser that rests on specific application subcomponents of typical location-based service architecture [6]. Although, several location-based systems exist, none of these systems integrate ontology formalism, as most existing location-based systems are those created from environmental information, trained and mapped to an area of interest [7].

This paper gained insights and motivation from the inconsistency in data obtained for reasoning with the spatial qualification logic [8]. Spatial qualification problem is well-known in artificial intelligence (AI), and is concerned with the non-recognition of agent's presence at a specific location at a particular time as a qualification for carrying out an action or participate in an event, given its known location antecedents [9]. The implementation of SQL however depends greatly on spatial geographical information system (GIS) data, and requires expensive GIS software and device to access, hence, introducing greater reasoning problems for big datasets [8].

3 Methodology

The Context-based Preposition-enabled Spatial ONTology (PeSONT), is an on-going project that provides spatial ontology – a classified repository of spatial (locational and temporal) concepts – based on some given contexts (textual or multimedia), which are to a great extent unstructured. The components of the proposed PeNLP are shown as subset components of the context-based PeSONT framework (see Fig. 1).

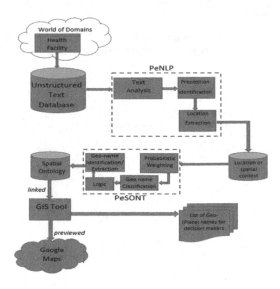

Fig. 1 The context-based PeSONT framework

The activity flow of the proposed PeNLP system includes the collection of unstructured public health data from several health facilities, be it textual or multi-media. The PeNLP process begins with text analysis, from where the relevant prepositions are identified, and the spatial contexts are extracted and storage in a spatial context repository. This repository then feeds the PeSONT component, which comprises a set of geographically-enabled tools for name identification and classification using formal representation logic. The extractions are finally stored in a spatial ontology database and linked to GIS tools for effective visualization and decision making purposes.

4   PeNLP Implementation and Evaluation

4.1   The PeNLP Algorithm

The PeNLP algorithm in Fig. 2 describes the human intelligent approach to placial noun identification. Using spatial reasoning, prepositions are first identified, before identifying words or phrases after the preposition. The algorithm splits the statements into sentences using a boundary marker (the period or full stop (.)), then the existence of verbs in each of the sentences are searched for (mostly the main verbs). In the absence of a main verb the auxiliary verb is retrieved before breaking the sentence into its subject and predicate. The algorithm then checks for prepositions in both the subject and the predicate. On finding any preposition, the word or phrase is extracted as the placial noun. This process is repeated for all sentences, and the placial nouns stored as spatial contexts in the repository. A formal representation of the part of speech (POS) and the classification of placial noun/spatial context based on Agarwal's structure is given using the following regular expressions:

<Sentence> = <Subject><Verb><Predicate>
<Subject> = <Noun Phrase>
<Predicate> = <Noun Phrase>
<Noun Phrase>= <Article><Preposition><Noun>
<Noun Phrase> = <GeoLocation><Location Description><Generic PlaceNames> ….

```
get unstructured text
split words into sentences using full stop
locate finite verb in sentence
if no finite Verb then
      locate Auxiliary Verb
      split Sentence into Subject and Predicate
      if Preposition exists in Subject then
            get Word or Phrase
      until "," or Auxiliary Verb or "?,!"
      else
                  if there is Preposition in Predicate then
                        get Word or Phrase
                  until "," or Auxiliary Verb or "?,!"
                  assign Phrase or Word to Placial Noun
                  store Placial Noun as Spatial Context
repeat until Sentence = ""
```

Fig. 2 PeNLP algorithm

The Agile software development lifecycle was followed during the development of the system. The process involved the building of the system prototype, testing, modification and re-building as need arises. A phase-wise approach was adopted for building the prototypes, with continuous update made to the existing prototype until the new system was obtained. The system programming tools used include the Java programming language, JXbrowser library, JavaScript, HTML, Cascading Style Sheet and Microsoft Access for spatial context database.

4.2   Evaluation Mechanism

The experimental plan features sample unstructured data collected directly from the temporary database, to accuracy. The unstructured data are textual data and the resulting geo-locations or placial nouns from the PeNLP is also textual but structured. The evaluation metrics we shall use to measure the correctness of the resulting spatial concept for the PeNLP and PeSONT include Precision and Recall, and are given in Eqs. (1) and (2) respectively [10]:

$$
Presision \ = \ \frac{correct \ + \ 0.5 \ * \ partial}{correct \ + \ spurious \ + \ partial} \tag{1}
$$

$$
Recall \ = \ \frac{correct \ + \ 0.5 \ * \ partial}{correct \ + \ missing \ + \ partial} \tag{2}
$$

The F-measure is used in conjunction with Precision and Recall, as a weighted average of the two. With the weight set to 0.5, both Precision and Recall are deemed equally important.

5   Conclusion

Empowering a community to collaboratively generate evidence that promotes better health decisions and better care is important and mission critical to improving health and healthcare services. This paper has proposed an ontology-based approach to formal characterization of unstructured data. Precise formal characterizations of all spatial relations assumed by PeNLP and PeSONT are necessary to ensure that the information embodied in the ontology can be fully and coherently utilized in a computational environment. The paper therefore serves as a springboard toward actualizing this goal, but more rigorous research along this line is required.

References

1. Gill, M.S., Ryan, P.B., Madigan, D.: Sparse coding for predictive modeling of observational health outcomes. In: Proceedings of OHDSI Symposium, Washington Hilton, pp. 1–2 (2016)
2. Crown, W.H.: Potential application of machine learning in health outcomes research and some statistical cautions. Value Health **18**(2), 137–140 (2015)
3. UN: United Nations general assembly draft outcome document of the United Nations summit for the adoption of the post-2015 development agenda. http://srsg.violenceagain stchildren.org/sites/default/files/documents/docs/A_69_L.85_EN.pdf. Accessed Sept 2017
4. Waller, L.A., Gotway, C.A.: Applied Spatial Statistics for Public Health Data. Wiley Series in Probability and Statistics. A Wiley Interscience. Wiley, Hoboken (2004)
5. Bennett, B., Agarwal, P.: Semantic categories underlying the meaning of 'place'. In: Winter, S., Duckham, M., Kulik, L., Kuipers, B. (eds.) COSIT 2007. LNCS, vol. 4736, pp. 78–95. Springer, Heidelberg (2007). https://doi.org/10.1007/978-3-540-74788-8_6
6. Donnelly, M., Bittner, T., Rosse, C.: A formal theory for spatial representation and reasoning in biomedical ontologies. Artif. Intell. Med. **36**(1), 1–27 (2006)
7. Wang, C., Shi, Z., Wu, F.: Intelligent RFID indoor localization system using Gaussian filtering based extreme learning machine. Symmetry **9**(30), 1–16 (2017)
8. Bassey, P.C., Akinkunmi, B.O.: An Alibi Reasoner based on the Spatial Qualification Model. In: Proceedings of ISKO International Conference on Transition from Observation to Knowledge to Intelligence, France, pp. 261–270 (2014)
9. Bassey, P.C., Akinkunmi, B.O.: Introducing the spatial qualification problem and its qualitative model. Afr. J. Comput. ICTs **6**(1), 191–196 (2013)
10. Maynard, D., Peters, W., Li, Y.: metrics for evaluation of ontology-based information extraction. In: Proceedings of the EON Workshop (2006)

Networks and Communications

Implementation and Performance Analysis of Trellis Coded Modulation in Additive White Gaussian Noise

Olawale Olapetan$^{(\boxtimes)}$ and Ifiok Otung

Faculty of Computing, Engineering Science, University of South Wales,
Pontypridd, Treforest CF37 1DL, UK
olapetanwale@yahoo.com, ifiok.otung@southwales.ac.uk

Abstract. Band-limited channels face a serious challenge in modern communication due to the need to increase transmission rate while bandwidth remains the same. Mobile communications including mobile satellite, wireless mobile and indoor wireless communication all need to transmit at a higher rate. Trellis-coded Modulation (TCM) is a modulation and error control scheme that allow band-limited and/or power limited channels to attain an efficient data rate without an increase in bandwidth. It is an advanced mode of convolutional coding that combines digital modulation and error correction coding in a single stage. This project sought to investigate the performance of TCM in Additive White Gaussian Noise, modelling a mobile wireless channel. To do this, trellis codes are digitally modulated with M-ary PSK and M-ary QAM using computer simulation (MATLAB) and the performance is evaluated when the modulated signals propagates through additive white Gaussian Noise. Experiments were also carried out on hardware equipment using Telecommunication Instructional Modeling System (TIMS). The plot of bit error rate against E_b/N_0 showed that there is a significant coding gain at no extra cost of bandwidth expansion.

Keywords: TCM · Bandwidth · AWGN · Coding gain · Power

1 Introduction

Trellis coded modulation (TCM) have developed over the last three decades as the modulation scheme that allows efficient data transmission for additive white Gaussian noise (AWGN) channel where bandwidth and power are limited. Lately, mobile radio and indoor mobile channels now make use of TCM and such channels are modelled as a fading channel. Trellis coded modulation was first proposed by Gottfried Ungerboeck in 1976 and following a more detailed publication in 1982 which led into thorough study of the subject to a point where a good knowledge and understanding of the theory and capabilities are achieved and then implemented [2].

The traditional forward error control (FEC) codes that were in use before TCM provides coding gain at the expense of increased bandwidth and power, for example block codes and convolutional codes etc. which is not an option for channels whose bandwidth is fixed and power limited like the microwave channels. The main attraction is that the technique combines forward error control coding and digital modulation in a

© ICST Institute for Computer Sciences, Social Informatics and Telecommunications Engineering 2018
V. Odumuyiwa et al. (Eds.): AFRICOMM 2017, LNICST 250, pp. 171–179, 2018.
https://doi.org/10.1007/978-3-319-98827-6_15

single stage to provide a significant coding gain over the traditional un-coded M-level modulation schemes. With channel bandwidth the same and the need for more data transmission increases, there exists an urgent need to either expand the bandwidth by finding an error correction code and a digital modulation scheme that would increase the data rate or switch to a whole new system that will provide the required bandwidth. In the late 1980s prior to the invention of TCM, modems operate over plain old telephone service, it is an analogue service with bandwidth between 56 and 64 kbps and can typically achieve a data rate of 9.6 kbps when employing QAM modulation with symbol rate of 2400 baud. Despite the efforts of researchers to improve data transmission the best that could be achieved was 14 kbps for a two-way communication which was approximately 40% of the bit rate Shannon theoretically predicted for this kind of communication medium.

1.1   Areas of Application

Trellis coded modulation has found application in telecommunication systems and it is commonly used in satellite communication where power is limited. Due to the distance signal has to travel to get to the earth station and attenuation that the signal suffers, only a fraction of the original signal is detected at the earth station, 10 pW at the best. This power might be too small for the receiver to be able to decode properly and can even make the error controlling scheme already implemented (if any) to insert more errors than it is correcting. TCM is also used on telephone lines to maximize the capacity of the channel and increases data rate and if an Asymmetry Digital Subscriber Line (ADSL) is used instead of the conventional voice modem then even faster bit rate can be achieved by making use of the frequencies that are not utilized by the telephone voice service. TCM has also found application in personal and mobile wireless communication which involves transmission of signals at microwave frequencies, these signals are severely affected by multipath propagation. It is preferred because of its ability to function at low power and delivers high data throughput while making use of the available bandwidth which are the characteristics of microwave transmission.

2   TCM Encoder

The coding techniques used prior to the advent of TCM provided error improvement at the expense of bandwidth because of the addition of redundant bits to the information bits. Examples are block code and convolutional codes where k information bits are inputted into the encoder and larger n code words are outputted requiring more bandwidth. For this singular reason, error control coding was not common especially for channels where bandwidth expansion is impracticable e.g. telephone lines. Unlike convolutional coding, TCM schemes uses redundant non-binary modulation in combination with a finite state encoder, the term finite state encoder refers to a device that has memory (Shift register) which can save information about the past signals and has limited and distinguishable number of these memories. The state of the encoder is the smallest bit of information that when combined with the present input can predict the output of the device. The state of this device carries information about the past signals and also restricts output to a set of possibilities limited by the past state [2]. This redundant non-binary modulation and finite state encoder governs the selection of modulation signals to generate the coded signal sequence. To improve error performance of the system, when k bits are to be coded, a convolutional encoder with a code rate of $\frac{k}{k+1}$ is used followed by a constellation mapper that maps k + 1 bits into 2^{k+1} signal sets (waveforms). Of course the individual symbols will be closer to one another on the signal space and one will tend to think that the signal is prone to error. One thing to keep in mind is that error performance is no longer measured by the Hamming distance but rather by the Euclidean distance. The encoder should be designed to achieve maximum free Euclidean distance.

TCM encoder consists of a convolutional encoder with code rate of $k/k+1$ and an M-ary constellation mapper combined as a single function. The M-ary signal mapper maps $M = 2^k$ into a larger constellation of $M = 2^{k+1}$ points [4]. It expands the signal points in order to accommodate coding bits rather than increasing the bandwidth, for instance, to code a 4-QAM, k = 2, there are two signal points on the un-coded system and M = 4. The constellation point will have to expand to k = 3 and M = 8, so the output of the encoder will be 8-QAM and code rate 2/3 (Fig. 1).

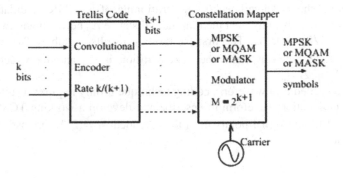

Fig. 1. TCM encoder

A convolutional encoder is characterized and can be fully described by the following parameters n, k, K and the generator polynomial. K is the constraint length and it specifies the number of shift register stages in the encoder. The encoder also contains modulo-2 adder whose output are interleaved to obtain the output code words. The connection of these modulo-2 adders to the shift registers fully describes the characteristics and behavior of a TCM encoder and this connection is generally represented by generator polynomial and are formally denoted in octet format. The input bits are streamed into the shift registers k bits at a unit time, k − 1 bit (which is the past output of the K − 1 shift register) together with the next input determines the next output (Fig. 2).

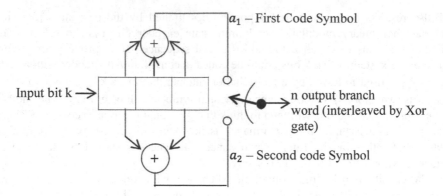

Fig. 2. Convolutional encoder, code rate, K = 3.

Ungerboeck in [3] pursed another TCM design method that seeks to maximize the free Euclidean distance based on a mapping rule called mapping by set partitioning. The rule follows that a modulation signal constellation is partitioned into signal subsets having an increasing minimum distance $\Delta_0 < \Delta_1 < \Delta_2...$ between the signals of these subset. Figure 3 shows Ungerboeck's set partitioning of a 8-PSK modulation, if the average signal power is unity then the minimum distance Δ_0 between any two adjacent signal is $2\sin(\pi/8) = 0.765$. The first partitioning results in subset B_0 and B_1 with distance $\Delta_1 = \sqrt{2}$ between them, the next partition is C_0 and C_1 which differ in distance by $\Delta_2 = 2$.

TCM is classified as a waveform coding technique it only requires a suitable trellis and a set of modulation waveform to describe and develop a working TCM code. To maximize the ED, the signal points from the extended $M = 2^{k+1}$ are assigned to the trellis transition.

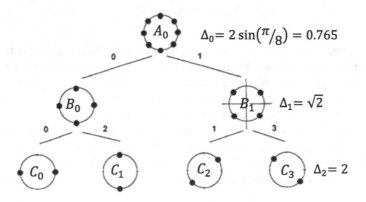

Fig. 3. Partition of 8-PSK channel signals into subsets with increasing minimum distance [1]

The design of trellis code can be done arbitrarily (theoretically) using a trellis diagram and Euclidean distance analysis. Practically, the code designed theoretically needs a circuitry if it is going to be implemented to actually encode and modulate information bits. Depending on the encoder, the circuitry may be easily designed where the choice of code words assignment gives rise to a simple encoder design. But a situation can arise where the choice of the code words assignment may not give rise to a simple encoder design and this may dictate an unwieldy encoder design [1].

3   TCM Decoder Using Maximum Likelihood Soft Decision Decoding

The major objective of a convolutional decoder is to track the path that the message received had traversed through in the encoding trellis. A convolutional encoder is a finite state machine that has memories, hence the optimum decoder for this type of encoder is a Maximum Likelihood sequence estimator which involves a search of the trellis for the most probable sequence. Following the rules for assigning trellis transition branches to waveforms, then all input message sequence should be equally likely. A decoder that will achieve minimum probability of error is the one that will compare the probability of the received sequence waveform with the most probable sequence waveforms and choose the maximum – this decision making criterion is known as maximum likelihood; it is a way of making decision when there is a statistical knowledge of the possibilities.

Significant coding gain is achieved by trellis coded modulation schemes at the expense of encoder and decoder complexities, complexities means extra processing time at both the encoder and the decoder which is interpreted as delay at the receiver. There is a processing delay when the encoder accumulates the input bit to generate the code word and another delay at the receiver when the decoder inspects a certain number of possible code words to arrive at a decision. Quality of service can be affected especially for services that are sensitive to delay such as telephone or video transmission if the delay is large enough to be perceived [5]. Therefore, the degree of TCM code complexities should be carefully chosen based on the kind on service it is intended for. A satellite link can endure the long delay introduced and also have large bandwidth to support higher code rates as an added advantage.

Figure 4 shows a transmitted sequence $U = \cdots U_1, U_2, U_3, \ldots$ path through the trellis and one probable sequence $V = \cdots V_1, V_2, V_3 \ldots$ The path of V is seen to be diverging from U and then remerge. For a binary sequence of L branch code word, there are 2^L number of possible sequences that could have been transmitted. Therefore, decoder chooses a sequence waveform as the transmitted sequence if its likelihood is greater than the likelihood of the other possible transmitted sequences. Assuming soft decision decoding is employed then an error event will occur if the received symbol is closer in Euclidean distance to some alternate V rather than U. The larger the free Euclidean distance between the signal waveforms, the lower the probability of error.

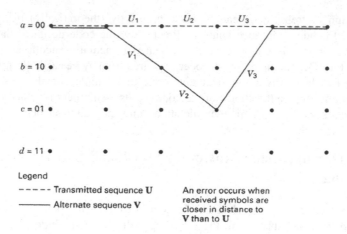

Fig. 4. Illustration of error event at the decoder.

3.1 Fading Channels

Communication channels linking one geographical location to another are bound to experience two major channels perturbations namely; Noise and fading due to multipath propagation. The TCM codes introduced earlier are designed to have a robust performance against Additive White Gaussian Noise but not equipped enough to overcome signal attenuation due to multipath fading.

Fading channels for mobile GSM are usually modelled using Rayleigh statistical model with its local mean following lognormal statistics and its phase distributed uniformly. This models a transmission that is basically multipath with no dominant line of sight. Another fading channel is Rician fading, here there is a dominant line of sight between the transmitter and the receiver. This can also be modelled statistically by using two Gaussian random variables – one with zero mean and the other with non-zero mean.

4 Results and Analysis

If a 2 level signal (ASK) is to be coded and transmitted, the code rate for the convolutional encoder will be ½ and the signal will be mapped into 2^2 signal sets, expanding the signal space to allow redundant bits and therefore transmitting a 4-ASK when a 2 level signal is received. A significant improvement to the error performance can be observed with a robust digital transmission against additive noise by 3 dB as seen in Fig. 5.

In Fig. 5 the error performances of an un-coded binary ASK is compared to that of trellis-coded modulated 4-ASK in an experiment (using Emona TIMS equipment). When the BER decreases the coding gain increases. The best that the bit error rate can go is 10^{-3} because TIMS equipment can only send a maximum of 10^6 pulses for evaluation and that explains why the results at higher power close to 5 dB are not reliable due to the fact that the pulses are simply not enough to reliably evaluate the corresponding BER. This places limits on the results obtained from the experiment.

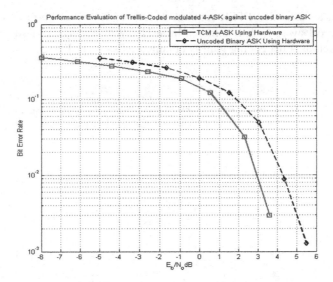

Fig. 5. Comparison of the performance of TCM coded 4-ASK with un-coded binary ASK

The maximum coding gain obtainable from this experiment is 1.35 dB at $= 3 \times 10^{-3}$. At $= 3 \times 10^{-4}$ the coding gain as compared to an un-coded binary ASK reference system is 2.4 dB which is close to the finding of Ungerboeck [2].

4.1 Simulation Results

The curve in Fig. 6 depicts that a system that is seeking to decrease the bandwidth of transmission will need to increase the transmission power and vice versa.

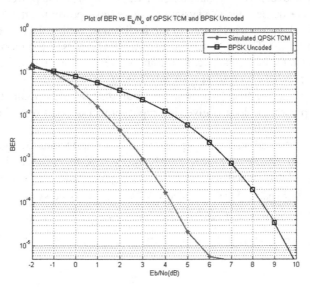

Fig. 6. Simulation results for BPSK un-coded and QPSK TCM systems

Typically, an un-coded BPSK requires E_b/N_0 of 9.6 dB at bit error rate of 10^{-5} which is 11.2 dB away from Shannon's limit [1]. With the aid of trellis coded modulation as much as 4 dB coding gain is obtained as show in Fig. 5.

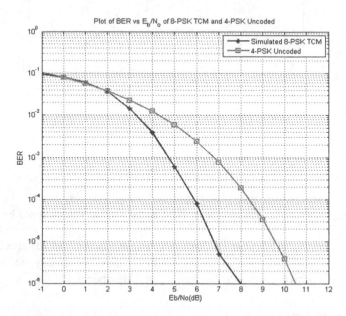

Fig. 7. Plot of BER versus E_b/N_0 of 8-PSK TCM (4 states) and 4-PSK un-coded system

From Fig. 7 above, it is seen that at higher values of BER, the power requirement is low; also the curve of the reference system requires more power to attain a certain BER on the coded 8-psk curve. This is due to the addition of coding which helps to reduce the power requirement. The TCM scheme used above accepts two symbols and outputs three symbols of information bits i.e. k = 2 and n = 3, i.e. code rate is 2/3 and it has N numbers of parallel transition signals with maximum distance between them.$N = 2^{m-2} = 2$. The free distance in this four-state 8-PSK is found to be $d_{free} = 2$ which when expressed in decibel gives an improvement of 3 dB over the un-coded 4-PSK whose $d_{free} = 2$ (Fig. 8).

The results achieved in figure agrees with several literatures, Ungerboeck [2] plotted a graph of simulated 8-PSK TCM and 4-PSK un-coded and got a similar results, also Sklar [1] obtained Asymptotic coding gain results for 4-state 8-PSK TCM by considering the expanded free distance which is 2 for coded system and $\sqrt{2}$ for un-coded system. The asymptote Coding gain $G = 10 \log_{10}\left(\frac{2^2}{\sqrt{2}^2}\right) = 3dB$, the coding gain of the above system at $BER = 10^{-5}$ is 2.7 dB.

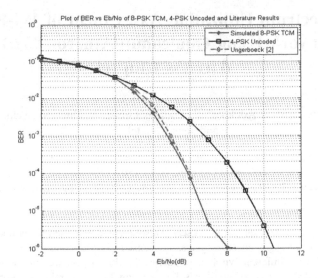

Fig. 8. Plot of BER versus E_b/N_0 of 8-PSK coded, 4-PSK un-coded and literature results

5 Conclusion and Further Work

The main contribution of this paper was to analyse trellis coded modulation in AWGN. A significant improvement can be observed using a simple 4-ASK four state TCM schemes that easily achieved coding gain of 3 dB and with more complex coding schemes, 6 dB is achievable. Signal can now be transmitted at a considerable lower *power* while maintaining the same *information rate* and even higher. *Bandwidth* can also be saved and trade-offs can be made between the choice of these three properties when designing a communication link (Link Budget).

Implementation of TCM in Rayleigh fading channel follows the same concepts as that of AWGN only that the signal gets to the receiver through a number of paths.

Further work should include the combination of TCM with other error correction codes e.g. block codes and turbo codes, this bring about further increase in coding gains and can also prove effective in fading channels. Further work will also include proper analyses of bandwidth efficiency and coding gain of TCM in fading channel and designing of optimum trellis codes for fading channel.

References

1. Sklar, B.: Digital Communications Fundamental and Application, 2nd edn. Prentice-Hall Inc., Upper Saddle River (2001)
2. Ungerboeck, G.: Trellis-coded modulation with redundant signal set part 1: introduction. IEEE Commun. Mag. **25**(2), 5–11 (1987)
3. Ungerboeck, G.: Channel coding with multilevel/phase signals. IEEE Trans. Inf. Theory **28**(1), 55–67 (1982)
4. Complex to real 2014 trellis-coded modulation. http://www.complextoreal.com/wp-content/uploads/2013/01/tcm.pdf
5. Otung, I.: Digital Communication principles and System. IET, Stevenage (2014)

Spectrum Utilization Assessment of Wi-Fi Network Using Qualcomm/Atheros 802.11 Wireless Chipset

Muyiwa Joshua Adeleke[✉], Andreas Grebe, Mathias Kretschmer, and Jens Moedeker

Technische Hochschule/Fraunhofer-Gesellschaft, Koln, Germany
muyiwa.adelekel@gmail.com, andreas.grebe@th-koeln.de,
{mathias.kretschmer,jens.moedeker}@fit.fraunhofer.de

Abstract. Wireless spectrum is a scarce resource and with the market boom of wireless technology over the years, unlicensed spectrum has become overcrowded with different wireless standards. In this paper, we proposed and demonstrated a proof of concept solution using FFT spectral scan with two methodologies: MaxHold-RMS approach and percentage ratio count approach. Both approaches could be used to detect a free/best channel from different scanned channel on the spectrum. The subsequent contributions were made to knowledge: an FFT based visual spectrum analyzer tool, an algorithm to classify different frequency channel on a spectrum, an algorithm which calculate frequency channel scores using weighted sum model, and channel ranking model. After different experimental evaluations coupled with the FFT spectral sampling timing, operation, a one(1) second scan duration is enough to detect signal transmission from a permanent device on the frequency spectrum since management and control frame signals are always transmitted periodically, while there is little chance for detecting a sporadic signal transmission from the non-permanent user since the FFT spectral scan is performed in passive mode. But to guarantee detection of such sporadic signals then scanning longer at different time segment of the day on the spectrum will increase the probability of detecting such some sporadic signals. Also, the FFT spectral scan capability has shown a high degree of probability for detecting non-WiFi signal on the shared spectrum using Qualcomm/Atheros chipset.

Keywords: Frequency channel · Fast Fourier transform · Wi-Fi
WiMAX · airFiber · LTE-U · Radar · WiBACK · OFDM · RMS
SNR · RSSI · 5 GHz spectrum · FFT bins · WSM

1 Introduction

It's a known fact that the unlicensed wireless spectrum such as Industrial, Scientific and Medical (ISM) radio bands with operating frequency of 2.4 GHz and Unlicensed National Information Infrastructure (UNII) radio bands with operating frequency of 5 GHz are by nature vulnerable to interference and limited in resources (e.g. frequency, time and space) with numerous users competing for the same resources to push their

© ICST Institute for Computer Sciences, Social Informatics and Telecommunications Engineering 2018
V. Odumuyiwa et al. (Eds.): AFRICOMM 2017, LNICST 250, pp. 180–191, 2018.
https://doi.org/10.1007/978-3-319-98827-6_16

data traffics on. These competitions are attributed to the recent growth in wireless technology which has brought about an heterogeneous network. In the unlicensed spectrum bands, interference is a major concern the user must contend with, and the predominant paradigm used against it is avoidance since you don't have control over the spectrum. Spectrum utilization assessment in the unlicensed spectrum is vital and should be given an utmost consideration because it would help in facilitating the sensing of signal energy on center frequency in bid to help determine how free or busy is a channel/frequency band, which is either a relative or an absolute measurement. This brings up the question of how to find the best frequency channel? With the 5 GHz unlicensed spectrum home to heterogeneous radio standards with different wireless technology such as WiMAX, AirMax/Airfiber, HiperLAN, LTE-U and Radar/DFS all sharing the same spectrum. The big question would now be, can 802.11 wireless chipsets detect the wireless frames signal from these heterogeneous radio standards?

Lastly, Qualcomm/Atheros 802.11xx chipset could scan in passive mode and report spectral samples using Discrete Fourier Transform (DCT) tool to compute Fast Fourier transform (FFT) in baseband, which could be used to detect wireless signals with inclusion of non-802.11 signals [1]. The question of how precise are Atheros/Qualcomm chipsets in terms of their FFT spectral scanning in power/energy sensitivity, signal spectral band, and signal duration need to be investigated. Looking at the foregoing, the above-listed motivations among others motivates us in carrying out this research work.

The remainder of the paper is structured as follows: Sect. 2 discussed the problem formulation, in Sect. 3 literatures was reviewed, Sect. 4 described proof of concept solution model, in Sect. 5 an experimental performance evaluation & analysis would be discussed, while Sect. 6 concludes the paper with conclusion & recommendation.

2 Problem Formulation

From the standpoint of this research paper objectives, background information and problem statement, the main scientific question shall be clarified, which is the best channel among a given set of channels?

To facilitate the answering of the main scientific question stated in the foregoing, the following scientific sub-questions were clarified as well:

i. What kind of interferers (WiFi, WiMAX, Airfiber, HiperLan, LTE-U and Radar/DFS) are expected and how to reliably detect them?
ii. What are the spectral characteristics of the signals/carriers for each interferer both in time and frequency domain?
iii. How precise are Atheros/Qualcomm chipset regarding FFT spectral analysis?
iv. What scan duration and FFT size are required to reliably detect likely expected wireless signals?
v. How to classify a channel and to compare them?

Based on the capability of hardware available for this research work which can report data from spectrum utilization using two scanning modes: WLAN scan and FFT spectral scan, several approaches were considered based on the aforementioned hardware capabilitz. In the context of this research two approaches (MaxHold-RMS and

Percentage count ratio) are proposed based on data samples reported from either FFT spectral scan mode alone or combination of both modes (FFT scan & WLAN scan).

3 Literature Review

There is a broad embodiment of literature on spectrum sensing techniques [2–5], with regards to the problem description of this paper quite a number of related work and state-of-the-art research can be found, but only a few of them would be reviewed because limited work in literature focused on the investigation of the possibilities of any non-IEEE802.11 wireless technology signals acting as a source of interference in the 5 GHz spectrum. This review was based on some requirements such as: (i) Only use the built-in radio and no external tool, (ii) FFT spectral scanner and/or WLAN scanner and (iii) Passive scanning mode.

Shravan et al. [2] proposed Airshark, a system that can detects non-WiFi RF devices (Microwave Oven, FHSS phone, Bluetooth, and ZigBee) signals operating in the 2.4 GHz Instrument, science and measurement (ISM) bands using the functionality provided by commodity WiFi hardware like Atheros AR9280 AGN wireless card. The paper detailed four steps used in the detection pipeline, namely spectral sampling, extracting signal data, generic feature extraction, and device detection. The authors used features such as pulse signature (duration, bandwidth, and center frequency), spectral signature, duty cycle, timing signature, pulse spread and device specific features were all used to detect devices. The authors in [2] evaluated the performance of Airshark using two metrics (detection accuracy and false positive rate). The authors claimed Airshark system has an average detection accuracy of 91–96%, even in the presence of multiple simultaneously active RF devices operating at a wide range of signal strengths (−80 to −30 dBm), while maintaining a low false positive rate. The major gap in this paper [2] was that no specifics on how to classify a channel as free or busy channel was provided. Likewise, the possibility of detecting non-WiFi signals in the 5 GHz band was left out as well.

Balid et al. [3] experimental work was performed using an energy detection technique providing systematics and experimental measurement of spectrum utilization using the concept of duty circle (DC) which was implemented in two stages by setting up two or three-pair 802.11b/g/n networks using Mikrotik router boards with Atheros chipsets. Authors [3] claimed noise level of −105 dBm was measured and provided two signal analysis process algorithms for time domain (TD) and frequency domain (FD) measurement. TD analysis algorithm process was proposed by the authors as follow: (i) calculation of instantaneous power values, (ii) smoothing the signal using moving average algorithm, that serves as a low pass filter (LPF), (iii) calculating the power signal threshold by determining the power histogram for data recording set, fitting a Gaussian distribution to the histogram's lowest power hill, and then setting the threshold five standard deviation from the peak, (iv) analyzing the entire data recording by comparing calculated power averages to the found threshold. The major gap in this paper was that the authors measured power from a vector spectrum analyzer and not from the Atheros wireless card. Likewise, no specific provision on how to classify a channel as free or busy was provided.

Xue et al. in [5] addressed an important problem in the wireless monitoring which is how to choose channels with best (or worst) qualities timely and accurately. They consider scenarios of one or more sniffers simultaneously monitoring multiple channels in the same area. Since the channel information is initially unknown to the sniffers, they adopted learning methods during the monitoring to predict the channel condition by a short time of observation. The authors [5] formulated this problem as a novel branch of the classic multi-armed bandit (MAB) problem, named exploration bandit problem, to achieve a trade-off between monitoring time/resource budget and the channel selection accuracy. The authors failed to describe which data from the sniffing monitoring tool was used for mean reward computation with no specific on how classify a channel as either free or busy in their work was provided, which are a gap in their work.

4 Proof of Concept Solution Model

In congruence with the problem statement of my paper alongside the aims & objectives of the research work, a proof of concept (POC) of my solution model as shown in Fig. 1 has five modules: spectral sample processing, statistics analysis/FFT sample data correction, decision making, multi-criteria decision making (MCDM), and channel ranking. Each of these modules would be briefly discussed in this section.

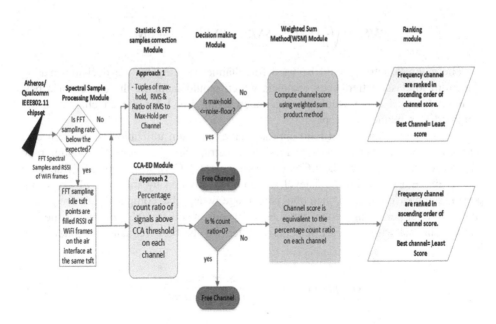

Fig. 1. Proof of concept architecture of the solution model

4.1 Spectral Sample Processing Module

This module describes how AthSpectralTool API spectral scan tool which is written in C++ programming language and built in Linux environment is used to activate FFT spectral scan features on any of the supported Atheros/Qualcomm chipsets on a frequency channel, in the context of this paper AR928x, AR9580 and QCA988x were evaluated. Spectral signal power was calculated based on [1] project using Eq. 1.1 on each FFT points frequency subcarrier using different FFT spectral coefficients from ath9k/ath10k driver.

$$SignalPower_i = nf + rssi + 10 * \log_{10}(b(i)^2) - 10 * \log_{10}(\sum_{i=1}^{56} b(i)^2). \qquad (1.1)$$

4.2 MaxHold-RMS and Percentage Count Ratio Approaches

With the MaxHold-RMS approach, the spectrum utilization assessment of wireless channel can be described using three metrics namely: maximum signal energy detected (max-hold), the computed root mean square (RMS) using Eq. 1.2 of all signal energy detected on each FFT subcarrier for any frequency channel, and the ratio of RMS to maximum signal energy detected to depicts utilization on the channel.

$$RMS_i = \sqrt{\frac{1}{n}(SNR_1^2 + SNR_2^2 + SNR_3^2 + \ldots + SNR_n^2)}. \qquad (1.2)$$

These three metrics could be used for channel ranking by the decision-making algorithm to classify frequency channels which would facilitate the choice of a best channel. Channel score would be calculated using Eq. 1.4 for each channel using weighted sum method concept.

For the percentage count ratio approach, the spectrum utilization assessment of a frequency channel can be described using a metric which is percentage count ratio which uses the concept of Clear Channel Assessment (CCA), from which FFT spectral power above a CCA threshold level are counted, divided by the total FFT spectral power samples computed, then the percentage would be computed per frequency channel. With percentage count ratio zero (0) indicates a free channel while the frequency channel with the least percentage is termed the best frequency channel using Eq. 1.3.

$$percentageCountRatio = \frac{SignalCount}{Total\,FTSamples} * 100. \qquad (1.3)$$

4.3 Multi-variable Decision-Making Module

This module explores the Weighted Sum Model (WSM) concept which is one of the multi-criteria decision-making methods presented by author [6], from which an algorithm was developed for WSM model using Eq. 1.4 where the alternatives are the sets of frequency subcarrier considered, while two criteria's (RMS and ratio) was proposed in this research work. The two criteria's (a_{ij}) are the factors affecting the preference of choice on the best alternatives using MaxHold-RMS approach, recalling that the alternatives are the sets of possible frequency subcarriers options to choose from.

$$ChannelScore_{wsm} = \sum_{i=1}^{n} a_{ij} * w_j. \tag{1.4}$$

From the Eq. 1.4 the relative weight (w_j) is a numerical value between 0 and 1 which depicts the relative importance of the criteria and their impacts on these alternatives [6]. The relative weight value attached to each criteria are based on subjective judgement, which are according to how significantly the criteria will impact the WSM score on each alternatives considered and by visual examination of different personal choice. Considering the two-subjective judgements used, relative weight of RMS value should be higher than that of ratio, since RMS indicates level of utilization on the channel while ratio is only a comparative metric between RMS and max-hold.

4.4 Ranking Module

This module takes care of the ranking of each frequency channel on a spectrum based on channel score computed using the concept described in Subsect. 4.3. Each frequency channel is ranked in ascending order of the scores computed, with the least score indicates the best channel while channel with highest score is classified as the busiest channel when considering either of the two approaches described in Subsect. 4.2.

5 Experimental Performance Evaluation and Analysis

In this section, an experimental performance evaluation would be carried out on the various Atheros/Qualcomm chipsets used in this research project.

5.1 Capability of Qualcomm/Atheros Chipset to Detect Narrowband Signals Such as Radar Signal with Good Power Sensitivity and Precision

This section describes the FFT spectrum scan capability of Atheros/Qualcomm 802.11x chipset to detect different narrow band signals since radar which are narrow band signal are expected on the 5 GHz frequency spectrum. In theory, a 20 MHz channel bandwidth with 64 FFT bins has frequency bandwidth of 312.5 kHz per bin, which implies that a single FFT bin is enough to capture narrow band signal between 1KHz-310 kHz. An experiment was set up with different signal generated using the generator provided by Rhode & Schwarz spectrum analyzer on frequency channel 5805 MHz at different power level instances (−50 dBm and −40 dBm). The signal generated has spectral bandwidth of 500 kHz, 100 MHz, 50 kHz, 20 kHz, 10 kHz, and 5 kHz respectively, at different power levels as shown on Figs. 2 and 3. For each signal generated at a particular power level, the FFT spectral scanner was initiated and the data sets are stored until all data are collected then the narrowband signal was plotted using the spectrum visualizer tool we designed. Figure 2 clearly shows narrowband signals captured from −50 dBm source power from the signal generator, where the blue, green, red, cyan, purple, and yellow lines are 500 kHz, 100 kHz, 50 kHz, 20 kHz, 10 kHz, and 5 kHz signals captured respectively.

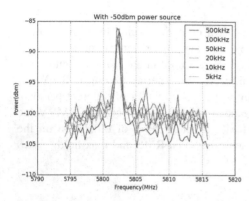 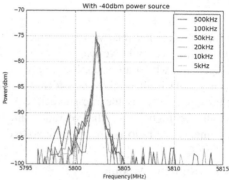

Fig. 2. Ath10k narrowband signal detection with −50 dBm source (Color figure online)

Fig. 3. Ath10k narrowband signal detection with −40 dBm source (Color figure online)

From Fig. 2 the highest signal was detected with −86 dBm from the signal generator at −50 dBm. Examining Fig. 3, increasing the signal power from the generator by 10 dBm to −40 dBm, the highest signal detected was about −76 dBm which is about 8 dBm ± 2 difference compared to the highest signal detected in Fig. 2. This clearly shows the capability of Qualcomm/Atheros chipset to detect narrowband signal such as radar signal with good power sensitivity and precision.

5.2 Finding the Best Channel

In the context of this paper, a free channel is one with its max-hold SNR value below 28 ± 3 dB (−96 dBm) decision threshold for MaxHold-RMS approach while for percentage ratio count approach is the one with signal count of zero(0) from the list of channels scanned for spectrum assessment as shown in Fig. 1, while the rest of the frequency channel are termed busy channel. From these busy frequency channels, one could compute channel score for each frequency channel with two metrics (RMS & duty cycle/ratio) for MaxHold-RMS approach and one metric (count of energy above threshold) for percentage count ratio approach using WSM concept. With the computed channel score, each frequency channel could be ranked in ascending order of their score, while the best channel is the one with the lowest channel score than the rest of the ranked frequency channel could be used by a wireless card in order of the rank.

A three-hops WiBACk wireless network with frequency 5310 MHz(40 MHz)/
5230 MHz(40 MHz) was used for this experiment with an iPerf UDP bi-directional
signal at data transmission rate of 70 Mb/s was initiated on the wireless link.

5.3 Evaluation of MaxHold-RMS Approach

Using AR928x and AR9580 chipsets to demonstrate the evaluation of this approach
which involves couple of statistical analysis and different computation as described at
Subsect. 4.2. While the iPerf UDP transmission is initiated on the wireless link, the
FFT spectrum scanner perform a 1-s scan on each center frequency using my designed
model, then statistical analysis was carried out on the FFT spectral samples on all
subcarriers of each channel. Each channel analyzed obtains a score which is calculated
using Eq. 1.4, with relative weight of RMS set to 0.7 dB and duty cycle/ratio set to
0.3 dB. The relative weight value chosen for each criterion are based on
observation/experience which is empirical in nature.

On Fig. 4 the blue line is the max-hold, green line is the RMS, while the dot on red
line, dot on the black line and the dot on the yellow indicates the average max-hold,
average RMS and ratio/duty cycle on each center frequency. It would be deduced from
the figure that the two center frequencies 5220 MHz and 5240 MHz that makes up the
40 MHz band for center frequency 5230 MHz used by one of the WiBACK wireless
links. By visual examination, none of these channels are free so using the decision-
making algorithm for calculating each channel score to help find the best channel from
the scanned spectrum (5170 MHz–5330 MHz). Using AR9580 FFT spectral data, my
algorithm will pick center frequency 5180 MHz as the best channel since it has the
lowest computed channel score as seen on Fig. 4.

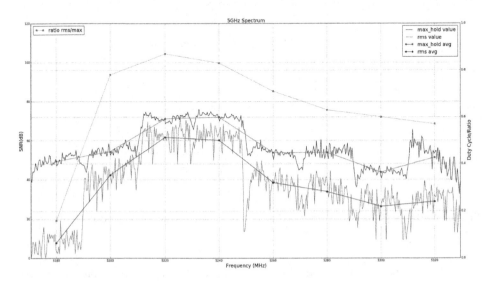

Fig. 4. AR9580 FFT spectral scan snapshot with MaxHold-RMS approach (Color figure online)

5.4   Percentage Ratio Count Approach

To perform this analysis the same FFT spectral samples collected in sub-Sect. 4.2 was used in percentage ratio count approach for counting of FFT spectral signal power above noise-floor (NF). Percentage ratio of signal counted on each frequency channel are computed by dividing the counted signal with the total FFT spectral samples. Each channel analyzed obtains a score which is calculated using Eq. 1.3 and afterwards ranking of channel are based on channel score, with lowest count percentage ratio indicating the least utilized/best channel while the highest value is the busiest channel.

Figure 5 shows spectrum utilization assessment using percentage count ratio approach which is the counting of signal power above a NF and averaging over the total FFT spectral samples received across each frequency channel. The blue, green, red, cyan and yellow lines represent percentage count ratio for different CCA threshold values of −95 dBm, −89 dBm, −83 dBm, −77 dBm, −71 dBm, −65 dBm respectively on each frequency channel. Presently ath9k & ath10k in the recent Linux kernel module has a fixed CCA value of −96 dBm, so the blue line which represents −96 dBm would be considered for the evaluation. Figure 5 clearly shows that at center frequency 5220 and 5240 MHz there you have the highest peak of signal counted for each NF value. This method is simple and doesn't require much computation and statistical analysis compared to MaxHold-RMS approach, but still yet depict same spectrum utilization status.

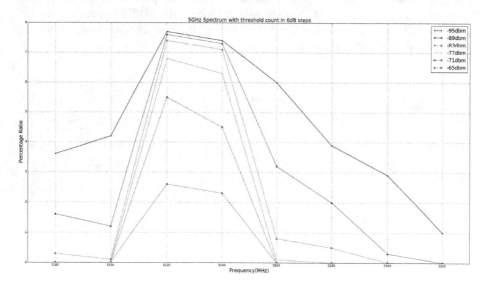

Fig. 5. AR928x FFT spectral scan snapshot with percentage count ratio approach (Color figure online)

Going by the count methodology in percentage ratio count approach, Fig. 5 depiction of the percentage ratio count on each frequency channel clearly shows the center frequency 5320 MHz is the best channel among the frequency channels scanned.

5.5   Scan Duration Required for Wireless Signal Detection on 5 GHz Spectrum

Scan duration is a vital metric which determines the percentage of certainty of signal detection, while going by the different modes of operation (access point (AP)-station, mesh, base station (BS)-subscriber station (SS)) of different wireless technologies there are management and control frames signals which are sent periodically even if there is no data frame transmission on the wireless link which are used for various management and control purposes. Each expected wireless technology uses similar concepts, but with varying signal durations. As described in the scope of this paper, only permanent device whose management/control frames are periodically sent are considered as non-permanent device's signal are only sporadically transmitted with no guarantee of detection during the scanning operation because such devices are non-permanent. A one second scan duration is sufficient to detect any signal from expected wireless technologies on the 5 GHz spectrum using FFT spectral scanning method.

5.6   Detection of Non-IEEE802.11 Wireless Signal

Expected non-802.11 signal on 5 GHz frequency spectrum (WiMAX, AirFiber, LTE-U, Radar) are of different wireless protocol which uses different technology. It is hard, if not practically impossible for an IEEE802.11 chipset from any silicon brand maker to decode any non-802.11 wireless signals on the shared spectrum by mere capturing of network traffic on its wireless interface using libPcap library in Unix-like system or winPcap in windows OS. FFT spectral scan features in Atheros/Qualcomm chipset has shown an ability detect non-802.11 spectrum on the 5 GHz spectrum going by experiments in Subsect. 5.1 where different narrow band were generated from a Rhode & Schwarz FSL spectrum analyzer using tracking generator features on the spectrum analyzer.

Considering the result from the experiment in Subsect. 5.1 and the time domain FFT spectral sampling capability of Qualcomm/Atheros Chipset as shown in Fig. 6, FFT spectral scanner samples a 20 MHz frequency band using sampling window duration of 4 µs, with 4 µs interval between successive sampling window and the chipset repeats these FFT sampling windowing sequence for 204 µs for each spectral scan mode until the scan duration elapses.

Each of the expected non-802.11 standard on the 5 GHz spectrum typically has different data frame and preamble durations: WiMAX (2.5 ms, 4 ms, 5 ms, 8 ms, 10 ms, 12.5 ms) [7], for Radar signals depending on the pulse width (0.6–1.9 µs) [8], HiperLan (8, 12, 16 µs) [9] and for LTE-U (5–10 ms) [10]. FFT spectral scan tool takes a snapshot of the whole 20 MHz in 4 µs with delay of 4 µs between successive FFT sampling window in a spectrum scan entry period of 204 µs. With the above-stated frame/subframe timing, alongside the FFT sampling timing then there is a high probability that these non-802.11 signals would be detected on the spectrum using the FFT spectral scan.

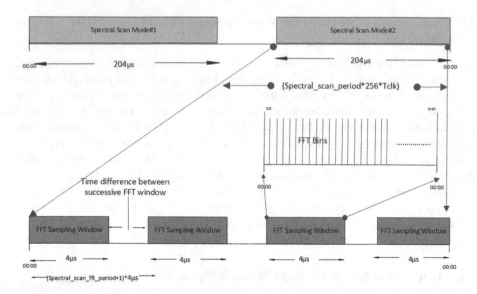

Fig. 6. Spectral scan timeline schematics for ath9k architecture

6 Conclusion and Recommendation

In this research work, which is all about "Spectrum Utilization Assessment of Wi-Fi Network using Atheros/Qualcomm 802.11 wireless chipset", a solution model was proposed using two approaches, where the spectrum utilization were analyzed using different Atheros/Qualcomm chipsets. FFT spectral samples was collected using AthSpectralTool from frequency subcarriers on each frequency channel using 64 FFT points, and the collected datasets for each channel was further analyzed using different statistical methods. With my proposed model, a free or busy can easily be figured out after scanning the spectrum using FFT spectral scan.

Summing up questions II to V, what are the requirements to detect any wireless signals on the 5 GHz spectrum? Answers to those research questions raised at Sect. 2 are provided based on results obtained from various experiments performed as follows:

- Signal time duration must be ≥ 1 µs
- Signal power level must be ≥ -60 dBm
- Periodic interval of the signals must be <1 s for 1 s scan duration
- Accuracy of assessment tools must have a value close to upper limit
- FFT size of 64 points are enough for detecting signals on 20 MHz frequency channel bandwidth.

The expected non-IEEE802.11 wireless technology signals on the 5 GHz spectrum are IEEE802.16 (WiMAX, airFiber, HiperLAN, Radar, LTE-U).

The research presented in this paper made a couple of discoveries on different Atheros/Qualcomm chipsets which are out of scope of my paper work, one notable is the drastic reduction on FFT spectral sampling rate experienced during continuous wireless frames injection on a frequency channel.

My contributions to knowledge in this field are as follows:

- Development of a visual spectrum analyzer tool.
- Development of an algorithm that could be used to find the most "free" or "best" channel from sets of frequency channel.
- Methods that could use to show utilization on the frequency spectrum.
- Discoveries on different behavior of Atheros/Qualcomm wireless chipset

Lastly, due to unavailability of the expected non-802.11 wireless devices at FIT laboratory environment, a future work would be testing the efficiency of FFT spectral scan tool in an environment where these expected non-802.11 signals are present.

References

1. Kalle, V.: ath9k spectral scan (2017). https://wireless.wiki.kernel.org/en/users/drivers/ath9k/spectral_scan
2. Shravan, R., Ashish, P., Suman, B.: Airshark: detecting non-WiFi RF devices using commodity WiFi hardware. In: ACM SIGCOMM Conference on Internet Measurement Conference, NY, USA, pp. 137–154 (2011). http://dx.doi.org/10.1145/2068816.2068830
3. Balid, W., Rajab, S.A., Refai, H.: Comprehensive study of spectrum utilization for 802.11b/g/n networks. In: International Wireless Communications and Mobile Computing Conference (IWCMC), Dubrovnik, pp. 1526–1531 (2015). https://doi.org/10.1109/iwcmc.2015.7289309, http://ieeexplore.ieee.org/stamp/stamp.jsp?tp=&arnumber=7289309&isnumber=7288920
4. Cisco System: Cisco Spectrum Expert WiFi (2007). http://www.cisco.com/c/en/us/products/collateral/wireless/spectru-expert/product_data_sheet0900aecd807033c3.html
5. Xue, Y., Zhou, P., Jiang, T., Mao, S., Huang, X.: Distributed learning for multi-channel selection in wireless network monitoring. In: 13th Annual IEEE International Conference on Sensing, Communication, and Networking (SECON), London, pp. 1–9 (2016). https://doi.org/10.1109/sahcn.2016.7732984, http://ieeexplore.ieee.org/stamp/stamp.jsp?tp=&arnumber=7732984&isnumber=7732953
6. Athanasios, K.: Multiple-Criteria Decision-Making (MCDM) Methods, p. 2 (2016). http://www.mdpi.com/1996-1073/9/7/566/pdf
7. IEEE Standard for Local and Metropolitan area Network Part 16: Air interface for fixed broadband wireless access system. IEEE802.16-2004, pp. 151–152, p. 307 (2004). http://standards.ieee.org/getieee802/download/802.16-2004.pdf
8. Radtec Engineering Inc.: Radar performance, p. 3 (2005). http://www.radarsales.com/PDFs/Performance_RDR%26TDR.pdf
9. ETSI: HiperLAN type 2 Physical Layer. ETSI TS 101 475 v1.2.2 (2005). http://www.etsi.org/deliver/etsi_ts/101400_101499/101475/01.02.02_60/ts_101475v010202p.pdf
10. Mathew, B.: LTE Advanced PHY layer (2009). ftp://www.3gpp.org/workshop/2009-12-17_ITU-R_IMT-Adv_eval/docs/pdf/REV-090003-r1.pdf

Resource Efficient Algorithm for D2D Communications Between Adjacent and Co-channel Cells of LTE Networks

Elias Ntawuzumunsi[1] and Santhi Kumaran[2(✉)]

[1] Faculty of Science and Technology, Catholic University, Butare, Rwanda
ntaweli2015@gmail.com
[2] African Center of Excellence in Internet of Things (ACEIoT),
College of Science and Technology, University of Rwanda, Kigali, Rwanda
santhikr@yahoo.com

Abstract. Device-to-device (D2D) communication has been a hot topic recently because of its potential advantages such as high data rates, spectrum-efficient, and energy-efficient. D2D communication has the advantage of maximum spectral usage, provides higher throughput. The idea in this paper is to design an algorithm for resource efficient D2D communications in adjacent and Co-channel cell of LTE networks. One of the methods used is cell splitting to make different adjacent and Co-channel cell, hence increasing cell capacity and offloading the base station. In this research work, we evaluate how to improve the Quality of service for the User Equipment by designing an algorithm of resource efficient for D2D communication within adjacent and Co-channel cells. As a result, different cells can reuse the same frequency resources in the LTE cellular network. The simulated results show that the proposed algorithm can largely improve the system capacity compared with other existing algorithm.

Keywords: LTE · D2D communications · Adjacent cell · Co-channel cell

1 Introduction

Recently, D2D communication is the topic for most of researchers in this field suggesting the possible means by which wireless communications can be enhanced. D2D communication is the way how two devices can communicate with or without base station (BS) to efficiently facilitate more high data rate services among nearby users and devices. In paper [1] different multiple access techniques which are used to allow many mobile subscribers to share finite amount of radio spectrum simultaneously has been introduced. There are several advantages of this kind of communication compared to traditional cellular network such as higher throughput, efficient spectral usage, extended network coverage improved energy efficiency, delays and fairness hence system capacity is improved [2]. In this type of communication, the user equipment sends the request to base station and then sends it to the receiver. The base station (BS) works as the middle point for both the sender and receiver to communicate [3]. Our focus in this paper is to design a resource efficient algorithm for D2D communication within adjacent and co-channel cells in LTE networks, so that the network provides better QoS

© ICST Institute for Computer Sciences, Social Informatics and Telecommunications Engineering 2018
V. Odumuyiwa et al. (Eds.): AFRICOMM 2017, LNICST 250, pp. 192–203, 2018.
https://doi.org/10.1007/978-3-319-98827-6_17

without overloading the network [4]. The rest of the paper is organized as follows: Sect. 2 focuses on the D2D communication based on the adjacent and co-channel cells in LTE networks. Section 3 describes the related works. Section 4 describes the proposed D2D algorithm design. Section 5, we show the analysis of simulation results and Sect. 6 describes conclusion and further works.

2 D2D Communication Based on Adjacent and Co-channel Cells in LTE Networks

D2D communication is the way how two devices can communicate with or without base station (BS) to efficiently facilitate more high data rate services among nearby users and devices. As illustrated in the Fig. 1, two adjacent cells (cell1 and cell2) where UE1 discover UE2 while they are located on two different cells. As explained in Sect. 1, you find that UEs are connected on base station for each cell, those base station was connected through the gateway. It is from that connection of base station where those two devices UE1 and UE2 are connected. If there are more UEs within those adjacent cells, the method of cell splitting and frequency reuse are applied for adjacent and co-channel cells in order to provide better QoS, better utilization of spectrum and avoiding of interference within the system.

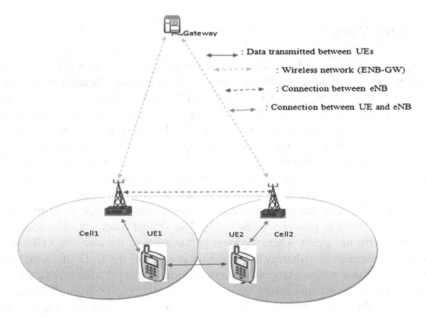

Fig. 1. Proposed system model of D2D communication within two adjacent cells in LTE network.

According to the Fig. 2, there is a complete network between different adjacent and co-channel cells, for example on the cluster 1, packets are transmitted between cell 7 and cell1.in addition, the packet are transmitted from cells located on two different cluster like for example on cell 2 within cluster 2 and cell 6 within the cluster one. The aim of this paper is to design and analyze a resource efficient algorithm for D2D communication within different adjacent and co-channel cells of a LTE network.

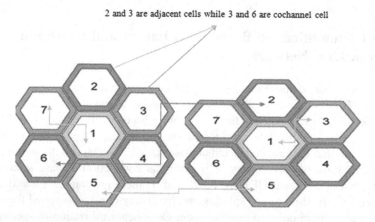

Fig. 2. Proposed system model of D2D communication within different adjacent and cochannel cells in LTE Network.

3   Related Works

Although a lot of work has been done on this topic but, most of them did not consider the system capacity of adjacent and co-channel cells as an issue. Reusing the resources of more than one cellular user were proposed in [5] but they do not indicate the way it will increase the system capacity. Three sharing modes are mentioned in [6] as non-orthogonal, orthogonal and cellular sharing modes but it focuses on optimization of power and energy. The spectrum reuse protocol where D2D users are only allowed to communicate with each other during the uplink (UL) frame of the network. This is due to the fact that during UL only the base station (BS) is exposed to interference by the D2D users but focuses on the spectrum sharing by analyzing and identifying the interference problem of the primary cellular network caused by the D2D transmitter during the UL and DL phases separately [7]. The system model in [8] contains the inner part and the outer part, where the inner part consists of the traditional UEs which communicate through BS whereas the outer part consists of the D2D UEs which have at least one neighbor within a targeted distance. The author in [9] assumes that the large number of resources in inner part is taken as infinite and Poisson point distribution is considered in this case for cellular UEs. The author in [10] assumes that the finite number of sources in outer part of the cell for D2D UEs and the corresponding model in this case is the Engset distribution and the number of sources in the inner part is distributed into small cell with a reuse factor of seven so that the number of resources is reduced and consider Engset distribution for both parts by applying the method of sharing available resource where each part uses dedicated resource but the author does not show how their model shall enhance the system capacity since this can accommodate more users. But in this paper our focus was for adjacent and co-channel cells where system capacity and throughput should have been considered to ensure better QoS. In this model, two adjacent cells are split into multiple small adjacent and cochannel cells, and an algorithm of resource efficient for D2D communication was designed to enhance the system performance. Also, based on Shannon's equation for capacity calculation, several formulas was used to design an algorithm of resource efficient for D2D communication within adjacent and cochannel cell in LTE network which helped to provide increased capacity for better performance and to increase the quality of service to the cellular users.

4 Proposed D2D Algorithm Design

In this paper, the concept is to analyze and design an algorithm of how two or more different devices located on two different adjacent cells or cochannel cells should be communicated. Two adjacent cells are split into multiple small adjacent and cochannel cell such that different UEs or Devices located on that two adjacent and cochannel cell are communicated. Due to that method of cell splitting and designed algorithm, the packet from the device located on one cell are transmitted to another device located on the other cell while those devices are located on two different cell which are adjacent or cochannel. A scenario is designed as follows, in each cell, there is a base station (Enode-B) to serve UEs located on that cell and for another cell there is a base station to serve the UEs located on that cell and those two base station was discovered one-another by the Gateway, if base station of one cell discover base station of another cell through the gateway, the device of one cell can discover another device of the other cell while those cell are adjacent or cochannel as it is illustrated on the Fig. 1.

4.1 Flowchart Representation of the Proposed Algorithm

In this paper, three parameters such as data, noise and error rate were proposed to test and it has been achieved because packets are transmitted successfully into different adjacent and co-channel cell. Noise is minimised and the error rate is very low. The following diagram indicate the flow of packets transmitted from different adjacent and co-channel cells. The overall algorithm is shown in the flowchart of system in Fig. 3. The flowchart representation for both adjacent and cochannel cell algorithm is shown in Fig. 3. As it is shown on the flowcharts below, we find the flow of how the packets were transmitted between different adjacent and cochannel cells in LTE network based on the proposed algorithms three parameters such as Data rate, Noise and Error rate was evaluated and it was achieved successfully as it is shown on the following algorithm. The proposed algorithm below help to set different devices within adjacent and co-channel cells in LTE network and help to check how transmission of packet are transmitted through different cells. The algorithm helps to minimize noise and error rate in order to provide good QoS.

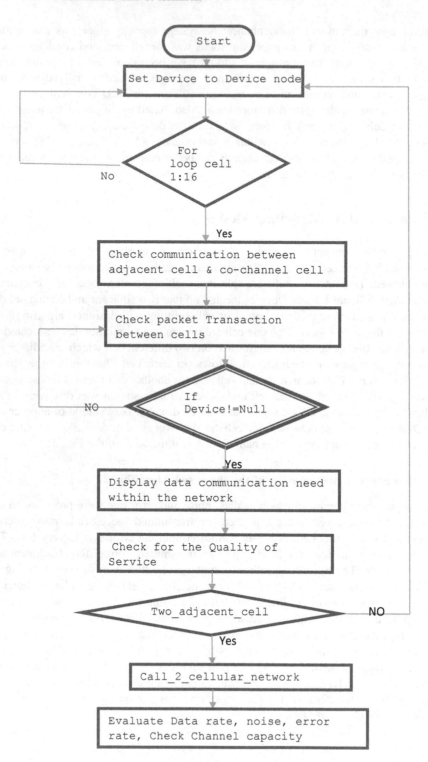

Fig. 3. Proposed flowchart of the system

4.2   Proposed Algorithm

```
1: Set Device to device cell
2: For loop cell 1:16
3: Check communication between adjacent cell & co-channel cell.
4: Check paket Transmission between nodes.
5: if (d1: Device! =null)
       {
   Print" data communication need within the network"
       }
6: check for the QoS;
7: Validating the network networkgrid.
8: if (two_adjacent_cell)
       {
   Cellular network= Call_2_cellular_network
       }
9: Evaluated Data rate, noise, error rate and Check Channel capacity
```

5   Simulation Results and Analysis

For evaluating the performance of the proposed algorithm, we simulated and showed the results in ns-2 where two adjacent cells split into multiple adjacent and cochannel cells to make LTE network. The cells are randomly deployed in a circular area. The number of cells varies from 8 to 17. The initial energy of normal node is 32 J. Table 1 summarizes the simulation parameters and their default values.

Table 1. Simulation parameters

Parameter	Value
Number of cells	17
Initial energy $E0$	32 J
Simulation time	2.00 ms
Channel type	Wireless channel
Network interface type	Physical
Bandwidth	100 Mbits/s
Delay	10.00 ms
Scenario size	240 m × 240 m

Figure 4 below shows how LTE network made by different cell was created, as you have seen on the interface bellow you find that two adjacent cell split into multiple cell which are adjacent and co-channel cell, in each cell there is a base station and the gateway to interconnect those two base station in order to facilitate communication between two UEs located on different cell. According to the Fig. 6 below, LTE network is divided into 15 adjacent and co-channel cells where two clusters, two base stations and one gateway is formed. For those two clusters there is 7 small cells for the first cluster and 6 small cell for the second cluster. Base station (E-NodeB) is located in each cell to serve the UEs located on that cell. Those two base station are located on two different cell and it is connected each other throughput gateway. Device from one cell discover another device for another cell if those two base stations was discovered each other through gateway and by D2D discovery mechanism. Figure 5 shows haw data transmission was transmitted for adjacent and cochannel cells.

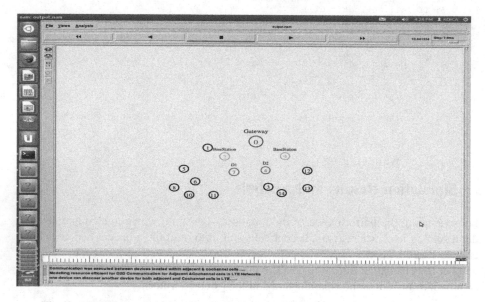

Fig. 4. LTE Network with cell splitting into multiple adjacent and co-channel cell

As it is shown on the Fig. 5 above, you find that packets are transmitted between devices located on adjacent and cochannel cells. As you have seen, cell 7 contain device D1 and it is located on the first cluster while cell 4 in the form of circle contain device D2. The data was transmitted from D1 to D2 while they located on two adjacent cells but it is possible because each device is connected to base station and if those two base stations were interconnected through gateway they will be the process of D2D discovery mechanism and those devices interconnect each other. As explained before, you find in Fig. 6, that there is a direct link between D1 and D2 while they are located on two different cells which are adjacent or cochannel. You find that the packets were transmitted from D1 to D2 while D1 is located on cell 7 and D2 on cell 4. This is due to the interconnection between those two base stations through the gateway.

According to the Fig. 6, the throughput is defined as total number of bits per second used by the user equipment excluding the number of bits per second used for control overhead. The throughput is calculated for both adjacent and co-channel cellular network. Here results are shown in form of lines, where red line shows the throughput of the adjacent and co-channel cell with D2D link in the proposed algorithm and green line shows the throughput of D2D communication in the existing algorithm. As you have seen for the proposed algorithm the throughput was increased much compared to the existing algorithm. As it is illustrated on the Fig. 10, the transmission of the packet is very high for the red line result while for the green line is low, thus the system

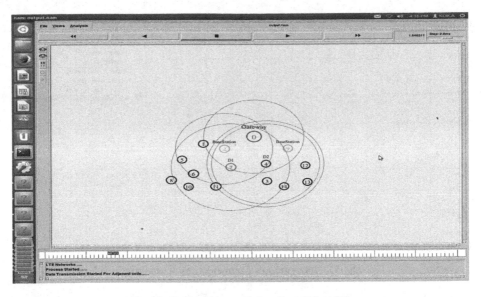

Fig. 5. Packets transmission from D1 to D2

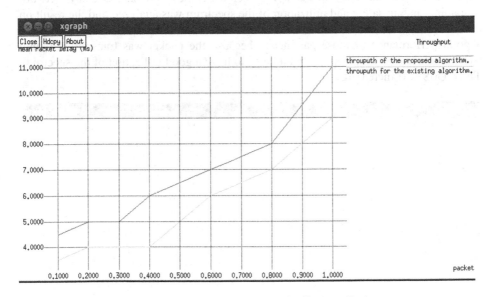

Fig. 6. Network throughput (Color figure online)

capacity is increased because different UEs located on adjacent and co-channel cell was communicated by D2D discovery mechanism in case base station was finished to set connection between them. For example for 0.30000 s the bit/s transmitted was still constant as it shown on green line while for red line was increased, hence the proposed algorithm gives better QoS than existing algorithm.

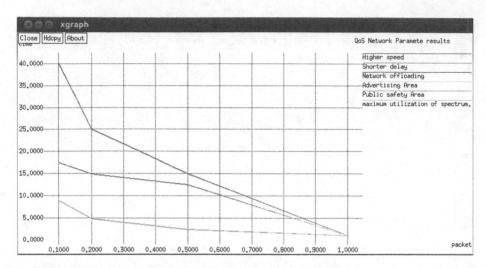

Fig. 7. Different QoS parameters result analysis

As it is shown on the Fig. 7 above, you find that different QoS parameters for both adjacent and cochannel cell was analyzed such as: High speed, shorter delay, network offloading, public safety and utilization of the spectrum was analyzed and the result on different lines indicated on the interface above shows that the proposed algorithm gives a good performance of those parameters because the packet was transmitted within shorter delay, a very high speed and it helps to have a good utilization of the spectrum. Thus, QoS was increased.

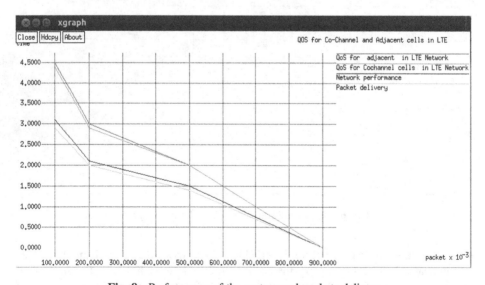

Fig. 8. Performance of the system and packets delivery

According to the Fig. 8 above, the result shows the performance of the system and the packets delivered within a time for both adjacent and cochannel cell. As it is indicated on the interface above, you find that many packets were transmitted within a short time. In addition, due to the good performance of the system, the more packets to be transmitted increased, the more time takes decreased. Thus, the proposed algorithm provides better quality of service than the existing algorithm.

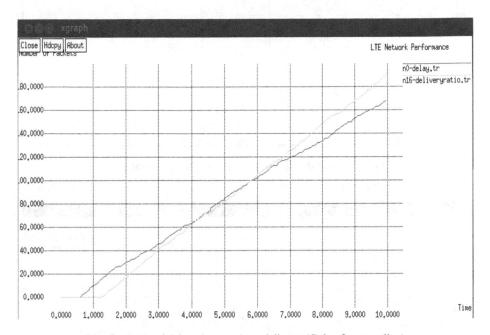

Fig. 9. Packets delayed vs packets delivery (Color figure online)

According to the Fig. 9 above, the results shows how the packets was delayed for the existing algorithm and delivered for the new algorithm within a time. As you have seen red line indicate the packet delayed result for the existing algorithm and green line shows the packet delivery for the proposed algorithm. The result on the green line indicates that more packets transmit on very high level within a time for the proposed algorithm while for the existing algorithm packets were delayed to be transmitted. Thus, the new algorithm provides better quality of service than the existing algorithm.

According to the Fig. 10 the result indicates on red line and green line that the more we have very high density of users, the more the system capacity also was increased because the proposed algorithm enhance the system capacity for both users located on adjacent and cochannel cells in LTE network and the more users was served, the more the quality of service was achieved and the problem of overloading the system will be resolved.

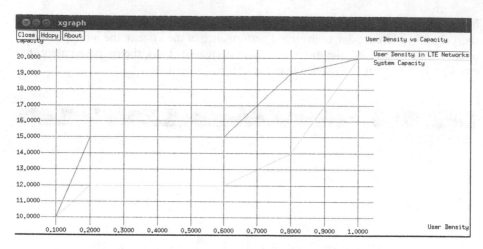

Fig. 10. User density vs. capacity (Color figure online)

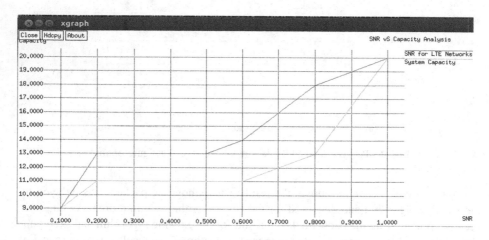

Fig. 11. SNR vs. capacity (Color figure online)

As it is indicated on the Fig. 11 the result of the new algorithm shows that the capacity increase as the target SNR increases as it is indicated by red and green lines of the Fig. 11 above. However, when D2D communication is used together with LTE more control overhead is required since the base station needs to make sure that all signaling information has been transmitted. In addition to that the discovery mechanism also requires some percentage. Once the capacity increase, thus QoS is achieved and many users was served by D2D link for both UEs located on adjacent and co-channel cells.

6   Conclusion and Further Works

In this paper, an algorithm was designed for how two or more different devices located on two different adjacent cells or co-channel cells should communicate between each other. Only one scenario of LTE cellular network, where two adjacent cell split into multiple small cells is tested. It is from those small cells where small adjacent and cochannel cells will be created. A resource efficient algorithm has been designed within the scenario. This algorithm improves the QoS in the adjacent and co-channel cells of the cellular network by increasing the capacity. We carried out analysis focusing on how the system capacity will be increased. The simulation results of the proposed algorithm shows that the QoS is achieved and the overloading problem of the system was resolved. In addition, the resource reuse is also the key for capacity enhancement in the way that reusing resources offloads BS between adjacent and co-channel cells and then other UEs can be served hence better QoS is achieved. In this paper several existing algorithms were evaluated and considered but our proposed algorithm works better than the existing approaches.

References

1. Yu, C.H., Doppler, K., Ribeiro, C.B., Tirkkonen, O.: Resource sharing optimization for device-to-device communication underlaying cellular networks. IEEE Trans. Wirel. Commun. **10**, 8–10 (2011)
2. Yu, C.H., Tirkkonen, O., Doppler, K., Ribeiro, C.: Power optimization of device-to-device communication underlaying cellular communication. In: Proceedings of ICC 2009, IEEE International Conference on Communications, Washington, vol. 2, pp. 92–96 (2009)
3. Tirkkonen, K. Doppler, H., Ribeiro, C.: On the performance of device-to-device underlay communication with simple power control. In: VTC Spring (2009)
4. Xing, H., Hakola, S.: The investigation of power control schemes for a device-to-device communication integrated into OFDM cellular system. In: 21st Annual IEEE International Symposium on Personal, Indoor and Mobile Radio Communications, New York, vol. 7, pp. 834–836 (2010)
5. Chen, T., Charbit, G., Hakola, S.: Time hopping for device-to-device communication in LTE cellular system. In: Proceedings of WCNC (2010)
6. Koskela, T., Hakola, T., Chen, T., Lehtomaki, J.: Clustering concept using device-to-device communication in cellular system. In: Proceedings of WCNC (2010)
7. Zulhasnine, M., Huang, C., Srinivasan, A.: Efficient resource allocation for device-to-device communication underlaying LTE network. In: WiMob (2010)
8. Mukherjee, A., Hottinen, J.: Energy-efficient device-to-device MIMO underlay network with interference constraints. In: International ITG Workshop on WSA, Sanfransisco (2012)
9. Jung, M., Hwang, K., Choi, S.: Joint mode selection and power allocation scheme for power-efficient device-to-device (D2D) communication. In: IEEE 75th VTC, Paris (2012)
10. Xu, Y., Yin, R., Han, G.: Interference-aware channel allocation for device-to-device communication underlaying cellular networks. In: IEEE ICCC, Noida (2012)

5G Dilemma of Supporting Contrasting Narrowband and Broadband Services

Mncedisi Bembe[1(✉)], Thierry Luhandjula[2], and George Sibiya[2]

[1] School of Computing and Mathematical Science, University of Mpumalanga,
Office 205, Building 5, University of Mpumalanga, Nelspruit 1200, South Africa
Mncedisi.bembe@ump.ac.za
[2] Meraka Institute, CSIR,
Building 43, Meiring Naude Road, Brummeria, Pretoria 0001, South Africa
{TLuhandjula,GSibiya}@csir.co.za
https://www.ump.ac.za/

Abstract. The 5th generation of cellular technology (5G), also known as IMT-2020, is seen as a game changer in mobile communication. One key characteristic of 5G is its consumer oriented emphasis, where the mobile user or user equipment is given utmost priority compared to previous generations. Its ongoing standardization is a result of the rapid growth of connected devices worldwide, an increased design complexity. Moreover, 5G has the vocation of providing wireless communication with almost no limitation, hence enhanced mobile broadband, but it also aims at enabling other applications such as IoT for which narrowband is used. This paper aims at investigating the challenges of accommodating both 5G broadband and 5G narrowband services in the same network.

Keywords: Narrowband · Broadband · Mobility · Internet of things
Data rates

1 Introduction

The aim of the 3rd Generation Partnership Project's (3GPP) 5G is to bring new developments including the support for enhanced mobile broadband, ultra-reliable and low latency communication, and support for connecting a massive number of machine type communication, resolving the limitation of 4G networks. However, the targeted services by 5G networks can be separated to both Narrowband and broadband services. Where enhanced mobile broadband services can be categorised as 5G broadband services, while ultra-reliable and low latency communications, and massive machine type communications can be classified as 5G narrowband services. 5G Narrowband services are seen as enablers of self-driven cars, mission critical application, industry automation and smart cities. 5G broadband services are targeting applications such as 3D video, ultra-high definition screens and cloud based game/work. However, the standardization is still ongoing and many issues are still being investigated by 3GPP. This paper aims at investigating the challenges of accommodating both 5G broadband and

© ICST Institute for Computer Sciences, Social Informatics and Telecommunications Engineering 2018
V. Odumuyiwa et al. (Eds.): AFRICOMM 2017, LNICST 250, pp. 204–209, 2018.
https://doi.org/10.1007/978-3-319-98827-6_18

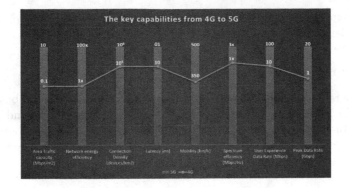

Fig. 1. The key capabilities between 4G and 5G networks [1].

5G narrowband services in the same network in terms of connectivity requirement, spectrum demand, and architecture requirement for 5G Radio Access Network.

The rest of the paper is organised as follows: Sect. 2 will give an overview of the requirements for realizing 5G and Sect. 3 presents the enabling technologies for the realization of a converged narrowband and broadband 5G network. Section 4 presents the current challenges encountered by the developers of 5G systems and will be followed by a conclusion in Sect. 5.

2 Requirements for Realizing 5G Systems

The aim of 4G was to increase support for broadband services. Networks beyond 4G are expected to further increase support for broadband services, by enhancing the peak data rate to multi-gigabits per second [2]. In addition to increased peak data rate, 5G also aims at increasing the user experience data rate, spectrum efficiency, mobility, latency, connection density, network energy efficiency and area traffic capacity as seen in Fig. 1. The following subsections will discuss the targets by 5G and their importance relevancy with respect to both narrowband and broadband services.

2.1 Enhanced Data Rates

The 3GPP standards beyond the current 4G standards will be expected to provide better throughput (average data rate) per connection as compared to its predecessors in order to meet the requirements of broadband services. There are three types of data rates: peak data rate, cell-edge and user experience data rate. Peak data rate is experienced on the base station, which refers to the highest theoretically achievable data rate in an error-free conditions and assignable to only one user-equipment (EU) when all the radio resource are utilized for the corresponding link. The peak data rates are expected to be in the range of 10–50 Gbps for user device at low speeds regardless of a user's location [3]. This is expected to solve the 4G cell edge problem of undesirable data rates. However, the equal improvement of data rate regardless of the UE location is what 5G aims to achieve [3].

2.2   Ultra-reliable and Low Latency

The latency requirement aims to reduce the time delay between the base station and the UE. 4G systems can achieve end-to-end latency of 50 ms and over-the-air latency of 10 ms. However, 5G systems are aiming to achieve an expected to end-to-end latency of 5 ms and over-the-air latency of 1 ms. Both services require low latency [4].

2.3   Very High Bandwidth Density

One of the envisioned 5G network improvement from its predecessor, is its ability to achieve wide coverage, while managing heavy traffic at a rate of 1000 fold of the system capacity per given area. The aim in the high bandwidth density is to achieve high area traffic capacity and high spectrum efficiency [6]. Conventionally, 3GPP broadband based networks are deployed in exclusively licensed spectrum, which has been shown to results to a minimum spectrum utility [5]. In response to this realization, the U.S. has adopted the use of the spectrum access system (SAS), which is a three-tier model between a permanent user, licensed opportunistic user and license-exempt users. A similar system is employed in the UK, which is a two-tier model [5].

2.4   Very High Connection Density

The introduction of 5G narrowband services is associated with a massive number of connected devices, which transmit sporadic and small amounts of data. The expectation is that these devices would be invisible and have less complexity, implying the need for lightweight radio-module design and efficient communication modes. The devices supporting 5G narrowband services should achieve a connection density of 10^6 [7].

2.5   Very High Mobility

5G will be required to support various high mobility environments, including trains, cars and airplanes, implying that most use case scenarios in 5G systems will require high mobility. This requirement is for both broadband and narrowband services.

2.6   Evolution or Revolution in the RAN

The architecture of 5G will be determined by the enabling technologies that will be adopted in the standard, which is still in its development as mentioned above. 5G will be a cornerstone for all broadband and narrowband based services

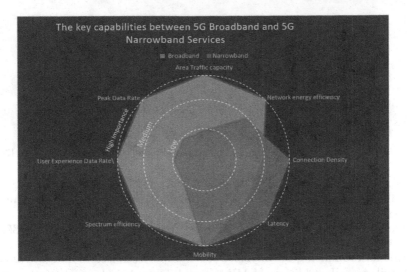

Fig. 2. The key capabilities between 5G's narrowband and broadband services.

and the definition of technologies that will be adopted in 5G will be concluded around 2020. These technologies will determine its fitting characterization as either evolution or revolution standard. 5G might therefore require the radio access network (RAN) and architectural level to be revolutionised. Moreover, the drastic change in the RAN will enforce a change in end-user devices [8].

3 Enabling Technologies for Broadband and Narrowband

In order for 5G systems to meet the services requirements as shown in Fig. 2, the following are the potential enabling technologies of such envisioned network or system: small cell deployment, utilization of the millimetre-wave band, M-MIMO, and beamforming.

3.1 Small Cells and Millimetre-Wave Band

With the anticipated increase in the rate of broadband services, network densification through the use of small cell networks seems to be an inevitable solution for 5G systems. Small cells are necessary for offloading traffic from macrocells. Their deployment can either be indoors or outdoors, which is associated with cost-effective solution to network capacity issues resulting from the massive growth in mobile traffic [8]. Smalls cells will definitely be part of the 5G networks, especially when considering that the World Radio Communications in 2015 conference made the spectrum at the 6-GHz band available [9] for use in mobile communication. Where it is understood that the coverage of millimeter-wave band will force the use of small cells. Millimetre-wave technology is investigated because of its wider bands provision and the saturation in lower bands. Still more spectrum is recommended to be allocated for 5G networks as shown in Fig. 3.

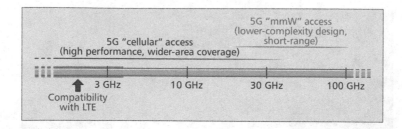

Fig. 3. The millimeter-wave band as a potential spectrum for 5G networks [7].

3.2 Massive Multiple-Input, Multiple-Output and Beamforming

Massive multiple-input, multiple-output (M-MIMO) is achieved by integration of advanced antennas with massive numbers of elements. M-MIMO is a useful technique for minimizing the intensity of RF imperfections and mitigate interference distribution. In addition, M-MIMO can be used to enhance the coverage for high-data-rate, especially given the number of narrowband devices anticipated. On the other hand, beamforming, which is achieved when multiple antenna elements are used to form narrow beams, is another vital technique for both 5G narrowband and broadband services.

4 Current Development and Challenges

4.1 Current Development

Current networks are able to provide data rates of more than 200 Mbps. SK Telecom in South Korea has heavily invested in 5G research and has about 29 million customers. This trial will heavily depend on M-MIMO use [10]. KT cooperation is preparing to launch its 5G trial service during the PyeongChang's Olympic Winter Games. KT's 5G network is based on the 28 GHz spectrum, different than SK telecom [11]. Furthermore, Fujitsu has managed to develop a millimetre-wave prototype receiver, achieving data rates at around 20-Gbps. In addition, Nokia has employed the 73-GHz carrier with 2-GHz bandwidth to achieve data rates of 10 Gbps, corresponding to a latency around of 1 ms [11].

4.2 Challenges Toward 5G Realization

Network planning and traffic management is vital in addressing the issue of adopting small cell and managing coordination between the different cells. Especially, given that network operators will be able to optimize the organization of macrocells and picocells. However, femtocells are self-organizing type of small cells. Moreover, there will be lot of handover taking place in 5G network if not well planned. The complication of the design will be escalated by the difficulty to estimate indoor network capacity.

M-MIMO have their own challenges, when deploying a number of RF chains is not realizable. Furthermore, the energy efficiency of M-MIMO, decreases with the increase in the number of RF chains, leading to the need for the development of channel estimation and beamforming algorithms that considers the limitation on the number of RF chains [12].

5 Conclusion

5G will increase efficiency, capacity, adaptability, innovation, and its ability to support narrowband and broadband services will provide access to information and sharing of data anywhere and anytime for anyone and anything. However, it will be a challenging task given the contrasting requirements between the two services. The evolution/revolution future network is necessary to meet the demands posed by the ever grown user equipment. This paper has shown the requirements of such networks and their enabling technologies with the associated challenges that still need to be addressed for its realization.

References

1. ITU agrees on key 5G performance requirements for IMT-2020. https://www.itu.int/en/mediacentre/Pages/2017-PR04.aspx
2. Sharma, S., Miller, R., Francini, A.: A cloud-native approach to 5G network slicing. IEEE Commun. Mag. **55**(8), 120–127 (2017)
3. Meng, X., Li, J., Zhou, D., Yang, D.: 5G technology requirements and related test environments for evaluation. China Commun. **13**(2), 42–51 (2016)
4. Benisha, M., Prabu, R.T., Bai, V.T.: Requirements and challenges of 5G cellular systems. In: 2016 2nd International Conference on Advances in Electrical, Electronics, Information, Communication and Bio-Informatics (AEEICB) (2016)
5. Licensed Shared Access (LSA) and Authorised Shared Access (ASA). https://www.gsma.com/spectrum/wp-content/uploads/2013/04/GSMA-Policy-Position-on-LSA-ASA.pdf
6. International Telecommunications Union, Recommendation ITU-R M.2083-0: IMT vision - framework and overall objectives of the future development of IMT for 2020 and beyond, Geneva, Switzerland (2015)
7. Dahlman, E.: 5G wireless access: requirements and realization. IEEE Commun. Mag. **52**(12), 42–47 (2014)
8. Al-Falahy, N., Alani, O.Y.: Technologies for 5G networks: challenges and opportunities. IT Prof. **19**(1), 12–20 (2017)
9. ITU towards IMT for 2020 and beyond. http://www.itu.int/en/ITU-R/study-groups/rsg5/rwp5d/imt-2020/Pages/default.aspx
10. SK Telecom Exec Talks 5G Tech, 2017 Trials. http://spectrum.ieee.org/tech-talk/telecom/wireless/executive-from-sk-telecoms-research-lab-talks-key-5g-technologies-2017-trials
11. KT to have trial run of 5G mobile network at PyeongChang Games. http://english.yonhapnews.co.kr/business/2017/03/14/0502000000AEN20170314004900320.html
12. Bogale, T.E., Le, L.B.: Massive MIMO and mmWave for 5G wireless HetNet: potential benefits and challenges. IEEE Veh. Technol. Mag. **11**(1), 64–75 (2016)

Design of Novel High Density, Fault Tolerant Protocol for Cluster Based Routing in Ad-Hoc Networks

Frodouard Minani and Santhi Kumaran[✉]

African Center of Excellence in Internet of Things (ACEIoT),
College of Science and Technology, University of Rwanda, Kigali, Rwanda
frodominani@gmail.com, santhikr@yahoo.com

Abstract. Clustering in ad-hoc networks is a widely used approach to ease implementation of various problems such as routing and resource management. Ad-hoc wireless networks perform the difficult task of multi-hop communication in environment without a dedicated infrastructure, with mobile nodes and changing network topology. In this article, after determining the cluster members and cluster head, distance and energy for each node are carried out per cluster head and cluster; data gathered from cluster members are relayed to the main server. The results showed that the proposed algorithm is scalable, has less number of dropped packets, uses high energy during the path discovery, and handles fault tolerance problem during the packets transmission. A new algorithm for clustering which merges network nodes to form higher level clusters by increasing their levels, their energy and their density is proposed. Its operations are provided in simulation environment of network simulation tool 2 (ns-2).

Keywords: Cluster density · Fault tolerance performance metrics
Network lifetime · Routing protocol · Throughput

1 Introduction

Ad-hoc network which is a local area network (LAN) that is built spontaneously as devices connect where there are a number of wireless nodes that are self-organized. The movement of the nodes enables them to generate multiple routes. Thus, accurate routes must be determined for those nodes. A new algorithm must therefore be developed to design a routing protocol that adapts to network topology changes. Clustering organizes the ad-hoc networks hierarchically and creates clusters of nodes which are geographically adjacent and each cluster is managed by a cluster head and other nodes may act as cluster gateway or cluster member [1]. Each node in the network or cluster also acts as a router forwarding data packets for other nodes. The cluster density is defined as the expected number of clusters per unit area [2]. Due to node mobility, there may be a chance of node or link failure and node have to consume more energy to transfer the packets from source to destination. Node failure occurs when there is a lack of power and it causes route failure in the network.

© ICST Institute for Computer Sciences, Social Informatics and Telecommunications Engineering 2018
V. Odumuyiwa et al. (Eds.): AFRICOMM 2017, LNICST 250, pp. 210–222, 2018.
https://doi.org/10.1007/978-3-319-98827-6_19

We proposed a novel high density, fault tolerant protocol for cluster based routing in ad-hoc networks with varying node's density which handles fault tolerance problem. The algorithm supports addition and deletion of dynamic nodes, ensuring the continuation of service despite the presence of failures [3]. Results were simulated using ns-2. The rest of the paper is organized as follows: Sect. 2 describes the related works. Section 3 talks about the proposed models, clustering algorithm and parameter metrics. Section 4 deals with the analysis of simulation results. Section 5 provides conclusion and future works.

2 Related Works

In Ad-hoc networks, many clustering algorithms have been proposed in the past. An algorithm called Linked Cluster Architecture (LCA) which was initially proposed by Baker and Ephremides [4]. A small variation to LCA was proposed by Ephremides, Wieselthier and Baker in [5] as a lowest ID algorithm. In this algorithm, a node which has the lowest ID among its neighbors is selected as the head node (Cluster-head). It retains its utility as a point of reference for producing reasonably stable cluster control architecture as written by Gerla and Tsai in Xue and Nahrstedt [6] confirmed that devising a fault-tolerant routing algorithm for ad-hoc networks is inherently hard. In [7], the authors designed an efficient algorithm, called the end-to-end fault tolerant routing (E2FT) algorithm, which is capable of significantly lowering the packet overhead, while guaranteeing a certain packet delivery rate. Following the work of Xue and Nahrstedt, Oommen and Misra proposed weak-estimation learning based fault-tolerant routing protocol for Ad-hoc networks.

In [8] Zhou, Xia proposed an algorithm called location based fault tolerant routing algorithm (FTRA). In this algorithm based on geographical location information networks divided in to grid, when faults occur, the proposed algorithm select alternate route from unused at hop in normal routing path, the route selection depends upon location information of its neighbors grids. In [9], Qin and Pang proposed fault-tolerance cluster head based (FTCH) routing protocol reduce misbehaving node in the network. If faulty node occurs, the proposed protocol provide packet delivery fraction guarantee and reduce routing overhead. In [10], they proposed a trusted fault tolerant (TFT) model based on location aided routing protocol along with user recovery features. It covers link failures during packet forwarding and location failures.

3 Proposed Models, Parameter Metrics and Clustering Algorithm

3.1 Proposed Model

As shown on Fig. 1, in this model, around 33 nodes and 3 clusters have been used where each cluster is composed of 11 nodes. Each node in the group communicates regularly with the leader by sending his information: identifier, energy level, neighboring nodes, number of times it stopped, and the directory replicas that exist in the node. It is assumed that each node has a unique address, called the ID_node, a line refers to one given. For each cluster, a cluster head (CH) is elected which initiates the communication among the others. To elect a cluster head, the cluster energy of a node is measured and calculated. During the packet transmission, when a fault occurs in the system, the algorithm designed searches for a new way so that the communication continues to happen by using the backup nodes. Every node in the network can communicate straightaway with the other nodes located in the transmission range.

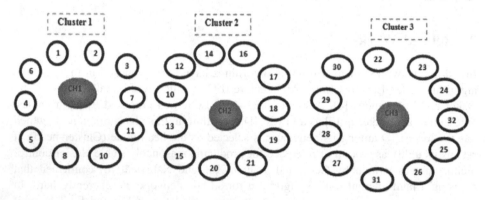

Fig. 1. Proposed model (cluster and cluster head formation)

The failure of some links and nodes is considered as criticism and can divide the network into several partitions. This reduces the data availability and leads to data inconsistency. To increase the data availability, a new protocol or algorithm has been designed to help the communication keeps going on within clusters. The model proposed for tolerating faults in the ad-hoc networks is a model which consists of four sub-services as shown in Fig. 2 below:

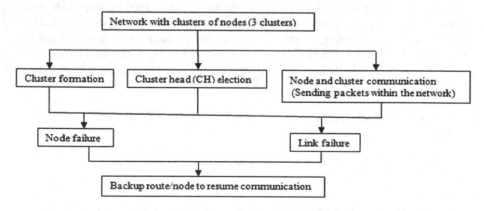

Fig. 2. Fault tolerance model of the algorithm

According to Fig. 2, the fault tolerance algorithm functions in two phases:

- Choosing the backup nodes or routes.
- Resume the communication of nodes within clusters.

3.2   Proposed Flowcharts

As shown in Fig. 3 of this model (flowchart), after forming nodes and clusters, cluster head for each cluster is selected. When faults (node or link failure) occur, the communication is resumed by choosing the backup routes or backup nodes. As indicated on Fig. 4, the average energy of the network is calculated; the nodes having energy more than average energy of network are added to the set of candidate cluster heads. Distance between each candidate cluster head and center is calculated. Candidate cluster head having lowest distance from the center is selected as cluster head for this cluster and remaining nodes from the candidate cluster head set becomes normal nodes.

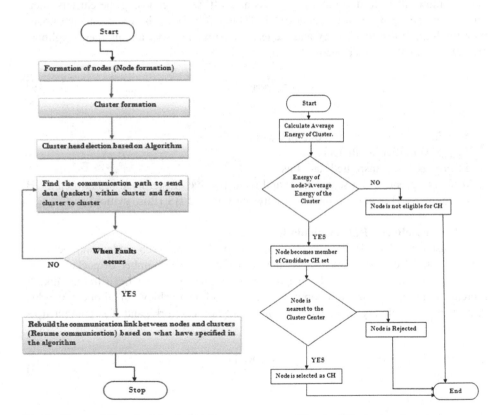

Fig. 3. Proposed flowchart for fault tolerance   **Fig. 4.** CH election flowchart

3.3 Parameter Metrics

(i) The Cluster Density

The experiment showed that the cluster density (ρ) i.e., the ratio of the number of cluster head (N) neighborhoods to cluster diameter (d) (if the given node become cluster head) is given by the following formula:

$$\rho = \frac{N}{d}.$$
(1)

(ii) Energy Consumed by Node within Cluster

Anode with higher energy consumption fails faster. When a cluster head depicts its energy, it fails and also shatters the whole cluster with its links and entails lots of maintenance costs. On the other hand, cluster heads have the highest responsibilities among other nodes. Therefore, they need and consume the highest energy in network and are more likely to drain the energy. As a result, when choosing the clusters, their remaining energy needs to be concerned. Taking this factor into account, the nodes with the highest residual energy and the least consumed energy among their neighbors are selected as the cluster heads. The factor is given as follows:

$$E_n = E_{amp} * k * d.$$
(2)

where:

E_n: Energy consumed by node in cluster
E_{amp}: Amplifier coefficient
k: Number of transmitted data bits
d: distance between a sensor node and its respective cluster head or between a CH to another CH nearer to the BS or between CH and BS (Base station).

(iii) Packet Delivery Ratio Calculation

The Cluster head (CH) initiates sending the packets between nodes and between clusters. The Packet delivery ratio is the ratio between the number of packets transmitted by a traffic source and the number of packets received by a traffic sink. It represents the maximum throughput that the network can achieve in ad-hoc networks. A high packet delivery ratio is desired in an ad-hoc networks and it is computed as follows:

$$PDR = \frac{\sum PRCD}{\sum PSCS} * 100.$$
(3)

where:

- PRCD: Packets received by cluster destination
- PSCS: Packets sent by cluster source
- PDR: Packets delivery ration.

(iv) End-to-end Delay Computation

Because of packets movement between nodes to nodes and clusters to clusters, delays can happen. End-to-end delay is the average time delay for data packets to reach from the source node to the destination node. It includes processing, queuing and propagation delay of the link. The performance is better when packet end-to-end delay is low. It is computed by the below formula:

$$EED = \frac{1}{N} \sum_{n=1}^{N} (TSn - TRn).\tag{4}$$

where

- TRn: Time at which data packets n has been sent
- TSn: Time at which data packets n has been received
- N: Total number of data packets received

(v) Throughput Calculation

For the cluster based routing, the parameter throughput has been taken into consideration which is the total packets successfully delivered to individual destinations over total time.

$$Tp = \frac{\sum P}{T}.\tag{5}$$

where:

- Tp: Throughput
- P: Number of packets successfully received at the cluster destination
- T: Unit time.

3.4   Clustering Algorithms

(i) Algorithm 3.3.1: Cluster Creation Algorithm

```
1: Begin
2: Cluster (N);
3: Set the position of N;
4: Calculate the speed of each node;
5: From N;
6:    If avg speed of each node is low then
7:       Form the cluster size smaller;
8:          Else make the cluster size bigger;
9:    Endif;
10: End;
```

(ii) Algorithm 3.3.2: Density-Based Algorithm

```
Step 1: Begin
Step 2: Create a graph whose nodes are the points to be clustered;
Step 3: For each core-point c, create an edge from c to every point
          in the □- neighborhood of c;
Step 4: Set N to the nodes of the graph;
          If N does not contain any core points then
             Terminate;
          Endif;
Step 5: Pick a core point c in N;
Step 6: Let X be the set of nodes that can be reached from c by going
        forward;
          Create a cluster containing X□{C};
          N=N/(X□{C});
          Continue with step 4;
        End;
```

As indicated in the Algorithm 3.3.2, c represents the core point and N represents a set of nodes of a graph. □ represents the edge of points in the cluster

(iii) Algorithm 3.3.3: Fault Tolerant Clustering Algorithm

```
Step 1: Begin
Step 2: Find the eligible node;
          For all the nodes in a cluster;
             If node=already (CH) then
                go to next node;
             Endif;
          Check the node status in memory table;
             If nodestatus=fail(trans_id) then
                go to next node;
              else node can be selected;
             Endif;
         move to step3;
         refresh;
       check for node availability for n sec;
         if NodeAvailability then
           Continue;
         select the next CH;
           else Put in (ListLow);
         Endif;
```

Step 3: Calculate the average threshold (Th_{avg});
For each node in cluster $C_1 \ldots C_n$;
Calculate threshold;

$$Th(n) = \left[\cfrac{p}{1 - p[r \bmod (\frac{1}{p})]}\right] \quad \text{if n belongs to G;}$$

Th(n)=0   if n doesn't belong to G;
Select nodes with values above the threshold value;

$$Th(avg) = \frac{\sum Th(n)}{n};$$

If Th(n)>=Th(avg)then
    put in (ListHigh);
        else put in (ListLow);
    Endif;

Step 4: Calculate the available node energy;
For all the nodes in the ListHigh;
    Energy=P*T;
Calculate the available energy of each node;
    $E_{avail}=E / E\max$;
Create a List $E_{availsort}$ in descending order;

Step 5: Calculate minimum distance and throughput;
For the first node in $E_{availsort}$;
Calculate minimum distance;

$$d = \sqrt{[(x_2 - x_1)_2 + (y_2 - y_1)_2]};$$

Calculate throughput;

$$Tp = \frac{Sp}{Tt};$$

If 2 nodes have same energy then
    Node with d_{min}=CH;
If 2 nodes have same energy and same minimum distance then
    Node with Tp_{max}=CH;
  Endif;
Endif;

Step 6: Check the link/node failure;
For the transmission;
    If node/link failure then
        Backup node/link;
        else system is down;
    Endif;
  End;

As shown in Algorithm 3.3.3, for finding the eligible nodes, we focus on the nodes past record of not being a cluster head already and not failed for the last n operations. The average threshold (Th_{avg}) of the node is the value for which the node will survive in the network. Before electing any node as CH, we take into account of its threshold value where in its formula, p is the prearranged percentage of cluster heads (e.g. $p = 0.1$), r is the current round of iteration and G is the set of nodes that have not been cluster heads in the last 1/p rounds and n is a random number between 0 and 1. For energy calculation, P is the power and T is the time. In the formula of distance, x_1, x_2, y_1 and y_2 are the coordinates. Throughput (Tp) is calculated as size of the packet (Sp) over the transmission time (Tt) while the available energy of each node equals to the current energy (E) over maximum energy (E_{max}).

4 Analysis of Simulation Results

In order to evaluate the performance of the proposed clustering algorithm, we simulated and showed the results in ns-2 [11]. The nodes are randomly deployed in a circular area. The number of nodes varies from 33 to 35. The initial energy of normal node is 35 J. Table 1 summarizes the simulation parameters and their default values.

Table 1. Simulation parameters

Parameter	Value
Number of nodes N	33–35
Initial energy E0	35 J
Simulation time	2.0 ms
Channel type	Wireless channel
End simulation time	10.0 ms
Scenario size	200 m × 200 m

Figure 5 shows the simulation environment where the nodes are formed and grouped into clusters as indicated. Each node is given a number in each cluster to be differentiated with others. The nodes are numbered from 0 to 34. It also shows the packets dropped from the network. Figure 6 indicates the CH election in each cluster based on the energy consumption of each node, the cluster head (CH) is the node with high energy and it is represented by red color.

Figure 7 indicates the process of fault tolerance (FT) which is the ability of a system to continue its operation after the failure of one of the nodes or link. When faults occur, choose the backup route or nodes to avoid the system failure and maintain the system functionality (availability). At the node 6 (with blue color) in the first cluster, there is a failure but the there is a backup route where data which was supposed to pass through that node tried to find another route to pass through. Figure 8 (X-axis: Number of nodes, Y-axis: size of the network area) shows the system performance with the parameter density. The algorithm indicates that when the size of the area increases while the number of nodes remains constant, the cluster density decreases while it increases when the area becomes big at the same time the number of nodes increases.

Figure 9 (X-axis: Node energy, Y-axis: Nodes) indicates the Cluster head selection graph where the node with high energy is selected as CH. The initial node energy was 0.0000 J and there was not CH cluster head elected but as long as the Energy of the node increases (many nodes which have the higher energy), many CHs are elected.

From Fig. 10 (X-axis: Time, Y-axis: Packet delivery ratio), we can see that when time increases, many packets are lost as well as they delay to reach the destination. The red line indicates dropped packets and green line shows the delayed packets. The delayed packets are implicitly increased when the time is moving but this delay starts at certain time after the packets transmission. You can see that the delay starts at 3.000 ms after the starting of the simulation and when the simulation time was 0.000 ms, no packet loss (PDR was 0.000).

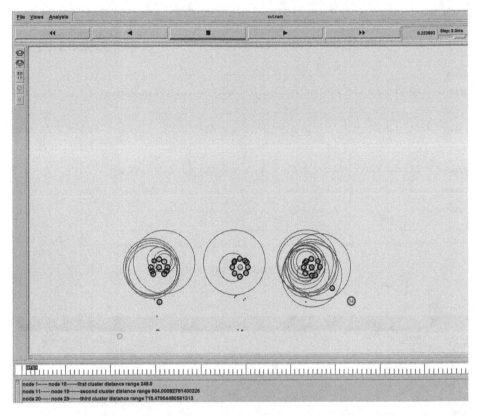

Fig. 5. Nodes with cluster formation and dropped packets

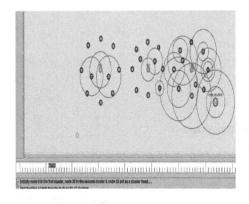

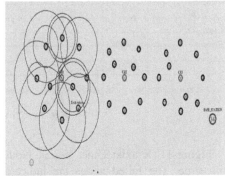

Fig. 6. CH election scenario (Color figure online)

Fig. 7. Node failure in cluster 1(Node 6) (Color figure online)

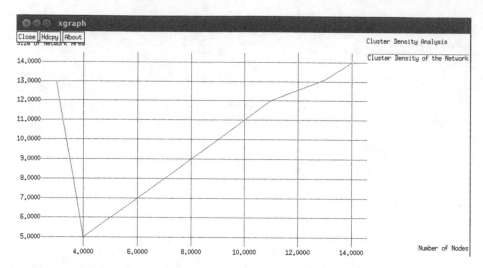

Fig. 8. Cluster density analysis

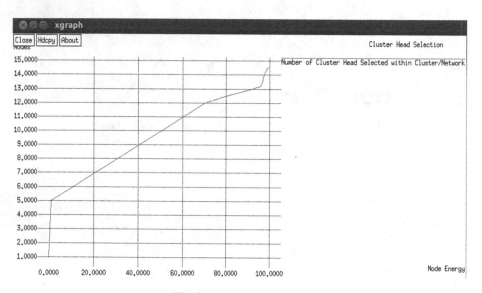

Fig. 9. CH selection graph

Figure 11 (X-axis: Time, Y-axis: Nodes) shows the number of dead (failed) nodes with time. The failed nodes are indicated by green line and the active nodes are represented by red line. It is indicating that as the time increases, active nodes are higher which means that during the packets transmission, small number of nodes failed to transmit as well as the backup nodes or routes is taking place to resume the communication.

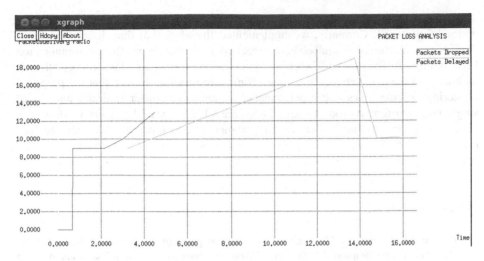

Fig. 10. Packet loss analysis within network vs. time (Color figure online)

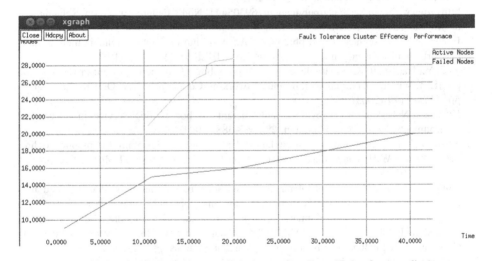

Fig. 11. Fault tolerance cluster efficiency performance (Color figure online)

5   Conclusion and Future Works

In this paper, the design of novel high density, fault tolerant protocol for cluster based routing in ad-hoc networks is about to increase the system performance when the faults occurs within nodes or within the transmission link and to test the system performance in case network nodes are increased within cluster (cluster density). Several network performance metrics have been tested such as the network throughput, the packets loss, the cluster density, the network lifetime to see how the new developed algorithm works. The goal was to investigate current research work on fault tolerance and to detect the faults in ad-hoc networks and test the system performance in case number of nodes is increased. Currently, we implemented the algorithm that detects the faults during data transmission and elaborate backup nodes/routes so that communication keeps going on. The energy of each node is considered in order to get energy efficient path to send the data between the nodes. Simulation results showed that the proposed clustering scheme gives better performance in terms of cluster size and number of single node clusters. As today, technologies are advancing, in the future work on this paper, we recommend to develop a routing algorithm which handles the fault tolerance problems and high density in other network technologies such LTE or LTE-Advanced where the cells act instead of having networks nodes as it is in ad-hoc networks.

References

1. Rezaee, M., Yaghmaee, M.: Cluster based routing protocol for mobile ad hoc networks. Department of Computer Engineering, Ferdowsi University of Mashhad, Iran, pp. 1–5 (2009)
2. Natsheh, E.: Impact of varying offered data load on density-based routing in mobile ad-hoc networks. J. Netw. Technol. **6**, 87–109 (2015)
3. https://www.researchgate.net/publication/269305441_Node_Failure_Effect_on_Reliability_of_Mobile_Ad-Hoc_Networks
4. Baker, D.J., Wieselthier, J.E., Ephremides, A.: A design concept for reliable mobile radio networks with frequency hoping signaling. Proc. IEEE **75**(1), 56–73 (1987)
5. Xue, Y., Nahrstedt, K.: Fault tolerant routing in mobile ad hoc networks. In: Proceedings of the IEEE Wireless Communications and Networking Conference, New Orleans, Louisiania, pp. 1174–1179 (2003)
6. Xue, Y., Nahrstedt, K.: Providing fault-tolerant ad hoc routing service in adversarial environments. Wirel. Pers. Commun. **29**, 367–388 (2004)
7. Zhou, J., Xia, C.: A location-based fault-tolerant routing algorithm for mobile ad hoc networks. In: WRI International Conference on Communications and Mobile Computing, vol. 2, pp. 92–96 (2009)
8. Qin, Y., Kong L.P.: A fault-tolerance cluster head based routing protocol for ad hoc networks. In: IEEE Vehicular Technology Conference, pp. 2472–2476 (2008)
9. Chandrasekaran, S., Udhayakumar, S., Mohan Bharathy, U., Jitendra Kumar Jain, D.: Trusted fault tolerant model of MANET with data recovery. In: 4th IEEE International Conference on Intelligent Networks and Intelligent Systems, pp. 21–24 (2011)
10. Hauspie, M., Simplot, D., Carle, J.: Partition detection in mobile ad-hoc networks. In: Proceeding of the 2nd Mediterranean Workshop on Ad Hoc Networks, Mahdia, Tunisia (2003)
11. The Network Simulator - ns-2. http://www.isi.edu/nsnam/ns/

ICT Applications for Development

SafeTransit: A Transit Safety Information Gathering Decision System

Korede Oluwafemi Lawrence and Victor Odumuyiwa[✉]

Department of Computer Sciences, University of Lagos, Akoka, Lagos, Nigeria
oluwafemikorede@gmail.com, vodumuyiwa@unilag.edu.ng

Abstract. The present situation of public transportation system in sub-Saharan Africa especially in Nigeria reveals to a large extent, a low level of effectiveness and safety. The need to provide safe transportation services to users in developing countries cannot be overemphasized. Hence, this paper provides a decision making model that helps users of public transport systems avoid unsafe transportation services (vehicles) by providing them with a community-aggregated information about vehicles and their personnel.

Keywords: Commuters · SafeTransit · PTS (Public transit systems/service)
Decision making

1 Introduction

Safety of Public Transit System (PTS) in Nigeria over the years has become an issue of great concern precipitating various calls for help from different institutions and corporate bodies towards ensuring a safe system. In view of the current rate of avoidable accidents happening as a result of technical faults or personnel skill and attitude, there is a need for an effective oversight of the public transport sector in order to guide the activities of the transport workers (mostly from the private sector) and also ensure safety of lives of road users. Transportation functions are an indispensable basis for any country's development and have the ability to provide benefits to the society.

With a current estimated human population of 180 million, Nigeria is a country with a high level of vehicular population estimated at over 7.6 million with a total road length of about 194,000 km (comprising 34,120 km of federal, 30,500 km of state and 129,580 km of local roads), Nigeria has suffered severe losses to fatal car accidents [1].

Nigeria's population density varies in rural and urban areas at about 51.7% and 48.3% respectively and translates to a population-road ratio of 860 persons per square kilometer, indicating intense traffic pressure on the available road network. This factor has contributed to the high road traffic accidents in the country [2].

Nigeria is ranked second highest in the rate of road accidents among 193 countries of the world [3]. According to a World Health Organization (WHO) report, one in every four-road accident deaths in Africa occurs in Nigeria. The WHO survey as well as the Federal Road Safety Commission (FRSC) report of 5,693 fatal road accidents in 2009 leave no doubt about the dangerous situations on Nigerian roads.

© ICST Institute for Computer Sciences, Social Informatics and Telecommunications Engineering 2018
V. Odumuyiwa et al. (Eds.): AFRICOMM 2017, LNICST 250, pp. 225–231, 2018.
https://doi.org/10.1007/978-3-319-98827-6_20

The causes of fatal car accidents are conventionally categorized into human, mechanical, and environmental factors. The human factor accounts for up to 90% of accidents [4], while mechanical and environmental factors account for the remaining 10%. The human factors include driver fatigue, poor knowledge of road signs and regulations, illiteracy, health problems, excessive speeding, drug abuse, and over-confidence while at the steering wheel. Among the mechanical factors that lead to fatal car accidents are poor vehicle maintenance, tyre blowouts, poor lights, un-roadworthy vehicles, and broken-down vehicles on the road without adequate warning. Environmental factors include heavy rainfall, harmattan winds, sun reflection, heavy wind, potholes, and un-tarred roads. These factors have independently and or collectively contributed to the high rate of fatal road accidents in Nigeria.

Road traffic crash is one of the causes of deaths in Nigeria as no day passes by without recording at least 20 crashes resulting in an average of 15 deaths [5]. According to a WHO fact sheet report, road injuries killed 1.3 million people in 2015 and are the leading cause of death among people aged between 15 and 29 years. These statistics coupled with the present nature of the PTS as well as the ineffective running of the system by the concerned bodies makes it imperative for users of the system to personally ensure their safety by making informed decisions.

Most PTS users depend on their intuition, formed from available information, in making decisions relating to their PTS choice. Information to support travel decisions is acquired actively (by reading, asking, listening) or passively (through experience) from various sources, and it is used, along with stored knowledge, to make choices. [6]. Access to public transit related information is a major component to any decision making process (human or artificial). It's been argued that drivers could save travel time by switching routes if they had information on current traffic conditions [7]. It has also been observed that information about road conditions and accidents provided by ATIS's allows travellers to make an informed route decision, more precisely, taking cautions or avoiding dangerous routes and choosing a safer path [8]. Reliance on intuition to help users make informed decisions is limited and this makes the need for a more robust and well informed decision making system imperative.

2   Related Works

2.1   LA Metro Transit Watch

LA Metro Transit Watch [9] is a smart phone security application built to report transit-related crimes. This application allows the public to assist law enforcement agents by reporting suspicious and criminal activity in a timely manner. This application is essentially a reporting tool to report incidents and does not prevent accidents or crime. It does not also alert commuters of the likely danger they could encounter as a result of boarding a particular vehicle. LA Metro Transit watch is available on the two major mobile platforms (Android and iOS).

2.2 Matserve Msafiri

This is a road safety application developed in Kenya [10] that analyses the speed of public transport vehicles. This helps in saving lives on the road and also to improve the quality of service in public transport. It is a road safety application built for the android platform that crowd sources speed feeds and reports from passengers on-board public service vehicles to help reduce the number of lives lost in road accidents due to avoidable human errors and impunity. The application detects the exact moving speed of a vehicle and instantly generates an alert and sends to relevant legal authorities if the allowed speed limit for the road is breached. This application allows users to report about reckless driving, overloading and over speeding among other challenges to mitigate accidents caused by human error and outright disregard for traffic laws. This application's central features include speed check and community policing.

3 Methodology

In developing SafeTransit, the methods employed include: (i) the development of a model highlighting the various phases that should be supported by the transit safety information gathering system; (ii) the implementation of the model as a mobile application for PTS users; and (iii) the preliminary evaluation of the system using few selected users.

4 SafeTransit Model and System Design

This paper proposes a model for transit safety information gathering and decision making. This model has six phases: (i) Source Validation: This phase ensures inputs to the system are accepted only from validated sources (users). (ii) Data Gathering: This phase determines how data about PTS vehicles and their personnel is to be gathered. (iii) Data Validation: Ensure only validated information supplied by users is allowed into the system; for example, the application can guard against gamification by getting global positioning system (GPS) coordinates at the point of data input. (iv) Data Analysis: Get trends from data supplied in phase two. (v) Transit Advice Generation: Propose decisions from patterns gotten from analyzed dataset and where possible taking into consideration the attributes of PTS personnel and users in making decisions. It has been noted that individual characteristics of PTS personnel impact on their decision making [11, 12]. Likewise the characteristics of PTS users influence their decision making process. Hence models (profiles) of the users should be inculcated in the advice generation phase. For example: the application can suggest best routes and PT systems based on current GPS location; the application rates each PTS and assigns a travel experience quotient. The application can then relay the comfort rating to the user on enquiry e.g. *"Hi, vehicle comfort rating is 45%. It is advised you look for a more suitable PTS"*. (vi) System Decision Validation: The application gets feedbacks on all application generated decisions and uses these to evaluate and improve the decision making process.

4.1   System Design and Implementation

In developing SafeTransit, all the phases from the proposed model were implemented. The application validates users by email and collects data about the vehicle, the route and user complaint or report about the trip or vehicle. In order to ensure correctness of input, users are blocked from adding more reports after two false or incorrect reports. The reports submitted by the users are validated by recognized regulatory bodies (in charge of ensuring vehicle's road-worthiness) whose task is to verify reports by checking out each reported vehicle, and reporting back the true state of the vehicle to the application.

The application has a public-facing website application (accessible on desktop and large-screen devices), mobile web (responsive for small and handheld devices) and a native mobile application for smartphones deployed on the android Operating System (OS). The web system's backend server is built using PHP for the business logic and MySQL for database. The application programming interface (API) gateway is implemented using the RESTFUL concept.

A simple use-case flow is itemized in the list below:

- A user who is about to board a PTS, checks the vehicle's plate number.
- The user types the number into the application to get information, if there is an existing report, the user can make his/her decision based on the generated advice.
- If no report is found, the user is left to use his intuition.
- The user can also add report en-route if an abnormality is observed.
- When a report is created, a notification is sent to the system administrator and the regulatory administrator using push notifications.
- The regulatory administrator checks the vehicle and also report back to the application.

A screenshot of the SafeTransit application is shown in Fig. 1.

(a)   (b)   (c)

Fig. 1. Safetransit screenshots (a) login page, (b) search result, (c) add report

4.2   System Architecture

The SafeTransit architecture as shown in Fig. 2 consists of the following modules: (i) Search: This functionality allows users to search the database for existing reports on a vehicle. (ii) Report: This function allows users to create a report about a vehicle and also allows the regulatory bodies to verify and attach a response to each user report or complaint. The module however does not allow the deletion of user-created report in order to maintain the integrity of the system. (iii) User Management: This functionality allows the system administrator to create, edit and delete users. Users of the system include commuters and government regulatory bodies and other administrators. (iv) Notifications: This feature is developed to manage the creation and sending of notifications and alerts using the mobile push notification. When users create a report, the report module generates an alert to be sent by the notification module to the regulatory bodies.

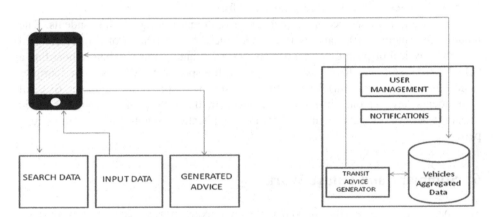

Fig. 2. Safetransit architecture

5   Evaluation and Feedback

To verify Safetransit's effectiveness and acceptance, an evaluation test was carried out among a group of twenty-five public transport users. The questions used in the evaluation are:

1. What are the factors considered before using a PTS?
2. Do you consider safety and security before using a PTS?
3. Have you ever regretted using a PTS due to safety/security factor?
4. How do you make meaningful deductions from listed response(s) in Q1?
5. Do you judge your observation mechanism employed in Q1 as being effective?
6. Do you think safetran provides a better mechanism for assessing PTS?
7. Can safetran bring some sanity into the public transport sector?
8. Can safetran help reduce the number of accidents on our roads?
9. Please give reasons to support your answer in 7 above.

10. Do you think the populace (Nigerians) will be willing to use safetran?
    (a) Yes, I am 100% percent sure.
    (b) Well, not too sure.
    (c) No, not too sure.
    (d) No, they won't be willing to use it.

The evaluation results showed that 50% of the respondents do not consider safety first when using a PTS and 90% agrees that their decision making hasn't always been effective. About 72% chose option B for question 10 above. This evaluation further proves the need for the SafeTransit system.

The evaluation results also showed that users' decision making processes are mostly influenced by the following: (i) Financial Capacity: Public transport users will likely go for the cheaper option. (ii) Time Constraints: Users will likely jostle for available options during rush hour periods. (iii) Religious beliefs: Religious beliefs can also make users ignore safety factors in making a decision. (iv) Physical Condition: Users will prefer a PTS that offers more comfort.

The results also showed some behavioral patterns among the respondents. The notable ones include: (i) Some users consider the safety condition of vehicle coupled with the physical disposition of the personnel (driver and conductor) before boarding a vehicle. (ii) Users will likely use a bad public transport vehicle for shorter journeys rather than long ones. (iii) Dependence on self intuition is not reliable. (iv) All respondents have at one time put themselves in danger's path by using a public transport service. (v) Use of the SafeTransit application is not feasible during rush periods.

6 Summary and Future Work

This paper work shows that human decision making process can be improved by exposing user to crowd sourced information. We plan to improve on Safetransit by introducing some intelligence into the application. Intelligence here means that the application will be able to learn from acquired data and make relevant recommendations to PTS users. We believe this will go a long way in bringing some sanity to the public transport sector and, directly and indirectly, reducing the number of accidents on our roads.

References

1. Ukoji, V.N.: Trends and patterns of fatal road accidents in Nigeria. Institute of African Studies, University of Ibadan. E-book (2014)
2. Federal Road Safety Commission. FRSC Annual Report (2012)
3. Agbonkhese, O., Yisa, G.L., Agbonkhese, E.G., Akanbi, D.O., Aka, E.O., Mondigha, E.B.: Road traffic accidents in Nigeria: causes and preventive measures. Civ. Environ. Res. 3(13), 90–99 (2013)
4. Joewono, T.B., Kubota, H.: Safety and security improvement in public transportation based on public perception in developing countries. IATSS Res. 30(1), 86–100 (2006)

5. Federal Road Safety Commission. FRSC Annual Report (2014)
6. Schofer, J.L., Khattak, A., Koppelman, F.S.: Behavioral issues in the design and evaluation of advanced traveler information systems. Transp. Res. Part C: Emerg. Technol. 1(2), 107–117 (1993)
7. Jones, E., Mahmassani, H., Herman, R., Walton, C.: Travel time variability in a commuting corridor: implications for electronic route guidance. In: Proceedings of First International Conference on Application of Advanced Technologies in Transportation Engineering, California, San Diego, pp. 27–32, February 1989
8. Kem, O., Balbo, F., Zimmermann, A.: Traveler-oriented advanced traveler information system based on dynamic discovery of resources: potentials and challenges. Transp. Res. Procedia 22, 635–644 (2017)
9. Transit Watch LA: Meet Our New LA Metro Transit Watch App. https://www.transitwatchla.org/app?device=desktop. Accessed 31 May 2017
10. Apps Africa: APPSKENYA: Road Safety App Aims to Change Transport in Africa. https://www.appsafrica.com/kenyan-road-safety-app-aims-to-change-transport-in-africa/. Accessed 31 May 2017
11. Wade, A.R., Ziedman, D., Rosenthal, T., Stein, A., Torres, J., Halati, A.: Laboratory assessment of driver route diversion in response to in-vehicle navigation and motorist information systems. Transp. Res. Rec. 1306, 82–91 (1991)
12. Mannering, F.L.: Poisson analysis of commuter flexibility in changing routes and departure times. Transp. Res. Part B: Methodol. 23(1), 53–60 (1989)

Tackling the Issues of Powering Mobile IoT Sensors and Systems Using Off-Grid Sources of Energy, the Case of the Real-Time Web-Based Temperature Monitoring System in Malawi

Alinafe Kaliwo[1,2(✉)] and Chomora Mikeka[1,2]

[1] Department of Electrical Engineering, The Polytechnic, University of Malawi,
Private Bag 303, Chichiri, Blantyre 3, Malawi
akaliwo@poly.ac.mw, chomora@gmail.com
[2] Department Physics, Chancellor College, University of Malawi, P.O. Box 280,
Zomba, Malawi

Abstract. Design and implementation of Internet of Things (IoT) devices and systems face the need of these systems to be self-powered. This is due to a number of characteristic and fundamental factors such as responsiveness, system mobility, portability, energy supply source adaptability. IoT covers a wide range of devices and systems, and an important subset of these involves real-time monitoring and control, particularly for both home and industrial applications. Other than just powering fixed sensor systems, the integration of such systems to mobile or transportation systems is a very important attributed characteristic but becomes a bit of a challenge to both designers and users in choosing the right option of power supply to the IoT systems. This paper illustrates some of such challenges and some of the efforts implemented to counter them in the design and implementation of a temperature monitoring system for transportation systems of dairy products in Malawi.

Keywords: Power source · IoT · Web-based · Temperature · Monitoring

1 Introduction

Various industry forecasts project that, by 2020, there will be around 50 billion devices connected to the Internet of Things (IoT), helping to engineer new solutions to societal-scale problems such as healthcare, energy conservation, transportation, etc. [1]. IoT devices are supposed to be deployed 'everywhere' and to be accessed 'any time' from 'anywhere' [2]. This attribute of IoT is the most fundamental application and ability of the very aim and objective of embracing IoT in sensing and monitoring. The fact that there are hundreds of sensors and actuators enables the implementation of IoT the best choice that replaces physical presence of human beings in monitoring and controlling systems.

A very good example of such systems is a temperature monitoring system for cold-chain management that was implemented in Malawi [3]. This system enables managers

© ICST Institute for Computer Sciences, Social Informatics and Telecommunications Engineering 2018
V. Odumuyiwa et al. (Eds.): AFRICOMM 2017, LNICST 250, pp. 232–238, 2018.
https://doi.org/10.1007/978-3-319-98827-6_21

to monitor their cold-chain assets using their mobile phones and laptops that are connected to the internet. The system also alerts the managers using the SMS service whenever high temperatures are detected. All this is done with an aim of reducing product damage and prevention of exorbitant losses.

The development of this Real-time, Web-based Temperature Monitoring System (RWTMS) has opened new opportunities for companies in Malawi, especially those in cold chain, to reduce their losses and expenses that arise due to poor monitoring of their both fixed and mobile cold chain assets. Although there are all these opportunities, the implementation of the RWTMS faces a very big bottleneck of an efficient source of power supply to power the system's operations like sensing, data processing and data communication.

In respect of paper structure, the rest of the paper is organized as follows: Sect. 2 presents methodology that was followed in coming up with a power supply system to the RWTMS. Analysis of the RWTMS power supply is outlined in Sect. 3 while Sect. 4 presents observations of results. Conclusions have been finally drawn in Sect. 5.

2   Methodology

2.1   Powering Mobile IoT Sensor Systems Using Off-Grid Power Supply Options

Study has shown that refrigerated shipments rise above the optimum temperature in 30% of trips from the supplier to the distribution centre, and in 15% of trips from the distribution centre to the stores [3, 4]. This calls for an innovative solution for monitoring the goods while in transit. Uninterrupted power supply is very crucial for the functionality of such a system.

In the implementation of the RWTMS, the power supply was approached in a very unique way. The following steps were employed: analysis of system's power needs and specification, brainstorming on the possible power supply options, implementation tests and use analysis of chosen power supply systems.

2.2   RWTMS System Power Supply Needs

The technology takes advantage of the presence of Open source technologies. Open-source software and hardware provide the opportunity to build low-cost information systems [5] that have brought to life new services and applications, made possible, directly or indirectly, by smart things.

The controller board was designed using Atmel programmable chips of designation ATMEGA 328/P which is a series of chips that are programmed using a wiring language of the calibre of c++ [6]. The board is enabled to transmit data wirelessly using a GSM adapter module that uses harnessed power of an inexpensive sim800L set of AT commands pre-programmed at the launch of the programme code into the micro-controller (Fig. 1).

Fig. 1. The SIM800L quad-band network mini GPRS GSM breakout module used in the RWTMS.

Temperature value signal is supplied to the board using high precision DS18B20 temperature sensors. This steel headed DS18B20 digital thermometer provides 9-bit to 12-bit Celsius temperature measurements and has an alarm function with non-volatile user-programmable upper and lower trigger points (Fig. 2).

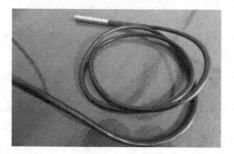

Fig. 2. The DS18B20 temperature sensor used in the RWTMS. (Source: Real-time, web-based temperature monitoring system for cold-chain management in Malawi)

The system was designed to be powered using a 12 V-direct current supply (12 VDC) to cover sensing (5 V sensor voltage), data processing (7–9 V Atmel chip voltage) and transmission (4.1 V GSM module voltage) power needs. This requires a minimum current specification of 1 Ampere (1 A).

2.3 Brainstorming Power Supply Options for the Transportation Monitoring Units

There were three power supply options that were suggested. The first one was the use of eight rechargeable 1.5 volts cells connected to form a 12-volt power supply. This would be charged prior to each and every deployment of the system into the refrigeration vehicle. The cells were Lithium ion battery type packed with terminals connected from negative to positive i.e. in series.

The second option was on the use of the same battery that is used to start the refrigeration system engine or the engine driving the vehicle. The last option was to use a solar panel connected to a 12-volt lead acid battery (Fig. 3).

Fig. 3. The 12 volts 7 AH battery used as a voltage supply for the system

3   The Analysis of the Adaptability of the Power Supply Options on the RWTMS

The power supply options were analyzed after running in-house tests and two options were tested on the refrigeration vehicles. The power supply options were tested based on three major factors namely: power specification, power recharge cycle intervals and easiness of use.

3.1   Power Specifications of the Power Supply Options

The system minimum requirements were identified to be 11 V at a flow of current of about 0.93 A. This was determined by varying the system input power parameters while checking the responsiveness of the system. Although this method proved to have some errors but it was noted that varying the power supply using a variable power adapter allowed good parameter analysis of the options of power supply.

Both the Arduino board and the Sim800L are provided with power light emitting diodes (LEDs). When the power being supplied is not adequate, the power LEDs lower their brightness. The other important indicator of the system's adaptability to power supply is the network LED found on Sim800L module. When power parametric specifications are below the minimum, the network LED keeps on blinking every half a second repeatedly. When the power supply is within the required range, the module finds the network and starts to blink at an interval of 3 s repeatedly.

It was noted that all the three options were able to produce enough power to drive the needed processes for the system. This is due to the fact that the power supply options' batteries were fully charged just before being connected to the system.

3.2   Power Recharge Cycle Intervals of the Power Supply Options

The power recharge cycle intervals were determined in terms of the time taken between two recharge actions for the battery to supply to the RWTMS. This factor can theoretically be predicted and practically proven using the Ampere-Hour rating of the power supply options. In general terms, the capacity of a cell/battery is the amount of charge that has been stored inside it expressed in ampere-hours (Ah). This is measured by discharging the battery at a constant current until it reaches a terminal voltage (usually 11 V for RWTMS) at standard room conditions.

It should also be emphasized here that the higher the battery capacity, the longer it takes to get it charged. This calls for a balance of the capacity and charging method capabilities of the source of the energy.

For the 1.5 V - 8 cells battery pack, the rated capacity was 2.8 Ah (2800 mAh). The battery that was being used to run systems on the vehicle had a rating of 40 Ah. The third option of the 12 V lead-acid battery was rated 7 Ah.

It was assumed that the RWTMS was drawing a constant 1.5 A of current. To find the time between recharges, the Ah rating was divided by the consumption rate of 1.5 A of the system. This yielded the following results as illustrated in the Table 1 below.

$$Recharge\ Time\ Interval = \frac{Ampere - hour\ rating\ (Ah)}{1.5\ A} \quad (1)$$

Table 1. The power consumption rate and recharge time interval for performance analysis of voltage supply for the system.

Power supply option	Ampere-hour rating (Ah)	Recharge time interval
1.5 V - 8 cells	2.8	1 h 52 min
Car battery	40	26 h 40 min
Lead acid battery	7	4 h 40 min

4 Results and Discussion

The following results were obtained. It was noted that the power coming from the battery pack was not enough to power the system for at least 1 h and 30 min. When the system was connected directly to the car battery, the system would consume much power to such an extent that when the vehicle engine was off for about 8 h, the engine of the vehicle would fail to start normally.

Lastly, the 12 V lead battery would power the system for about 5 h which is approximately the result that was achieved out of the theoretical solving of the recharge time interval.

4.1 Easiness of Use of the Power Supply Options on the RWTMS

The measure of easiness is based on the amount of time taken per recharge cycle and how that affects other systems on the vehicle. In reference to the results, it could be observed that the battery pack power option was not suitable for this application as travel time might exceed 1 h and 30 min in most cases. The car battery was also not very good an option because there are many systems that use the same power supply, e.g. indicator lights, head lamps, mirrors etc. It was abserved that the vehicle could start on a hard-start as the power had been depleted by the RWTMS hence clients could not accept the system be installed on their vehicles. The 12 V lead acid battery seemed a viable option because it could act as a separate power silo for the system to stay on for about 5 h.

Possible power charge and enhancement systems were proposed so that the system could be powered continuously while it is being used. Two options were proposed: vehicle alternator system and a solar panel system. The arrangement proposed was to use a hybrid type of charging system by combining the solar and alternator charging power so that it charges the 12 V lead acid battery. A very efficient power charging with cut-off circuit was designed and incorporated so that it could cut-off the charging power supply whenever the battery was fully charged. The input power to the RWTMS was equipped with a power surge protection circuit using a voltage regulation method of using an adjustable three-terminal positive-voltage regulator capable of supplying more than 1.5 A over an output-voltage range of 1.25 V to 37 V. This voltage regulator is known as LM317 (Fig. 4).

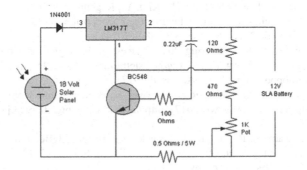

Fig. 4. The solar charging circuit for 12 volts battery used in the voltage supply for the system

4.2 Cost Evaluation on the Final Power Option for the RWTMS

This power supply was made using materials bought from an electrical store. The most expensive part was the battery which was bought at a cost about Twenty Five United States Dollars (US$ 25). The solar panel was bought at US$ 18 and the support electronics were acquired at a cost of US$ 10. The total sum of money spent on this power supply option was US$ 53.

4.3 Challenges Encountered in the Design, Implementation and Operation of the Power Supply Option for the RWTMS

One of the most prevailing challenges that were faced was to do with interoperability of system units for the achievement of an efficient source of power supply to power operations like sensing, data processing and data communication by RWTMS. The challenge was on how the 12 V lead acid battery could be connected to two power sources and be charged while it is supplying to the RWTMS.

5 Conclusion

In this paper, an efficient source of power supply to the real-time web-based temperature monitoring system for cold-chain management has been presented. This RWTMS power supply option has demonstrated a huge potential in tackling issues that arise lack of proper power supply to IoT sensors and systems more especially when they are mounted in equipment that is in transit. Our solution allows the hybridized charging system with a very good automatic cut-off and voltage regulation circuit. This work-in-progress will end up realizing some best savings in investment of power supply to efficient IoT systems.

References

1. Jayakumar, H. Lee, K., Lee, W.S., Raha, A., Kim, Y., Raghunathan, V.: Powering the internet of things. In: Proceedings of the 2014 International Symposium on Low Power Electronics and Design, New York, NY, USA, pp. 375–380 (2014)
2. Somov, A., Giaffreda, R.: Powering IoT devices: technologies and opportunities, 09 November 2015. https://iot.ieee.org/newsletter/november-2015/powering-iot-devices-technologies-and-opportunities.html. Accessed 2017
3. Kaliwo, A., Mikeka, C., Pinifolo, J.: Real-time, web-based temperature monitoring system for cold chain management in Malawi (2017). http://article.sapub.org/10.5923.j.jwnc.20170703.01.html
4. Ruiz-Garcia, L., Barreiro, P., Robla, J.I., Lunadei, L.: Testing ZigBee motes for monitoring refrigerated vegetable transportation under real conditions. Sensors (2010). http://www.mdpi.com/1424-8220/10/5/4968/htm. Accessed 2017
5. Yi, Q., et al.: Integrating open-source technologies to build low-cost information systems for improved access to public health data. Int. J. Health Geograph. 7, 29 (2008)
6. Saldaña Ruiz de Villa, L.: Sistema de control y alimentación para un robot ápodo modular e hiper redundante (2017)

A Novel Mobile Phone Contact List Based on Social Relations

Ibraïma Dagnogo, Rashid Ben Amed Charles Zongo, Pasteur Poda[✉],
and Théodore Tapsoba

École supérieure d'Informatique, Université Nazi BONI,
01 BP 1091, Bobo-Dioulasso 01, Burkina Faso
ibradagnos@yahoo.fr, zongorashid@gmail.com, pasteur.poda@univ-bobo.bf,
tmytapsoba@yahoo.fr

Abstract. Social ties are of a great importance in African societies. Obviously, they are the major provider of entries in the mobile phone contact list. However, the contact lists of mobile devices, as they are designed until now, do not efficiently take into account the social connections between contacts. They do not allow to efficiently retrieve/remember a contact who is forgotten or concerned by homonymy. Inspired by African social and cultural practices, this paper is about a new vision of the contact list design by integrating social ties. Preliminary results of the implementation of this vision clearly show that the proposed contact list is a convenient instrument of contacts reminder and homonymy resolver.

Keywords: Contact list · Mobile phonebook · Social ties
Social software

1 Introduction

One of the basic features offered on a mobile phone is the contact list. The contact list is used to store contact information (names and surnames, phone numbers, etc.) of the mobile phone owner's contacts. Primarily, it serves for allowing people to call contacts without having to remember and dial their phone numbers. Nowadays, smartphones offer contact lists with more elaborated input fields that serve to identify and remember a contact entry. However, none of them is provided with input fields for explicitly describing the relationships that could exist between contacts of the same contact list. It seems evident that relationships existing between people in the social life (i.e., social ties) can explain how a contact list is populated. For example, a frequently observed social practice in African societies is that when a problem has to be solved, people use to resort to an acquaintance who, will in turn resort to his own acquaintance and so on until the right one who can actually help solving the problem. In that endeavor

© ICST Institute for Computer Sciences, Social Informatics and Telecommunications Engineering 2018
V. Odumuyiwa et al. (Eds.): AFRICOMM 2017, LNICST 250, pp. 239–245, 2018.
https://doi.org/10.1007/978-3-319-98827-6_22

to solve the problem, several types of social ties (mainly family and friendly) are activated and can spontaneously give rise to the creation of new entries in the contact lists. In this way, a mobile phone can be easily "crowded" with hundreds even thousands of contacts. In African societies in general, the way people do to recognize someone is mostly based on social considerations. Social ties are thus more useful than the classical contact information whenever a contact entry has to be matched to the individual of the real life that it represents. This is further true insofar the "crowding" of contact lists increases the number of the rarely called contacts and gives rise to more homonyms occurrences. The integration of social ties in the design of the contact list software can help facing such a problem of contact matching. The paper in [1] stood for this new vision of the contact list and looks for providing African people with a mobile phone which looks like them in the sense of their social and cultural practices. In the present proposal, the purpose is to deal with preliminary results of the implementation of this new vision.

In the remainder of this paper, we deal in Sect. 2 with a brief review of works with close research interest. We present in Sect. 3 the new design of the contact list, deal with the associated software architecture and illustrate a few screen shots of the developed software. We conclude the paper with Sect. 4.

2   Brief Review of Related Works and Inventions

Since the decade of the 2000s, the design of social software involving the mobile phone contact list has been an active field of research. Several related research works and inventions covered systems built based on the concept of awareness and besides many other issues. Some of them consist of mobile recommendation systems based on situation-awareness [2]. Associating mobile awareness to initiation of group communications, a community-aware mechanism was proposed in [3] for efficient creation of groups of contacts. Works that associate mobile awareness and collaboration are also found. Based on psychological findings, the smartphone contact list was redesigned [4] to provide cues for the design of mobile awareness application that is capable to disclose information about users' presence. Many other works addressed contact information update and exchange. They gave birth to inventions consisting of methods for updating automatically mobile phone contact list entries [5] and improved systems for providing phonebook and bookmarked links to web sites for mobile users [6]. A system [7], that proceeds with synchronization and updates through communications between the mobile phone and a data service provider, enables the mobile phone to initiate according to the circumstances the appropriate form of communication with one of the contacts. Regarding contact information exchange, a method [8] of sending contact list data from one mobile phone to another mobile phone allows to eliminate the need to re-key individual contact data. A messaging service is used to exchange contact data between mobile phones within a group. In [9], a solution was proposed to take advantage of social relationship and context information to provide recommendations for users of social networks. Inspired by African social and cultural practices, this paper is about the integration of social ties in the design of mobile phone contact list. In [10], the cultural model of African countries was considered in the design of opportunistic networks for facilitating the collection and synthesis of agricultural information.

3   New Vision of the Contact List

The proposed new vision of the mobile devices contact list was described in details in [1]. The contact list is modeled as a graph; its nodes representing the contacts and its edges the social ties that link them. Any type of social tie can be considered. In the particular context of African societies, family ties that are of usual and cultural considerations are more meaningful: *"Is the father of"*, *"Is the daughter of"*, *"Is the sister of"*, *"Is the cousin of"*, etc. In this new vision, the classical usual CRUD (Create Read Update Delete) functionalities of the contact lists are preserved and the emerging social software (recommendation systems, group communications, ...) based on mobile contact list can continue working. In addition, the proposed design of the contact list enables some novel functionalities that make it a practical instrument of reminder, homonymy resolver and cultural values promoter. It also makes available, through the social ties, new cues that can be used in mobile awareness applications.

3.1   Software Architecture

Our approach for implementing the new vision of the contact list is based on the software architecture of Fig. 1. The user interface of this architecture has been developed using Java programming language. The knowledge base is for the contacts information storing and accessing. It consists of an ontology of the social ties populated by individuals and a set of rules of inference. We implemented the knowledge base using Protégé, an open-source ontology editor [11], to create an OWL (Web Ontology Language) [12] file that contains the description of the concepts related to the social ties. The inference engine is in charge of the reasoning and is so the support of the intelligent functionalities that could involve the contact list. The inference engine has been based on Apache Jena, an open-source Java framework for semantic web and linked data applications building [13]. For the queries management between the knowledge base and the user interface, the SPARQL protocol and query language [14] has been used.

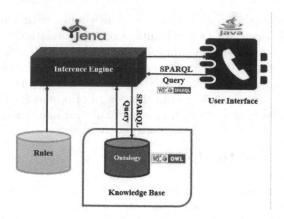

Fig. 1. Technical architecture of the contact list software

3.2   Views of the Developed Contact List Software

We developed the proposed contact list software based on the architecture of Fig. 1. The software is provided with both the classical CRUD functionalities and novel functionalities that are inherent to the new design. For the purpose of the demonstration, we registered in the contact list software six contacts including two homonyms with name and surname "Dagnogo Ibraïma". The resulting sample of the contact list is as given in Table 1.

Table 1. A sample of the contact list content

1	**Dagnogo Ibraïma** is the brother in law of **Poda Pasteur**
2	**Dagnogo Ibraïma** is the cousin of **Dagnogo Binta**
3	**Poda Pasteur** is the colleague of **Tapsoba Théodore**
4	**Tapsoba Théodore** is the friend of **Dagnogo Ibraïma**
5	**Poda Pasteur** is the friend of **Zongo Rashid**
6	**Zongo Rashid** is the colleague of **Dagnogo Ibraïma**

One of the novel functionalities makes the contact list an effective reminder. Indeed, in the particular case of a rarely contacted contact for instance, the simple visualization of his contact information is not sufficient to remember who he is in the real life. However, based on the social ties, we are able to remember that rarely contacted contact and then initiate any form of communication with him. This is illustrated by the view of Fig. 2a where the fact of knowing that the contact "Dagnogo Ibraïma" is a brother in law of the contact "Poda Pasteur" can help remember who "Poda Pasteur" is in the real life.

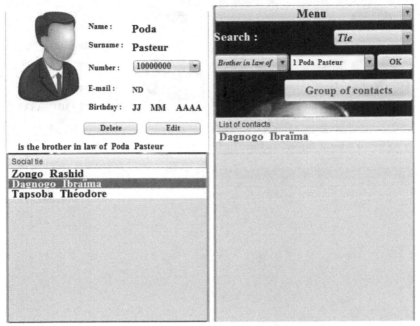

(a) Exhaustive listing of contacts of   (b) Vague search of a contact
any social tie with a given contact

Fig. 2. Some views of the contact list software

A second novel functionality is such that we have to retrieve a contact (e.g.: "Dagnogo Ibraïma") whose contact information are forgotten and that fortunately we remember one of his contact (e.g.: "Poda Pasteur"). Vaguely, knowing that latter contact, we can try by selecting any type of social tie (e.g.: "*is the brother in law of*") and then search for the corresponding contacts who share that social tie with him. This search operation can be iterated, if needed, with another type of social tie until the contact who is searched for (i.e., "Dagnogo Ibraïma") is retrieved or not. This is illustrated in the view of Fig. 2b.

Another situation where the new design of the contact list can help is the need to efficiently discriminate between several contacts that are involved by homonymy. In this case, before initiating a communication with the desired contact, we need to select the right one. For each homonym, the developed software offers the possibility to display his social ties with other contacts so that by browsing the list of homonyms, the right contact with whom we want to communicate can be identified. In Fig. 3, we illustrate how the two homonyms with name and surname "Dagnogo Ibraïma" can be discriminated based on social ties. In Fig. 3a, we are about the contact "Dagnogo Ibraïma" who has "Poda Pasteur" as brother in law. In the same contact list we have a second contact "Dagnogo Ibraïma" who has "Dagnogo Binta" as cousin.

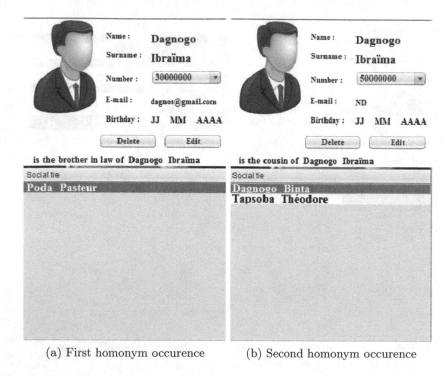

(a) First homonym occurence   (b) Second homonym occurence

Fig. 3. Views of the contact list software relative to homonimy resolving

4   Conclusion

This paper was about the implementation of a new vision of mobile contact lists. Taking into account the particular context of African social practices, the new design of the contact list consists of integrating social ties existing between people in the real life. To implement the proposed contact list, we built a system comprising a knowledge base, an inference engine and a graphical user interface. Well known Java programming tools and emerging linked data technologies were used to develop the software. A few views of the developed software were provided to illustrate functionalities regarding contacts reminder and homonymy resolver.

References

1. Poda, P., Compaoré, A.J., Somé, B.M.J.: Redesigning mobile phone contact list to integrate African social practices. In: Bissyande, T., Sie, O. (eds.) AFRICOMM 2016. LNICST, vol. 208, pp. 26–32. Springer, Cham (2018). https://doi.org/10.1007/978-3-319-66742-3_3
2. Plessas, A., Georgiadou, O., Stefanis, V., Komninos, A., Garofalakis, J.: Assessing physical location as a potential contextual cue for adaptive mobile contact lists. In: IEEE International Conference on Computer and Information Technology; Ubiquitous Computing and Communications; Dependable, Autonomic and Secure Computing; Pervasive Intelligence and Computing, pp. 1316–1324 (2015)

3. Grob, R., Kuhn, M., Wattenhofer, R., Wirz, M.: Cluestr: mobile social networking for enhanced group communication. In: ACM International Conference on Supporting Group Work, pp. 81–90 (2009)
4. Oulasvirta, A., Raento, M., Tiitta, S.: ContextContacts: re-designing SmartPhone's contact book to support mobile awareness and collaboration. In: ACM 7th International Conference on Human Computer Interaction with Mobile Devices and Services, pp. 167–174 (2005)
5. Henri, F.M., Stephanie, L.W., Tong Y., Yingxin, X.: Method of and System for Updating Mobile Telephone Contact Lists Entries. U.S. Patent Application No 11/867, 287 (2009)
6. Guedalia, I., Guedalia, J.: System and method for dynamic phone book and network content links in a mobile device. U.S. Patent Application No. 11/638,272 (2006)
7. Apfel, D.A.: Unified Contact List. U.S. Patent No. 7,139,555. U.S. Patent and Trademark Office, Washington, DC (2006)
8. Northcutt, J.W.: System and Method of Sharing a Contact List Among Mobile Phones. U.S. Patent No. 7,613,472. U.S. Patent and Trademark Office, Washington, DC (2009)
9. Gao, Y., Zhang, C., Wang Y., Sun, L.: A directed recommendation algorithm for user requests based on social networks. In : 9th IEEE/IFIP International Conference on Embedded and Ubiquitous Computing, pp. 457–462 (2011)
10. Ouoba, J., Bissyandé, T.F.: Leveraging the cultural model for opportunistic networking in Sub-Saharan Africa. In: International Conference on e-Infrastructure and e-Services for Developing Countries, pp. 163–173 (2012)
11. Protégé. http://protege.standford.edu
12. McGuinness, D.L., Van Harmelen, F.: OWL web ontology language overview. W3C recommendation (2004)
13. Jena. https://jena.apache.org
14. Prud, E., Seaborne, A.: SPARQL query language for RDF. W3C recommendation (2008)

Design of a Secure Public Accounts System for Enhanced War Against Corruption Using Intelligent Software Agent

Olugbemiga Solomon Popoọla[1](✉), Kayọde Boniface Alese[2],
Ayọdele Solomon Kupoluyi[2], Caleb Ayọdeji Ehinju[2],
and Adebayọ Olusọla Adetunmibi[2]

[1] Computer Science Department, Ọsun State College of Education Ila-Ọrangun,
Ila-Ọrangun, Nigeria
`popsol7@yahoo.com`, `popsol777@gmail.com`
[2] Computer Science Department, Federal University of Technology, Akurẹ,
Akurẹ, Nigeria

Abstract. Transparency of methods is a measure of accountability in governance. Availability of public data is a measure of transparency. However, confidentiality and integrity are mandatory requirements for the security of public data, which consequently enhances accountability. Maintaining public data availability, while optimal degree of their integrity and confidentiality are ensured, is a paramount preoccupation of any good government. Among such data are the public bank accounts. Treasury Single Account (TSA) is a measure towards the security of public funds; but it constitutes liquidity challenge to the banking sector of the economy. This paper presents a leakage-blocking public finance management (PFM) mechanism; a secured multiplatform for receipts and payments system, which is liquidity-friendly to the commercial banking industry. A web (Internet) platform is required for all transactions. Software intelligent agents are employed in monitoring receipt and payment processes made by the clients of the revenue-generating Ministries, Departments and Agencies (MDAs) of the government. The mechanism ensures that the centralized bank account's transactions are logged; and appropriate heads and subheads are updated accordingly after every successful transaction. Thus the inflow of revenue would be tracked, and illegal bank accounts reported promptly. Therefore, public accounts would be under intensive surveillances, guaranteeing the accountability of every kobo generated.

Keywords: Accountability · Availability · Integrity · Confidentiality
Public accounts · Treasury Single Account

1 Introduction

A financial reform process of the present Nigeria democratic dispensation conceived and nurtured the Treasury Single Account (TSA) as an alternative approach towards fighting financial leakages and corruption being perpetrated through the government fragmented Revenue Bank Accounts (RBAs), which has hitherto been in operation [1].

© ICST Institute for Computer Sciences, Social Informatics and Telecommunications Engineering 2018
V. Odumuyiwa et al. (Eds.): AFRICOMM 2017, LNICST 250, pp. 246–252, 2018.
https://doi.org/10.1007/978-3-319-98827-6_23

Coincidentally, TSA has provisions in sections 80 and 162 of Nigeria constitution of 1999 (as amended). It maintains a single account, where all receipts are paid, and from where all payments are made.

Liquidity in the banking sector of the economy is a major challenge of TSA [2]. In a developing democracy with developing economy, running the commercial banks out of cash is dangerous to small and medium scale industries. The present implementation of TSA has given highest premium to where/who keeps government money; with the presumption that it is only a centralized reservoir of funds that could be managed centrally. But, the true spirit of Public Financial Management (PFM) is how government funds could be managed efficiently and cost-effectively.

This paper presents a revised implementation of TSA, which is liquidity-friendly to the commercial banking industry. The design is a distributed reservoir of government funds whose management is centralized. The design also captures all categories of government funds holistically.

2 Current Implementation of TSA

Under the present arrangement, MDAs are categorized into eight, based on budgetary and/or funding status. Based on the categories, some MDAs would use an electronic collection platform – Government Integrated Financial Management Information System (GIFMIS) – through the Deposit Money Banks (DMBs) to remit receipts into the TSA; while some others would open a sort of Sub-accounts with CBN where their receipts would be remitted through Remita, the CBN payment gateway [3].

MDAs are to voluntarily close all existing RBAs, and forward evidence of such closure to OAGF. Those categories that require Sub-accounts with CBN are to channel the request to open such account through the OAGF. After request is granted, such MDA has to register in order to use Remita. Even, they could register to spend part of the collection made to the Sub-accounts through the same CBN payment gateway (Remita). Receipts and payments reports have to be forwarded to OAGF manually. Criteria for exemption from TSA are not explicit, because opportunities are opened to MDAs to apply for exemption [4].

Summarily, the payer visits MDA to obtain some sort of codes; go to a DMB, which must use Remita to process the remittance; the DMB generates payment evidence for the payer, which he takes to the appropriate MDA to effect the delivery of the goods and/or services paid for. At the close of each working day, the DMBs clear the revenue account into the CBN designated TSA, maintaining a zero-balance account for the RBAs [4].

2.1 Current Challenges of TSA

Zero-balance accounts would pose a serious liquidity challenge in the banking industry: Reducing the DMBs lending power. Cash-crunch might lead to work force downsizing; a negative trend that is looming in the banking industry [2].

Remita's monopoly of government funds remittance negates the spirit of competitiveness in a supposedly deregulated market. Monopoly would definitely hamper appropriate computing standards upon which adequate benchmarking of solution of such magnitude of importance should be anchored. This has led to charges, which is currently based on a certain percentage of funds collected; instead of a uniform charge, which should be based on volume of transactions [5].

The nature of the fragmented public accounts requires an automated system for the confirmation of their closure, which does not feature in the current implementation. Threats of sanctions through government circulars do not guarantee a faithful closure of all these bank accounts. Even new fraudulent bank accounts could still be opened in the future if not prevented.

3 Best Security Practices for Information Systems

All risks, threats and vulnerabilities are measured for their potential capability to compromise confidentiality, integrity and availability of information. Hence, all security controls, mechanisms and safeguards are designed and implemented to provide confidentiality, integrity and/or availability. Certainly, the strength of any system is not greater than its weakest link. Defense-in-depth security strategy is integrated, by building up, layering on and overlapping modular security measures. This provides security compensations: If one defensive measure fails, there are other defensive measures in place that continue to provide protection. The weakness of one security measure is compensated for by the strength of others. Hence, vulnerability of a single weak link would not aid successful exploitation of the system [6].

Separation of duties (SoD) is the concept of having more than one person required to complete a task. It is alternatively called segregation of duties, or division of labour, or separation of powers. Literatures from the Information Systems Audit and Control Association (ISACA) report that SoD specifies that no single individuals should have controls over two or more phases of an operation, so that a deliberate fraud is more difficult to occur; because it would definitely require collusion of two or more individuals or parties. Therefore, potential damage from the actions of a single person is reduced [7].

Need-to-know principle gives access rights to a person to perform their job functions. This principle is used in the government, when dealing with different clearances. Even though two employees in different departments have a top-secret clearance, they must have a need-to-know in order for information to be exchanged. Within the need-to-know principle, network administrators grant the employee least amount privileges to prevent employees' access, so that they cannot do more than what they are supposed to [6]. Moreover, least (minimal) privilege principle requires that in a particular abstraction layer of a computing environment, every module (i.e. a process, a user or a program) based on the layer being considered, must be able to access only such information and resources that are necessary to its legitimate purpose and duty [7].

To be effective, security controls must be enforceable and maintainable. Effective policies ensure that people are held accountable for their actions. All failed and successful authentication attempts must be logged, and all access to information must leave some type of audit trail [6]. Reports of all suspicions to the technical/surveillance stakeholders must be automated, online, and real-time.

4 The All-Sectors Accommodating TSA

Reengineering the current TSA implementation would eliminate most of, if not all, the challenges being experienced in some sectors of the economy. In preparation for a smooth deployment of a robust solution, some actions and processes need be carried out on the core stakeholders.

The MDAs should be tagged on per branch bases. Interested electronic payment platforms (ePays) should be registered. DMBs should be registered on per branch bases. Comprehensive coding of goods and services would address all forms of government businesses and activities. Every transaction is assigned a unique code, which is automatically translated to the goods/service descriptions on the goods/service request form and payment invoice.

At the takeoff, the basic databases would include MDAs, DMBs, E-Transaction Systems, Economy Sectors, Receipts, Payments, Treasury Subheads, Goods, Services, Donations, Foreign Currency Receipts, Foreign Currency Payments, Raised Funds, Grant and Counterpart Funds. Databases are expected to grow over some time until the working conditions of the system satisfy set objectives. The need for necessary visibility of unusual and/or unauthorized actions to some kind of law enforcement agents such as Economic and Financial Crimes Commission (EFCC) (as may be modified to fit into contemporary forensic technologies) might account for such growth. Also, availability of authentic public data to the general public through the media houses might justify expansions of databases. Local and remote backups of databases are automated in accordance with some timely schedules (Fig. 1).

The CBN hosts a GIFMIS; the receipts and payments management and coordinating platform. It generates invoices, verifies payments, issues payment evidences, manages databases, maintains electronic ledgers, and coordinates multiple backups for preventive purposes. The CBN gives feed-backs to appropriate MDAs, Payers and DMBs on every transaction. The GIFMIS hosts intelligent agents and tamperproof subsystems for keeping constant surveillance on the system so that automated real-time reports of tamper-attempts are ensured. The intelligent agent specifically scans the intranet of appropriate DMB for possible fraudulent duplication and/or opening of bank accounts for MDAs.

The package in Fig. 2 is wirelessly connected and integrated into the DMBs' intranets, through which they are connected to each other (i.e. extranet) and the Internet. There is a single common program for processing all payment transactions of the government, eliminating the duplications that are usually occasioned by policy-specific programs such as for the aviation industry and foreign currency donor/counterpart funds. Goods and services setup and corresponding subheads are defined as parameters. Goods and services could be added/modify very easily.

Only authorized users have access to the system, and such could perform only authorized tasks. It is a multi-user system with user-defined security levels; and there is no restriction on the number of users. Every change in the database requires authentication of the administrator, the CBN governing body and electronic audit moderating body; and the system keeps audit trail of all changes. Transactions reports link is only accessible at the appropriate time.

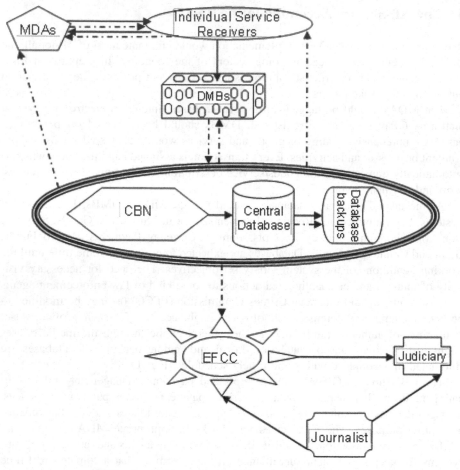

Fig. 1. Architecture of a corruption-fighting TSA

The intelligent agent searches for existing MDAs' bank accounts, which were fraudulently kept from being closed. Suspected existence or duplications of bank accounts are automatically detected and reported to the system administrator and/or the EFCC for appropriate actions (Fig. 2).

4.1 Security Features

User access to database is through the package only. All updates are carried out using stored procedures after proper validations, data integrity checks, and transaction auditing. Users have only execute permission to the stored procedures, and only when called via the package (Fig. 2). Every transaction is monitored by the system; and also keeps an audit trail for the same. Before processing reports, the system ensures that all expected data is received and all databases are updated.

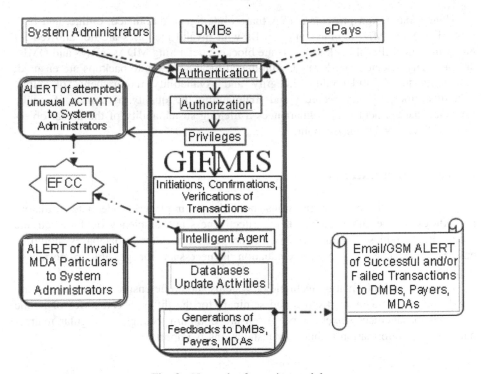

Fig. 2. Network of security modules

Apart from the physical network access security, the package has its own User Access system. The system administrator has the highest authority level and access to all options of the package. He can create Supervisory Users and grant them access to restricted work options. The security of the information systems are audited on timely basis with automated mechanism. Every change in the database bears the signature of the transaction point and the supervisor in charge.

5   Conclusion

Information security is the process of exercising due care and due diligence to protect information and information systems, from unauthorized access, use, modification, destruction, disclosure, distortion, disruption or distribution. This makes information security an indispensable part of all business operations across different domains.

This design focused on financial security issues as they feature right from issuing of invoice to clients by the MDAs till payments/receipts transactions are updated on the databases at the CBN. New data concerning any MDA is entered only once. Goods/services per MDA per DMB per Treasury subhead are mapped with very high level of consistency. There is a single program and common databases for all users. Integrity and availability of data are guaranteed.

Hence, the design presents a TSA that is intelligent, automated, online, and real-time. Therefore, MDAs, ePays and DMBs with invalid identities are not allowed for any transaction; illegal bank accounts are blocked; defaulting MDAs, ePays and DMBs are promptly detected and located. Automated local and remote backups are ensured; enhancing the Confidentiality, Integrity and Availability requirements of public accounts processes and records; and maintaining the quality assurance of public financial management, which guarantees a lifelong sustainability of the actual objectives of Treasury Single Account.

6 Recommendations

Appropriate security policy legislations should be put in place for adequate regulatory procedures for the enhancement of the effectiveness and efficiency of the electronic processing activities. Adequate security of the remote backups of databases should be ensured; and scheduled system evaluation is necessary for possible performance upgrade.

Proper use of information technology systems should be ensured through relevant, regular and up-to-date workshops and seminars for the different categories of public financial management stakeholders. To ensure optimum throughput, regular maintenance of any information technology installations is important.

References

1. Ifeanyi, M.: Treasury single account (in Nigeria) issues and implications. Covenant University, Canaanland, Ọta, Nigeria (2015)
2. Eme, O.I., Chukwurah, D.C., Emmanuel, N.I.: An analysis of pros and cons of treasury single account policy in Nigeria. Arab. J. Bus. Manag. Rev. (OMAN Chapter) 5(4), 20 (2015)
3. Ọtunla, J.O.: Introduction of e-Collection of Government Receipts. Federal Treasury Circular, Ref: Nọ TRY A1 & B1/2015/OAGF/CAD/026/V.1/253 (2015)
4. Accountant-General of the Federation (AGF): Guidelines on the Implementation of TSA/e-Collection. Office of the Accountant-General of the Federation (2015)
5. Taiwo, O.: TSA and Taxation (2015). www.pwc.com/nigeriataxblog
6. Popoọla, O.S., Ajayi, O.D., Salawu, A.K.: Electronic processing of examinations for educational systems (EPEES): a security framework. KWASU (Kwara State Univ.) Int. J. Educ. (KIJE) 2(1), 193–206 (2014)
7. David, H., et al.: Enterprise resource planning (ERP) security and segregation of duties audit: a framework for building an automated solution. Inf. Syst. Audit Control Assoc. (ISACA) J. 2, 11–25 (2007)

Decision Support

A User-Centric Decision Support Model for Cloud of Things Adoption Using Ellipsoidal Fuzzy Inference System

Ademola Olaniyi[✉], Babatunde Akinkunmi, and Olufade Onifade

Department of Computer Science, University of Ibadan, Ibadan, Nigeria
ademola.olaniyi@gmail.com, ope34648@yahoo.com,
olufadeo@gmail.com

Abstract. Cloud adoption for Internet of Things is gaining attention among researchers and organizations. The decision to choose a Cloud vendor is complicated and dynamic in nature. The majority of the existing Decision support systems designed to support migration to the Cloud have limitations. They mostly provide information to support evaluation and selection of vendors with cost being the main factor while some fundamental issues had been left unsupported. This work proposes a robust User-Centric Cloud of Things Decision Analytic Model using Ellipsoidal Fuzzy Inference System. The proposed model supports real time decision making process for the adoption of Cloud computing in Internet of Things by comparing User-defined Application demand and Cloud Decision attributes. The results of this work are expected to contribute to the acceptance of Cloud of Things services.

Keywords: Decision support · Cloud computing · Cloud of Things
Internet of Things · Ellipsoidal · Fuzzy

1 Introduction

The Internet of Things (IoT) permits communication between different sensors connected to the Internet and the use of their services towards relevant applications [1]. Cloud concepts are integrated with IoT so that storing and computation is done in the Cloud [2]. Essentially, the Cloud acts as intermediate layer between the things and the applications, where it hides all the complexity and the functionalities necessary for implemention [3]. The introduction of IoT to Cloud Computing gave birth to the concept called Cloud of Things (CoT).

As IT administrators take proactive measures to mesh IoT with their Cloud deployments, it becomes a great deal of concern which Cloud provider to adopt for IoT deployment [4]. The majority of the existing Decision Support Systems mostly provide information to support evaluation and selection of vendors with cost being the main factor [5]. This paper proposes a model that will evaluate CoT attribute parameters based on Cloud user experiences and IoT application security demands. The proposed model will help in choosing which Cloud vendor to adopt for any CoT deployment service.

© ICST Institute for Computer Sciences, Social Informatics and Telecommunications Engineering 2018
V. Odumuyiwa et al. (Eds.): AFRICOMM 2017, LNICST 250, pp. 255–261, 2018.
https://doi.org/10.1007/978-3-319-98827-6_24

2 Related Works

Considering the availability of various Cloud providers, IoT users find it challenging to select the most appropriate secured Cloud for a Cloud IoT application. Several researchers have proposed several decision support systems for migrating to the Cloud. [6] proposed a solution based on user parameters for the migration of applications to the Cloud. [7] considered the characteristics of services provided by Cloud providers such as storage, intra-Cloud, cost, and so on. [8] developed the CloudGenius framework that provides a multi-criteria approach in decision support for selecting providers for IaaS in migrating a web server to the Cloud. [9] presented a Cloud adoption toolkit for Infrastructure as a Service (IaaS) that aids decisions on suitability of the technology. [10] considered various properties, security and availability to determine the best Cloud service provider for a particular application.

[11] proposed a model to support user decision-making by calculating the optimal amount of internal Cloud computing resources and expected cost reductions of strategic public Cloud deployment. [12] proposed a model that help decision makers consider whether and which forms of Cloud computing would operate best for their organization. It provides an estimate of the operational costs of adopting a Cloud system. [13] presented a system that can predict the costs for a Cloud deployment of an application. It provides expected trade-offs between cost and performance.

3 Methodology

The methodology to this research study entails classifying various Cloud of Things Attribute parameters (Decision Attributes) based on their characteristics and strength. This classification will be done under five (5) categories. These categories will be used as "decision criteria" for choosing the most appropriate Cloud resource for an IoT application deployment. From the features obtained from any category, a fuzzy based Cloud of Things decision system will be developed using user experiences of various Cloud resource providers while comparing it with "user defined" application demand by an IoT application.

[14] identified twenty security considerations for Cloud-supported Internet of Things. According to [15], Skyhigh network in conjunction with Cloud Security Alliance (CSA) also presented and evaluated 50 attributes that defines the rating of a Cloud service. These works formed a basis for identifying various CoT attributes across five categories defined thus; (1) Defense Capability Attributes (α), (2) Access Control and Device Attributes (β), (3) Data Attributes (γ), (4) Service, Business and/or Legal Attributes (δ), and (5) Primary Security Attributes (λ). Figure 1 below depicts an overall architecture for the proposed model.

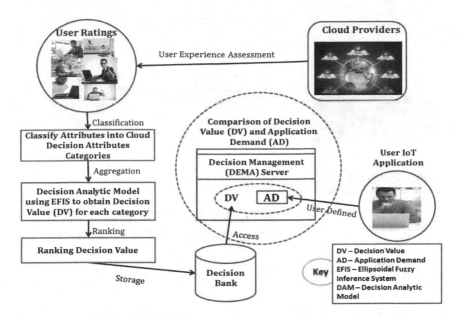

Fig. 1. Overall system architecture

The system architecture above depicts various stages of work to be carried out. The primary source of data for this work will be obtained from Cloud user ratings. A questionnaire will initially be designed and posted across various Cloud user and IoT forums to garner information about various Cloud providers as perceived by the users. Secondarily, CoT experts, Researchers and IoT developers will also be required to answer some questions about their Cloud resource usage experiences. The garnered information will then be categorized into five Decision Attribute categories (Defense Capability Attributes, Access Control and Device Attributes, Data Attributes, Service, Business and/or Legal Attributes, Primary Security Attributes).

The information for each category will then be used as input for developing the Decision Analytic Model Ellipsoidal Fuzzy Inference System (DAMEFIS). The result obtained for each category of decision criteria will be ranked in order of most suitable Cloud provider depending on the specified user-defined Application Demand.

3.1 Decision Analytic Model Ellipsoidal Fuzzy Inference System (DAMEFIS)

The proposed model is specifically designed for the evaluation of Decision attributes in Cloud of things. This model applies Ellipsoidal fuzzy inference system to evaluate the Decision value (DV) for any Cloud resource provider and compares it with the user-defined Application Demand for IoT applications. The aim is to aggregate each Decision attribute of Cloud resource sites into a single value output as illustrated in Fig. 2 below:

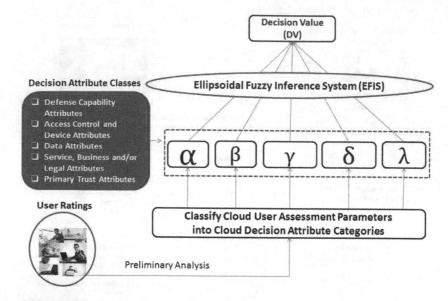

Fig. 2. Aggregation of decision criteria parameters into decision value

On the other hand, A CoT application issues an Application demand (AD) depending on the expected level of service for the application. The Application demand is based on important parameters as defined in the application. These include; authentication, access control, data integrity, data encryption and so on which has been categorized into five classes. These parameters are aggregated into a single value defined as the Application demand (AD) for the CoT application.

The aggregated values are then used for Decision Support in determining the most suitable Cloud resource provider for any CoT application.

3.2   Vector Spaces and Ellipsoidal Fuzzy Rules

This work proposes that Cloud attributes can be defined as a vector space hence every Cloud resource maintains a Decision vector (DVEC) defined as:

$$V_i = (A_1, A_2 \ldots \ldots \ldots A_n)^T \text{ for } 1 \le i \le n \tag{1}$$

Where V_i = Decision Vectors for the Cloud and A_i = Decision Attributes for CoT.

It should be noted that the Decision Vector is an aggregate of all related Decision Attributes in the Cloud. It is made up of each of the five (5) attributes classes. Each Cloud attribute parameters are the Decision attributes.

The whole Cloud can thus be defined by a Decision Matrix (DM) defined as an aggregate of all Decision vectors (V_i) in a Cloud as an n × m matrix.

$$\mathbf{DM} = \left(\mathbf{V_1, V_2, \ldots \ldots V_m}\right)^{\mathbf{T}} \tag{2}$$

$$\mathbf{DM} = \begin{matrix} \mathbf{A_{11}} & \mathbf{A_{12}} \ldots & \mathbf{A_{1j}} \\ \mathbf{A_{21}} & \mathbf{A_{22}} \ldots & \mathbf{A_{2j}} \\ \cdots & \cdots & \cdots \\ \mathbf{A_{n1}} & \mathbf{A_{n1}} \ldots & \mathbf{A_{nm}} \end{matrix} \tag{3}$$

Regarding EFIS, the covariance of the Matrix identifies ellipsoidal rules. In particular, each rule is represented by an ellipsoid covering a portion of inputs-outputs space and they overlap. Geometrically, an ellipsoid z can be represented by Eigenvectors and Eigenvalues of a definite matrix DM: If n and p are the number of inputs and outputs respectively, $q = n + p$ represent the dimension of the ellipsoid. Its columns are the unitary eigenvectors.

Let R = Diagonal matrix of Eigen values of DM
       S = Orthogonal matrix that orient the ellipsoid
Then

$$\mu^2 = (\mathbf{z} - \mathbf{c})^{\mathbf{T}} \mathbf{R}(\mathbf{z} - \mathbf{c})$$
$$= (\mathbf{z} - \mathbf{c})^{\mathbf{T}} \mathbf{S} \wedge \mathbf{S}^{\mathbf{T}}(\mathbf{z} - \mathbf{c}) \tag{4}$$

Where:

$$\mu = \in R^+$$

c = Centre of ellipsoid
Each ellipsoid represents a fuzzy rule and then, its projection on each possible values axis represents the support of membership function.

3.3 Evaluation and Ranking

Finally, the result obtained for each category of decision attribute will be aggregated into a single Decision Value (DV) for any Cloud provider. The DV is normalized as a single real number with 0 representing the Cloud with a condition of low acceptance and 1 representing the condition high acceptance.

The normalized DV will be used to rank Cloud providers based on users Application Demand (AD) in order to recommend the most suitable Cloud provider. The DV is then compared with the Application demand (AD) such that DV > AD. This will in turn be used for decision making. For example, if a user defines the Application Demand for an IoT based application to be 0.7, it is assumed that this value is obtained from the normalized weighted average of the priority score given to various critical decision attributes by the user.

4 Conclusion

Cloud adoption for Internet of things is gaining attention among researchers and organizations. The decision to choose a Cloud vendor is complicated and dynamic in nature. This paper proposed a model to support the decision making process for the adoption of Cloud computing in IoT. This system mainly provides an efficient method for decision making purposes using soft computing methodology and is aimed to be highly beneficial to any individual or organization. As a future work, extended efforts are being made to enhance the model by integrating service level agreements (SLA) from Cloud providers into the decision making process. Works can also be done to ensure that metrics to measure the Quality of Service (QoS) for CoT by Cloud Providers is integrated.

References

1. Suciu, G., Vulpe, A., Todoran, G., Cropotova, J., Suciu, V.: Cloud computing and Internet of Things for smart city deployments. University POLITEHNICA of Bucharest, Faculty of Electronics, Telecommunications and Information Technology (2011)
2. Suchetha, K.N., Guruprasad, H.S.: Integration of IoT, cloud and big data. Glob. J. Eng. Sci. Res. **2**, 251–258 (2015). ISSN 2348 – 8034 Impact Factor-3.155
3. Liu, Y., Dong, B., Guo, B., Yang, J., Peng, W.: Combination of cloud computing and internet of things (IoT) in medical monitoring systems. Int. J. Hybrid Inf. Technol. **8**(12), 367–376 (2015)
4. Christoforou, A., Andreou, A.S.: A cloud adoption decision support model using influence diagrams. In: Papadopoulos, H., Andreou, A.S., Iliadis, L., Maglogiannis, I. (eds.) AIAI 2013. IAICT, vol. 412, pp. 151–160. Springer, Heidelberg (2013). https://doi.org/10.1007/978-3-642-41142-7_16
5. Alkhalil, A., Sahandi, R., John, D.: Migration to cloud computing: a decision process model. Faculty of science and Technology, Bournemouth University (2014)
6. Andrikopoulos, V., Song, Z., Leymann, F.: Supporting the migration of applications to the cloud through a decision support system. In: IEEE Sixth International Conference on Cloud Computing, pp. 565–572. IEEE (2013)
7. Li, A., Yang, X., Kandula, S., Zhang, M.: CloudCmp: comparing public cloud providers. In: The 10th ACM SIGCOMM Conference on Internet Measurement, pp. 1–14. ACM (2010)
8. Menzel, M., Ranjan, R.: CloudGenius: decision support for web server cloud migration. In: Proceedings of the 21st International Conference on World Wide Web, pp. 979–988. ACM (2012)
9. Khajeh-Hosseini, A., Sommerville, I., Bogaerts, J., Teregowda, P.: Decision support tools for cloud migration in the enterprise. In: IEEE International Conference on Cloud Computing, pp. 541–548 (2011)
10. Chan, H., Chieu, T.: Ranking and mapping of applications to cloud computing services by SVD. In: IEEE/IFIP, pp. 362–369 (2010)
11. Lilienthal, M.: A decision support model for cloud bursting. Bus. Inf. Syst. Eng. **5**(2), 71–81 (2013)
12. Khajeh-Hosseini, A., Greenwood, D., Smith, J.W., Sommerville, I.: The cloud adoption toolkit: supporting cloud adoption decisions in the enterprise. Softw.-Pract. Exp. **42**(4), 447–465 (2012)

13. Perez-Palacin, D., Calinescu, R., Merseguer, J.: Log2Cloud: log-based prediction of cost-performance trade-offs for cloud deployments, pp. 397–404 (2013)
14. Singh, J., Pasquier, T., Bacon, J., Ko, H., Eyers, D.: Twenty security considerations for cloud-supported Internet of Things. IEEE Internet Things J. **3**, 269–284 (2015). https://doi.org/10.1109/JIOT.2015.2460333
15. Musthaler, L.: Is your trust in the Cloud services misplaced or true? Find out with a cloud trust rating (2016). www.networkworld.com

Enhancing Business Decision Making Through Actionable Knowledge Discovery Using an Hybridized MCDM Model

Lucky Ikuvwerha[1(✉)], Taiwo Amoo[1(✉)], Victor Odumuyiwa[1(✉)],
and Olufunke Oladipupo[2]

[1] Department of Computer Sciences, University of Lagos,
Akoka, Lagos, Nigeria
ogagatilucky@gmail.com, amootaiwo01@gmail.com,
vodumuyiwa@unilag.edu.ng
[2] Department of Computer Science, Covenant University, Ota, Ogun, Nigeria
funke.oladipupo@covenantuniversity.edu.ng

Abstract. In recent years, with the increase in the usage of internet-enabled electronic devices and information systems, the upsurge and availability of volumes of high dimensional data have become one of the sources of high business value. The need for businesses to make informed decisions by leveraging on the patterns from the multi-dimensional data have become paramount. However, the major issue is whether or not the patterns can optimize business decision making process to increase profit. Hence, there is need for actionable knowledge discovery (AKD). Therefore, this paper proposed an hybridized interval type-2 fuzzy Multi Criteria Decision Making (MCDM) model for evaluating patterns based on three subjective interestingness measure which are unexpectedness, actionability and novelty. The interval type-2 Fuzzy Analytical Hierarchy Process (AHP) was employed to weigh the patterns and Compensatory AND approach was utilized for ranking the patterns using the three subjective interestingness measures. The proposed model depicts its applicability in identifying and ranking the patterns which are more relevant for enhancing business decision making.

Keywords: Actionable knowledge discovery
Fuzzy analytic hierarchy process · Multi-criteria decision making

1 Introduction

Business organizations are using Information and Communication Technologies (ICT) to gather and store data in high dimensional volumes. All these data hold valuable knowledge in form of patterns or trends, which can be used to advance business strategies in today's competitive business environment. Businesses require measures that will drive productivity, increment profits, improve customer satisfaction and the likes. One of the processes that can be employed to achieve this is knowledge discovery process. Knowledge Discovery Process is defined as non-trivial process of identifying valid, novel, potentially useful, and ultimately understandable patterns in

© ICST Institute for Computer Sciences, Social Informatics and Telecommunications Engineering 2018
V. Odumuyiwa et al. (Eds.): AFRICOMM 2017, LNICST 250, pp. 262–271, 2018.
https://doi.org/10.1007/978-3-319-98827-6_25

data [1]. However, the patterns discovered can be so many, and as a result may not be actionable, that is, the end user cannot act on it or take action. Hence, the domain knowledge of the experts is required to extract useful and actionable patterns. This has led to the paradigm shift from traditional Knowledge discovery process to Actionable knowledge discovery process (AKD).

Actionable knowledge discovery is based on interestingness measure. Interestingness measure can be generally divided into two categories: objective measure which is based on the strength of the statistical method of the data mining criteria and subjective measure based on the user's beliefs or expectations of the particular problem domain. In recent years, different approaches have been proposed as an extension of knowledge discovery processes to transcend to better actionable patterns [2, 3]. However, these studies lack consideration for the inter-uncertainties/imprecision that may be involved in preference elicitation from decision makers [6]. Therefore, using a model that will improve the subjective interestingness measure is of great importance.

MCDM models are techniques that analyse decision makers' preferences concurrently in the presence of multiple and conflicting criteria to arrive at an optimized decision out of all alternatives concerned [4]. However, the classical MCDM approaches cannot handle the imprecision and ambiguities that are involved in decision making processes [8]. Consequently, as an extension of the classical MCDM approaches, the hybridization of type-1 fuzzy and the interval type-2 fuzzy set was proposed [4, 7]. Therefore, in this paper, a novel interval type-2 fuzzy MCDM model based on explicit data intervals of the decision makers is proposed for the subjective interestingness measure of discovered patterns.

2   Preliminaries

This section describes the basic concept of actionable patterns and the interval type 2 fuzzy definitions used in this paper.

Definition 1.1. Actionability of a pattern: Given a pattern P, its actionable capability $act()$ is described as to what degree it can satisfy both technical and business interestingness.

$$\forall x \in I, \exists P: x.tech\_int(P) \wedge x.biz\_int(P) \rightarrow act(P) \tag{1}$$

where $x.tech\_int(P)$ is the technical or objective interestingness measure and $x.biz\_int$ (P) is the business or subjective interestingness measure.

Definition 1:2. The type-2 fuzzy set A can be represented as follows [5]:

$$\tilde{\tilde{A}} = \int_{x \in X} \int_{u \in J_x} \mu_{\tilde{\tilde{A}}}(x, u)/(x, u) \tag{2}$$

where $J_x = [0, 1]$ and $\int$ denote union over all admissible x and u.

Definition 1.3. If all $\mu_{\tilde{\tilde{A}}}(x, u) = 1$, then $\tilde{\tilde{A}}$ is called an interval type-2 fuzzy set. An interval type-2 fuzzy set $\tilde{\tilde{A}}$ can be considered as a special case of a type-2 fuzzy set, which is represented as [8] :

$$\tilde{\tilde{A}} = \int_{x \in X} \int_{u \in J_x} 1/(x, u), \tag{3}$$

where $J_x = [0, 1]$ and $\int$ denote union over all admissible x and u.

Definition 1.4. The upper membership function (UMF) and the lower membership function (LMF) of an interval type-2 fuzzy set are type-1 membership functions, respectively [6].

$$\begin{aligned}
\tilde{\tilde{A}}_1 = \left(\tilde{A}_i^U, \tilde{A}_i^L\right) = &\left(\left(a_{i1}^U, a_{i2}^U, a_{i3}^U, a_{i4}^U, H_1\left(\tilde{A}_i^U\right), H_2\left(\tilde{A}_i^U,\right)\right),\right. \\
&\left. \left(a_{i1}^L, a_{i2}^L, a_{i3}^L, a_{i4}^L, H_1\left(\tilde{A}_i^L\right), H_2\left(\tilde{A}_i^L\right)\right)\right)
\end{aligned} \tag{4}$$

where $\tilde{A}_i^U$ and $\tilde{A}_i^L$ are type1 fuzzy sets, $a_{i1}^U, a_{i2}^U, a_{i3}^U, a_{i4}^U, a_{i1}^L, a_{i2}^L, a_{i3}^L, a_{i4}^L$ are the reference points of the interval type-2 fuzzy $\tilde{\tilde{A}}_i$; $H_j(\tilde{A}_i^U)$ denotes the membership value of the element $a_{i(j+1)}^U$ in the upper trapezoidal membership function $\tilde{A}_i^U; 1 \leq j \leq 2, H_j(\tilde{A}_i^L)$ denotes the membership value of the element $a_{i(j+1)}^L$ in the lower trapezoidal membership function $\tilde{\tilde{A}}_i^L; 1 \leq j \leq 2, H_j(\tilde{\tilde{A}}_i^L)H_1(\tilde{\tilde{A}}_i^U) \in [0, 1], H_2(\tilde{\tilde{A}}_i^U) \in [0, 1], H_1(\tilde{\tilde{A}}_i^L) \in [0, 1], H_2(\tilde{\tilde{A}}_i^L) \in [0, 1]$ and $1 \leq i \leq n$. The arithmetic operations between the trapezoidal interval type-2 fuzzy sets is described in [7]. The defuzzification of trapezoidal type-2 fuzzy sets (DTraT) proposed by [8] was defined for the defuzzification process.

3 Methodology

In this section, the methodological flow is described as follows:

3.1 Stage One: Pattern Generation

At this stage, rules were generated from the decision tree. These are the rules that show how the decision tree was able to classify the model based on the label. We used these rules as patterns because it is possible to gain more insight from them on how the decision tree was able to classify the model [3].

3.2 Stage Two: Pattern Ranking

The rules generated which were represented as patterns were passed into this stage as input to be ranked using the three subjective interestingness measures (unexpectedness, actionability and novelty) as a combined measure. Consequently, the interval type-2 fuzzy Analytical Hierarchy and Compensatory AND approach were proposed for weighting the criteria and ranking the patterns accordingly as follows:

Interval Type 2 Analytical Hierarchy Process
The AHP was proposed by [9]. The proposed main steps for defining criteria importance are as follows:

Step 1: Collect data intervals for all the words used in eliciting criteria importance from the decision makers (DM).

Step 2: Perform the pre-processing of all the data intervals for each linguistic term (word) based on [6].

Step 3: Translate the data intervals from all subjects for each word to their respective UMF and LMF fuzzy parameters using [6] and plot the fuzzy set for each word.

Step 4: Construct a fuzzy pair-wise comparison matrix between criteria for each decision maker, k using the interval type-2 fuzzy numbers derived in **Step 3.**

Step 5: Perform arithmetic operations on the pair-wise comparison matrices of the evaluators/DMs and derive an average.

Step 6: Defuzzify the averaged type-2 fuzzistics pair wise comparison matrix, A_{ave} using DTrat defuzzification method [8].

Step 7: Perform the Eigenvector technique on the defuzzified comparison matrix A to derive final weight of each criterion.

The criteria weights of the interval type-2 fuzzy AHP are inputs to the ranking MCDM method below to finally rank the patterns concerned. The patterns were ranked according to their interestingness based on the following criteria: unexpectedness, actionability and novelty.

Compensatory AND Approach: The compensatory AND is defined by Zimmerman and Zynso [10] as:

$$\mu_\theta = \left(\prod_{i=1}^{m} \mu_i \right)^{1-\gamma} * \left(1 - \prod_{i=1}^{m} (1 - \mu_i) \right)^{\gamma} \quad 0 \leq \mu \leq 1; \ 0 \leq \gamma \leq 1. \tag{5}$$

If it is desired to introduce different weights for the sets in question, μ_i and $1 - \mu_i$ could for instance be replaced by $\mu_i = \left(\frac{\vartheta_i}{n} \right)^{\delta_i}$ and $1 - \mu_i = \left(1 - \left(\frac{\vartheta_i}{n} \right) \right)^{\delta_i}$ where ϑ_i are the (raw) membership values, δ_i, their corresponding weights and $\gamma = 0.6$, which indicate the degree of compensation. The sum of weights δ_i should be equal to the number of sets connected. That means $\sum_i \delta_i = m$.

4 Experiments

The dataset used in this research is from the University of California, Irvine (UCI) benched mark dataset [11]. The dataset contains 45,211 records, 17 attributes and a class label attributes. This dataset is related to the direct marketing campaigns from a Portuguese bank which was done by phone call. The goal is to predict if the customer will subscribe or not for a new deposit package. This study uses RapidMiner studio version 7.0 edition for model training and testing. The decision tree obtained from the dataset is shown below:

Decision Tree
duration > 827.500
| pdays > 495.500: no {no = 2, yes = 0}
| pdays $\leq$ 495.500: yes {no = 744, yes = 1036}
duration $\leq$ 827.500
| age > 89.500
| | age > 93.500: no {no = 2, yes = 1}
| | age $\leq$ 93.500: yes {no = 0, yes = 5}
| age $\leq$ 89.500: no {no = 39174, yes = 4247}
Several patterns were generated as shown in Table 1:

Table 1. Rules generated as patterns

Rules generated
if duration $\leq$ 410.500 and month = aug and pdays $\leq$ 0 and duration > 183.500 then no (1444 /113)
if duration $\leq$ 410.500 and month = aug and pdays $\leq$ 0 and duration $\leq$ 183.500 and job = admin. then no (174 /3)
if duration > 410.500 then no (4801 /2742)
if duration $\leq$ 410.500 and month = apr then no (1959 /331)
if duration $\leq$ 410.500 and month = aug and pdays > 0 and duration > 159.500 then yes (107 /146)
if duration $\leq$ 410.500 and month = aug and pdays > 0 and duration $\leq$ 159.500 and duration > 106.500 and job = admin. and pdays > 100.500 then no (12 /0)

Three rules as patterns from the above rules with higher right classification and lower wrong classification covered by the rule were chosen. These patterns are labelled pattern A to C according.

Pattern A: if duration $\leq$ 410.500 and month = aug andpdays > 0 and duration > 159.500 then product = yes

Pattern B: if duration $\leq$ 410.500 and month = aug and pdays $\leq$ 0 and duration $\leq$ 183.500 and job = technician then product = no

Pattern C: if duration $\leq$ 410.500 and month = jun and contact = unknown and duration $\leq$ 368.500 and age > 24.500 then product = no

where pdays is numbers of day when the client was last contacted. Duration is the time in seconds when the client last contacted.

After generating the patterns, we proceeded to weigh the patterns: Assume we have k decision makers, $\{DM_1, DM_2 \ldots DM_k\}$ and also set of criteria F where F = {Unexpectedness(UN), Novelty(NO), Actionability(AC)} which are established to be hierarchical in nature. Also, a definition of a set T of linguistic terms, T = {Moderately more important = MI, Extremely more important = EXI, Equally more important = E, Very Strongly more important = VSI, Strongly more important = SI} was proposed for eliciting criteria importance from decision makers as shown in Table 2.

Table 2. Pairwise comparison matrix obtained from DM 1

	AC	NO	UN
AC	E	MI	1/SI
NO	1/MI	E	EXI
UN	SI	1/EXI	E

Additionally, a set X of linguistic terms, X = {Dissatisfied = D, Very satisfied = VS, Fair = F, Very Dissatisfied = VD, Satisfied = S} was defined for evaluating the patterns by the decision makers as shown in Table 3. Lastly, a set Y of competing alternatives which comprise of 3 patterns were proposed where Y = {Pattern A, Pattern B, Pattern C}.

Table 3. Performance matrix of pattern A

	AC	NO	UN
DM 1	F	F	F
DM 2	S	S	S

In order to rank the patterns Y in relation to subjective interestingness, the following MCDM approaches, interval type-2 fuzzy analytical hierarchy process and the Compensatory AND approach were utilized. Using Steps 1-7 in the Interval Type-2 Fuzzy Analytical Hierarchy Process, the linguistic terms of the pairwise comparison matrix are transformed to their respective (UMF) and (LMF) parameters using Table 4. Similarly, their respective interval type-2 plots for each word are depicted in Fig. 1, and the determination of weights of the criteria, F are derived as shown in Table 5.

In deriving the ranked patterns with respect to its subjective interestingness, the Compensatory AND approach was utilized as defined in Eq. (5). The set X of linguistic terms, X = {Dissatisfied = D, Very satisfied = VS, Fair = F, Very Dissatisfied = VD, Satisfied = S} was defined for evaluating the patterns by the decision makers as shown in Table 3. Consequently, set X was transformed to their corresponding interval type-2 fuzzy numbers using Table 6 and aggregation was done using arithmetic operations defined in Eq. (4). Defuzzification was carried out accordingly using the DTrat approach. Furthermore, their respective interval type-2 plots for each word in X are depicted in Fig. 2. Then, using Eq. (5), the patterns were ranked as depicted in Table 7.

Table 4. Words used for eliciting criteria importance (weights) and their interval type-2 fuzzy numbers

Linguistic labels	Corresponding interval type-2 fuzzy numbers
Equally important	(0,0,1.1918,4.6077; 1,1)(0,0,0.1376,1.9747; 1,1)
Moderately more important	(2.5858, 4, 4.5, 5.4142; 1,1)(3.7929, 4.3333, 4.3333,5.2071; 0.7643,0.7643)
Strongly more important	(4.4822,5.7500,7,8.4142; 1,1)(5.8136,6.2857,6.2857,6.8107; 0.4949, 0.4949)
Very strongly more important	(6.0858,7.2500,8.2500,9.1692; 1,1) (7.3308,7.7773,7.7773,8.0864; 0.4857,0.4857)
Extremely more important	(6.7088,9.7706,10,10; 1,1)(9.3418, 9.9541,10,10; 1,1)

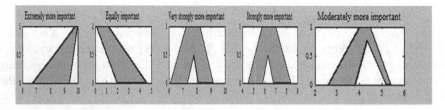

Fig. 1. Plots of the fuzzy sets for each word used in eliciting criteria performance

Table 5. Weight derived for each criterion

Criteria	Weight	Rank
Actionability	0.2941	2
Novelty	0.4261	1
Unexpectedness	0.2798	3

Table 6. Words used for eliciting performance of each pattern and their interval type-2 fuzzy number

Linguistic labels	Corresponding interval type-2 fuzzy numbers
Very Dissatisfied	(0, 0,0.2753,3.9495; 1,1)(0,0,0.0918,1.3165; 1,1)
Dissatisfied	(0.98,2.5,3.25,5.0178; 1,1)(2.29,2.8,2.8,3.18; 0.5757, 0.5757)
Fair	(2.98,4.5,5.25,7.01; 1,1)(4.39,4.71,4.71,5.10; 0.697,0.697)
Satisfied	(4.27,6,7.5,9.22; 1,1)(6.21,6.75,6.75,7.20; 0.4697,0.4697)
Very satisfied	(6.70,9.77,10,10; 1,1)(8.6835, 9.9082, 10,10; 1,1)

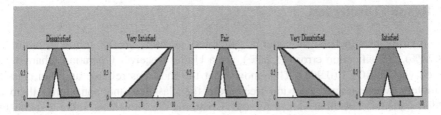

Fig. 2. Plotting of the fuzzy sets for each word used in eliciting patterns' performance

Table 7. The final ranked patterns using the interval type-2

Pattern	Compensatory AND values	Rank
Pattern A	0.4066	3
Pattern B	0.4375	2
Pattern C	0.4604	1

Table 8. The final ranked patterns using the type-1 fuzzy

Pattern	Compensatory AND values	Rank
Pattern A	0.5227	2
Pattern B	0.5137	3
Pattern C	0.5654	1

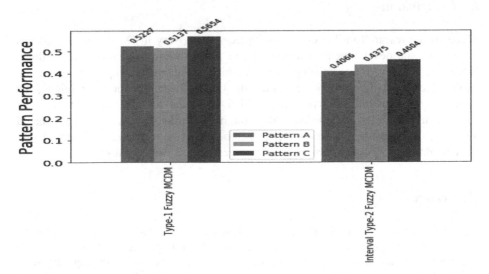

Fig. 3. Comparison of ranked patterns between the type-1 fuzzy MCDM and the proposed interval type-2 fuzzy MCDM approach

5 Results/Discussion

The performance metrics of patterns generated as rules are as follows: Accuracy (88.74%), Classification error (11.22%), Area Under Receiver Operating Characteristics curve (AUROC) (0.904). This shows that the model is reliable and can classify accurately. We extracted decision trees from the classifier and considered them as hidden patterns. The final values for the 3 patterns are shown in Table 7 using the Compensatory AND approach. These values are derived in terms of aggregated consideration of the 3 criteria defined i.e. (novelty, actionability and unexpectedness) which were then evaluated by the decision makers with respect to each pattern. Pattern C was the best with the overall value of 0.4604 followed by Pattern B with an overall value of 0.4375 while the least useful pattern was adjudged to be Pattern A with the overall value 0.4066. This gives an indication of the most critical patterns that decision makers can act on to drive business performance to the organization. Meanwhile, the overall weighted value of each criterion is depicted in Table 5 which shows the importance of each criterion in relation to the other. The Novelty of a pattern was adjudged to be the most critical feature in extracting useful insight from patterns mined with the weighted value of 0.4261 followed by Actionability with 0.2941 and Unexpectedness with 0.2798. Meanwhile, the type-1 fuzzy ranking of patterns showed a slight change between Pattern A and B as opposed to the interval type-2 as shown in Fig. 3. This could be as a result of both inter and intra uncertainties that cannot be accommodated sufficiently by the type-1 fuzzy. However, both confirmed pattern C as the most actionable (Tables 7 and 8).

6 Conclusions

Much of the research in the area of Knowledge Discovery in Databases (KDD) has focused on the development of more efficient and effective data mining algorithms. However, recently, issues relating to the usability of these techniques in extracting exploitable knowledge from databases has drawn significant attention. Therefore, this work proposed an interval type-2 fuzzy MCDM model for exploiting and ranking patterns in their order of subjective interestingness. Further research could be geared towards extending other variants of AHP methods with the interval type-2 fuzzy using the enhanced interval approach in order to be compared with our results.

References

1. Chen, F., Pan, D., Jiafu, W., Daqiang, Z., Athanasios, V., Xiaohui, R.: Data mining for the internet of things: literature review and challenges. Int. J. Distrib. Sens. Netw. (2015)
2. Amruta, L., Balachandra, k.: Performance evaluation of actionable knowledge discovery (AKD) framework under the decision making system. Int. J. Adv. Res. Comput. Sci. Eng. **3** (9) (2013)

3. Chiang, R.-D., Chang, M.-Y., Keh, H.-C., Chan, C.-H.: Mining unexpected patterns by decision trees with interestingness measures. In: 1st International Conference on Artificial Intelligence, Modelling and Simulation (AIMS), pp. 117–122. IEEE (2013). 978-1-4799-3251

4. Baykasoğlu, A., İlker, G.: Development of an interval type-2 fuzzy sets based hierarchical MADM model by combining DEMATEL and TOPSIS. Expert Syst. Appl. **70**, 37–51 (2017)

5. Mendel, J.M., Robert, I.J., Feilong, L.: Interval type-2 fuzzy logic systems made simple. IEEE Trans. Fuzzy Syst. **14**(6), 808–821 (2006)

6. Wu, D., Jerry, M.M., Simon, C.: Enhanced interval approach for encoding words into interval type-2 fuzzy sets and its convergence analysis. IEEE Trans. Fuzzy Syst. **20**(3), 499–513 (2012)

7. Chen, S., Li-Wei, L.: Fuzzy multiple attributes group decision-making based on the interval type-2 TOPSIS method. Expert Syst. Appl. **37**(4), 2790–2798 (2010)

8. Kahraman, C., Başar, Ö., İrem, U.S., Ebru, T.: Fuzzy analytic hierarchy process with interval type-2 fuzzy sets. Knowl.-Based Syst. **59**, 48–57 (2014)

9. Saaty, Thomas L.: The Analytic Hierarchy Process: Planning, Priority Setting, and Resource Allocation. MacGraw-Hill, New York International Book Company, New York (1980)

10. Zimmermann, H.J., Zysno, P.: Latent connectives in human decision making. Fuzzy Sets Syst. **4**(1), 37–51 (1980)

11. UCI Machine Repository Data. http://archive.ics.uci.edu/ml/dataset/Bank+Marketing

Comparative Analysis of Supervised Learning for Sentiment Classification

Afusat O. Muyili[✉] and Oladipupo A. Sennaike

Department of Computer Sciences, University of Lagos, Lagos, Nigeria
muyiliafusat@gmail.com, osennaike@unilag.edu.ng

Abstract. Sentiment analysis is an active research area which deals with information extraction and knowledge discovery from text using Natural Language Processing and Data Mining techniques. Sentiment analysis, also known as opinion mining, plays a major role in detection of customer's attitude, response and opinion towards a product or service. The aim of this paper is to perform sentiment analysis on a particular service to discover how users perceive the service automatically. Data is extracted from twitter, pre-processed and classified according to the sentiment expressed in them: positive, negative or neutral using five supervised learning classifiers-The Naïve Bayes, Multinomial Naïve Bayes (MNB), Bernoulli Naïve Bayes (BNB), Linear Support Vector Machine (SVM) and Decision Tree classifiers. Finally, the performance of all the classifiers is compared with respect to their accuracy. In addition, the results from the classifiers show that supervised learning classifiers perform excellently in sentiment classification.

Keywords: Sentiment analysis · Twitter · Feature extraction · Naïve Bayes
Decision Tree · Linear Support Vector Machine · Multinomial Naïve Bayes
Bernoulli Naïve Bayes

1 Introduction

Social media have completely changed the way people communicate and have become a large part of daily lives in most societies. This development has led to the creation of huge amounts of data which is useful for analysis of users' opinion such as evaluating a written or spoken language to determine if the expression is favourable, unfavourable or neutral and to what degree.

Over the years, business organizations have experienced exponential growth in the use of online resources, particularly social media and microblogging websites like Facebook, Twitter, Tumbler, YouTube, etc. Such organizations highly depend on these resources as a rich mine of marketing knowledge unlike the conventional methods (interviews, questionnaires and survey) which are highly expensive and time consuming in gaining insight and feedbacks into how customers perceive their products or services due to poor design and environmental factor. Hence, there is need of a system that can automatically generate users' opinions (sentiment analysis) from huge amount of data.

© ICST Institute for Computer Sciences, Social Informatics and Telecommunications Engineering 2018
V. Odumuyiwa et al. (Eds.): AFRICOMM 2017, LNICST 250, pp. 272–278, 2018.
https://doi.org/10.1007/978-3-319-98827-6_26

Sentiment Analysis (SA) is the process of classifying the emotion conveyed by a text as negative, positive or neutral. It has a wide variety of applications in e-business and e-government as it extracts people's opinions, sentiments, appraisals, attitude towards entities such as products, services, organizations and their attributes using various machine learning techniques and natural language processing (NLP).

This paper applies sentiment analysis to analyze customers' opinions and reviews about two companies: Arik Airline and Guarantee Trust Bank using comparative analysis of supervised learning approach. To achieve this, specified tweets about these companies are extracted from twitter and pre-processed. The system architecture applied in this paper is shown in Fig. 1. Section 2 discusses the existing methods in sentiment analysis. Section 3 presents our research methodology. Section 4 covers discussion of results and Sect. 5 contains the conclusion.

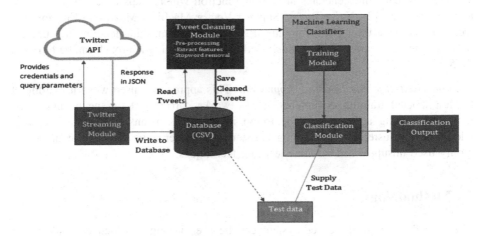

Fig. 1. Proposed system architecture

2 Data Mining and Sentiment Analysis

The objective of data mining is to extract information or knowledge from dataset and transform it into a structure that can be understood Dodd in [1] pointed that data mining focuses on discovering patterns in data while sentiment analysis focuses on discovering patterns in text that can be analyzed to classify the sentiment in that text.

2.1 Twitter Sentiment Analysis

Twitter is a micro-blogging service which enables users to send and read short text messages usually in 140 characters or less, known as "**tweet**". Twitter begun as a backup project for a failed project and today it is one of the highest growing social media websites in the world with huge amount of accumulated unstructured data written in natural language. Sentiment analysis on twitter posts is the process of accessing tweets for a particular topic as these tweets give us a rich and varied source of opinions on product reviews or the individual state of mind with the help of different machine learning algorithms.

2.2 Sentiment Analysis Classification Techniques

Generally, researches on sentiment analysis require very fast and concise information to make accurate decisions which mostly depends on machine learning algorithms. Machine learning algorithms consist of two approaches: Supervised and Unsupervised machine learning approach.

Supervised Machine Learning Approach: This approach derives a function from labelled training examples consisting of a large set of examples about a particular topic. Each training example occurs as a pair of input and output (target) value. The algorithm analyzes the data and generates an output function which maps a new dataset to its appropriate class [2]. Naïve Bayes, Support Vector Machine, Maximum Entropy and Decision Tree are the most commonly used supervised machine learning techniques. Some of the work carried out on supervised machine learning approach can be found in [3–5, 6].

Unsupervised Machine Learning Approach: This approach is used when it is difficult to find labeled training documents. Major works carried out on the unsupervised machine learning approach can be found in [7, 8]. K-means, Spectral Clustering, Hierarchical Clustering, Partitioning Clustering and Semantic Orientation are commonly used unsupervised machine learning techniques.

3 Methodology

The workflow of the proposed system can be seen in Fig. 2 which consists of the following steps:

Step 1: Tweet Collection
The training data for the proposed system were collected from twitter with the help of the twitter streaming API. The dataset consists of roughly 6000 short messages collected on daily basis for the month of April 2017. They were stored and pre-processed for mining.

Step 2: Tweet Pre-processing
The aim of pre-processing tweet is to remove any piece of information within the tweet that will not be useful for the machine learning algorithm in assigning class to the tweets. The main pre-processing steps adopted in this paper include:

i. **Lowercase Conversion:** All tweets were converted to lower case.
ii. **Removal of URLs, @user and retweets:** All URL links (E.g. https://t.co/99GCMKVxHx), usernames (@omojuwa which indicates the user name) and special words (e.g. RT meaning Retweet) were removed with regular expressions to increase the accuracy of our classifiers.

iii. **Removal of stop-words:** Stop-words like *the, and, before, to, on, while* were eliminated. We built a custom list and added it to the list of stop-words available in the NLTK library.

iv. **Removal of duplicates and repeated characters:** People sometimes repeat letters to stress their emotion. Words like hunggrryyy, are used in place of 'hungry', haapppyyy instead of 'happy'. Such repeated letters were replaced by only two occurrences.

v. **Punctuation and whitespace Removal:** Punctuations in each word, words which do not start with an alphabet were removed while multiple whitespaces were replaced with single whitespace.

Step 3: Feature Extraction

We used the bag-of-words model to create the feature vector. Each tweet in the training dataset was split into words and each word added to the feature vector, some of the words which do not indicate the sentiment of a tweet were filtered out.

Step 4: Classifiers Used

Naïve Bayes, Multinomial Naïve Bayes (MNB), Bernoulli Naïve Bayes (BNB), Linear Support Vector Machine (SVM) and Decision Tree classifiers were used.

Naive Bayes

Naïve–Bayes are probabilistic classifier, it relies on the application of Bayes theorem given as

$$p = \left(\frac{c}{d}\right) = \frac{p(c) * p(c/d)}{p(d)}. \tag{1}$$

We used the Naïve Bayes Classifier and its variants from NLTK to train and test the data.

Support Vector Machine

The SVM is a non-probabilistic binary linear classifier. It plots the training data in a multidimensional space and discovers a hyper plane which separates the documents as per the sentiment, and the margin between the classes. A python package known as the Linear SVM from the Sci-kit learn was utilized to classify the tweet as NLTK does not provide libraries for SVM.

Decision Tree

A decision tree classifier is a tree whose nodes are labeled by the features as it categorizes a document starting at the tree node through the branches until it reaches the leaf using the information gain. The edges that leave these nodes are labeled by the class. The information gain measures how the input values will be organize once they are divided with a given feature using the formula

$$H = -\sum p(l) \times \log_2(l). \tag{2}$$

The decision tree ensures that each feature from the training set is checked in a particular order and to achieve this, the decision tree classifier in the NLTK library was used (Table 1).

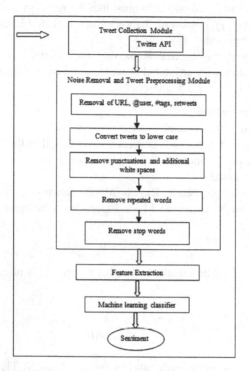

Fig. 2. Sentiment analysis process flow

4 Discussion of Results

The supervised machine learning model was designed using the Hold Out validation method which separates the dataset into two sets called the training set and the test set. We trained with 3600 tweets (60%) and test with 2375 tweets (39.5%). Each tweet is classified to be positive, negative or neutral based on a query term and polarity classification, the percentage accuracy of each classifier was calculated using a python library and confusion matrix. Table 2 depicts the confusion matrices and accuracies of our classifiers.

Table 1. Confusion matrix

		Predicted		
		Positive	Negative	Neutral
Actual	Positive	True Positive (TP)	False Positive (FP)	False Positive (FP)
	Negative	False Negative (FN)	True Negative (TN)	False Negative (FN)
	Neutral	False Neutral (FNeu)	False Neutral (FNeu)	True Neutral (TNeu)

Table 2. Confusion matrices with classifier accuracies

	GTBank			Arik Airline		
	Positive	Negative	Neutral	Positive	Negative	Neutral
Linear SVM						
Positive	557	0	5	106	0	0
Negative	0	319	2	0	57	0
Neutral	0	0	1039	0	0	285
Classifier accuracy = 99.62				99.99		
Naïve Bayes						
Positive	550	5	46	102	0	8
Negative	7	304	75	0	53	10
Neutral	0	10	925	4	4	267
Classifier accuracy = 92.56				94.19		
Multinomial Naïve Bayes						
Positive	500	301	58	97	1	8
Negative	47	301	150	6	54	12
Neutral	10	9	838	3	2	265
Classifier accuracy = 92.61				92.86		
Bernoulli Naïve Bayes						
Positive	550	3	60	97	5	26
Negative	4	315	71	6	50	40
Neutral	3	1	915	3	2	219
Classifier accuracy = 85.28				81.69		
Decision Tree						
Positive	104	0	0	548	4	65
Negative	1	57	0	1	315	92
Neutral	1	0	285	8	0	889
Classifier accuracy = 91.16				99.55		

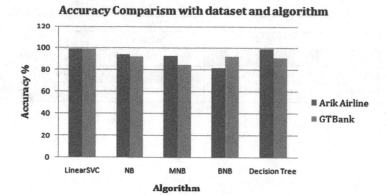

Accuracy Comparism with dataset and algorithm

5   Conclusion

The results of the analysis show that, the machine learning classifiers works correctly. Evaluation of the different algorithms shows that the Linear Support Vector Machine had the highest accuracy on all the datasets with short processing time. The Decision Tree classifier had the second highest.

References

1. Dodd, J.: Twitter sentiment analysis (2014). http://trap.ncirl.ie/1868/1/johndodd.pdf. Accessed 18 Mar 2017
2. Garg, P.: Sentiment analysis of Twitter data using NLTK in Python, June 2016. http://dspace.thapar.edu:8080/jspui/bitstream/10266/4273/4/4273.pdf. Accessed 15 Feb 2017
3. Pak, A., Paroubek, P.: Twitter as a corpus for sentiment analysis and opinion mining. In: Proceedings of LREC (2010)
4. Read, J.: Using emoticons to reduce dependency in machine learning techniques for sentiment classification. In: Proceedings of the ACL Student Research Workshop, pp. 43–48. Association for Computational Linguistics (2005)
5. Parikh, R., Movassate, M.: Sentiment analysis of user-generated Twitter updates using various classification techniques (2009)
6. Kharde, V., Sonawane, S.: Sentiment analysis of Twitter data: a survey of techniques. Int. J. Comput. Appl. **139**(11), 5–15 (2016)
7. Suresh, A., Bharathi, C.R.: Sentiment classification using decision tree based feature selection. IJCTA **9**(36), 419–425 (2016)
8. Turney, P.: Thumbs up or thumbs down? Semantic orientation applied to unsupervised classification of reviews. In: Proceedings of the 40th Annual Meeting on Association for Computational Linguistics, pp. 417–424. Association for Computational Linguistics (2002)

e-Business and e-Services

An Empirical Study on the Adoption of Consumer-to-Consumer E-commerce: Integrating the UTAUT Model and the Initial Trust Model

Kwame Simpe Ofori[1(✉)], Kwabena G. Boakye[2],
John Agyekum Addae[3], George Oppong Appiagyei Ampong[3],
and Adolph Sedem Yaw Adu[1]

[1] Department of Computer Science, Ho Technical University, Ho, Ghana
kwamesimpe@gmail.com, aadu@htu.edu.gh
[2] Department of Logistics and Supply Chain Management,
College of Business Administration, Georgia Southern University,
Statesboro, GA, USA
kboakye@georgiasouthern.edu
[3] Ghana Technology University College, Accra, Ghana
{jagyekum, gampong}@gtuc.edu.gh

Abstract. With the ever-increasing internet penetration in Ghana, e-commerce development seems to be on the ascendency. However, users are reluctant to patronize these online sites due to the lack of trust. While literature is inundated with numerous B2B and B2C e-commerce studies, little is known about C2C e-commerce. Thus, our study contributes to the e-commerce literature, seeking to extend knowledge by integrating the Unified Theory of Acceptance and Use of Technology (UTAUT) model with the Initial Trust Model (ITM) to explore user adoption of C2C e-commerce in an emerging market. Data was collected from 193 university students who have had some experience with some Ghanaian C2C websites and analyzed using the Partial Least Squares approach to Structural Equation Modelling (PLS-SEM). Results from the model showed that Performance Expectancy had the most significant effect on Behavioral Intention, followed by Trust. Behavioral Intention was also found to significantly predict Actual Usage. In all, our model accounted for about 51% of the variability in Actual Use. The proposed model is useful in understanding trust in the C2C context. Results from this work could inform strategies to be taken by these C2C websites to attract visitors to such websites.

Keywords: E-commerce · PLS-SEM · UTAUT · ITM · Structural assurance
Situational normality · C2C

1 Introduction

The increasing internet penetration rate in Ghana is opening avenues for businesses and individuals to transact businesses online. E-commerce affords users (sellers and buyers) a 24-hour access to the storefront from any location. Even though e-commerce offers

© ICST Institute for Computer Sciences, Social Informatics and Telecommunications Engineering 2018
V. Odumuyiwa et al. (Eds.): AFRICOMM 2017, LNICST 250, pp. 281–292, 2018.
https://doi.org/10.1007/978-3-319-98827-6_27

some great advantages to shoppers, recent research shows that due to the space and time separation between the buyer and the seller, trust has become an important issue [1, 2].

There are mainly three e-commerce business models: Business-to-Business (B2B), Business-to-Customer (B2C) and Consumer-to-Consumer (C2C). C2C e-commerce is a type of e-commerce that allows individuals to come together to buy and sell goods/services through a third party platform provider. C2C is fast becoming the most popular form of electronic commerce. In China, C2C e-commerce accounted for about 64% of all online shopping transactions in 2013 [3]. The platform providers often play an inactive role in the transaction, only mediating the transaction between the seller and the buyer. Unlike B2B and B2C where the business host its own platform, the platform for C2C is hosted by a third party and hence trust in C2C becomes a major issue. Issues of trust range from buyers not being able to hold the platform provider responsible for any inappropriate products sold to the buyer and the inability to return the products or receive a refund. As more and more individual consumers buy from and sell to other individual consumers, it is imperative to understand consumers' purchasing and selling behaviors in relation with trust and other factors that influence them to participate in C2C transactions.

Sustaining C2C business is important since C2C providers face intense competitive pressure as their website and ideas can easily be replicated by competitors [4]. In addition, the entry barriers for other providers and switching cost for sellers who advertise on the platform is low. Although the C2C market is the fastest growing, only a few studies have investigated the motives for adopting this e-commerce model. Additionally most research in this area have concentrated on developed countries. Hence, by integrating the Unified Theory of Acceptance and Use of Technology [5] and the Initial Trust Model [6] our study seeks to identify the factors that influence a user's decision to adopt C2C e-commerce in an emerging market.

2   Literature Review and Hypotheses Development

2.1   C2C E-commerce

E-commerce relates to buying and selling through electronic means, using web-based and other related technologies to support necessary activities for firms to perform effectively [7]. E-commerce facilitates shopping 24/7, anywhere, anytime, and all year round. In recent times due to increasing access to the web, potential for cost-savings and availability of a limitless selection of products and services, C2C has grown in popularity. In 2013, C2C sales were responsible for about 64% of the online shopping market in China [3].

Whereas B2C transactions involve well established businesses, same cannot be said of C2C. B2C online businesses have policies that protect customers that are not satisfied with the products they buy [2]. C2C on the other hand cannot promise such protection since the third party listing website or forum only provides a platform for buyers and sellers to interact but does not have any control over the seller [8]. As more people resort to C2C, it is important to understand issues that relate to trust and consumer behavior in this segment.

2.2   The Unified Theory of Acceptance and Use of Technology (UTAUT) Model

In a bid to improve the predictive power of technology adoption models, Venkatesh et al. [5] examined eight previous models and came out with the UTAUT. The rationale for developing the UTAUT model stemmed from the fact that variables from the previous models were similar and therefore, it was logical to map and integrate them to create a unified model [5]. The UTAUT model proposes four key constructs namely; performance expectancy, effort expectancy, social influence, and facilitating conditions. The model postulates that these four key constructs significantly influence behavioral intention and ultimately actual use behavior. The UTAUT model has drawn the attention of many scholars and has been applied to a varied number of technological innovation under different settings including, including internet banking [9, 10], mobile banking [11], e-governance [12], and e-learning [13].

Performance Expectancy (PE). In our study, we define performance expectancy as user's perception of outcome improvement after adopting a new technology. It is expected that user's perception of how C2C retailing websites would improve shopping convenience, and efficiency has an influence on user's adoption intentions. Previous studies have affirmed significant relationship between performance expectancy and technology adoption [14, 15]. We therefore posit that:

H₁: Performance expectancy positively affects behavioral intention
H₂: Performance expectancy positively affects trust

Effort Expectancy (EE). Effort expectancy connotes the degree of ease associated with using a system. In-built systems complexity deter adoption. Hence, when a user feels that buying and selling online is easy and it does not require specialized mental and physical efforts, then effort expectancy becomes a strong predictor of intention to use C2C. Empirically, the link between effort expectancy and behavioral intention has been supported by many authors [9, 14, 16]. In line with this, we posit that:

H₃: Effort expectancy positively affects behavioral intention

Social Influence (SI). Social influence is the degree to which an individual's intention to adopt a technological innovation is influenced by referent others [16]. Users/potential users are more likely to adopt a new technological innovation when important people like family members, friends and colleagues advise them to do so. There have been some mixed findings in the literature on the effect of social influence on behavioral intentions. Previous researchers have shown that social influence has a significant effect on behavioral intention [5, 16]. For example, Lian and Yen [17] found social influence to significantly affect intention among both old and young online shoppers. However, in a study of user acceptance of mobile wallet, Shin [18] found no support for the relationship between social influence and behavioral intention. In view of this we propose:

H$_4$: Social influence positively affects behavioral intention.

Facilitating Conditions (FC). According to Venkatesh et al. [5], facilitation conditions relate to consumer's perception about the existence of resources and support system to promote the use of technology. If users believe that there exists adequate resources, help-lines, and support services (both organizational support and technical infrastructure), they would be more likely to adopt. Thus, if users are not in a position to provide the necessary resources (financial, software and hardware) and its associated know-how, they will most likely not adopt C2C e-commerce. Hence, we hypothesize that:

H$_5$: Facilitating conditions positively affects actual use.

Behavioral Intention (BI). This construct is derived from the Theory of Planned Behavior, which posits that an individual's behavior is driven by his/her intention to engage in that behavior. A number of studies have found behavioral intention to be a strong predictor of actual use [5, 19]. In line with previous research we expect behavioral intention to have a positive influence on the actual use of C2C website and therefore propose the following:

H$_6$: Behavioral intention positively affects actual use.

2.3 Initial Trust and Its Antecedents

The inability of consumers to touch and inspect products as well as the lack of cues such as body gestures, the tone of voice, facial expressions, etc. makes trust an important issue in e-commerce. In B2C e-commerce, vendors may protect consumers with return or refund policies and warranties. Unfortunately, this is not the case for C2C since the C2C platform provider is only responsible for creating a platform for buyers and sellers to interact and does not play an active role in the transaction.

In B2C trust is built over time through the consumer's experiences developed from using the B2C website, e-WoM and the reputation of the B2C vendor. In contrast to B2C, trust in C2C website is based on the initial interaction the buyer has with the seller on the platform and not experiences since no relationship would have been formed yet between the buyer and the seller. In the context of e-commerce, McKnight et al. [20] proposed a typology of trust which included the following: dispositional trust, institutional trust, and interpersonal trust. In this study, we concentrate on institutional trust. Institutional trust can be decomposed into two components – situational normality and structural assurance.

Situational Normality (SN). Situational normality is belief that the environment is in order and that success is likely because the situation is normal [20]. Consumers are expected to have high trust in the website if they believe that the nature of the transaction and the information required from them by the C2C website is what they expect. On the other hand, consumers are likely to develop distrust towards the website if the interface is suspicious or are required to go through procedures that are atypical. We therefore hypothesize that:

H_7: Situational normality of website positively influences the user's initial trust in C2C e-commerce website.

Structural Assurance (SA). Structural assurance is the belief that structures like guarantees, regulations, promises, legal recourse are in place to support success [21, 22]. Consumers are likely to develop trust in the website if they believe that there are enough safeguards, legal structures and technological features that support the success of their online transactions. In the C2C e-commerce environment where there is little direct interaction with the seller, structural assurance is expected to play an important role in the trust building process. Thus,

H_8: Structural assurances positively influence the user's initial trust in C2C e-commerce website

Initial Trust (TRST). Previous research in e-commerce shows a positive relationship between trust in websites and behavioral intention to engage in transactions on the website [23]. Trust can be categorized as initial trust and continuance trust [23]. Initial trust is most applicable in the context of C2C e-commerce since users lack previous experience with the seller. Initial trust in the C2C website leads users to believe that the website has the ability to perform as expected. Once users develop trust, it is the expectation that they would have positive intentions towards adoption. Thus:

H_9: Initial trust positively influences the user's intention to adopt C2C e-commerce.

3 Methodology

3.1 Measurement Instrument

Items for Performance Expectancy, Effort Expectancy, Social Influence, Facilitating Conditions and Behavioral Intention were derived from Venkatesh et al. [5] Situational Normality was also derived from Gefen et al. [22], while the items used to measure Structural Assurance were derived from Kim et al. [24]. Items on Trust were also derived from Koufaris and Hampton-Sosa [25]. Finally Actual Use was measured with three items adapted from Kim [26]. All measurement items used in the current study were presented in English and measured using a 5-point Likert scale anchored between Strongly Disagree (1) and Strongly Agree (5).

3.2 Sample and Data Collection

Students from three private universities in Ghana were sampled and asked whether they had C2C e-commerce usage experience. Respondents who answered in the affirmative were given questionnaires to fill, using their previous experience in C2C e-commerce business. A total of 320 questionnaires were handed out. Out of this number, 221 were returned, representing a response rate of 69.1%. Of these responses, 28 were dropped

Table 1. Demographic information of the sample.

	Option	Percentage %
Gender	Male	52.8
	Female	47.2
Age	<20	18.5
	20–29	39.2
	30–39	32.6
	>39	9.7
Educational level	Undergraduate	58.7
	Graduate	41.3
Preferred C2C website	Kaymu.com	15.6
	Olx.com.gh	23.8
	Tisu.com	7.9
	Jumia.com.gh	19.5
	Tonaton.com	33.2

because they contained too many missing values. As a result, 193 valid responses were used for data analysis. Of the valid responses, 47.2% were females and 52.8% were males. Table 1 provides information on the demographic characteristics of respondents.

4 Analysis

4.1 Measurement Model

Reliability was assessed using both Cronbach's alpha (α) and composite reliability (CR). For variables to exhibit satisfactory levels of reliability, it is recommended that values for both Cronbach's alpha and Composite Reliability must be above 0.7 [27].

Table 2. Results for testing reliability and convergent validity.

Construct	Item	Std. Loading	t-Statistics	AVE	CR	α
Behavioral intention	BI1	0.931	79.80	**0.867**	**0.951**	**0.923**
	BI2	0.942	102.77			
	BI3	0.921	61.46			
Effort expectancy	EE1	0.856	26.68	**0.748**	**0.922**	**0.888**
	EE2	0.878	33.64			
	EE3	0.860	26.58			
	EE4	0.866	41.41			
Facilitating conditions	FC1	0.898	50.45	**0.724**	**0.887**	**0.81**
	FC2	0.836	23.90			
	FC3	0.816	23.39			

(continued)

Table 2. (*continued*)

Construct	Item	Std. Loading	t-Statistics	AVE	CR	α
Performance expectancy	PE1	0.884	41.97	**0.781**	**0.934**	**0.907**
	PE2	0.889	46.53			
	PE3	0.870	37.13			
	PE4	0.891	47.93			
Structural assurance	SA1	0.873	37.55	**0.717**	**0.91**	**0.868**
	SA2	0.849	32.69			
	SA3	0.864	34.29			
	SA4	0.800	21.77			
Situational normality	SN1	0.866	34.85	**0.764**	**0.907**	**0.846**
	SN2	0.892	47.57			
	SN3	0.863	36.09			
Social influence	SI1	0.919	26.24	**0.821**	**0.902**	**0.783**
	SI2	0.893	26.63			
Trust	TRST1	0.889	54.24	**0.809**	**0.927**	**0.882**
	TRST2	0.901	59.24			
	TRST3	0.908	67.56			
Actual use	USE1	0.944	123.23	**0.876**	**0.955**	**0.929**
	USE2	0.933	90.01			
	USE3	0.931	76.74			

From Table 2, it is evident that all constructs are reliable. Convergent validity is assessed with average variance extracted (AVE) measure and factor loadings of items. Variables with AVE greater than 0.5 are seen to have satisfactory levels of convergent validity [27]. From Table 2, it can be seen that AVE for each construct is above 0.5 indicating that our measurement model exhibits good convergent validity.

Table 3. Test for discriminant validity using the Fornell- Larcker criterion

	USE	BI	EE	FC	PE	SN	SI	SA	TRST
USE	**0.936**								
BI	0.697	**0.931**							
EE	0.633	0.596	**0.865**						
FC	0.483	0.500	0.630	**0.851**					
PE	0.449	0.516	0.586	0.510	**0.804**				
SN	0.566	0.589	0.527	0.391	0.470	**0.874**			
SI	0.33	0.349	0.319	0.28	0.326	0.326	**0.906**		
SA	0.600	0.520	0.389	0.268	0.322	0.605	0.329	**0.847**	
TRST	0.766	0.655	0.587	0.561	0.449	0.643	0.348	0.642	**0.899**

Note: Square root of average variance extracted (AVEs) are shown on diagonal and off-diagonals are inter-construct correlations.

Discriminant validity on the other hand was assessed using the Fornell- Larker criterion [28]. According to this Fornell and Larcker [28] discriminant validity is exhibited when the AVE of each latent construct is greater than the squared correlations between any other construct. Evidence of discriminant validity is presented in Table 3. Based on our results, we conclude good psychometric properties for our latent constructs.

4.2   Structural Model

Once the measurement model has been shown to be reliable and valid, the structural model can then be assessed. Using a bootstrap resampling procedure with 5000 sub-samples drawn with replacements from the initial sample of 193 samples, the significance of the path coefficients was tested. We found Performance Expectancy ($\beta = 0.496$, $p < 0.001$) to have the most significant effect on Behavioral Intention, providing support for H_1. In support for H_3, Effort Expectancy ($\beta = 0.132$, $p < 0.05$) was found to predict Behavioral Intention. Social Influence ($\beta = 0.037$, $p > 0.1$) was however found not to be a significant predictor of Behavioral Intention. Trust ($\beta = 0.243$, $p < 0.01$) was found to be the second most significant predictor of Behavioral Intention. In all, our model was able to account for 62.3% of the variability in Behavioral Intention. Performance Expectancy ($\beta = 0.359$, $p < 0.001$), Situational Normality ($\beta = 0.223$, $p < 0.01$), and Structural Assurance ($\beta = 0.343$, $p < 0.001$)

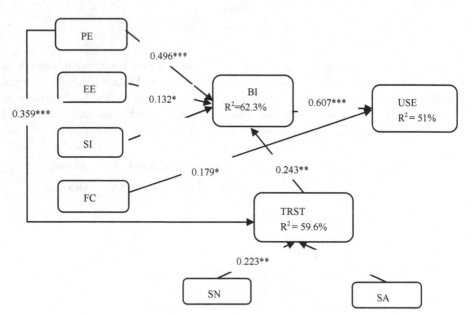

*** Significant at $p = 0.001$ **; significant at $p = 0.01$; *significant at $p = 0.05$; ns not significant

Fig. 1. PLS results for structural model

Table 4. Path coefficients and their significance

Hypotheses	Path	Path coefficient	t-Statistics	p-values	Results
H_1	PE→BI	0.496***	6.772	0.000	Supported
H_2	PE→TRST	0.359***	6.010	0.000	Supported
H_3	EE→BI	0.132*	2.156	0.031	Supported
H_4	SI→BI	0.037 ns	0.736	0.462	Not supported
H_5	FC→USE	0.179*	2.585	0.010	Supported
H_6	BI→USE	0.607***	10.386	0.000	Supported
H_7	SN→TRST	0.223**	3.204	0.001	Supported
H_8	SA→TRST	0.343***	5.152	0.000	Supported
H_9	TRST→BI	0.243**	3.314	0.001	Supported

*** significant at $p = 0.001$; ** significant at $p = 0.01$; *significant at $p = 0.05$; ns not significant

were found to be significant predictors of Initial Trust, providing support for H_2, H_7 and H_8 respectively. These variables jointly explained about 59.6% of the variability in trust. As expected, Behavioral Intention ($\beta = 0.607$, $p < 0.001$) was found to be a significant predictor of Actual Use. Besides, Facilitating Conditions ($\beta = 0.179$, $p < 0.05$) was also found to be a significant predictor of Actual Use. Both Facilitating Conditions and Behavioral Intention accounted for 51% of the variability in Actual Use. Results for the structural model assessment are presented in Table 4 and Fig. 1.

5   Discussion and Implications

Of the UTAUT constructs, performance expectancy was found to have the strongest effect on behavioral intention to adopt C2C e-commerce websites as established in the literature [11]. C2C platform providers should therefore strive at developing more user-friendly interfaces that would meet the performance expectations of their customers. While most of the C2C providers do not allow the use of credit or debit cards, the inclusion of this feature would go a long way to improving the users' perception of the usefulness of the C2C websites. Consistent with Venkatesh et al. [16], the study found effort expectancy to be a significant predictor of behavioral intention. This implies that if users found the C2C easy to navigate they were more likely to form positive behavioral intention towards the adoption of the platform. Our results could be due to the fact that our sample was drawn from young university students who are technology savvy. Our study did not find social influence to be a significant predictor of behavioral intention. A plausible reason for this insignificant relationship is that, e-commerce transactions are personal and since users would not want to lose their privacy in such transactions, the need to impress peers and others who are important to the user is overshadowed by the need to keep the transactions confidential.

Structural assurance and situational normality were found to have a strong effect on initial trust. This result is consistent with numerous studies in the IT adoption literature [11, 21, 29]. In C2C, trust becomes an important issue since the chance of returning items bought is non-existent. Platform providers could improve trust by improving the quality of their website as this would enhance users' perception of situational normality. Because there are currently no specific laws for internet-based fraud in Ghana, users may be skeptical in adopting C2C e-commerce if they feel that the legal framework for online shopping is not well developed to address their concerns should they encounter one. Also, since trust is based on the ability of the service provider, users who find the website useful in their online purchases would develop trust in the system. As is the case with previous research [16], our study also found support for the link between behavioral intention and actual use and that it was stronger than the link between facilitating conditions and actual use. Altogether, facilitating conditions and behavioral intention accounted for 51% of the variability in actual use. Based on the findings, we argue that, when users have a behavioral intention to adopt and the facilitating conditions such as support from friends and technical infrastructure are present, they would want to adopt C2C e-commerce websites.

From a theoretical perspective, this study makes several important contributions to the body of knowledge. First, this study synergistically integrates two theories in information systems research; the UTAUT model and the Initial Trust model to predict user adoption of C2C e-commerce websites in an emerging market. In addition to the significant direct effect that performance expectancy has on behavioral intention, performance expectancy was also found to have an indirect effect through trust. This suggests that intrinsic factors such as trust should be incorporated into models of adoption.

Results from our analysis suggest that performance expectancy is the most significant predictor of behavioral intention. Since consumers cannot verify the quality of the products sold on these C2C e-commerce websites, managers must design their websites to reflect the quality of the product being sold and also manage the evidence of quality as presented by the seller. A well-designed website would also reduce the uncertainties associated with online purchases and improve trust in the system. It will also reduce the time effort used to navigate the platform thereby improving users' perception of effort expectancy.

Results from the study also show that initial trust is a strong predictor of usage intention. Thus, it is important for platform providers to find ways of improving initial trust that potential users have in the system. This could be achieved by focusing in on the antecedents of trust. Platform providers should devote much effort to designing quality websites as it would improve users' perception of situational normality. Platform providers should strive to develop websites that are usable since usability reduces the risks of uncertainty thereby increasing the trust that users have in the system. To improve the interaction between the sell and buyer and build trust, the platform providers could also include an instant message feature on their websites.

5.1 Limitations

Firstly, while our research participants reflect a fairly typical band of actual users of C2C e-commerce, they may not be representative of all C2C e-commerce users. It is therefore important to be cautious in generalizing these results. Secondly, the authors did not consider the moderating effects of demographic variables such as age and gender, in future research it would be interesting to examine the effects of these variables. Thirdly, the authors made no distinction between sellers and buyers on the C2C e-commerce platform. Finally, the study used cross-sectional data, further research could employ longitudinal data. It would be particularly interesting to explore how the effect of trust on behavioral intention will change with time.

References

1. Teo, T.S.H., Liu, J.: Consumer trust in e-commerce in the United States, Singapore and China. Omega **35**, 22–38 (2007)
2. Yoon, H.S., Occeña, L.G.: Influencing factors of trust in consumer-to-consumer electronic commerce with gender and age. Int. J. Inf. Manag. **35**, 352–363 (2015)
3. CNNIC: Statistical report on internet development in China, p. 57 (2013)
4. Chen, J., Zhang, C., Xu, Y.: The role of mutual trust in building members' loyalty to a C2C platform provider. Int. J. Electron. Commer. **14**, 147–171 (2009)
5. Venkatesh, V., Morris, M.G., Davis, G.B., Davis, F.D.: User acceptance of information technology: toward a unified view. MIS Q. **27**, 425–478 (2003)
6. McKnight, D.H., Cummings, L.L., Chervany, N.L.: Initial trust formation in new organisational relationship. Acad. Manag. Rev. **23**, 473–490 (1998)
7. Lefebvre, L.-A., Lefebvre, É., Elia, E., Boeck, H.: Exploring B-to-B e-commerce adoption trajectories in manufacturing SMEs. Technovation **25**, 1443–1456 (2005)
8. Kwahk, K., Ge, X., Park, J.: Investigating the determinants of purchase intention in C2C e-commerce. Int. J. Soc. Behav. Educ. Econ. Bus. Ind. Eng. **6**, 497–501 (2012)
9. AbuShanab, E., Pearson, J.M.: Internet banking in Jordan: the unified theory of acceptance and use of technology (UTAUT) perspective. J. Syst. Inf. Technol. **9**, 78–97 (2007)
10. Martins, C., Oliveira, T., Popovič, A.: Understanding the internet banking adoption: a unified theory of acceptance and use of technology and perceived risk application. Int. J. Inf. Manag. **34**, 1–13 (2014)
11. Oliveira, T., Faria, M., Thomas, M.A., Popovič, A.: Extending the understanding of mobile banking adoption: when UTAUT meets TTF and ITM. Int. J. Inf. Manag. **34**, 689–703 (2014)
12. Loo, W.H., Yeow, P.H.P., Chong, S.C.: User acceptance of Malaysian government multipurpose smartcard applications. Gov. Inf. Q. **26**, 358–367 (2009)
13. Dečman, M.: Modeling the acceptance of e-learning in mandatory environments of higher education: the influence of previous education and gender. Comput. Human Behav. **49**, 272–281 (2015)
14. Slade, E., Williams, M., Dwivdei, Y.: Extending UTAUT2 to explore consumer adoption of mobile payments. In: 23rd UK Academy for Information Systems Conference Proceedings (2013)
15. Dulle, F.W., Minishi-Majanja, M.K.: The suitability of the unified theory of acceptance and use of technology (UTAUT) model in open access adoption studies. Inf. Dev. **27**, 32–45 (2011)
16. Venkatesh, V., Thong, J.Y.L., Xu, X.: Consumer acceptance and use of information technology: extending the unified theory of acceptance and use of technology. MIS Q. **36**, 157–178 (2012)
17. Lian, J.-W., Yen, D.C.: Online shopping drivers and barriers for older adults: age and gender differences. Comput. Human Behav. **37**, 133–143 (2014)

18. Shin, D.H.: Towards an understanding of the consumer acceptance of mobile wallet. Comput. Human Behav. **25**, 1343–1354 (2009)
19. Davis, F.D.: Perceived usefulness, perceived ease of use, and user acceptance of information technology. MIS Q. **13**, 319–340 (1989)
20. McKnight, D.H., Choudhury, V., Kacmar, C.: Developing and validating trust measures for e-commerce: an integrative typology. Inf. Syst. Res. **13**, 334–359 (2002)
21. Yousafzai, S.Y., Pallister, J.G., Foxall, G.R.: Strategies for building and communicating trust in electronic banking: a field experiment. Psychol. Mark. **22**, 181–201 (2005)
22. Gefen, D., Karahanna, E., Straub, D.W.: Trust and TAM in online shopping: an integrated model. MIS Q. **27**, 51–90 (2003)
23. Zhou, T.: An empirical examination of initial trust in mobile banking. Internet Res. **21**, 527–540 (2011)
24. Kim, H.-W., Xu, Y., Koh, J.: A comparison of online trust building factors between potential customers and repeat customers. J. Assoc. Inf. Syst. **5**, 392–420 (2004)
25. Koufaris, M., Hampton-Sosa, W.: The development of initial trust in an online company by new customers. Inf. Manag. **41**, 377–397 (2004)
26. Kim, B.: The diffusion of mobile data services and applications: exploring the role of habit and its antecedents. Telecommun. Policy **36**, 69–81 (2012)
27. Henseler, J., Ringle, C.M., Sinkovics, R.: The use of partial least squares path modeling in international marketing. Adv. Int. Mark. **20**, 277–319 (2009)
28. Fornell, C., Larcker, D.F.: Evaluating structural equation models with unobservable variables and measurements error. J. Mark. Res. **18**, 39–50 (1981)
29. Kim, G., Shin, B., Lee, H.G.: Understanding dynamics between initial trust and usage intentions of mobile banking. Inf. Syst. J. **19**, 283–311 (2009)

A Conceptual Model to Guide the Evaluation of E-Business Value in Small and Medium-Sized Enterprises in Botswana

Meduduetso Tsumake[(✉)] and Michael Kyobe

University of Cape Town, Private Bag X3, Rondebosch 7701, South Africa
mlatsumake@gmail.com, michael.kyobe@uct.ac.za

Abstract. The implementation of electronic business (e-business) in organisations has led to a major improvement in business performance in both developed and developing countries. This improvement as well as market forces have put pressure on Small and Medium-sized Enterprises (SMEs) to adopt e-business. However, the e-business models adopted by SMEs are often abstruse and poorly represented, which leads to time consumption and miscommunication between the stakeholders involved, the business operations and Information Technology (IT) functions. These unclear e-business models make it difficult to evaluate its value. In Botswana, SMEs are the major drivers of the economy. This research examines the elements necessary for this e-business value creation and draws from different disciplines and theories to create a comprehensive model for e-business evaluation in SMEs. This model can help (1) stakeholders investigate, communicate and make appropriate decisions and (2) aid SMEs to successfully integrate e-business in their business processes and practices.

Keywords: E-business · E-business value · SMEs · Evaluation
Conceptual model · Botswana

1 Introduction

The continued use of the internet has become a predominant game changer in business practices in both developed and developing countries [1]. More companies have had to re-think how they conduct business, which is a result of the major investments made in Information and Communication Technology (ICT) adoption in businesses today. With the rapid growth of electronic business (e-business) and as more companies adopt and invest in it, it is crucial to investigate its value creation, more so in Small and Medium-sized Enterprises (SMEs) as they have become significant contributors to employment creation and helpers of local improvement and innovation [2]. In Botswana, [3] conducted a study that revealed that ICT SMEs help the Botswana government immensely with over 80% of business activity. However, with this significant growth of SMEs in Botswana and e-business, little has been done to measure the value created in e-business adoption in Botswana SMEs.

It is essential to better understand the post-adoption differences in usage and value [4] of e-business in order for companies to appreciate this value and to fully enjoy it.

© ICST Institute for Computer Sciences, Social Informatics and Telecommunications Engineering 2018
V. Odumuyiwa et al. (Eds.): AFRICOMM 2017, LNICST 250, pp. 293–303, 2018.
https://doi.org/10.1007/978-3-319-98827-6_28

This study argues that there is no conceptual model that measures this e-business value creation in SMEs in Botswana. Such a model could assist stakeholders of SMEs in Botswana that have adopted e-business, or would like to adopt e-business to recognise the essential elements that are critical to the company and an e-business model and to understand e-business operations in order to create e-business value.

This paper will therefore learn and acquire from different viewpoints to create a comprehensive model that evaluates the value of e-business in SMEs in Botswana. It aims to develop a comprehensive model by providing an answer to the question: How is the value of e-business in SMEs in Botswana evaluated? Such a model could also assist SMEs to be able to successfully integrate e-business in their business processes and practices, and to avoid the failure of e-business.

1.1 Definitions

E-Business: According to [5], e-business is defined as the use of internet to conduct or support business activities along the value chain [6].

SMEs: The criteria for the definition of an SME differs from country to country [7]. In Botswana, an SME is defined as an entity that takes on less than 25 employees and has an annual turnover of between P60,000 and P1,500,000, and a medium-sized enterprise with less than one hundred workers including the owner and an annual turnover of between P1,500,000 and P5,000,000 [8]. Because this study is focused in Botswana, it will adopt the definition provided by BICA.

E-Business Value: [9] define e-business value as the effect of using e-business for firm performance. Furthermore, they discuss that the firm's performance is determined by the downstream sales, upstream procurement and internal operations along the value chain. These are the major activities of the value chain, and this suggests that value is created if e-business adoption within the firm results in an increase in sales and a better customer service, a reduction in costs of purchasing business goods and products, improvement in coordination with the suppliers and employee effectiveness and efficiency of inter-organizational processes.

2 E-Business in Botswana

When it comes to e-business development, research shows that the common challenges that most developing countries encounter are based on a lack of economic, infrastructural, social and political factors. [10] categorise these factors under e-readiness, which they suggest is lower in developing countries than developed countries. E-readiness is defined as the degree to which a country or organisation is willing to adopt ICT for value creation and competitive advantage [11]. [12] argue that, based on a recent study conducted by [13] on e-readiness in Africa, Botswana has one of the best performing economies in Africa, and that on a five-point scale, and an African e-readiness mean of 2.22, it comes in second after South Africa with a score of 2.47. However, even with this good score of e-readiness, Botswana still encounters challenges when it comes to adopting e-business activities.

Most studies on the adoption of e-business in Botswana identify technological, environmental and organisational factors as major impediments to e-business development. [3] adopt a technology-organisation-environment framework in their paper, as well as the owner/manager challenge. They argue on technological challenges in Botswana such as slow internet speed, organisational challenges such as the way in which organisations prefer to do business, for example by face-to-face interactions, environmental challenges such as economic and political instability in the country as well the owner/managers' lack of visionary leadership and entrepreneurial ability, as major impediments to e-business adoption in organisations in the country. Although organisational challenges are discussed in their paper, little is discussed in terms of internal business challenges as inhibitors of e-business, such as the business mission and strategy as well as business processes.

Another study conducted by [14] on e-commerce technology adoption by SMEs in Botswana aims to assess the adoption of e-commerce in the country. The findings of their study revealed that to create e-business value in terms of return on investments, support of SMEs is essential in areas such as financial resources, capability of users and technology. However, these authors looked at this value creation and support from a technological point of view, and discussed the need for financial resources and capable users in support of this technology. From the existing literature, it is evident that the majority of the studies conducted on e-business and e-commerce in Botswana discuss and focus more on the technological, environmental and external organisational aspects of the business. Little research has been done in evaluating e-business from an internal business perspective. The Table 1 below shows the gaps identified in literature in the Botswana context.

Table 1. Gaps identified in literature

Source/study	Business mission and strategy	Business processes	Entrepreneurial drive	Management capabilities	Financial resources	Users capabilities	Technology	E-Business value
Shemi and Proctor (2013)			X	X	X	X	X	
Olatokun and Kebonye (2010)		X	X	X	X	X	X	X
Mutula and van Brakel (2006)		X			X	X	X	
Uzoka and Seleka (2006)		X					X	
Nkwe (2012)		X		X	X	X	X	
Mutula and Mosbert (2010)			X	X	X	X	X	
Chinyanyu Mpofu and Watkins-Mathys (2011)			X	X	X	X	X	
Ntozintle Jobodwana (2009)			X	X	X	X	X	X
Dlodlo and Dhurup (2010)			X	X	X	X	X	X

*X represents what's covered in the study

3 E-Business Value

There are several approaches that explain e-business value. [15] Value-Chain Model focuses on the economic implications (i.e. costs and value) of business functions and activities by identifying the primary activities (which have a direct impact on value creation) and support activities (which affect value through their impact on the primary activities performance) and the value they add in the chain. If all these activities add value to the chain, overall value is created. The Resource-Based View is another approach that explains value. Here, value is created by using various resources that are economically valuable, difficult to imitate, or imperfectly mobile across firms [16, 17]. This means that e-business value is created by focusing on using e-business resources in a firm that are efficient and effective, cannot be copied by any other firm, and cannot be moved across the firm. This approach fits well with the needs of SME managers and owners, as they are able to strategically focus on resources that are critical to the company and align them with the company's strategic intent (which is developed by the company's management), resulting in value creation through key performances or successes [18]. Economic theory suggests that value is created by looking at the supply, i.e. large capital investments on Information Systems and demand side: increase of users of information technology, taking into consideration the uncertainty of actual benefits of the technology and switching costs [19]. This assumes that value is created by using Information Systems on a large scale, and where the demand to use technology is high. Each approach looks at value from a different perspective. While Porter's Value-Chain Model looks at value from a business activity perspective, the Resource-based view focuses on the resources of the firm. The economic theory, on the other hand, looks at demand and supply of IS/IT. The aim of this study is to come up with a framework that measures the overall value created in SMEs. It will therefore encompass some dimensions from each of these theories.

4 Determinants of E-Business Value

When it comes to discussing e-business requirements, this paper uses the viewpoints discussed in the paper by [20]. They state that in the development of IS, three major perspectives have to be considered. These are the value viewpoint which represents the creation of economic value, the process viewpoint which suggests the use of business processes for the operationalization of the value perspective, and lastly, the system architecture viewpoint, which is the IS that enables and supports e-business processes. However, [21] suggests that for there to be competitiveness in the buying and selling of goods over the internet, resources, capabilities, processes or firm knowledge that provides firm performance have to be involved. Therefore aside from the viewpoints of [20], this paper also recognises and incorporates the human factor capabilities, the business mission and strategy as well as the resources available.

Value Viewpoint. This can be understood from the economic theory perspective. [20] suggest that there are various dimensions or aspects which form the e^3-value ontology. This paper considered some of these value aspects which are (1) the actor (an independent economic entity capable of making a profit, for example. an individual, an entrepreneur an SME etc.); (2) the value object (the service, product, money or consumer experience that is exchanged between actors); (3) the value port (an interface or a connection point that interconnects actors so that they may exchange value objects); (4) the value interface (a mechanism that allows two or more actors to communicate or interact e.g. a website); (5) the value exchange (the act of giving value objects and receiving them in return or trading value objects between actors); (6) the value offering (the act of giving an actor the opportunity to exchange a value object) and (7) the value activity (the act of performing a process that is profitable between two or more actors). These value aspects are interlinked in that each one is dependent on another and each is necessary for value creation. For instance, the actor instigates value activity by creating value objects, which are then offered (value offering) to other actors for exchange (value exchange). These value objects are offered to other actors through value interfaces, and value exchange is enabled by value ports as they aid with this interconnection. Therefore if all of these aspects are present in an e-business model, they form e-business value.

Process Viewpoint. According to [20], the process viewpoint discusses the operationalization of the value viewpoint by using business processes. This simply means integrating the business processes with the value viewpoint. This integration can clearly be explained by the value chain theory [15], as it looks at value-adding activities within the firm. The value chain theory predicts that overall value is created if each of the primary and support activities within an organisation add value. [22] discuss [23] PIT model of ICT Adoption by SMEs. This model consists of processes used by SMEs through the adoption of ICT. For the availability, interaction and exchange of these processes within the e-business, channels in which these processes are transferred from one end to another must be in place. [24] discuss that this exchange and interaction of services, products and information sharing can occur between channels such as the business-to-business (B2B), business-to-consumer (B2C), business-to-employee (B2E), business-to-government (B2G) and a Hybrid of B2B and B2C models. Although they discuss other channels of e-business such as consumer-to-consumer (C2C), this study focuses only on those that are directly impacted by the business. Overall, if the e-business process is effectively and efficiently integrated with the value viewpoint, this results in e-business value creation.

Architecture Viewpoint. In this paper, the architecture perspective implies the technology used to support these business activities. [20] discuss this viewpoint as an IS/IT enabler and supporter of the e-business processes. This is explained by the technology theory, specifically the theory of ICT as an enabler. [25] predicts that five (5) levels of IT-enabled business configuration should exist in an organization for there to be added value. These levels include the IT functionality within a business, leveraging IT throughout the entire business, business process integration, business network integration and business scope integration. These levels explain how technology is used to support and enable internal and external business processes as well as the organization as a whole for added value. [24] discuss the specific technologies that support and enable e-business as being the electronic data interchange (EDI) and internet. Both these technologies use telecommunication infrastructure for electronic connections which enable information transactions.

Furthermore, [24] discuss how the availability of broadband channels, which are cables or fibre optic lines that allow more and faster data transfer, have been the final breakthrough for the enablement of e-business. With this advanced technology, e-business processes are better supported and enabled, which results in e-business value creation within organisations.

Human Factor. This factor is explained by the entrepreneurship theory discussed by [26]. According to this theory, entrepreneurs need to possess an entrepreneurial orientation consisting of certain methods, practices and organizational behaviours in order to keep the firm competitive. The human factor discusses this entrepreneurial orientation. For the successful adoption and value creation of e-business, an SME needs to have visionary and capable leaders. These leaders include the entrepreneur and managers. [27] argues that for the success of IS, entrepreneurs have to possess certain qualities and traits that distinguish them from others. Furthermore, he suggests that behaviour characteristics such as attitude to technology, risk taking, commitment and control over resources influence the entrepreneur's ability to effectively respond to technology adoption. [28] also suggest that the entrepreneur's knowledge of IT and outlook of innovation drive this e-business adoption. The SMEs' managers also need to possess these traits. They should have the relevant ICT information good managerial skills and should be able to allocate their time, resources and encouragement for the use of IS within the firm [29]. If the human factor within an organization consists of all these traits and capabilities, e-business is more likely to be adopted and efficiently implemented in the organization, resulting in the creation of e-business value.

Business Mission and Strategy. Stakeholders of SMEs need to be able to understand the business mission (what the business is about) so that they can develop and implement proper and innovative business strategies that support, drive and help the business to achieve this mission. The business mission provides the overall direction in which the business is going. Both the business mission and strategy are explained by the strategic management theory. [30] discusses innovation in strategic management as a fundamental consideration in adding value in a business. This means that for an organization to create and add value, it needs to have innovative strategies that support the business mission. According to [24], IT managers need to be aware of the business strategy and e-business plan in order to develop the right e-business technology to support the business processes. [31] discuss strategic competencies as those that establish a direct link with customers, use technology to stand out from the rest of the companies and develop and provide new products and services. It is hence essential to be able to understand and know these competencies when developing the business strategy, so as to ensure proper alignment with the e-business plan and technology. This alignment drives e-business adoption and influences e-business value.

Availability of Resources. In order for companies to fully experience e-business value, it is essential for them to stay interactive and maintain the e-business. This element is explained by the resource-based view [16, 17], which discusses the use of resources that are efficient and effective, cannot be copied by any other firm, and cannot be moved across the firm. This paper focuses on financial resources and the users of the e-business for the creation of e-business value. [31] discuss the need for financial resources which are necessary to invest in the right technology, to be able to regularly maintain the business websites, to integrate the company's information management systems and to provide proper interfacing with customers. To stay interactive with the e-business, companies also need to have employees in place who ensure that this interaction is maintained. [32] suggest that these employees need to possess some IT knowledge, IT technical capability, technical expertise and an intellectual resource (the employee's educational qualification and work experience that distinguish them from the others). These traits make it easier to train these employees when adopting the new system, and makes them more aware in determining the value created by the system. This is especially necessary in SMEs, as they are characterized by a smaller number of employees. With the use of financial resources and capable employees, the e-business is well maintained and stays interactive, which results in e-business value.

5   Evaluation of E-Business Value

In order to improve business performance by using e-business in SMEs, it is important to evaluate the elements that lead to its value creation. [33], define evaluation as the decisive assessment of defined entities, based on a set of criteria, to solve a given problem. In this study, the evaluation process will involve a critical assessment of some elements of the value creation approaches and determinants of e-business value discussed above, in the context of Botswana, which, if exist in a business, create e-business value. [34] suggest that evaluation be achieved by examining (i) outset situations (organisational norms and values, IS project contingencies and IS project resources), (ii) the business development process (for example IS development and procurement) and (iii) the outcomes (for example. success of IS implementation, investment and functionality). This e-business value evaluation will furthermore examine the outset situations of e-business (for example. the organizational mission and strategy, the processes involved, technology and e-business resources), and its outcomes and post-adoption (i.e., the e-business value created).

6   Research Framework and Propositions

Following the above discussion, the conceptual model below (Fig. 1) has been developed to evaluate the value of e-business in SMEs in Botswana. It adopts some dimensions from each of the theories discussed, which are specific to the nature of SMEs, as defined in this study. It aims to fully capture the overall value created in e-business for SMEs. Following the conceptual model, Table 2 below summarizes the constructs used, their definitions, the theories they discuss and their sources.

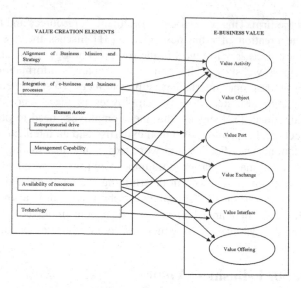

Fig. 1. A research model of the elements that create e-business value

Table 2. Constructs, explanations and sources

Construct	Explanation	Theory	Source
Business mission and strategy	Competent and innovative strategies support and aid the achievement of the business mission which leads to the growth and development of the business	Strategic Management Theory	[15, 24, 31]
E-business and business processes	This is the integration of business processes with the e-business so as to operationalize the e-business model. For example, using e-business to order and purchase inventory online and generate automated billings	Value Chain Theory	[10, 12, 14, 15, 20, 22–24]
Human actor	Consists of the entrepreneur's drive to adopt technology and management's capabilities which ensure the smooth integration of this e-business adoption within the SME	Entrepreneurship Theory	[3, 14, 15, 27–29]
Availability of resources	This is the use of financial resources that support, maintain and enable e-business, as well as employees who are skilled, experienced and have knowledge of ICT to use the e-business for business processes	Resource – Based Theory	[3, 10, 14, 16, 17, 19, 31, 32]
Technology	This is the technology needed to support and enable the business processes in the e-business	Technology Theory	[3, 10, 12, 14, 19, 20, 24]
E-business value	This is the tangible and intangible value created in e-business. Value is broken down into actors, value activities, value objects, value interfaces, value ports, value exchanges and value offerings	Economic Theory	[14–17, 19–21]

From the research model above, the following propositions have been formulated:

Proposition 1: The more aligned the business strategy is with the business mission in an SME, the greater the value activity.

Proposition 2: The stronger the integration of e-business is with the business processes in an SME, the greater the development of value objects and occurrence of value activity.

Proposition 3a: The more the capabilities of the human actor are in an SME, the greater the value activity and better the value interface.

Proposition 3b: The more the capabilities of the human actor are in an SME, the greater the value offering and value exchange.

Proposition 4a: The more the financial resources and employees there are in an SME, the greater the development of value objects and occurrence of value activity.

Proposition 4b: The more the financial resources and employees there are in an SME, the greater the value offering and value exchange.

Proposition 5: The more the technology there is in an SME, the greater the value ports and better the value interface.

Proposition 6: The more value creation elements there are in an SME, the greater the e-business value.

7   Conclusion

The main objective of this study was to develop a conceptual framework that evaluates the value of e-business in SMEs in Botswana. In order to achieve this, the literature review drew from several different disciplines and theories, and identified gaps which led to the development of this multi-theoretical model. The model reveals some factors that have not been looked at in previous research. Most studies show that the main challenges that impede e-business adoption and value are technological challenges, lack of resources such as financial and user capabilities and challenges in business processes. However, there are other factors which have not been sufficiently explored in previous research such as a misalignment of business mission and strategy, lack of entrepreneurial drive and management capabilities, which also greatly impede e-business adoption and value creation. While this study focuses in Botswana, the developed model is not just limited to the country, but is also applicable to other countries as well. This model can also guide further research in assisting stakeholders in SMEs on e-business operations and elements necessary for the smooth running of the e-business. Such studies will have implications in practice as it can help guide government policies and initiatives in order to encourage the diffusion of new ICT technologies in Botswana. There is also a need to educate and train entrepreneurs and managers on the benefits of e-business as well as technology as a whole, as they are drivers of the business. Such training would help them possess competent capabilities necessary for them to make informed and innovative decisions on the business mission and strategy, processes and practices. On a theoretical level, such research will advance theories such as the economic theory, value chain theory, resource-based theory, entrepreneurship theory, strategic management theory and technology theory and show how they can be applied to the e-business value context.

References

1. Mann, L., Graham, M., Friederici, N.: The Internet and Business Process Outsourcing in East Africa: Value Chains and Connectivity-Based Enterprises in Kenya and Rwanda. Oxford Internet Institute, Oxford (2014)
2. Jones, P., Packham, G., Beynon-Davies, P., Pickernell, D.: False promises: E-Business deployment in Wales' SME community. J. Syst. Inf. Technol. **13**, 163–178 (2011)
3. Shemi, A., Proctor, C.T.: Challenges of E-Commerce adoption in SMEs: an interpretive case study of Botswana. Botswana J. Bus. **6**, 17–30 (2013)
4. DeLone, W.H., McLean, E.R.: Information systems success: the quest for the dependent variable. Inf. Syst. Res. **3**, 60–95 (1992)
5. Barua, A., Konana, P., Whinston, A.B., Yin, F.: Driving E-Business excellence. MIT Sloan Manag. Rev. **43**, 36–44 (2001)
6. Michael, P.: Strategy and the Internet. Harv. Bus. Rev. **79**, 63–78 (2001)
7. OECD: Financing SMEs and Entrepreneurs an OECD Scoreboard. OECD Publishing, Paris (2013)
8. BICA: Promoting the Growth of Small and Medium Enterprises. African Congress of Accountants Business Case (2013). http://acoa13.com. Accessed September 2014
9. Zhu, K., Kraemer, K.L., Dedrick, J.: Information technology payoff in E-Business environments: an international perspective on value creation of E-Business in the financial services industry. J. Manag. Inf. Sys. **21**, 17–54 (2004)
10. Mutula, S.M., van Brakel, P.: E-Readiness of SMEs in the ICT sector in Botswana with respect to information access. Electron. Libr. **24**, 402–417 (2006)
11. Hung, W.H., et al.: E-Readiness of website acceptance and implementation in SMEs. Comput. Hum. Behav. **40**, 44–55 (2014)
12. Uzoka, F.M.E. Seleka, G.G.: B2C E-Commerce development in Africa: case study of Botswana. In: 7th ACM conference on Electronic commerce, pp 290–295. ACM, New York (2006)
13. Ifinedo, P.: Measuring Africa's E-Readiness in the global networked economy: a nine-country data analysis. Int. J. Educ. Dev. ICT **1**, 53–71 (2005)
14. Olatokun, W., Kebonye, M.: E-Commerce technology adoption by SMEs in Botswana. Int. J. Emerg. Technol. Soc. **8**, 42–56 (2010)
15. Porter, M.E.: Competitive advantage: creating and sustaining superior performance. Free Press, New York (1985)
16. Barney, J.: Firm resources and sustained competitive advantage. J. Manag. **17**, 99–120 (1991)
17. Peteraf, M.A.: The cornerstones of competitive advantage: a resource-based view. Strateg. Manag. J. **14**, 179–191 (1993)
18. Rangone, A.: A resource-based approach to strategy analysis in small-medium sized enterprises. Small Bus. Econ. **12**, 233–248 (1999)
19. Bakos, J.Y., Kemerer, C.F.: Recent applications of economic theory in information technology research. Decis. Support Syst. **8**, 365–386 (1992)

20. Gordijn, J., Akkermans, H.: Designing and evaluating E-Business models. IEEE Intell. Syst. **16**, 11–17 (2001)
21. Sahim, C.: Competitiveness of E-Commerce companies: an integrated approach. Int. J. Ebus. Egover. Stud. **4**, 13–22 (2012)
22. Taylor, M., Murphy, A.: SMEs and E-Business. J. Small Bus. Enterp. Dev. **11**, 280–289 (2004)
23. Foley, P., Ram, M.: The use of online technology by ethnic minority businesses: a comparative study of the West Midlands and UK. SBS Research Directorate, Sheffield (2002)
24. Chen, E.T., Lewis, D.: Adopting E-Business in small and medium enterprise. Commun. IIMA **10**, 29–41 (2010)
25. Venkatraman, N.: IT-enabled business transformation: from automation to business scope redefinition. Sloan Manag. Rev. **35**, 73–87 (1994)
26. Miller, D.: The correlates of entrepreneurship in three types of firms. Manag. Sci. **29**, 770–791 (1983)
27. Kyobe, M.: The impact of entrepreneur behaviours on the quality of E-Commerce security: a comparison of urban and rural findings. J. Glob. Inf. Technol. Manag. **11**, 58–79 (2008)
28. Chatzoglou, P., Chatzoudes, D.: Factors affecting E-Business adoption in SMEs: an empirical research. J. Enterp. Inf. Manag. **29**, 327–358 (2016)
29. Petter, S., DeLone, W., McLean, E.R.: Information systems success: the quest for the independent variables. J. Manag. Inf. Syst. **29**, 7–62 (2013)
30. Drucker, P.F.: The discipline of innovation. Harv. Bus. Rev. **76**, 149–157 (1998)
31. Chaston, I., Badger, B., Mangles, T., Sadler-Smith, E.: Knowledge-based services and the internet: an investigation of small UK accountancy practices. J. Small Bus. Enterp. Dev. **9**, 49–60 (2002)
32. Bordonaba-Juste, V., Lucia-Palacios, L., Polo-Redondo, Y.: Antecedents and consequences of e-business adoption for European retailers. Internet Res. **22**, 532–550 (2012)
33. Ammenwerth, E., Graber, S., Herrmann, G., Burkle, T., Konig, J.: Evaluation of health information systems – problems and challenges. Int. J. Med. Informatics **71**, 125–135 (2003)
34. Hallikainen, P., Chen, L.: A holistic framework on information systems evaluation with a case analysis. Lead. Issues ICT Eval. **9**, 57–64 (2006)

Blockchain Consensus Protocols

Towards a Review of Practical Constraints for Implementation in Developing Countries

Hadja F. Ouattara[1], Daouda Ahmat[2], Fréderic T. Ouédraogo[3],
Tegawendé F. Bissyandé[1,4(✉)], and Oumarou Sié[1]

[1] Université Ouaga I Pr. Joseph Ki-Zerbo, Ouagadougou, Burkina Faso
hadja.ouattara@gmail.com, oumarou.sie@gmail.com
[2] Virtual University of Chad, N'Djamena, Chad
daouda.ahmat@uvt.td
[3] Université Norbert Zongo de Koudougou, Koudougou, Burkina Faso
ouedragoft@gmail.com
[4] SnT, Université du Luxembourg, Esch-sur-Alzette, Luxembourg
tegawende.bissyande@uni.lu

Abstract. There is currently a big rush in the research and practice communities to investigate the blockchain technology towards leveraging its security, immutability and transparency features to create new services or improve existing ones. In developing countries, which are seen as a fertile ground for field testing disruptive technologies, blockchain is viewed as the "trust machine" that is necessary for accelerating development. Unfortunately, the internal working of blockchain as well as its constraints are often overlooked in the design of services. This, in conjunction with a poor regulatory framework, slows down any concrete attempt to build upon the technology. In this paper, we contribute towards accelerating the concrete adoption of blockchain by making explicit the constraints that affect their practical use in the context of developing countries such as African sub-saharan countries. Overall we recommend that the technology should be adjusted to the real-world constraints, in particular those that we currently witness on network latency, computation power as well as cultural gaps.

Keywords: Blockchain · Developing countries · Adoption constraints

1 Introduction

The history of technology has shown that any of its revolutions can drastically change societies [1,2]. For the first time in the history of information technology (IT) revolutions, a single one, beyond the Internet revolution, has the potential "to act on the top-down and centralised authority that States exercise on currency, that banks exercise on financial transactions, that notaries exercise on

© ICST Institute for Computer Sciences, Social Informatics and Telecommunications Engineering 2018
V. Odumuyiwa et al. (Eds.): AFRICOMM 2017, LNICST 250, pp. 304–314, 2018.
https://doi.org/10.1007/978-3-319-98827-6_29

real-state transfers, that energy monopolies exercise on electricity and fuel distributions"[1]. No other technology before the advent of blockchain has provided so many opportunities to rethink existing trust processes.

Briefly summarized, blockchain is a technology for information storage and transmission, which presents three key features: transparent, secured and decentralized. Actually, a blockchain is an immutable digital database that supports facilities for consensual validation of transactions into the database. blockchain appeared concurrently with the Bitcoin cryptocurrency in 2008. Indeed, the blockchain—originally block chain [3]—was first defined as the virtual infrastructure that enables the mining and transfer of bitcoins.

Because blockchains are *secured by design*, and shows high byzantine fault tolerance, they are increasingly used in various industries, most notably the security-sensitive financial domain. The immutability property is also relevant for establishing permanent records of any transaction. Finally, the transparency in the distributed model is essential for setting up public (e.g., national) databases accessible to all stakeholders including citizens.

This paper focuses on a central element in blockchain implementation: the *consensus protocol*, which eventually allows *people/machines who do not know or trust each other, to build a dependable ledger*. Our main contributions include:

- a comparative enumeration of state-of-the-art consensus protocols
- an assessment of consensus protocols with regards to the contextual constraints in developing countries
- suggestions of a roadmap for the sustainable adoption of the blockchain technology across Africa

The remainder of this paper is organized as follows. Section 2 quickly overviews the fundamentals of blockchain working. Section 3 describes a few use cases that are relevant to the developing world. Section 4 describes the consensus protocols and develops their strengths and weaknesses. Section 5 discusses the insights as well as related work. Finally Sect. 6 concludes this paper.

2   Understanding the Blockchain Technology

Similarly to how the concept of "world wide web" has been long assimilated to the internet, blockchain is currently mostly reduced to its cryptocurrency application. Blockchain can however be used to build a broader range of applications involving transactions.

At the core of the blockchain technology is a distributed ledger or decentralized database which keeps records of digital transactions. Instead of implementing a central administrator as in traditional databases (e.g., a bank, the government, an accountant), a distributed ledger has a network of replicated databases, synchronized via the internet and visible to anyone within the network.

---

[1] cf. Preface of Joël de Rosney in the book "La blockchain décryptée - les clefs d'une révolution" by Blockchain France.

Whether they are private with restricted membership (similar to an Intranet) or public and accessible to every one (similar to the Internet), blockchain networks work in the same way as depicted[2] in Fig. 1. When a digital transaction is carried out, it is sent to the network and validated cryptographically by a node, then grouped together in a cryptographically protected block with other transactions that have occurred in the last time frame (generally about 10 min) and sent out to the entire network. When a block is created, all participants in the network evaluate the transactions and, through mathematical calculations, determine whether they are valid, based on agreed-upon rules. When "consensus" has been achieved, typically among more than 50% of participating computers, the transactions are considered verified.

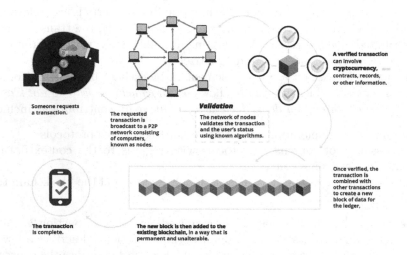

Fig. 1. Typical blockchain working process - Schema courtesy of ©BlockGeeks

By design, blockchains are inherently resistant to modification of the data. Once recorded, the data in any given block cannot be altered retroactively without the alteration of all subsequent blocks and a collusion of the network majority.

3   Blockchain Use-Cases

As largely hinted in previous section, a blockchain mainly solves the pervasive problem of manipulation in transactions and data. Vitalik Buterin, inventor of the Ethereum, was reported to having said the following about manipulation: "when I speak about it in the West, people say they trust Google, Facebook, or

---

[2] Figure elements borrowed from https://blockgeeks.com/guides/what-is-blockchain-technology/.

their banks. But the rest of the world doesn't trust organizations and corporations that much – I mean Africa, India, the Eastern Europe, or Russia. It's not about the places where people are really rich. Blockchain's opportunities are the highest in the countries that haven't reached that level yet" [4].

In the following, we introduce concrete use-cases where blockchain technology can contribute to solving most pressing citizens and governments concerns. We present three families of use-cases, where the first focuses on leveraging the historical objective of blockchain infrastructure, the second considers the features of distribution and transparency of the database, and the third explores advanced automation services.

3.1   Cryptocurrencies and Payments

Historically, blockchain technology is associated with currency. Indeed, after Bitcoin, the main applications of blockchain were the creation of new cryptocurrencies, including Litecoin, Dogecoin, Namecoin.

Generally, fragile economies in developing countries may not be ready for currencies that are "mined" (almost out of thin air) based on computing power. Nevertheless, cryptocurrency systems have desirable properties for solving important issues in developing countries, especially for tracking money flows. Thus, blockchain can be leveraged to develop *digital fiat currency* systems which will be systematically pegged to the national currency (i.e., one would give 1 token from fiat currency in exchange of one crypted digital token). Such digital currencies can be used to properly implement transparent crowdfunding, follow and assess the use of development aid. Finally, cryptocurrencies, because, if needed, they can be traced back in all its exchange paths, can be leveraged to ensure tax contributions by all merchants. This last possibility could be instrumental in more rapidly transforming the informal economy of developing countries into a formal one.

The main advantages that can be gained with this application of blockchain are the reduction of cost for handling cash, collecting taxes, as well as the speed for transactions and reporting.

3.2   Identification/Authentication

Current development of blockchain applications beyond cryptocurrencies, focus on the immutability of its database. In developing countries, this property can be leveraged to solve rooted problems related to identification and authentication based on immutable registries. For example, a common concern lies in tracking land ownership. Another concern for promoting democracy is the count of citizen's vote, ensuring that it is protected and non-temperable.

The main advantage that such applications bring is their openness and flexibility properties, with possibilities to empower users and deliver new business models.

3.3 Smart Contracts

Recently, a new term, *Blockchain 2.0* [6], has been coined to refer to new kinds of applications of the distributed blockchain database. Smart contracts are one possible implementation of this second-generation programmable blockchain which come with "a programming language that allows users to write more sophisticated smart contracts, thus creating invoices that pay themselves when a shipment arrives or share certificates which automatically send their owners dividends if profits reach a certain level" [7].

In developing countries, smart contracts can be heavily relied upon to avoid the dictatorship of intermediates in handling insurance claims or dealing with notary needs. For example, they could serve to manage family trusts and reduce the number of issues that are increasingly seen around inheritance sharing.

The main advantages that this type of applications provide are the autonomy of execution as well as the irrefutability of the transactions. Speed and cost are also incidentally improved.

4 Consensus Models

The consensus mechanism is the most critical feature of a blockchain. It ensures that all participants involved in maintaining a distributed ledger are on the same page, and further enables the distributed network of peers to remain reliable for circulating information even if some of the peers keep failing.

4.1 Recap: Byzantine Generals Problem

To better summarize the challenge to reach consensus, we recall the Byzantine generals problem detailed by Lamport et al. [5]. The following is an excerpt from the seminal 1982 paper on byzantine fault tolerance:

"Several divisions of the Byzantine army are camped outside an enemy city, each division commanded by its own general. The generals can communicate with one another only by messenger. They must decide upon a common plan of action. However, some of the generals may be traitors, trying to prevent the loyal generals from reaching agreement. The generals must have an algorithm to guarantee that:

C_1: All loyal generals decide upon the same plan of action.

The loyal generals will all do what the algorithm says they should, but the traitors may do anything they wish. The algorithm must guarantee condition C_1 regardless of what the traitors do. The loyal generals need to reach agreement and agree on a reasonable plan that also ensures that

C_2: A small number of traitors cannot cause the loyal generals to adopt a bad plan"

Such an algorithm is known as the *consensus protocol*. The goal of this protocol in a public blockchain network is indeed to let many different computing nodes to agree on the current state of the blockchain even though they don't trust each other or any central authority. Therefore, the protocol serves two roles: (a) to ensures that the added block in a blockchain is the one and only version of the truth (i.e., the actual, un-tampered, transaction that was requested), and (b) to prevent adversarial nodes, even when they are computationally powerful, from derailing the system and successfully forking the chain (i.e., creating another chain of transactions). In the remainder of this section, we present a few common protocols implemented in existing blockchain infrastructure initiatives.

4.2 State-of-the-Art Consensus Protocols

Proof-of-Work (PoW) – In this pioneer protocol [8,9], participating nodes "work" to solve difficult mathematical problems, and then broadcast the results in the network. PoW use the number and difficulty of solutions being found to measure what percentage of the network agrees on the state of the blockchain.

To prevent legitimate nodes from coming to agreement about the state of the blockchain, an adversary must control a large portion of the involved computing power in order to seed his/her opinion as the real consensus, or work for perpetual disagreement in the network.

Bitcoin was the first to implement this consensus protocol in a real-world case for cryptocurrencies [10]. Although the requirement for actual resources (computing power, electricity, time) is a strong point for PoW protocols to guarantee efficacy in deterring adversaries, it is also the weak point for efficiency since it involves a constant expenditure and resources to work normally (i.e., even when no one is actually trying to interfere with the blockchain).

Proof-of-Stake (PoS) – The energy inefficiency of PoW protocols have motivated a new consensus protocol [11,12] where agreement within the blockchain network is not measured on the basis of the computing power that is spent to validate a blockchain state, but rather on the basis of the amount of cryptocurrencies that are in agreement with the current state. Thus, a block in the blockchain is now created by a node selected in a deterministic, i.e., pseudo-random, way with a probability that is correlated with its wealth (i.e., its stake). Therefore, mining is done by stakeholders in the ecosystem who have the strongest incentives to be good stewards of the system [13]. PoS has been implemented for the Ethereum blockchain.

PoS-based currencies have been shown to be up to several times more cost-effective than PoW currencies. Unfortunately, simulations have already proven theoretically that simultaneous forging of several chains is possible [14] and can be abused to attempt to double-spend "for free".

Byzantine Fault Tolerant (BFT) – Since blockchain are distributed systems, they can leverage the state-of-the-art practical byzantine fault tolerance (PBFT) [15] for the consensus mechanism. Each blockchain node publishes its public key, and messages coming through the node is signed by the node to verify its format. If a majority of responses are identical, then the blockchain network consensually agrees that the message is a valid transaction.

PBFT was originally designed for low-latency storage systems, and its properties have been argued to be valuable in blockchain use-cases where digital asset-based platforms do not require a large amount of throughput, but instead see a large number of transactions [16]. Hyperledger[3] is an example of blockchain system that relies on PBFT.

Federated Byzantine Agreement (FBA) – Implemented in the Stellar Consensus protocol [17] the FBA model relies on a small sets of trusted parties to achieve quorum: the assumption is that a given node "knows" a subset of nodes in the network. Thus, nodes in the blockchain network agree to accept information from a group of nodes (a.k.a, quorums or slices which are believed will not collude among themselves). Consensus is then formed as these quorums form collective agreement on the information.

Proof of Elapsed Time (PoET) – Introduced by Intel focusing on efficiency, PoET uses secure CPU instructions in processor chips to ensure the safety and randomness of a leader election without requiring costly investment on power and/or hardware. Concretely, every node in the blockchain network requests a wait time from an trusted function. The node with the shortest wait time for a given transaction block is then elected validation leader. The algorithm is said to meet the criteria of a good lottery algorithm where leader role can be bestowed randomly to any of the node with a distribution similar to lottery algorithms where the probability to be selected is proportional to the resources contributed (i.e., how many chips with the trusted functions you have).

The main limitation of the PoET algorithm is that it implicitly moves the trust problem to a single authority, the chip maker, which implements the trusted functions. Nevertheless, PoET can be effective in a private enterprise blockchain setup.

Many other consensus protocols have been directly derived from Proof-of-Work and Proof-of-Stake to address some of their limitations (mainly security guarantees). Among them we can quickly cite Proof-of-Activity (PoA) [18], Proof-of-Burn (PoB) [19] and Proof-of-Capacity (PoC) [20]. We encourage the reader to find more details on these protocols in the literature. We will focus our comparison on the mainstream protocols presented above.

4.3   Comparative Assessment

In this section we discuss a high-level comparison of consensus protocols based on several essential blockchain properties that can be related to the context of developing countries. We first enumerate features regrouped in families following the assessment of Vukolic [16].

---

[3] https://www.hyperledger.org/.

- *Identity management*: This feature relates to how blockchain node identities are managed by the consensus protocols. For example, while PoW implements an entirely *decentralized control* allowing anyone to participate in the blockchain, BFT protocols typically requires every node to know the entire set of its peer nodes participating in the blockchain. The first type of protocols are useful for creating "public" **permissionless** blockchains, while the latter allow to create **permissioned** blockchain.
- *Scalability*: This feature relates to the numbers of nodes that can participate in the blockchain and of clients that can simultaneously send transactions to the system.
- *Performance*: This regroups features related to the latency (how fast are transactions), throughput (how many transactions per unit of time can be submitted) and the amount of power consumed. As an example, Bitcoin shows very limited performance: up to 7 transactions per second, 1-h latency with 6 block confirmation. Furthermore, according to a bitcoin mining-farm operator, energy consumption totaled 240 kWh per bitcoin in 2014 (i.e., approximately the equivalent of 16 gallons of gasoline) [23].

4.4   Property-Based Comparison

Although the properties listed above are not exhaustive for characterizing Blockchain consensus protocols, they allow to differentiate clearly most state-of-the-art algorithms, and are assessment dimensions that are representative for the context of developing countries.

Table 1 provides a comparative listing of the protocols. Positive markings +++, ++ and + indicates that the protocol more or less takes this property into account. Negative markings ---, -- and -, on the other hand, indicate that the design of the consensus protocol was more or less detrimental to this aspect. For example *energy performance* of PoW will be marked as --- while BFT protocol, which shows a very low latency, will be marked as +++ for this aspect.

Table 1. Blockchain consensus protocols

Feature		Consensus protocols				
		PoW	PoS	BFT	FBA	PoET
Decentralized control		+++	+++	---	+++	-
Scalability	Nodes	+++	+++	--	+	+
	Clients	+++	+++	+++	+++	+++
Performance	Latency	---	+	+++	+	++
	Throughput	--	+	+++	+++	++
	Energy	---	++	+++	+++	+++

4.5   Constraints of Developing Countries

Developing countries, including those in sub-Saharan, have specific constraints related to network latency, to the trustworthiness of governments (and their infrastructures), to energy scarcity, and to increasing demographics.

Decentralized control is an essential feature for any blockchain that must truly offer trust to citizens and stakeholders. Unfortunately, PoW, wwich is the most adapted for public, permissionless, fully decentralized blockchain, has numerous caveats with regards to computing power and energy consumption, as well as with regards to latency and throughput. Similarly, although BFT presents desirable properties for latency, its low throughput makes it less interesting for many use cases.

Roadmap: As can be viewed in the comparison table of previous section, all consensus protocols present different strengths and weaknesses. Some consensus protocols are further token-based (e.g., cryptocurrency-oriented blockchains) while some may not be (e.g., general purpose blockchains). It is thus necessary when contemplating the implementation of a blockchain application to consider the expected scenarios and the contextual constraints. This requires a very good understanding of blockchain fundamentals, as well as practical hands-on experience into the inner working of consensus protocols. This work is a stepping stone towards eliciting all parameters to take into account when selecting a blockchain system: e.g., for an online voting system in developing countries, given the instability and corruption risks, it may be suitable to consider only fully decentralized control. For implementing payment systems on the other hand, it may be interesting to focus on permissioned, low-latency, high-throughput blockchains.

5   Insights and Related Work

In January 2017, in response to Sarah Underwood's article 'Blockchain Beyond Bitcoin' [21], Ingo Mueller pointed that many blockchain proponents fail to raise the right questions. He then went on to protest that "Instead of focusing on *what block-chain could do*, one should address *what blockchain can do better than other technologies*. As described above, the underlying consensus algorithms even predate the blockchain phenomenon. For example, Proof-of-work-alike protocol was proposed 15 years before the Bitcoin, while the recent Hyperledger system is developed on top of PBFT which was developed for operating system storage management.

Our work is a step towards asking the right questions about blockchain for developing countries. This article is a first of a series where we aim to explore the applicability of blockchain with regards to developing countries contents. We have so far focused on technical constraints. However, as Mueller pointed out, although blockchain is often credited with the ability to solve tough long-standing problems (e.g., digital identity), one should keep in mind that various attempts to solve such challenges, including state-of-the-art approaches (e.g.,

Public Key infrastructure for digital identity) "have often failed due to non-technical aspects of human relationships, including trust, social, cognitive, economic, and even physical".

With regards to related work, although there is currently a number of blog and websites providing details on the blockchain technology, very few academic work provide a comprehensive view of the current state-of-the-art on blockchain consensus protocols. Jesse et al. [22] have recently presented a systematic literature review of research on blockchain technology. However, the particular of consensus protocols has not been addressed.

6 Conclusion and Future Work

Development of blockchain across various industries is an opportunity for developing countries research and practice around ICT for development. Nevertheless, there is a huge gap between the promise of blockchain and its eventual real impact on our processes. We have contributed in this work with a first look at what options present themselves today with regards to the consensus protocols, the core element of blockchain.

In this article we have focused on the theory of how the protocols are designed. In future work, we plan to experiment with the available software for a better view of the technological readiness level of the different systems. We further plan to enumerate the various non-technical aspects in our societies which can challenge the use of blockchain, and for which there may be a need to develop ad-hoc consensus protocol that is culturally-aligned [24] with developing countries context.

References

1. Latour, B.: Technology is society made durable. Sociol. Rev. **38**(1–suppl), 103–131 (1990)
2. Bell, D.: The coming of the post-industrial society. Educ. Forum. **40**(4), 574–579 (1976)
3. Brito, J., Castillo, C.: Bitcoin: A Primer for Policymakers. Mercatus Center at George Mason University, Arlington (2013)
4. Vitalik buterin about ethereum, smart contracts, and himself, May 2016. https://goo.gl/C58nJZ
5. Lamport, L.: The byzantine generals problem. ACM Trans. Program. Lang. Syst. **4**(3), 382–401 (1982). http://dl.acm.org/citation.cfm?id=357176
6. Bheemaiah, K.: Block chain 2.0: the renaissance of money. Wired, January 2015
7. Economist Staff: Blockchains: the great chain of being sure about things. The Economist, 31 October 2015. https://goo.gl/PwLDsw
8. Dwork, C., Naor, M.: Pricing via processing or combatting junk mail. In: Brickell, E.F. (ed.) CRYPTO 1992. LNCS, vol. 740, pp. 139–147. Springer, Heidelberg (1993). https://doi.org/10.1007/3-540-48071-4_10
9. Jakobsson, M., Juels, A.: Proofs of work and bread pudding protocols. In: Communications and Multimedia Security, pp. 258–272. Kluwer Academic Publishers (1999)

10. Nakamoto, S.: Bitcoin: a peer-to-peer electronic cash system, October 2008. https://bitcoin.org/bitcoin.pdf
11. Popov, S.: A probabilistic analysis of the Nxt forging algorithm. Ledger **1**, 69–83 (2016). https://doi.org/10.5195/LEDGER.2016.46. ISSN 2379–5980
12. Vitalik, B.: What proof of stake is and why it matters. Bitcoin Mag
13. Narayanan, B.: Bitcoin and Cryptocurrency Technologies. Princeton University Press, Princeton (2016)
14. Chepurnoy, A.: PoS forging algorithms: formal approach and multibranch forging. https://www.scribd.com/doc/248208963/Multibranch-forging
15. Castro, M., Liskov, B.: Practical byzantine fault tolerance. In: OSDI, vol. 99 (1999)
16. Vukolić, M.: The quest for scalable blockchain fabric: proof-of-work vs. BFT replication. In: Camenisch, J., Kesdoğan, D. (eds.) iNetSec 2015. LNCS, vol. 9591, pp. 112–125. Springer, Cham (2016). https://doi.org/10.1007/978-3-319-39028-4_9
17. Mazieres, D.: The stellar consensus protocol: federated model for internet level consensus. Stellar Development Foundation (2015)
18. Bentov, I.: Proof of activity: extending Bitcoin's proof of work via proof of stake. ACM SIGMETRICS Perform. Eval. Rev. **42**(3), 34–37 (2014)
19. P4Titan: Slimcoin: a peer-to-peer crypto-currency with proof-of-burn, May 2014. http://www.slimcoin.club/whitepaper.pdf
20. BURST's proof of capacity mining. Bitcoin Talk. https://bitcointalk.org/index.php?topic=731923.0
21. Underwood, S.: Blockchain beyond bitcoin. Commun. ACM **59**(11), 15–17 (2016)
22. Yli-Huumo, J., et al.: Where is current research on blockchain technology? A systematic review. PLoS one **11**(10) (2016)
23. CoinDesk: Carbon footprint of bitcoin. http://www.coindesk.com/carbon-footprint-bitcoin/
24. Ouoba, J., Bissyandé, T.F.: Leveraging the cultural model for opportunistic networking in sub-saharan Africa. In: Jonas, K., Rai, I.A., Tchuente, M. (eds.) AFRICOMM 2012. LNICST, vol. 119, pp. 163–173. Springer, Heidelberg (2013). https://doi.org/10.1007/978-3-642-41178-6_17

Exploring E-Procurement Adoption in the Context of a Developing Country: The Case of Lesotho

Nteboheleng Pitso, Salah Kabanda(✉), and Meke Kapepo

University of Cape Town, Private Bag X3, Rondebosch 7701, South Africa
{Nteboheleng.Pitso,salah.kabanda,
meke.kapepo}@uct.ac.za

Abstract. An E-Procurement system allows organizations to automate and streamline the internal procurement processes and also allow them to integrate and share information with their suppliers and customers for better business results. Despite these and other benefits promised by E-Procurement systems, their adoption remains a challenge in most organizations in developing countries, and in Africa in particular. This could be partly because of the fact that the phenomenon has not received sufficient attention in Africa, and as a consequence, adoption is enacted in a manner that is exclusive of contextual challenges the organizations face. It is also not clear whether E-Procurement benefits in literature do translate into actual benefits by African public organizations. The purpose of this study is therefore to identify the perceived benefits and contextual challenges posed during the implementation of an E-Procurement system in the Lesotho electricity sector. Following an interpritivist approach, grounded in the study context; the study identified two key perceived benefits of efficiency and transparency. The challenges faced includes the organizational lack of adequate training, system failure, employee resistance and lack of project management skills by top management. There were consistent reports of a lack of expertise from the external market to address implementation issues and that perceived knowledgeable agents such as consultants were not able to deliver what was tasked of them.

Keywords: E-Procurement · Adoption · Developing countries · Lesotho

1 Introduction

The use of information technology systems to automate procurement processes such as ordering and tendering, with the objective of improving efficiency, quality and transparency within such processes is now an important aspect for all organizations. This process, known as E-Procurement integrates and links buyers and sellers by automating the requisitioning, approval, ordering and account management processes [1]. The use of these systems has been associated with stronger search abilities, faster and more accurate data transmission and better information that assists inter-organisational integration leading to low communication and coordination costs. As such, E-Procurement is now regarded as a strategic tool that can be used to optimise the business operations [2].

© ICST Institute for Computer Sciences, Social Informatics and Telecommunications Engineering 2018
V. Odumuyiwa et al. (Eds.): AFRICOMM 2017, LNICST 250, pp. 315–326, 2018.
https://doi.org/10.1007/978-3-319-98827-6_30

Despite these benefits, there remains minimal adoption of E-Procurement systems in organizations in developing countries, particularly in Africa [3]. As for those that have adopted the technology, they report minimal benefits from its use [4]. This could partly be because the phenomenon has not received sufficient attention in Africa, and as a consequence, adoption is enacted in a manner that is exclusive of political, legal, social, and cultural contextual factors. According to Jarzabkowski (2004, 10), 'while communities may have some broad similarities, each community has specific social interactions that constitute a unique interpretative context'. This is truer on the African continent where different countries and even tribes have different interpretive repertoire and challenges. On this note, this study explores perceived benefits and challenges associated with E-Procurement systems in public organizations in the developing country context. The study is situated in the Kingdom of Lesotho and the case is a public institution hereby named LesothoOrg which automated its procurement processes in 2010. This study is arranged as follows: Sect. 2 will provide a literature review on E-Procurement and how it has been perceived in other African countries. Section 3 describes and discusses the research approach, paying attention to how the data was collected and analysed. The report on the field research findings are documented in Sect. 4. An extrapolation of the field research findings in the context of the literature is made in Sect. 5. Finally, Sect. 6 concludes and provides recommendations and future research work.

2 Theoretical Background

2.1 E-Procurement

A procurement process is defined as the whole process of acquiring goods or services. It begins with the request to acquire an item or service by the user department, approved by the head of that department, and goes through to receiving the goods and ultimately disposing that item after its useful life. This process is guided by procedures and rules set out to achieve procurement performance [10]. Procurement is a subset of supply chain management process which includes activities such as goods and services sourcing, order processing, invoicing, inventory management and customer service [11]. When the procurement process becomes automated (E-Procurement), it becomes an important strategic focus that is perceived as having the potential to improve the organizational performance, increase process efficiency, reduce the purchasing activity cost and improve process transparency [2, 12]. An E-Procurement system allows organizations to automate and streamline the internal procurement processes and also allow them to integrate and share information with their suppliers and customers for better business results [13–15].The use of these systems have been associated with stronger search abilities, faster and more accurate data transmission and better information that assists inter-organisational integration leading to low communication and coordination costs.

Studies on E-Procurement have been in various industries although most have rested in the manufacturing domain. For example, Abdullah and Halim [16] investigated the impact of dependency among supply chain members on the diffusion of an E-Procurement adoption system; and Li [17] investigated the major determinant factors for the successful adoption of E-Procurement by Chinese manufacturing enterprises. From the hospitality sector, Au et al. [18] explored the key factors that are associated with the low adoption of E-Procurement specifically in the hotel industry in Hong Kong, a major tourism destination in Asia. Their findings show that (1) technical factors, (2) perceived benefits, (3) conflicts between hotel owners and management, (4) resistance to change, (5) product diversity, and (6) rumours were the main factors that determined adoption.

2.2   E-Procurement in Africa

Although the body of knowledge on E-Procurement is vast, there remains limited attention paid to the adoption and implementation of the innovation in Africa. And as a consequence, Africa's lessons on E-Procurement could potentially be based on the developed economies context which is significantly different from the African context. Studies in Africa on E-Procurement have been conducted in the Nigeria building sector and there is report of technical and infrastructure challenges which are common barriers in most developing countries [4]. This is a problem because innovations such as E-Procurement are reliant on an IT infrastructure that is reliable, accessible, and of high-speed. Technical and infrastructure include telecommunication infrastructure, networks, Internet services, hardware and software which could be perceived as costly and therefore deter adoption [19]. Other findings in Nigeria include political, social, and cultural issues. Their findings show that organisations failed to see the evidence of the benefits of E-Procurement and hence there was minimal top management support [4]. Top management support and commitment is important and has often been considered crucial in the adoption and deployment of technology, as they provide the financial resources necessary and cultivating an organisational climate conducive to the adoption of the technology and for the management and achievement of organisational goals, values and beliefs [20, 21]. In most cases, top management is granted if they can perceive the benefits of adoption and less of the challenges of innovation such as the costs involved in respect of the adoption of technology, for example, for hardware, software, Internet access, or the availability of alternative technologies and developmental innovations [22, 23].

Other challenges that potentially affect management's intention to support the adoption of a new innovation include their perception of the complexity and compatibility of the innovation with organizational goals. Innovation complexity has an effect on adoption because the more difficult an innovation is to understand and more difficult to implement, the less likely will be adopted, but if less complex, a faster adoption is predicted [24, 25]. Despite the perceived complexity and cost involved in adopting an innovation, if it is perceived to be compatible with the organization's strategy it can be adopted. Compatibility of an innovation refers to 'the degree to which an innovation is perceived as being consistent with the existing values, past experiences, and needs of potential adopters' [24]. Technological incompatibilities between organisations may pose challenges that inhibit organisations from adopting E-Procurement systems [26]. The organisational legacy systems may not be technically compliant with E-Procurement systems and thus forcing organizations to change such applications before acquisition and implementation. Decision to change legacy systems normally take a lot of discussions and time to conclude. Technical skills to implement and support the systems may also be a barrier of adoption [26–28].

In South Africa, reports of limited use of E-Procurement in the construction sector are noted [29]. The authors attribute this to (1) lack of a definite government policy to implement E-Procurement; (2) reliability of ICT infrastructure; (3) high costs of installing and operating E-Procurement systems; and (4) perceived negative impact of E-Procurement adoption on smaller firms and employment of people in the departments. Several studies have confirmed that the size of an organization, its financial capability and characteristics have a critical effect on the adoption of E-Commerce and technological systems [30]. The organisational size is one of the predictors of an organisation's intentions to adopt IS innovations on the premise that larger firms have a greater need for them, as well as resources, skills and experience and the ability to survive failures, than smaller firms [31]. Ntawanga and Coleman [32] presented a lightweight mobile E-Procurement application for small scale retailers in a rural areas of South Africa. Their application, allowed businesses to conduct their operations, specifically stock replenishment, efficiently and cost-effectively. In Kenya, the adoption of E-Procurement among large scale manufacturers is examined by [33], and five critical success factors reported: employees and management commitment to success of adoption; reliability of information technology and supplier performance; monitoring the performance of E-Procurement systems; user acceptance of E-Procurement systems and top management support. The authors also found the following challenges: resistance to change from employees, lack of E-Procurement approval by company board, existence of old IT equipment among the firms that need overhaul and lack of managerial sup-port. From the public sector, Adebayo and Evans [34] examined the level of adoption of E-Procurement in Nigeria and arrive at the conclusion that at an operational level, public sector organisations are yet to fully attain the full benefits of E-Procurement. In Kenya, Ndumbi and Okello [35] point to the need for staff training in the use of E-Procurement because staff training influences compliance to regulatory instruments such as the public procurement and disposal act in Kenya.

The experience and the knowledge that organisations have about the intended innovation play an important role in decisions regarding adoption [24]. ICT expertise are critical as the task of managing the IT infrastructure and resources continues to grow more complex as businesses rely more and more on it. This complexity requires governance – a framework for making strategic, tactical and operational decision regarding rights and accountabilities, and stipulating clearly who is entitled to make major decisions, who has input and who is accountable for implementing those decisions, so as to encourage desirable behaviour in the use of IT [19]. Appropriate governance and the adoption of best governance practices enables organisations to ensure that their enterprise's IT sustains and extends their strategies and objectives [14] and fully harnesses the benefits of IT investments [25]. Table 1 documents the challenges faced by organizations in Africa in the adoption of E-Procurement.

Table 1. Challenges faced by African organization in the adoption of E-Procurement.

Country	Industry	Challenges
Nigeria	Building and construction	Technical and infrastructure
		Political
		Social and cultural issues
		Lack of perceived benefits
		Minimal top management support
	Public sector	Lack of perceived benefits
Kenya	large scale manufacturers	Resistance to change from employees
		Lack of E-Procurement approval by company board
		Lack of managerial support
		Existence of old IT equipment among the firms that need overhaul
	Public sector	Lack of staff training and ICT expertise in conformance to regulation
South Africa	Building and construction	Lack of a definite government policy to implement E-Procurement
		Reliability of ICT infrastructure
		High costs of installing and operating E-Procurement systems
		Perceived negative impact of E-Procurement on smaller firms

3 Methodology

The study adopted an interpretivist research philosophy and using a single case study, it examined the contextual challenges faced by the LesothOrg in its implementation of the E-Procurement system. A case study approach is more suitable to studies where the researcher desires to gain better insight and deep understanding of the processes being investigated [36]. Data was collected using semi-structured interviews from eight participants (see Table 2) who were with the organization from the adoption to the implementation phase of the project. Although the sample size is small, it should be borne in mind that qualitative studies are more concerned with in-depth understanding of the phenomenon from its natural setting as perceived by participants [37]. In this study, saturation point was reached with eight participants.

The literature review and the challenges identified in Africa with regards to E-Procurement informed the research instrument. Of these eight participants, three were in the project implementation team, representing Finance, Procurement and Information technology departments. These are the people who motivated for the project and were involved in the implementation. They observed and have information of the change management strategies that were applied, challenges faced and why the particular application was implemented. The Finance department representative is also a member of the LesothOrg execute management team who is mostly affected by this system. The remaining five participants include one stores department employee, one

Table 2. Respondent profile

Respondent # and Position		Gender	Line manager
1	Transmission and distribution manager	Female	General manager engineering
2	Acting operations manager	Male	General manger engineering
3	Stores controller	Male	Procurement manager
4	Procurement manager	Female	General manager finance
5	Financial accounting manager	Male	General manager finance
6	Operations and administrator	Male	Information technology manager
7	General manager finance (acting)	Female	Managing director
8	Section engineer planning & projects	Male	Planning and projects manager

financial accounting department employee, and three representatives for the three engineering departments who use the different modules of the system and were present both before and after the system implementation.

These participants are mainly the users of the systems and therefore have a better understanding of the benefits and challenges associated with the system use. All participants are based at the LesothOrg Headquarters in Maseru, Lesotho; and all interviews were recorded. Data analysis commenced with the process of transcribing the recordings from the audio tapes to a Microsoft Word document. Then, the main author went through the process of rereading each interview transcript with the purpose of familiarising oneself with the data and embedding herself into the situated context by relieving the interview experience. Each time an interview transcript was read, initial codes were identified and documented in MS Excel. Different colours were then used to highlight words, sentences and paragraphs that gave similar meanings, and helped the researcher compare similarities across respondents and thus identify initial patterns across the different interview scripts. Then, the process of aggregating and collapsing themes that talk about the same concepts followed so as to reduce the number of themes that emerged and avoid redundancy.

4 Findings

4.1 Perceived Benefits

One of the perceived benefits the study finds is the ability to automate various activities so as to *"achieve an acceptable level of efficiency"* (Respondent 5). There was a consistent remark that automation was the driver for the adoption of e-procurement, although for some employees this was not explicitly stated. For example, the Transmission and Distribution Manager (Respondent 1) was informed that the purpose of e-procurement was to move from the manual system to the electronic system. Although she quickly indicates that *"the manager did not explicitly tell us the purpose, maybe he did to our senior management"*. The Acting Operations Manager was also given the impression that *"the new system that they wanted would make it easier for people to order things because, you know before it used to be difficult be-cause the people at procurement used to throw away papers if they see that they cannot find what you are looking for, they just throw them away"* (Respondent 2). The Stores Controller who reports directly to the procurement manager was confident in the anticipated benefits and reports that *"The intention was to try to automate some of the processes in order to achieve shorter errrrrr turnaround time and to respond to the user requirements but mostly our requirements were about that"* (Respondent 3). Respondent 6 strongly highlights the benefits that he finds important from his department's perspective: *"because the requisitioning process has been fully automated, the requisition books or leaflets no longer get lost"*. This was believed to be a significant advantage because it improved their efficiency, thereby making their *"customers happier and the queries that we used to have, have been reduced a lot. Even for unhappy customers, we are able to explain with the support from the system. Also there used to be a lot of stock shortages before, we no longer have that"*.

Finally, one of the additional benefit cited by managers was the need to improve transparency. Respondent 8 clarifies: *"quotations we used to give to customers were different in every district and varied daily or from whoever the quotation was issued because the project estimator was just a spreadsheet that was not linked to other users. You can now trace your order easily with this system in place"*. Respondent 4 agrees that *"for now, we have a clear record of transactions, with times and days, we can know when a requisition was initiated, and when it was completed and by whom"*

4.2 Lack of Expertise

The Acting Operations Manager (Respondent 2) was of the view that employees lacked adequate training of the system and believed that *"more training is needed for them in order to understand what they are doing"*. Similar sentiments are made by The Stores Controller (Respondent 3) who indicates that all employees needed training of the system. He indicates that training was only given to a few because of the budget constraints. Respondent 7 confirms this challenge and indicates that the problem was not only a budget issue but the quality of the trainees that were employed. She states that through her observations, *"the consultants kept on recommending stuff, some of which they could not deliver or do themselves and then recommended that LesothOrg subcontract their other partners in the project"*. According to Respondent 2 *"the consultant was a little bit of err he was also learning himself"*. This was not well received by the management team as they perceived low confidence in the project implementers and brought pressure on employees to learn the system as they go.

4.3 System Problems

Although LesothOrg was able to accrue some benefits from the E-Procurement system, there were some challenges they experienced with the system itself, which were not related to the lack of training on the employee's part. Respondent 1 explains: *"From my office every week I get a complain/request from the regional manager requesting IT intervention because either the system is not allowing them to raise a purchase requisition, it is slow or it is not allowing them to register the customers when they apply and then causes long customer queues"*. Respondent 6 confirms that *"the system itself had too many problems and could not eliminate all the manual challenges we experienced and so sometimes we had to go manual"*. This was not well received by the LesothOrg management because *"all these IT problems"* (respondent 7) were putting strain on the most important goals and objectives of why the system was implemented in the first place – that of achieving efficiency and transparency.

4.4 Employee Resistance

The findings show that despite the advantages the E-Procurement system brought into LesothOrg, evidence of employee resistance were noted. Respondent 5 noted *"resistance by some departments, especially engineering who say that the system belongs to Finance"*. There was consistent lack of ownership of the system and Respondent 4 attributed this to the fact that *"people were not adaptive to change, they were not well trained and most were not told what the system was to do and how it will affect them directly with regards to their daily work activities"*. According to respondent 2, the challenge was to provide proper information for the system to operate well – findings this proper information was problematic, given that people were not trained. Thereby confirming observations made by respondent 4 that most people in her department thought the *"new system has now created more job for them"*.

4.5 Lack of Project Management Skills and Support

According to respondents, the LesothOrg management lacked project management skills and the project eventually suffered scope creep problems. Management were also perceived not to be knowledgeable in E-Procurement and therefore were not able to solicit the right development team for the implementation (respondent 2). According to respondent 7, *"LesothOrg did not really know what they wanted and depended on the consultant to tell them what they can offer ... and so it was more like signing a blank cheque, and in every project meeting, something else came up"*. Respondent 6 confirms, noting that *"the tendering process was never followed for the whole process so basically there was not even a business case or anything...and unfortunately that exercise was done when some of the executive management do not want to hear anything about this project even though the project had already begun operation"*. Thus the lack of project management skills and top management support was perceived to be a barrier to successful implementation of E-Procurement.

5 Discussion

The findings in this study show that the most realized benefits associated with E-Procurement in the LesothOrg context were efficiency and transparency. The following challenges were identifies: lack of expertise, system problems, employee resistance and lack of project management and support. Although most of these challenges have been identified in literature, thereby confirming our findings to be more generalizable to other developing countries; the challenges that stands out in the Lesotho context are (1) the lack of project management skills by the management team and (2) the lack of knowhow of the consultants brought in to provide development and training.

The lack of project management skills is a problem, especially in the LesothOrg context that lacked "*a business case*" which is crucial to lay the foundation of clear objectives and how these are aligned to the business strategy. Several studies have reported that for business process initiatives to be successful there needs to be a clear link between the business processes and the business strategy [38–40]. Also, the skills portal of South Africa [41] has advised Africa that "a project-oriented mindset needs to be developed in the state sector" so as to address and redress current project failures and challenges. Our findings regarding the role of consulting companies in this study deviates from those attributed in literature. According to many studies, the role of consultants includes technology transfer, technology assessment, the articulation of needs, the exploration and appropriation of technologies, as well as acquisition, implementation and learning [42]. Consultants are perceived to possess the expertise and experience and so many organizations are advised to "spend money and time on getting the relevant advice from ICT experts and consultants in order to set up the ICT strategy, based on the SME's business strategy" [43].

However, this advice becomes problematic in Africa and more specifically in the Lesotho context were ICT consultants are perceived to be lacking in ICT knowledge, thereby jeopardizing the successful completion of the project. According to [44] "ICT consultants with general ICT skills and specific ERP skills in particular are in short-supply world-wide....and the lack of quality ERP expertise, skills and knowledge affects ICT project success and may prevent organisations from achieving the potential benefits of implementing ERP". This study therefore calls for the public institution to redress the lack of expertise and consider putting measures in place of reevaluating consultants on a periodical basis to assess their relevance to the agile ICT market.

6 Conclusion

The purpose of this study was to identify the perceived benefits and contextual challenges posed during the implementation of an E-Procurement system in the Lesotho electricity sector. Following an interpritivist approach, grounded in the study context; the study identified two key perceived benefits of efficiency and transparency. The challenges include the lack of adequate training, lack of expertise from the external market, system failure, employee resistance and lack of project management skills by top management. The study further identifies the lack of expertise and skill sets required by top management with respect to managing a project of the magnitude of an E-Procurement system. It was strongly suggested by all respondents that top management should, and in this case did not, possess project management skills that are necessary to drive an ICT project to its fruition. The study has presented insights into the challenges and potential benefits accrued from e-procurement. Future studies can work towards increasing the sample size, and using a theoretical lens that can provide a richer understanding of the E-Procurement in Lesotho.

References

1. Zunk, B.M., Marchner, M.J., Uitz, I., Lerch, C., Schiele, H.: The role of E-Procurement in the Austrian construction industry: adoption rate, benefits and barriers. J. Ind. Eng. Manag. **5** (1), 13–20 (2014)
2. Alvarez-Rodríguez, J.M., Labra-Gayo, J.E., de Pablos, P.O.: New trends on E-Procurement applying semantic technologies: current status and future challenges. J. Comput. Ind. **65**, 800–820 (2014)
3. Gardenal, F.: A model to measure E-Procurement impacts on organizational performance. J. Public Procure. **13**, 215–242 (2013)
4. Aduwo, E.B., Ibem, E.O., Uwakonye, O., Tunji-Olayeni, P., Ayo-Vuaghan, E.K.: Barriers to the uptake of e-procurement in the Nigerian building industry. J. Theor. Appl. Inf. Technol. **89**(1), 133–147 (2016)
5. Feinberg, S., Hill, T.L., Darendeli, I.S.: An institutional perspective on non-market strategies for a world in flux. In: The Routledge Companion to Non Market Strategy. Routledge (2015)
6. Zhang, C., Dhaliwal, J.: An investigation of resource-based and institutional theoretic factors in technology adoption for operations and supply chain management. J. Prod. Econom. **120**, 252–269 (2009)
7. Liang, H., Saraf, N., Hu, Q., Xu, W.: Assimilation of Enterprise systems: the effect of institutional pressures and the mediating role of top management. J. MIS Q. **31**, 59–87 (2007)
8. Kaynak, E., Tatoglu, E., Kula, V.: An analysis of the factors affecting the adoption of electronic commerce by SMEs: evidence from an emerging market. Int. Mark. Rev. **22**, 623–640 (2005)
9. Oruezabala, G., Rico, J.C.: The impact of sustainable public procurement on supplier management—The case of French public hospitals. Ind. Mark. Manag. **41**, 573–580 (2012)
10. Amemba, C.S., Nyaboke, P.G., Osoro, A., Mburu, N.: Challenges affecting public procurement performance process in Kenya. J. Res. Manag. **4**, 41–55 (2013)
11. Vaidya, K., Campbell, J.: Multidisciplinary approach to defining public E-Procurement and evaluating its impact on procurement efficiency. J. Inf. Syst. Front. **18**, 333–348 (2016)
12. Chang, H.H., Wong, K.H.: Adoption of E-Procurement and participation of e-marketplace on firm performance: trust as a moderator. J. Inf. Manag. **47**, 262–270 (2010)
13. Piera, C., Roberto, C., Giuseppe, C., Teresa, M.: E-Procurement and E-supply chain: features and development of E-collaboration. IERI Procedia **6**, 8–14 (2014)
14. Piotrowicz, W., Irani, Z.: Analysing B2B electronic procurement benefits: information systems perspective. J. Enterp. Inf. Manag. **23**, 559–579 (2010)
15. Vaidyanathan, G., Devaraj, S.: The role of quality in E-Procurement performance: an empirical analysis. J. Oper. Manag. **26**, 407–425 (2008)
16. Abdullah, N., Halim, N.A.: 5th International Conference on Business and Economic Research (5th ICBER 2014), Pullman Hotel, Kuching Sarawak Malaysia (2014)
17. Li, Y. H.: An empirical investigation on the determinants of E-Procurement adoption in Chinese manufacturing enterprises. In: 15th Annual Management Science and Engineering Conference Proceedings, ICMSE, pp. 32–37. IEEE (2008)
18. Au, N., Ho, C.K., Law, R.: Towards an understanding of E-Procurement adoption: a case study of six hotels in Hong Kong. J Tour. Recreat. Res. **39**, 19–38 (2014)
19. Lin, C., Huang, Y.A., Jalleh, G., Liu, Y.C., Tung, M.L.: An exploratory study of factors affecting adoption and implementation of B2B E-Commerce in Australian health care organizations. J Electron. Commer. Stud. **1**, 77–96 (2010)

20. Teo, T.S., Lin, S., Lai, K.H.: Adopters and non-adopters of E-Procurement in Singapore: an empirical study. J. Omega **37**, 972–987 (2009)
21. Hashim, F., Alam, G.M., Siraj, S.: Information and communication technology for participatory based decision-making-E-management for administrative efficiency in higher education. Int. J. Phys. Sci. **5**, 383–392 (2010)
22. Ho, S.C., Kauffman, R.J., Liang, T.P.: A growth theory perspective on B2C E-Commerce growth in Europe: an exploratory study. J. Electron. Commer. Res. Appl. **6**, 237–259 (2007)
23. Iddris, F.: Adoption of E-Commerce solutions in small and medium-sized enterprises in Ghana. Eur. J. Bus. Manag. **4**, 48–57 (2012)
24. Rogers, E.: The Diffusion of Innovations, 5th edn. The Free Press, New York (2003)
25. Othman, M.F.I., Chan, T., Foo, E., Nelson, K.J., Timbrell, G.T.: Barriers to information technology governance adoption: a preliminary empirical investigation. In: Proceedings of 15th International Business Information Management Association Conference, pp. 1771–1787, Cairo, Egypt (2011)
26. McCue, C., Roman, A.V.: E-Procurement: myth or reality? J. Public Procure. **12**, 221–248 (2012)
27. Quesada, G., González, M.E., Mueller, J., Mueller, R.: Impact of E-Procurement on procurement practices and performance. J. Benchmarking **17**, 516–538 (2010)
28. Toktaş-Palut, P., Baylav, E., Teoman, S., Altunbey, M.: The impact of barriers and benefits of E-Procurement on its adoption decision: an empirical analysis. J. Production Econom. **158**, 77–90 (2014)
29. Laryea, S., Ibem, E. O., Pagiwa, R., Phoi, R.: Electronic procurement in the South African construction sector: case study of government departments in the Gauteng Province. In: Proceedings of the DII-2014 Conference on Infrastructure Investments in Africa, Livingstone, Zambia 25–26 2014 (2014)
30. Simmons, G., Armstrong, G.A., Durkin, M.G.: A conceptualization of the determinants of small business website adoption: setting the research agenda. J. Small Bus. **26**, 351–389 (2008)
31. Ramdani, B., Kawalek, P., Lorenzo, O.: Predicting SMEs' adoption of enterprise systems. J. Enterp. Inf. Manag. **22**, 10–24 (2009)
32. Ntawanga, F., Coleman, A.: A lightweight mobile E-Procurement solution for rural small scale traders implemented using a living lab approach. In: IST-Africa Conference, 2015, pp. 1–10). IEEE (2015)
33. Mose, J.M., Njihia, J.M., Peterson, O.M.: The critical success factors and challenges in E-Procurement adoption among large scale manufacturing firms in Nairobi. Kenya. J. Eur. Sci. **9**, 375–401 (2013)
34. Adebayo, V.O., Evans, R.D.: Adoption of E-Procurement systems in developing countries: a Nigerian public sector perspective. In: 2nd International Conference on Knowledge-Based Engineering and Innovation, Tehran, Iran, pp. 20–25. IEEE (2015)
35. Ndumbi, C.W., Okello, B.: Effect of staff training on level of compliance to public procurement system in Parastatals in Kenya. J. Econom. Commer. Manag. **3**, 613–626 (2015)
36. Saunders, M., Lewis, P., Thornhill, A.: Research Methods for Business Students, 5th edn. Pearson Education Ltd., London (2009)
37. The applications of qualitative methods to social research. In: Qualitative Research Practice: A Guide for Social Science Students and Researchers (2003)
38. Ariyachandra, T.R., Frolick, M.N.: Critical success factors in business performance management - striving for success. J. Inf. Syst. Manag. **25**, 113–120 (2008)
39. McGee-Abe, J.: The business performance excellence summit (2016). http://www.businessperformanceexcellencesummit.com

40. Jeston, J.A.: Business Process Management: A Practical Guide to Successful Implementations. Elsevier, Oxford (2006)
41. Skillsportal.co.za (2016). http://www.skillsportal.co.za
42. Janssen, W., Bouwman, H., van Buuren, R., Haaker, T.: An organizational competence model for innovation intermediaries. Eur. J. Innov. Manag. **17**, 2–24 (2014)
43. Modimogale, L., Jan, H.: The role of ICT within small and medium enterprises in Gauteng. In: Communications of the IBIMA (2011). http://www.ibimapublishing.com/journals/CIBIMA/cibima.html
44. Calitz, A., Greyling, J., Cullen, M.: The problems experienced within the e-skills value chain in South Africa. In: Proceedings E-Skills Summit, Cape Town, South Africa, pp. 1–10 (2010)

Smartphone Usage Among Millennial in Finland and Implications for Marketing Segmentation Strategies: Lessons for Nigeria

Sunday Adewale Olaleye[1(✉)], Ismaila Temitayo Sanusi[2],
Dandison C. Ukpabi[3], and Oladapo Aina[4]

[1] Marketing, Management and International Business,
University of Oulu, Oulu, Finland
sunday.olaleye@oulu.fi
[2] Philosophical Faculty, University of Eastern Finland, Joensuu, Finland
ismails@uef.fi
[3] Digital Marketing and Communication Research Group,
University of Jyväskylä, Jyväskylä, Finland
dandison.c.ukpabi@jyu.fi
[4] Kingfisher Plc, Chandler's Ford, Eastleigh, UK
oladapo@aina.me

Abstract. The study examines smart phone usage by millennial based on different criteria of operating system, Wi-Fi, text messaging, internet surfing and social media. The study used quantitative methodology and data were gathered with online questionnaires with 391 young smartphone users in Finland. The Millennial were clustered into five levels. The results reveal the prominent status of profiling in a developed market and how marketers in emerging markets can apply segmentation and targeting strategies using instant messaging, text messages, email, mobile app, gamification and social media based on the profile of each segment. Nigerian policy makers should adopt a framework to make smartphone affordable for people as it constitutes a goldmine for marketing professionals on their segmentation and targeting strategies.

Keywords: Smartphone · Millennial · Social media · Segmentation
Targeting

1 Introduction

Mobile technologies are gaining rapid increase globally. These technologies such as computers and mobile telephones have revolutionized communication and by extension interpersonal relationship hence influencing intimacy and the closeness that exist between people [1]. Mobile device usage is more relevant in all aspects of our daily lives, especially with significant impact in the business sector. As mobile phones get more and more popular, their capabilities increase as they are no more simple voice centric handsets; they rather provide mobile computing power that can be used for several purposes [2]. Smartphones especially as stressed by the authors, represent a possibility of moving appropriate applications from the PC to mobile devices, as they mostly provide large bandwidth wireless network access, office tools, and the

© ICST Institute for Computer Sciences, Social Informatics and Telecommunications Engineering 2018
V. Odumuyiwa et al. (Eds.): AFRICOMM 2017, LNICST 250, pp. 327–341, 2018.
https://doi.org/10.1007/978-3-319-98827-6_31

possibility of installing third party programs. According to [3], smartphones with multi-touch screens have been widely adopted all over the world and become one of the fastest spreading technologies of mankind since the introduction of the first ever iPhone in 2007 [4]. Reference [5] pointed out in a graph showing smartphone penetration by age where only 62% of young people between the age 18–24 have smartphones and 66% of young people (25–34) have smartphone out of the 48% of mobile subscribers in USA using smartphone as at the time. This shows high rate of smartphone usage by young people in the US.

The primary objective of this study is to examine the degree of smartphones usage by the young people with focus on Finland. To get the clear picture of this objective, the study explores the nature of smartphone, motivating factors for its frequent usage, its benefits and limitation to the youth. Characteristics of the young people that affect the usage of smartphone positively or negatively were also discussed. The effective use of smartphone is determined by the features and functions of available applications on the phone which are already in use or proposed to use. The types of smartphone used, the operating systems, the number of applications installed and the frequent of usage are also examined. Additionally, this study shows the rapid usage of smartphone among the young people and its implication on other sectors like smartphone manufacturers, network operators and the advertisers. Online survey in form of questionnaire is conducted to the young people within the age bracket 16 to 30 to determine the extent of degree the young people use their smartphones. The survey takes place to know the young people motivation towards smartphone usage. As the youth typify the frequent usage of the smartphone, the questionnaire was administered to different young people in different location to assess the extent of their smartphone usage. Finally, this research resulted into pertinent findings and provides astute recommendations on smartphone usage by the young people. To accomplish the researchers' objective for this study, a research question was formulated as to what degree do young people use their smartphone?

2 Literature Review

2.1 Theory of Segmentation and Targeting

Overtime, marketing theorists have posited a given market as constituting consumers with varying demand patterns, lifestyles, needs, values, motivations and interests [6, 7]. Thus, marketing segmentation is defined as the process of dividing homogenous market into groups to understand their product and service preferences and then developing the right marketing mix such as product, pricing, delivery channel and promotional strategies for those segments [8]. According to [8], segmentation criteria could be geographic, demographic, psychographic and behavioural. Scholars have also argued that a condition for effective segmentation implies that the segment must be measurable, accessible, sustainable, profitable and actionable [6]. Similarly, targeting has been defined as the concentration of the marketing mix elements into selected segments that matches the marketers' offerings [7]. With the emergence and diffusion of the information and communication technology (ICT), scholars have adopted different segmentation and targeting strategies to effectively reach users. In evaluating the users of mobile phones in Finland, [9] attitudinally segmented the Finnish mobile phone market into conservatives, medium and innovatives with female users dominating in the conservatives and medium segments. Majority of pensioners were also in the conservatives segment while those possessing smartphones dominated in the innovative segment. Additionally, [10] using a latent class analysis for measuring smartphone usage reported that major segments such as traditionalists, career-makers, socially concerned and Yuppies exhibited different behavioural typologies in their use of smartphones.

2.2 Smartphone and Young People

For young people, they can go to any extent to secure a smartphone even when their budget is tight. Remarkably, this group whose income is also lower than the older ones own the greatest volume in the smartphone market [10]. The research conducted by [11] further supports the claim that more young people own a smartphone compared to adults. It was also noted in their research that more teens are highly addicted to their smartphones. This addiction has led them ignoring or participating less in other activities such as watching TV and reading books. Reference [12] used Emily Hooley as an example of an addicted smartphone user. Emily once recalled an event which she narrated by saying, "We went to Wales for a week at half term to revise. There was no mobile, no TV, no broadband. We had to drive into town just to get a signal. It was hard, knowing people were texting you, writing on your Wall, and you couldn't respond. Loads of my friends said they'd just never do that." Young people in the age bracket of consideration love to talk together among their peers and most particularly to share their daily experience through call, text messages and mobile chat. Communication is a strong affinity among the youth and since smartphone has multiples features and functions, many youths can do anything to buy a smartphone so that they can fit in to their youthful status. Ariel Young, a 20 years old biology student from George Washington University participated in [13] survey and confirmed that she exchanged a text messages with her peers for about 75 times in a day. Reference [14] observed that gender play a dominant role in smartphone usage as he pointed out that girl's converse more than the boys but [15] believed that young males are getting Smartphone's than the young females and based his result on "53% as against 47%". The youthful age is a point of developing emotion and love for the opposite sex, both boys and girls seize this opportunity for familiarity and to fulfil their love desire. They are trying to shift their attention from physical contact relationship to online mobile love. Reference [16] opined that above 70% of the young people use their smartphone to take decision.

Another important factor that makes the youth the focus of smartphone is its ubiquity. Youth do not need to make a trip before they make a call, send text messages or chat with their peers. Reference [17] observed that smartphone usage among the young people in Scotland is diminishing their interest in obtaining driver's license and to make use of taxi services since smartphone is helping them to reach their friends at distance. It was further noticed by [18] that "young people off cars" is a contributory factor to high insurance and fuel costs in Scotland. Reference [15] discovered that youthful age is a period that the youth desire independence and freedom from parental control. Some of them prefer to communicate with their parents at distance with a smartphone, therefore avoiding having a physical contact with their parents and the author concluded that smartphone usage can build home or break it. Reference [19] in their study designed a mobile telephone model and group the factors that motivate the young people in using smartphone into three, they are "appropriation criteria, which emphasize social management, critical mass, lifestyle organizer, leisure, security and contact." The authors opined that these factors are appropriate to the young when considering the usage of smartphone because they love to manage their social life, they want to organize their lifestyle, and they want to use the phone for their pastime. They also want to use it for safety by using the mobile application for tracking messages and goods. Reference [19] also talk about "disadvantage criteria which entails usage costs, health, reception, usability and ease of learning." The authors mentioned these factors as the negative criteria that can discourage the young people to maximize the usage of smartphone. Though smartphone is nice and have multiple functions but it cost a lot at the end of the month when the bill rolls in, most especially if it is contractual. It was also argued by [20] that smartphone applications cause a lot of distraction for the young people while driving. It was observed that the young people are fascinated with smartphone applications and thus making using of it on the wheel (Fig. 1).

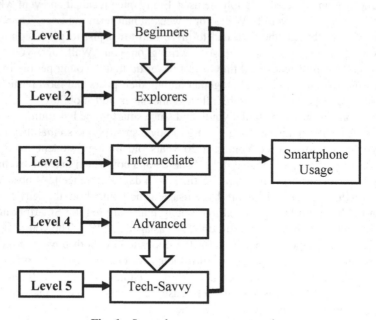

Fig. 1. Smartphone usage segmentation

The youth are prompt to learning new things, but if the design of the smartphone is too cumbersome, it may be discouraging. Smartphone usage hazard to health of its users is another point of consideration by the authors [19]. Non-appropriation is another criteria considered by [19] and it was divided into attractors and repellents.

According to the authors "purchase cost, convenience, usefulness, fashion, adaptability and familiarity are factors that determine the usage of smartphone by the young people." In their opinion factor like cost will repel smartphone usage while convenience will attract its usage. The researchers' assume most companies are aware that the younger generations consist of the greatest revenue booster. Reference [21], reports that HTC's market target is divided into two, which are the young enthusiast and pragmatic business users (p. 15). With their primary focus being on the young ones between the ages of 18–34. They have chosen segment because they are the highest users and most enthusiastic about technology. While the surge of purchases of smartphones by young people seems to be good revenue for mobile vendors to make profit, this also comes with some problems. PR Newswire in 2012 reported that, a survey conducted by a car insurance company, Ingenie, indicates that 58% of people between the ages 17–25 have been distracted by their smartphone application while driving.

3 Methodology/Data Collection and Description

The study utilized descriptive-quantitative methodology based on observation and survey distributed among the millennials. Descriptive data technique concentrates in reporting mean, median, mode, central tendency, percentage, correlation and draw inferences from the descriptive statistics output. The study research questions, design and data analysis align with the descriptive-quantitative methodology and the goal of the study is to describe, explain and validate different levels of smartphone users. To find out the level of usage of smartphone by young people, a questionnaire was designed and made accessible online to young people, with various characteristics. The total number of respondents was 391, with 69.8% being male and 30.2% females. Majority of the respondents are students, they have a university education and earn less than 10,000 euros per annum. The most common data subscription is flat rate, and monthly subscriptions are usually below 10 euros. Android is the most commonly used operating system making up for approximately 33%, iOS occupying close second at approximately 32%, third is Symbian at approximately 14%. Approximately 95% of respondents would buy a smartphone over a cell phone if they were to purchase a phone today.

The most common reason for choosing their present smartphone is Wi-Fi functionality. Touch screen, camera, and possibility to install application follow closely. TV and anti-virus were the least desired functionalities. 80% of the respondents believe that a smartphone should have a Wi-Fi, 76% are in support of E-mail and good battery life, while TV with 10% and Symbian operating system with 5% take the last positions. 92.4% have downloaded software, games or other application on their smartphone, with 41% downloading only free applications, and 51.3% having both free and paid application. The respondents often use their mobile vendor's app store to find and download applications and sources from their mobile operator being the least used. Usefulness of the smartphone is the most important feature followed by usability, while social aspect and entertainment value takes the least position. More than half of the respondents update their operating systems, and most agreed it was easy and fast to update. More time was spent on the smartphone doing something else than surfing the internet. About 85% agreed downloading application has increased the functionality of their smartphone and would gladly recommend smartphones to others. The most used functionalities daily are text messaging, internet surfing, and social media, while gambling is the least. Music player is the highest number of device completely replaced by the smartphone, followed by navigation devices and camera. The laptop and PC are the least affected and the smartphone complements them the most. To reach the objective of this research, the collected data was examined. Based on our observation and user characteristics, five distinctive level of users were identified, with level 5 being the highest level of use and level 1 being the lowest level use of smartphones.

4   Results

4.1   Observations of Users on Each Level

The total data collected was 391, while the usable data was 390. The distributions of the correspondence into their respective level of use are shown in Fig. 2 below.

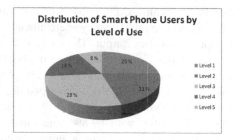

Fig. 2. Percentage of level of use from the total sample

4.2   Level 1 (Beginners) Observation

The users on this level consists of 66% male and 34% female, about half of them use a flat rate data and just about the other half do not use a flat rate data as shown in Fig. 3.

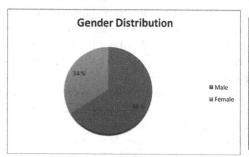
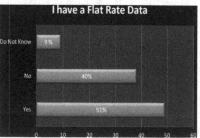

Fig. 3. Level 1 users by gender and data plan

Mainly consisting of beginners, majority of level 1 user will buy a smartphone if they have a chance to buy a phone today, as depicted in Fig. 4. The most used operating system is Android followed closely by Symbian, with Windows Mobile and Windows Phone being the least used as shown on Fig. 5.

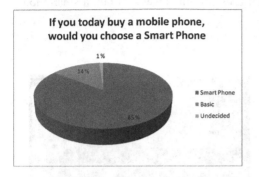

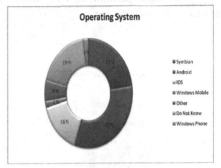

Fig. 4. Level 1 users by potential purchase of mobile phone

Fig. 5. Level 1 users by operating system

For Level 1 users, their smartphone has not replaced other devices such as Desktop, Laptop, and Game Console. Camera, however, seems to have been partially replaced for many, while navigation devices have the highest number of users who use their mobile as a complete replacement. Other comparisons are visible on Fig. 6.

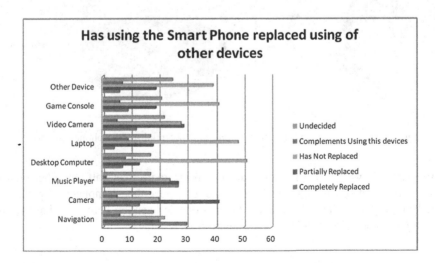

Fig. 6. Level 1 devices replaced by smartphone

4.3   Level 2 (Explorers) Observation

As illustrated on Figs. 7 and 8, these constitute explorers, with more than half of them made up of male and 61% have a flat rate data. The most used operating system is Android, followed closely by iOs and Symbian respectively, with Window Phone taking the least position at 1%. Almost all users on this level will buy a smartphone ahead of a basic phone.

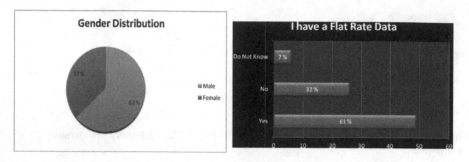

Fig. 7. Level 2 users by gender and data plan

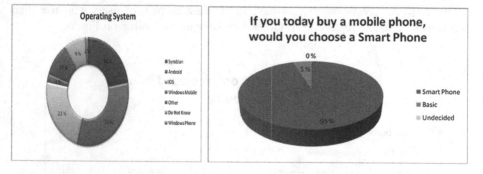

Fig. 8. Level 2 users by operating system and potential mobile phone purchase

Figure 9 shows that, for the users in this group, more than half have their Music player, video camera, navigation devices and camera either completely replaced or partially replaced by their smartphone. Game console, desktop computer, laptop, and other devices are irreplaceable by their smartphones.

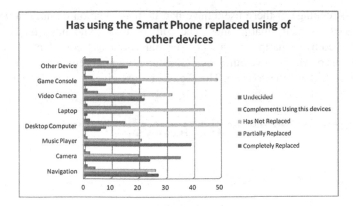

Fig. 9. Level 2 devices replaced by smartphone

4.4   Level 3 (Intermediate) Observation

About three quarter of the users in these group are male, and 79% using a flat rate data plan as illustrated on Fig. 10. From Fig. 11, as intermediate users, we found that almost all the users on this level will buy a smartphone if they are opportune to buy one today. Three quarter of these users are either using an iOS or android based operating system, with iOS having the majority share.

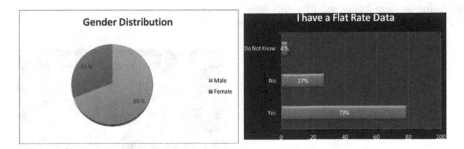

Fig. 10. Level 3 users by gender and data plan

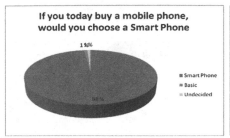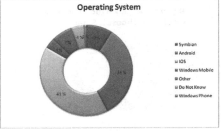

Fig. 11. Level 3 users by potential phone purchase and operating system used

A great percentage of these users have had their navigation device, camera, music player replaced by their smartphones. The sum of users who have had their laptop partially replaced by a smartphone or who see smartphone as a complement to it seem to be more than users who believe otherwise. Desktop computer remains irreplaceable with smartphone, so is the game console. The Fig. 12 below gives a more detailed overview.

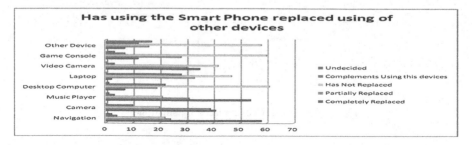

Fig. 12. Level 3 devices replaced by smartphone

4.5 Level 4 (Advanced) Observations

After analysing the data of users in level 4, the following deductions were made as shown in Figs. 13 and 14; more than three quarter of users in level 4 are male, with 80% using a flat rate data plan. Almost all respondent in this group will choose a smartphone over a basic phone, with only 1% undecided. iOs and android are the major operating system being used by this level of users.

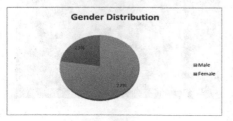

Fig. 13. Level 4 users by gender and data plan

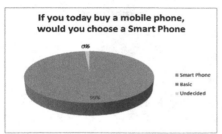

Fig. 14. Level 4 users by potential phone purchase and operating system used

Figure 15 gives us a more detailed overview of devices which are being replaced by a smartphone. At this level, navigation devices, camera, music player have almost being completely or partially replace by a smartphone. High percentage of users believe that their smartphone complements their laptop. Game console and other devices still remains highly irreplaceble.

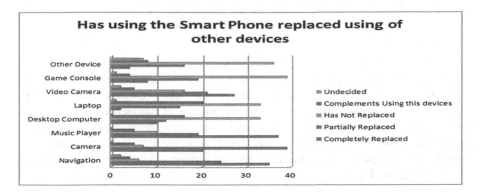

Fig. 15. Level 4 users' devices replaced by smartphone

4.6 Level 5 (Tech-Savvy) Observations

Figure 16 indicates that level 5 users are mainly male, and most have a flat rate data plan. Almost all of them will choose a smartphone again as seen on Fig. 17, while 3% will go for a basic phone. iOs and android are still the dominant operating system, with iOS being the most used of the two.

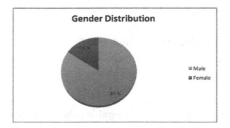 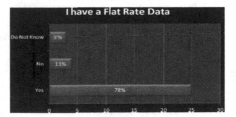

Fig. 16. Level 5 users by gender and data plan use

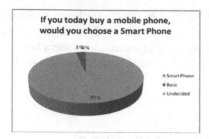
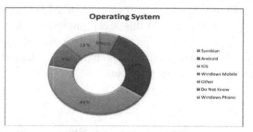

Fig. 17. Level 5 users by potential phone purchase and operating system in use

They are the most sophisticated group of users. At this level, music player seem to be the most used functionality, since it has almost being completely replaced by a smartphone. One can also observe that the summation of number of users who have their smartphone as a partial or complete replacement for all listed devices outweighs the number of users who think otherwise. Hence, majority of this users find all devices partially or completely replaceable with their smartphone. All these variables are further illustrated on Fig. 18.

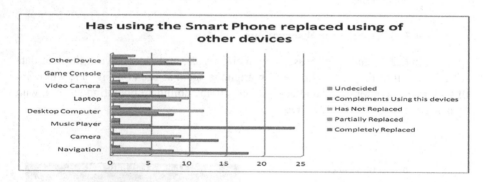

Fig. 18. Level 5 users by devices replaced by smartphone

5 Implication and Conclusion

The result reveals the prominent status of profiling in international market and how businesses can target the millennial with different promotional strategy most especially advertising through instant messaging, text messages, email, mobile app, gamification and social media based on the profile of each segment. About a quarter of young Finnish smartphone users fall into beginners (level 1), who do not use most of the advanced functions of their smartphones. The higher users who are on level 4 or 5 only consist of 26% of the total respondent. This demonstrates that most young Finnish smartphone users do not actually make use of the advanced functionality of their smartphone. Some identified reasons include choice or operating system and data plan. The smartphone operating system of Finnish youth seems to also be a determining factor for the level of usage. We assume that the more the usage of advanced functionality, the more value-added service the operating system has provided. For instance, the use of Symbian operating system is only noticeable on the lower levels of users (level 1 and 2) and becomes obscure as we move to higher level of users. Thus, the Symbian operating system is perceived to have little value-added services. The Android operating system is noticeable in all level of usage and it remains the most used operating system in total. iOS became more visible as we progressed to higher level of users, which indicates that the operating system provides more quality value-added services compared to another operating system.

The data plan being used has also proven to be a determining factor while accessing the level of usage of smartphone. Nearly half of the least users (level 1), do not have a flat rate data and just more than half of level two users. Also, a quarter of the mid-range users at level 3, do not use a flat rate. For the high-level users, approximately 80% are on flat rate data plan. Most common advanced functionalities being used on smartphone by young Finns are navigation devices, music player, and camera. Advanced smartphone functionalities have not, however, being able to replace devices such as laptop, desktop computer and game console. The study conclude that the young Finns do not use majority of the advanced functionalities of a smartphone. To increase the level of usage of smartphone for young Finns, quality value added services should be provided on various mobile operating systems, as observed in the case of iOS. Flat rate data plan should also be encouraged, through bundling with smartphone purchase and attractive pricing regime. These findings have lots of implications for marketing planners and most importantly Nigeria as an emerging market. The user of smartphones in level 1 (beginners) can be reached with mere sending of promotional messages to their phones since basically they do not necessarily perform more than one functional activity on their smartphone, daily or weekly. For level 2 (explorers) users, business owners can target this set of millennia by sending text as well as making their brand visible online since these set of users can surf the net for information. The level 3 (intermediate) users can receive and send an email which means that these set of users can receive messages through their emails in form of newsletters and advertisement on product or services. Level 4 (advanced) users aside from the fact that they can be contacted for promotion of products and services through the means in other 3 levels, they can be engaged via downloading of games or using social media such as Twitter or Facebook where products are on display and there is an opportunity to interact and bargain. To reach the tech-savvy users (level 5), the youth can be targeted using all the strategies employed in all other levels as the users of this level perform with their smartphones what the other level users does as well. Generally, the users in every level can be contacted through text messaging with promotional messages. This profiling insight will benefit emerging market such as Nigeria.

Managerially, the businesses can target the millennial with different promotional strategies most especially advertising through instant messaging, text messages, email, mobile app, gamification and social media based on the profile of each segment. Mobile commerce merchants and vendors can create a niche market for the smartphone online shopper. The implication for the Nigerian economy is that policy makers should come up with a blueprint on how to make smartphone affordable to people especially the young people who use it for educational, social and business transactions. The government should work on the internet connectivity tariff and lessen the burden of erratic internet connection and it became obvious through this study that smartphone will be less enjoyable without internet connectivity being a multifunctional mobile device.

5.1 Conclusion

Segmentation and targeting are critical elements of successful marketing strategy. As identified in our study, there are different levels of users of smartphone based on their knowledge and income. The type of smartphone and their functionalities determine what they use it for. Marketers with a good knowledge of these different users will apply the right marketing strategy to reach them. Our study is therefore important and extends knowledge on this research stream as it does not only identify different ways millennials use smartphone, it also profiles and segments them serving as a hands-on tool for marketing professionals.

5.2 Limitations

The study is not without limitations as the focus rest only on the millennials without considering other generation. Also, the study employs descriptive-quantitative methodology, it will be insightful if future studies could adopt the structural equation modeling as an extension of this study and compare different generations. Additionally, future studies can explore cross-market antecedents of smartphone use and how marketers can segment smartphone users for effective marketing programmes.

References

1. Elegbeleye, O.S.: Prevalent use of global system of mobile phone (GSM) for communication in Nigeria: a breakthrough in interactional enhancement or a drawback? Nordic J. Afr. Stud. **14**(2), 193–207 (2005)
2. Aubrey-Derrick, S., Frank, P., Florian, L., Christian, S., Seyit, C., Şahin, A.: Monitoring smartphones for anomaly detection. Mob. Netw. Appl. **4**(1), 92–106 (2009)
3. Michael, D.: Are Smartphones Spreading Faster than Any Technology in Human History? http://mashable.com/2012/05/09/smart-phones-spreading-faster/.Retrived. Accessed 12 Feb 2013
4. Mathew, H.: Apple unveils iPhone, 9 January 2007. http://www.macworld.com/article/1054769/iphone.html. Accessed 31 Jan 2013
5. Nielsen, D.: Survey new U.S smartphone growth by age and income. http://www.nielsen.com/us/en/newswire/2012/survey-new-u-s-smartphone-growth-by-ageand-income.html. Accessed 15 Feb 2013
6. Dolnicar, S., Lazarevski, K.: Methodological reasons for the theory/practice divide in market segmentation. J. Mark. Manag. **25**(3-4), 357–373 (2009)
7. Quinn, L., Dibb, S.: Evaluating market-segmentation research priorities: targeting re-emancipation. J. Mark. Manag. **26**(13-14), 1239–1255 (2010)
8. Jones, S.C., et al.: Using market segmentation theory to select target markets for sun protection campaigns (2005)

9. Sell, A., Mezei, J., Walden, P.: An attitude-based latent class segmentation analysis of mobile phone users. Telemat. Inform. **31**(2), 209–219 (2014)
10. Hamka, F., et al.: Mobile customer segmentation based on smartphone measurement. Telemat. Inform. **31**(2), 220–227 (2014)
11. Kessler, S.: Even on $15,000 a Year, Most Young People Buy Smartphones [STUDY]. Mashable, 20 February 2012. http://mashable.com/2012/02/20/smartphones-young-people/. 05 May 2012
12. Ofcom: A Nation Addicted to Smartphones. Ofcom, 4 August 2011. http://media.ofcom.org. uk/2011/08/04/a-nation-addicted-to-smartphones/. 05 May 2012
13. Henley, J.: Teenagers and Technology: 'I'd Rather Give up My Kidney than My Phone'. The Guardian. Guardian News and Media, 15 July 2010. http://www.guardian.co.uk/ lifeandstyle/2010/jul/16/teenagers-mobiles-facebook-social-networking. 05 May 2012
14. Freudenheim, M.: As Smartphones Become Health Aids, Ads May Follow. New York Times, April 2012. http://www.nytimes.com/2012/04/02/technology/as-smartphones-become-health-aids-ads-may-follow.html?_r=1. Accessed 5 May 2012
15. Villar, E.A.: Revista De Estudios De Juventud. A.G. Luis Perez, Spain (2002)
16. Entner, R.: Smartphones to Overtake Feature Phones in U.S. by 2011. Nielsenwire (2010). http://blog.nielsen.com/nielsenwire/consumer/smartphones-to-overtake-feature-phones-in-u-s-by-2011. Accessed 5 May 2012
17. Dan: 77% of young people use a Smartphone to help decide what film to watch. Digital Stats (2012). http://digital-stats.blogspot.com/2012/02/77-of-young-people-use-smartphone-to.html. Accessed 5 May 2012
18. McKim, C.: Smartphones linked to decreasing number of young Scottish drivers. Deadline (2012). http://www.deadlinenews.co.uk/2012/04/29/smart-phones-linked-to-decreasing-number-of-young-scots-drivers/. Accessed 5 May 2012
19. Carroll, J., Howard, S., Peck, J., Murphy, J.: A field study of perceptions and use of mobile telephones by 16 to 22 year olds. J. Inf. Technol. Theory Appl. **4**(2), 49–61 (2002)
20. Cummins, D.: Smartphone Apps Creating More Distraction for Young Drivers on the Road. Ingenie (2012). http://finance.yahoo.com/news/smartphone-apps-creating-more-distraction-120000091.html. Accessed 5 May 2012
21. Kleinmann, T., Chen, X., Jaderstrom, B., Pinkerton, J., ONeil, S.: HTC Marketing Plan, p. 15 (2012) http://www.grin.com/en/catalog/business-economics/business-economics-marketing-corporate-communication-crm-market-research/?display=50

Internet Measurement

Measuring IPv6 Adoption in Africa

Ioana Livadariu[1(✉)], Ahmed Elmokashfi[1], and Amogh Dhamdhere[2]

[1] Simula Research Laboratory, 1364 Fornebu, Norway
{ioana,ahmed}@simula.no
[2] CAIDA/UCSD, La Jolla, CA 92093, USA
amogh@caida.org

Abstract. With the current IPv4 scarcity problem, deploying IPv6 is becoming increasingly important. This paper provides a first look at the state of IPv6 deployment in Africa. Using BGP routing data, we assess various aspects of IPv6 adoption. We find that, although most African countries suffer a deficit in IPv4 addresses, only 20% of African autonomous systems advertise IPv6 prefixes. IPv6 adoption is strong in Southern and Eastern Africa and weak elsewhere.

Keywords: IPv6 adoption · African Internet

1 Introduction

In the past six years all Regional Internet Registries (RIRs), except AFRINIC, have allocated IPv4 blocks from their last /8 address block. Moreover, in 2015 ARIN completely exhausted its available IPv4 addresses. AFRINIC, however expects to run out of addresses in 2019. This places Africa in a good position to orderly manage the transition to IPv6. However, Africa faces two key challenges in the coming decades. First, the continent population is projected to grow exponentially [10]. Second, the Internet penetration rate is expected to grow by 25% in the coming three years. Addressing these challenges and pushing the Internet penetration even further requires a swift deployment of IPv6. Thus, AFRINIC has put considerable effort into educating Internet practitioners on the continent about IPv6. It has, in fact, organized over 200 training sessions in 45 countries. However, there is a lack of a comprehensive study that tracks the outcome of these efforts. In this paper, we take a small step in this direction. Using BGP routing data we track the number of African Autonomous Systems (ASes) that deploy IPv6, compare different economic regions, investigate the stability of IPv6 prefixes, and check whether African IPv4 prefixes are being transferred outside the continent.

We find that most African countries have far fewer IPv4 addresses than Internet users. However, IPv6 deployment in Africa remains at an abysmal 20%, a percentage that is lower than most of the other regions except for the Middle East. South and East African countries lead the adoption, while Northern and Western countries lag further behind. We also find that, currently, the routing

© ICST Institute for Computer Sciences, Social Informatics and Telecommunications Engineering 2018
V. Odumuyiwa et al. (Eds.): AFRICOMM 2017, LNICST 250, pp. 345–351, 2018.
https://doi.org/10.1007/978-3-319-98827-6_32

stability of African IPv6 prefixes is comparable to the rest of the IPv6 Internet. African IPv4 prefixes seem to largely remain in Africa, indicating that the global exhaustion has a weak impact on Africa. Our findings point to avenues for improvements and underscore the need for a more comprehensive study of the African Internet in general and IPv6 in particular.

2   Related Work

Recently, there has been a growing interest in characterizing different aspects of Internet connectivity in Africa. Chetty *et al.* [2] studied the performance of mobile and fixed broadband connectivity in South Africa and underscored the importance of peering decisions. Gupta *et al.* [6] collected traceroutes between South Africa, Kenya, and Tunisia to investigate the interconnectivity between African Internet Service Providers (ISPs). The study underscored the poor connectivity between African ISPs and that most of them were more likely to be present at European IXPs than regional IXPs. This resulted in circuitous routing paths and consequently higher round trip delays. Zaki *et al.* measured webpage loading performance for users in Ghana and found that DNS resolution delay is the largest contributor. The measurement studies by Fanou *et al.* [4,5] offered a wider view of the AS level topology interconnecting African ISPs, using data collected in 2014 from RIPE Atlas probes located in multiple African countries. The authors found differences in the transit and peering practices of ISPs across the African continent that depend on socio-economic factors. They also reported an extreme lack in Internet peering between African ISPs - most of the African ISPs peer with networks outside the continent, directly impacting the Internet quality-of-service and resilience. Our paper is the first to investigate the deployment of IPv6 in Africa.

3   Datasets

In this section we briefly describe the datasets we employ in our study.

BGP Data: University of Oregon's Routeviews [3] and RIPE NCC's Routing Information System [8] collect Internet routing data from a set of route collectors that establish BGP peering sessions with routers in different networks. We leverage information from these two data repositories to investigate the IPv6 deployment and stability of the routed prefixes within AFRINIC.

World Bank Data: Through its open data initiative, World Bank publishes 237 datasets that cover a large variety of topics [15]. In Sects. 4 and 6, we use data on the Internet penetration rate and population per country [15] to contextualize our results.

4   IPv4 vs IPv6 Topologies

Figure 1(a) shows the number of African ASes originating IPv4 and IPv6 prefixes over time. The number of IPv6 ASes has started increasing rapidly since mid-2011. In general, the number of African ASes comprises a small fraction of the overall number of ASes in the Internet ≈1 in 50. Overall, 1089 and 203 ASes are advertising IPv4 and IPv6 prefixes, respectively. Figure 1(b) compares IPv6 deployment in Africa to Latin America and the Middle East[1] Since 2014, IPv6 deployment in Latin America picked up and rapidly surpassed the other two regions. Note that LACNIC entered the post exhaustion phase in 2014. Further, IPv6 deployment in Africa is almost double that in the Middle East.

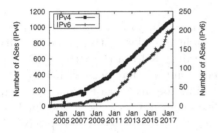
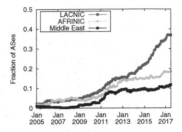

(a) Number of IPv4 and IPv6 deploying ASes within AFRINIC.

(b) Fraction of dual stack ASes within AFRINIC, LACNIC and Middle East.

Fig. 1. Evolution of IPv4 and IPv6 topologies over time.

We further use the United Nations geoscheme [9] to divide Africa into sub-regions and compare IPv6 deployment across them. These sub-regions represent economical and cultural blocks. In the map in Fig. 2(a), we delimit with dark lines the five African sub-regions. In the same figure, we show the number of ASes deploying IPv6 in different sub-regions. Except for the central sub-region, the different sub-regions include comparable numbers of ASes that deploy IPv4.

Since 2011, most of the IPv6 deploying ASes appear to be registered in countries located in the *Southern* and *Eastern* sub-regions. These sub-regions account for more than 75% of the overall number of ASes in the AFRINIC IPv6 graph. Notably, North and West Africa lag behind despite their large populations. We further compare IPv6 adoption across countries as of July 2017. Figure 2(b) presents the number of ASes that deploy IPv4 and IPv6, respectively, per country. Overall, only 34 countries out of 54 deploy IPv6. We measure large discrepancies between countries. Most ASes in South Africa, Tanzania, and Kenya deploy IPv6. Egypt and Nigeria reflect an opposite trend. Both countries have a large number of ISPs and populations but IPv6 uptake is low. Interestingly, IPv6

---

[1] We exclude Egypt from the Middle East region [12] as it is registered within AFRINIC.

adoption rate is higher for countries with small number of ASes (less than 10). These numbers again highlight the slow adoption in North and West Africa. To further understand the observed discrepancies, we use the Internet Penetration[2] per country collected from World bank [13]. We find that countries that deploy IPv6 have a higher Internet penetration rate. On average the Internet penetration rate is 27% and 11.6% for countries that deploy IPv6 and those that do not deploy it, respectively. Note that countries in the Northern sub-region have the highest Internet penetration rate, followed by the Southern and Eastern sub-regions. Hence, the lag of the Northern countries shows that IPv6 deployment is not mainly driven by Internet usage.

5   Stability of IPv6 Prefixes

Another key aspect of IPv6 deployment is the stability of the routed IPv6 prefixes compared to the IPv4 prefixes. To gain insight into the control plane stability of African IPv6 prefixes, we use BGP update dumps from the RIPE RIS RRC00 collector. We first identify 8 dual-stacked monitors that peer with RRC00 and provide a full routing table. Second, we count the number of updates per prefix sent by each of these monitors to the collector in six two-week periods in Jan'15, July'15, Jan'16, July'16, Jan'17, and July'17. Finally, we divide prefixes into African and non-African and compute the mean daily updates per active prefix for each period. The panels in Fig. 3 show the average daily prefix updates for African and non-African prefixes, for IPv4 and IPv6 respectively. African IPv4 prefixes exhibit a slightly higher average than non-African prefixes. Since the difference is very small, a plausible explanation could be differences in the length of convergence sequences, i.e., path exploration. Until July 2016, three monitors experienced a large mean daily updates for African IPv6 prefixes. This seems to normalize since January 2017, where African IPv6 prefixes start to exhibit

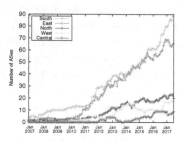
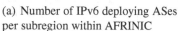
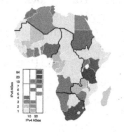

(a) Number of IPv6 deploying ASes per subregion within AFRINIC

(b) July 2017: IPv6 deploying ASes per country

Fig. 2. Number of IPv6 deploying ASes within the AFRINIC region.

---

[2] The Internet Penetration within a country is given as percentage of the country's population.

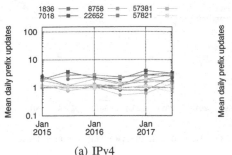
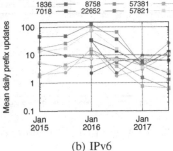

(a) IPv4   (b) IPv6

Fig. 3. Mean daily updates per active prefix - African (squares), others (circles).

daily means that are comparable to the rest of the Internet. Overall, IPv6 prefixes exhibit larger daily means compare to IPv4 prefixes. Our results, do not indicate that African IPv6 prefixes are particularly more unstable than the remainder of the IPv6 Internet.

6   Outlook and Impact of IPv4 Exhaustion

In this section, we assess the distribution of IPv4 addresses across Africa, which will be a key factor as AFRINIC enters the exhaustion phase. We also investigate the impact of mobility of African IPv4 prefixes. This is interesting since all other regions have entered the post exhaustion phase, which may encourage different actors to acquire prefixes that are allocated by AFRINIC.

6.1   Routed Address Space

African ASes contribute less than 4% and 11% to the global advertised IPv4 prefixes and IPv4 addresses, respectively. To understand whether IPv4 addresses are fairly distributed across Africa, we compute for each country the number of advertised IPv4 addresses over the number of Internet users. We obtain the latter value by using the World Bank's Internet penetration rate and the population of each country [13,14]. Figure 4 shows the median, quartiles, maximum, and minimum value of this fraction per subregion and over time. Countries in the Southern sub-region have a larger fraction of IPs per user compare to other sub-regions. Almost all countries have fewer IPs than users, which indicates that ISPs in these countries are already resorting to IP-sharing schemes to serve their customers. Resorting to such solutions, however, may cause a number of issues for end-users (e.g., low performance of file transfer and video streaming sessions [1]). The projected rapid increase in the Internet penetration in African will likely exacerbate this sharing.

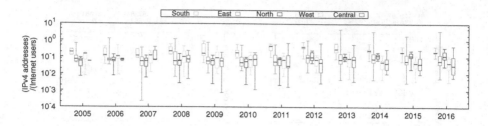

Fig. 4. Advertised IPv4 addresses/Internet users per region over time.

6.2 BGP Movements

We employ the BGP-inferring methodology detailed in [7] to analyze IPv4 address space movements between AFRINIC and the other four RIRs (i.e., APNIC, ARIN, LACNIC, RIPE) that occur in the post exhaustion period. From 2011 to 2015, we identify 461 IP address space movements involving ASes registered in AFRINIC; 71% and 21% of these movements come from/to RIPE and ARIN, respectively. For the latter registry, most of the address blocks are exchanged between the US and different African countries. In the RIPE region, the top country in terms of IP movements is Great Britain, followed by Netherlands and Israel; 57.57% of the BGP movements in this region come from ASes registered in these three countries.

Reasons for the observed IP space movements include complex organizational changes or IP address space management. In June 2015, we infer 72 prefixes that move from AS33770 (Kenya Data Networks) to AS30844 (Liquid Telecommunications); the sender AS is registered in Kenya, while the receiver AS is registered in Great Britain. Investigating further these organizations we find that Kenya Data Networks was acquired by Liquid Telecommunications in 2013 [11]. Thus, the observed IP movements appear most likely due to organizational changes within Liquid Telecommunications. We find the same organization (i.e., Liquid Telecommunications) involved in another IP address space movement that occurred in July 2014; one /24 block moved from AS3300 (BT Global Services) to AS36937 (Neotel/Liquid Telecommunications South Africa). The /24 block is registered in RIPE but has been collocated for BT via Neotel (organization acquired in 2017 by Liquid) in the AFRINIC region since May 2015. So far, our analysis does not point to an alarming rate of prefixes movements from Africa.

7   Discussion and Conclusions

Using BGP routing data, this paper has taken a first look at IPv6 adoption in Africa. We find that only 20% of African ASes advertise IPv6 prefixes. Most of these ASes are in Southern and Eastern Africa. Surprisingly, countries with large populations in Northern and Western Africa lag behind. Further, there is no evidence that IPv6 adoption is picking up in Africa. We have not found any evidence that African IPv6 prefixes are particularly less stable. There is also no indication that ASes from other continents are attempting to acquire prefixes allocated by AFRINIC. Next, we plan to have a closer look at African routing stability, and IPv6 performance.

References

1. RFC 7021: Assessing the impact of Carrier-Grade NAT on Network Applications (2013). http://tools.ietf.org/html/rfc7021
2. Chetty, M., Sundaresan, S., Muckaden, S., Feamster, N., Callandro, E.: Measuring broadband performance in South Africa. In: Proceedings of the 4th Annual Symposium on Computing for Development (2013)
3. Meyer, D.: University of Oregon Route Views Project (2014). http://www.routeviews.org/
4. Fanou, R., Francois, P., Aben, E.: On the diversity of interdomain routing in Africa. In: Proceedings of Passive and Active Measurement Conference (PAM) (2015)
5. Fanou, R., Francois, P., Aben, E., Mwangi, M., Goburdhan, N., Valera, F.: Four years tracking unrevealed topological changes in the African interdomain. Elsevier Comput. Commun. J. **106**, 117–135 (2017)
6. Gupta, A., Calder, M., Feamster, N., Chetty, M., Calandro, E., Katz-Bassett, E.: Peering at the internet's Frontier: a first look at ISP interconnectivity in Africa. In: Proceedings of Passive and Active Measurement Conference (PAM) (2014)
7. Livadariu, I., Elmokashfi, A., Dhamdhere, A.: On IPv4 transfers markets: analyzing reported transfers and inferring transfers in the wild. Elsevier Comput. Commun. J. **111**, 105–119 (2017)
8. RIPE: Routing Information Service (RIS) (2014). http://www.ripe.net/ris/
9. United Nation: Standard Country or Area Codes for Statistical Use. https://unstats.un.org/unsd/methodology/m49/
10. United Nation: World Population Prospects. https://esa.un.org/unpd/wpp/Publications/Files/WPP2017_KeyFindings.pdf
11. Wikipedia: Kenya Data Networks. https://en.wikipedia.org/wiki/Kenya_Data_Networks
12. Wikipedia: Middle East. https://en.wikipedia.org/wiki/Middle_East
13. Worldbank: Individuals Using the Internet (% of Population). http://data.worldbank.org/indicator/IT.NET.USER.ZS
14. Worldbank: Total Population. https://data.worldbank.org/indicator/SP.POP.TOTL
15. Worldbank: World Bank Open Data. https://data.worldbank.org

Reputation Rating Algorithm
for BGP Links

Hospice Alfred Arouna[1(✉)], Lionel Metongnon[1,2], and Marc Lobelle[2]

[1] Université d'Abomey-Calavi, Abomey-Calavi, Benin
hospice.arouna@uac.bj
[2] Université Catholique de Louvain, Ottignies-Louvain-la-Neuve, Belgium
{lionel.metongnon,marc.lobelle}@uclouvain.be

Abstract. BGP is a dynamic protocol used by Autonomous Systems (AS) constituting the Internet to exchange information in order to set up or remove links between AS. It takes into account the status of existing links and the internal policy of the AS. New links can be either legitimate or malicious. Having an objective way to detect route-leaks and/or route-hijacks could be a good starting point for deciding to accept or reject newly advertised links. In this work, an algorithm has been developed to evaluate link reputation on the basis of metrics. The work proceeded in three steps: first, BGPStream is used to overcome difficulties related to the collection of BGP record files from various collectors and projects. In the analysis phase (second phase), the algorithm is applied on collected data. The final phase is to visualize the results with a modified version of BGPlayJs to display the links reputation by coloring them from green to red. This algorithm could be used for baseline leak/hijack detection.

Keywords: BGP · Algorithm · Link · Reputation · Visualization

1 Introduction

BGP is the *de facto* inter-domains routing protocol used to maintain and exchange routing information on Internet. AS_PATH is one of the most important attributes of BGP [13]. BGP peers implicitly trust each other [2,9]. Any AS may announce and/or update any prefix (*i.e.*, IP address blocks) even if this prefix has already been assigned and/or announced by another AS or is a bogon (illegal prefix) [7]. This implicit trust is the fertile breeding ground for malicious activities, censorship and configuration errors. Various solutions have been proposed to improve the security of the protocol, but most of them remained at the project stage [2,9]. Since then, visualization solutions with their user-friendly analysis approach stand out and get popular. However most of those graphical solutions are not algorithm-based and are useless to detect if a link is legitimate or malicious [1]. The goal of this paper is to develop a BGP link reputation algorithm. For each link on each AS_PATH, a reputation will be computed based on other metrics. The rest of the paper is organized as follows.

© ICST Institute for Computer Sciences, Social Informatics and Telecommunications Engineering 2018
V. Odumuyiwa et al. (Eds.): AFRICOMM 2017, LNICST 250, pp. 352–357, 2018.
https://doi.org/10.1007/978-3-319-98827-6_33

Section 2 summarizes related work. Section 3 explain our methodology. Section 4 give details about our approach. Section 5 presents tests cases and the results. Section 6 introduce African perspective while Sect. 7 concludes the paper.

2 Related Work

Studies [4,5,15] are related to ASes trust. Konte et al., [10] focused on malicious ASes fully dedicated to supporting cybercrime while Sankar et al., [14] developed a framework to detect suspicious deviation in the AS_PATH between a source and destination. The linkrank project from UCLA was using only one metric. However, Lad et al. show in [11] the need to have more than one metric to evaluate link reputation. The linkrank project from UCLA is a rare example of graphical tool that is algorithm based and allows BGP routing dynamics observation [11]. Although, this project was abandoned since July 2011, the idea has been taken up during the linkrank challenge from the Center for Applied Internet Data Analysis (CAIDA) BGP hackathon [3]. The objective of CAIDA linkrank, was to find a solution to help discriminate legitimate from malicious link information. The algorithm described in this paper combines different metrics to determine link reputation and clear the CAIDA linkrank challenge.

3 Methodology

This paper presents a proof of concept for link reputation computation. With the huge amount of BGP data available, *BGPStream* [12] is an efficient tool for processing large amounts of distributed and/or live BGP measurement data, enabling rapid prototyping and large-scale monitoring applications building. The JavaScript version of *BGPlay* [6]; *BGPlayJS* is used to visualize the algorithm results. With those 2 tools already available, our solution can focus on the algorithm part. In phase 1, *BGPStream* is used to collect BGP data during a defined time interval. The last phase is about results where a modified version of *BGPlayJS* is used to display the reputation of links by coloring them from green to red. Red means that link has bad reputation while green means the opposite. Phase 2 is the principal part where our intuition has been implemented in mathematical functions and algorithms. Our implementation has been evaluate with existing tests cases.

4 Approach

This study is based on the intuition that links with good reputation have a majority of BGP announcements with little amount of bogon and that most peers use those links. From this intuition, three metrics has been defined and combine to compute the link reputation at a specific time: (i) `link stability` (number of announcements vs withdrawn), (ii) `bogon degree` (number of bogon per link) and finally (iii) `link sensibility` (number of prefixes - new and/or modified - per link between t_2 and t_1). Those metrics have been converted first to mathematical functions and then as algorithms. For example, in an oriented graph $G = (V, E)$ where $V = \{v | v \in path_i\}$ (nodes are ASN on specific AS_PATH) and $E = \{\langle a, b \rangle | \langle a, b \rangle \in path_i\}$ (edges between ASN), the bogon degree is given by the following formula:

$$
bogons_t(\langle a, b \rangle) = \begin{cases} \sum_{i=0}^{n} 1, & \text{if } prefix_{ti} \bigcap bogon_{set} \\ 0, & \text{otherwise} \end{cases}
\tag{1}
$$

where n is the total number of prefixes on link $\langle a, b \rangle$ for event t. For each event (BGP annoncement) at time t and for each prefix i seen on link $\langle a, b \rangle$ between ASes a and b, a positive counter is incremented by one if $prefix_{ti}$ is present in bogon database ($bogon_{set}$ from *Team Cymru*). With link stability, link behavior is observed on each event by removing the number of withdrawn prefixes from the number of announced prefixes. link sensibility metric is the one used by the linkrank project from UCLA. This metric helps us to observe the link utilization by peers and is taken as it is [11].

BGPStream helped us filter collected BGP events related to our tests cases. For each of those test cases, a specific list of BGP events is available. For the purpose of our study, a data structure called record has been added to each BGP event result. Each record contains a list of links which represents each link observed on the current AS_PATH. In each link data structure, elements like prefixes_list and as_path_list are present.

Input: events list
Output: link_reputation
1 **while** *we still have event* **do**
2   **foreach** *record in event* **do**
3   **foreach** *link in record* **do**
4   link_stab $\leftarrow$ Stability(*link*)
5   link_bogon $\leftarrow$ Bogons(*link*)
6   link_sens $\leftarrow$ Sensibility(*link*)
7   link_reputation
                $\leftarrow 1 + \text{link\_stab} - \text{link\_bogon} + \text{link\_sens} - \text{link\_stab}^{link\_bogon}$
8   **end**
9   **end**
10 **end**

Algorithm 1. Link Reputation (Main algorithm)

In the main algorithm (Algorithm 1), while there are BGP events (line 1) and record (line 2) from *BGPStream*, link reputation can be compute for each link (line 3). link stability metric result is saved on link_stab variable (line 4). On line 5, bogon degree metric result from function Bogon apply formula

1 and the last metric `link sensibility` result is obtain on line 6. With all components, the link reputation is compute by combining those metrics using the formula on line 7. The last part this formula express exponential impact of correlation between announcement and the type of prefixes. The 1 is a fallback to make sure we have *positive cost* when others parts of the formula gives 0. We have evaluated other formulas to combines those metrics without conclusive results. Our tests shows that the current formula is quite acceptable as shown in Sect. 5.

5   Results

Due to resources limitation, our implementation has been tested on four cases: censorship (Youtube hijack), malicious activities (Link Telecom hijack), configuration error (Malaysia Telekom route leaks) and country-wide outage on Egypt. For each case, two states has been observed: one *incident* state and one control state, called *normal* state. For the purpose of this paper, only Egypt country-wide outage case will be discuss.

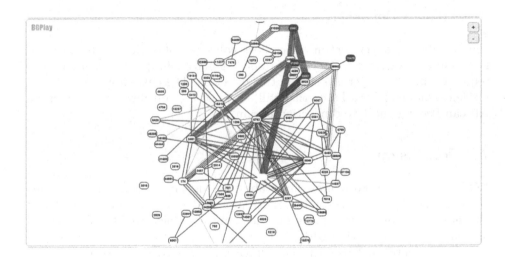

Fig. 1. Internet in Egypt offline (incident state)

Figure 1 presents the *incident* state where majority of the 3089 prefixes (196.219.246.0/24, 81.21.104.0/24 and 193.227.0.0/18 are monitored for this analysis) assigned to Egyptian Ases have been withdrawn on January 27th, 2011 [8]. We can notice a majority of red lines between `Origin AS` and transit/peers Ases, helping us verify our intuition: a majority of the links have *bad reputation*.

Figure 2 is the *normal* state of this case (February 2nd, 2011). Here we have mixed link color. Some have *good reputation* while other have *bad reputation*. Since Egyptian Ases started advertising theirs prefixes as before the censorship, reputation of those links is gradually migrating from *bad* to *good*.

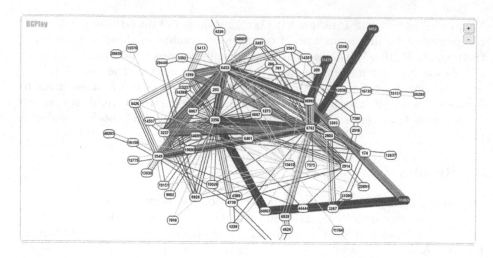

Fig. 2. Egypt back online (control state) (Color figure online)

6   African Perpective

The low density of Internet in Africa does not lower BGP threats in the continent. On the other hand, the lack of resources makes cheap security solutions a requirement. This paper is a step in this direction. The next step is a real time implementation of our solution that will be tested with operators we met during African Peering and Interconnection Forum.

7   Conclusion

BGP is a resilient protocol providing stable inter-domain routing since late 1993. BGP threats are well known but most proposed solution require significant changes to be applied worldwide for the protocol, which would require global agreement. However living with BGP threats is possible if these threats can be quickly identified. This work is a response to the need expressed by linkrank projects (UCLA and CAIDA). In this work a graphical link detection algorithm-based tool has been introduced, to easily provide baseline leak/hijack detection. However there is space for improvement. BGP is a large scale protocol, so massive data analysis tools like machine learning algorithms has to be used to increase the efficiency of the algorithm. Those technologies will also help to evaluate the number of links detected with correct/expected reputation. There is also the need to develop a more appropriate viewer, since *BGPlayJS* was not designed to display only one line between ASes.

References

1. Biersack, E., et al.: Visual analytics for BGP monitoring and prefix hijacking identification. IEEE Netw. **26**(6), 33–39 (2012)
2. Butler, K., Farley, T.R., McDaniel, P., Rexford, J.: A survey of BGP security issues and solutions. Proc. IEEE **98**(1), 100–122 (2010)
3. CAIDA: List-of-challenges. https://github.com/CAIDA/bgp-hackathon/wiki/List-of-Challenges#linkrank-1
4. Chang, J., et al.: AS-TRUST: a trust quantification scheme for autonomous systems in BGP. In: McCune, J.M., Balacheff, B., Perrig, A., Sadeghi, A.R., Sasse, A., Beres, Y. (eds.) Trust 2011. LNCS, vol. 6740, pp. 262–276. Springer, Heidelberg (2011). https://doi.org/10.1007/978-3-642-21599-5_20
5. Chang, J., et al.: AS-CRED: reputation and alert service for interdomain routing. IEEE Syst. J. **7**(3), 396–409 (2013)
6. Colitti, L., Di Battista, G., Mariani, F., Patrignani, M., Pizzonia, M.: Visualizing interdomain routing with BGPlay. J. Graph Algorithms Appl. **9**(1), 117–148 (2005)
7. Cymru, T.: The bogon reference. http://www.team-cymru.org/bogon-reference.html
8. Dainotti, A., et al.: Analysis of country-wide internet outages caused by censorship. In: Proceedings of the 2011 ACM SIGCOMM Conference on Internet Measurement Conference, IMC 2011, pp. 1–18. ACM, New York (2011). https://doi.org/10.1145/2068816.2068818
9. Huston, G., Rossi, M., Armitage, G.: Securing BGP - a literature survey. IEEE Commun. Surv. Tutor. **13**(2), 199–222 (2011)
10. Konte, M., Perdisci, R., Feamster, N.: ASwatch: an as reputation system to expose bulletproof hosting ASes. ACM SIGCOMM Comput. Commun. Rev. **45**(4), 625–638 (2015)
11. Lad, M., Zhang, L., Massey, D.: Link-Rank: a graphical tool for capturing BGP routing dynamics. In: 2004 IEEE/IFIP Network Operations and Management Symposium, NOMS 2004, vol. 1, pp. 627–640. IEEE (2004)
12. Orsini, C., King, A., Giordano, D., Giotsas, V., Dainotti, A.: BGPStream: a software framework for live and historical BGP data analysis. In: Proceedings of the 2016 ACM on Internet Measurement Conference, pp. 429–444. ACM (2016)
13. Rekhter, Y., Li, T., Hares, S.: A border gateway protocol 4 (BGP-4) RFC 4271. Technical report (2005)
14. Prem Sankar, A.U., Poornachandran, P., Ashok, A., Manu, R.K., Hrudya, P.: B-Secure: a dynamic reputation system for identifying anomalous BGP paths. In: Satapathy, S.C., Bhateja, V., Udgata, S.K., Pattnaik, P.K. (eds.) Proceedings of the 5th International Conference on Frontiers in Intelligent Computing: Theory and Applications. AISC, vol. 515, pp. 767–775. Springer, Singapore (2017). https://doi.org/10.1007/978-981-10-3153-3_76
15. Yu, H., Rexford, J., Felten, E.W.: A distributed reputation approach to cooperative internet routing protection. In: 1st IEEE ICNP Workshop on Secure Network Protocols (NPSec), pp. 73–78. IEEE (2005)

Internet Performance Measurements
for Education and Research Network in Kenya

Kennedy Odhiambo Aseda[✉] and Meoli Kashorda

Kenya Education Network, P.O. Box 30244, Nairobi 00100, Kenya
{kaseda,mkashorda}@kenet.or.ke

Abstract. KENET operates the national research and education network (NREN) of Kenya and has deployed Internet Measurement tools that are used for network performance monitoring. This paper focuses on the deployment of perfSONAR and how it has been utilized for end-to-end network performance measurements by researchers in Kenya who need to collaborate with researchers in other parts of the world. perfSONAR is a widely-deployed test and measurement infrastructure that is used by science networks around the world to monitor and ensure network performance. The paper introduces some of the measurement metrics that can be queried from the openly accessible data archive provided by the infrastructure based on real measurements done from within the KENET network. End-to-end measurement metrics provided by the deployed infrastructure is important for researchers, policy makers and regulators especially in Africa where such measurement metrics are not openly available or collated.

Keywords: KENET · Internet measurement · perfSONAR · ESNET
TCP throughput measurement · One-way ping · Latency measurement

1 Introduction

The Kenya Education Network (KENET)[1] is the National Research and Education Network (NREN) of Kenya. It operates the national network that interconnects universities and research institutions. The national network is in turn connected to the global research networks through the regional research and education network (RREN) for East and Southern Africa, UbuntuNet[2]. UbuntuNet in turn is connected to GEANT[3] in Europe as well as the commodity Internet service providers. This research network allows Kenyan researchers to collaborate with other researchers in any of the global research networks such as CENIC[4] in California or TENET[5] in South Africa. To effectively support the researchers in Kenya, KENET has put in place internet performance measurement tools that are able to provide required visibility to the network operations center (NOC). These tools assist KENET engineers to quickly diagnose and

---

[1] Kenya Education Network, https://www.kenet.or.ke
[2] Ubuntunet Network, https://www.ubuntunet.net/network-topology
[3] GEANT, https://www.geant.org/
[4] CENIC, http://cenic.org/about/about-overview
[5] TENET, http://www.tenet.ac.za/

© ICST Institute for Computer Sciences, Social Informatics and Telecommunications Engineering 2018
V. Odumuyiwa et al. (Eds.): AFRICOMM 2017, LNICST 250, pp. 358–367, 2018.
https://doi.org/10.1007/978-3-319-98827-6_34

isolate network performance problems before they impact the service level agreements of the member institutions.

Most data network performance measurements deployed in networks are geared towards passive collection of metrics. These metrics mainly provide an indication of the network connectivity utilization and performance, which are used to ensure the achievement of service level agreements (SLAs). Passive measurements such as Simple Network Management Protocol (SNMP) [1] and Netflow [2] measure real traffic and/or provide metrics related to the real traffic traversing the network. However, these tests do not inject substantial traffic into the measured network.

There are situations which require that the network under measurement be stressed to ascertain the capacity limitations or to find subtle signs of impending faults in the network. These measurements not only require injection of measurement traffic into the test network but also active measurement of the test packets to ascertain the performance of the network. Specifically, active measurements are employed when measurements traverse networks that are not controlled by the entity conducting the tests [11].

Research networks are designed to be able to effectively handle large data transfers between research centers and facilities, or to support real-time applications. Examples of research facilities that require large data transfers include grid computing facilities, high performance computing (HPC) centers and open access data repositories (OADRs). Real time applications include telemedicine application and high-definition video conferencing that support research collaboration. These applications are very sensitive to packet loss and jitter. Packet loss may result in loss of communication for a telemedicine procedure, or lead to ineffective access of the shared computing infrastructure due to inability to adequately scale the TCP window [3]. To effectively equip a network operations center (NOC) of a research network with the visibility to support real time applications, both active and passive measurements tools must be used.

Active measurements such as accurate TCP throughput tests are essential in determining situations when the network is congested or losing packets. TCP throughput measurements based on the IEFT RFC6349 [4] are affected by several factors like packet loss, cross-traffic, end-to-end delay, throttling, test device resource contention, and TCP buffers.

End-to-end delay and packet loss affect the TCP throughput measurements in diverse ways. Delay coupled with TCP receive window configuration of the test devices can limit the maximum throughput measurement even on a lossless path. It is therefore imperative that the end-to-end delay measurement be as accurate as possible to ensure integrity of the TCP throughput measurement result. Delay measurements on the other hand require accurate time measurement between the test devices thus a need to ensure synchronized time in the test devices.

Finally, packet loss can affect TCP throughput measurement by limiting the ability of the TCP window to scale to a level that allows for measuring the full capacity of the network under test. Additionally, TCP window scaling can be affected by the TCP implementation of the software being used; for instance, different operating systems have different implementations of TCP with recent releases of operating systems and kernels enabling TCP auto-tuning feature by default. Other improvements to the TCP stack implementations such as TCP New Reno [5], Binary Increase Congestion Control

(BIC) [6] and CUBIC [7] that exhibit better TCP congestion control in high bandwidth-high delay connections [9], also known as long-fat networks (LFNs).

One of the widely deployed toolkits that is designed to facilitate the measurement and collection of active performance metrics is perfSONAR. perfSONAR is an Internet measurement toolkit that is designed to provide end-to-end network measurement traversing multiple networks under the same or different management domains [8, 13]. The infrastructure is deployed in developed country NRENs and Science Networks because it not only helps to identify and isolate problems in real-time but also enhances the network operations and support functions of network providers.

This paper discusses KENET's deployment of the perfSONAR measurement nodes and how they have been used to support Kenyan researchers collaborating with other researchers in other countries with similar deployments. The paper highlights the perfSONAR internet measurement infrastructure setup at KENET, the applications that support the internet measurements and a few use cases. Finally, the paper summarizes the benefits of the measurement infrastructure and the need to deploy more perfSONAR internet measurement nodes in Kenya and Africa in general.

2   Internet Measurement Infrastructure at KENET Network

As the NREN of Kenya, KENET's first objective in the internet measurements sphere is to provide Internet users and regulators with tools of measuring the quality of broadband Internet. Secondly, KENET purposes to support internet engineering and policy research by graduate students and faculty. Finally, KENET aims to provide the global Internet community with tools that can be used to measure the quality of Internet in Kenya.

To achieve the mentioned objectives, KENET has put in place open source Internet measurements tools [10] such as Measurement Lab[6], RIPE Atlas Probes[7] and perfSONAR. Each tool provides a different functionality and in some cases, the tools complement each other. For the purposes of research data transfers and real-time connectivity, KENET extensively uses the perfSONAR toolkit. The toolkit is used to provide automated measurements that are scheduled and fully integrated with the out-of-band alerting system (e.g., using Mobile GSM network, SMS alerts are sent to NOC technical teams). This has greatly improved the response time of the KENET NOC in the event of a performance degradation on KENET's in country connectivity or international capacities.

In an effort geared towards ensuring the correct metrics are measured, KENET has put in place scheduled measurements of critical network performance metrics like network throughput, loss rates, delay and jitter. The results obtained from these measurements are stored in a searchable database to provide point-in-time analysis of performance events on the network. Performance metrics are collected using seven (7) dedicated distributed

---

[6] Measurementlab.net, https://www.measurementlab.net

[7] RIPE Atlas - RIPE Network Coordination Centre, https://atlas.ripe.net

measurement nodes placed strategically on the KENET network at the geographical Points of Presence (PoPs). Two (2) nodes are located at KENET data centers hosted in two (2) separate universities in Nairobi. The other nodes are located at KENET PoPs hosted by different universities in the Kenyan towns of Nakuru, Eldoret, Kisumu, Mombasa and Meru as shown in the KENET network coverage map in Fig. 1.

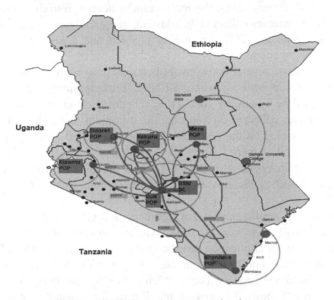

Fig. 1. KENET measurement node placement

The perfSONAR toolkit is designed to provide scheduled or on-demand measurement with the ability of incoming measurement control to reduce resource contention on the measurement host. In addition, the toolkit has the ability of measurement archiving that allows querying of the collected metrics on-demand based on the data access policies of the hosting institution(s). Some of the test measurements possible on the framework include both TCP and UDP throughput measurements; one-way delay measurements [12]; round trip time; and one-way packet loss among others.

For researchers, the toolkit provides archived open access data that can be queried and analyzed for policy and research purposes. With a large data set, queries done against archives in different countries can facilitate access to unique open internet measurement data.

3   KENET perfSONAR Implementation

KENET set up the perfSONAR measurement infrastructure in the year 2015 with support from International Networks group at Indiana University (IN@IU)[8] and the Network Startup Resource Center (NSRC)[9]. The infrastructure is composed of dedicated measurement equipment. The selection of the hardware and base system configuration was done to ensure that the measurement devices introduce no bottlenecks that would affect the metrics collected. In addition, the test devices are installed with an Operating System that has TCP auto-tuning enabled and a test scheduler to avoid concurrent tests being conducted.

On the base system, several software applications have been enabled on the nodes and other supporting applications within KENET. Each application contributes to the full functionality of the system by conducting scheduled or on-demand measurement. Whenever the metrics collected do not meet the minimum thresholds set, an alarm is raised. The tools enabled on the perfSONAR toolkit installed at the seven nodes are powstream[10], owampd[11], iperf[12], iperf3[13], bwctl[14], pScheduler[15] and ntp[16]. Other supporting software independent of the test nodes are esmond[17] for data archiving, MaDDash[18] dashboard application for data visualization, Nagios Core[19] and SMS Server Tools[20].

The visualizations are organized as a summary in a grid[21] and allows for interrogation of the data collected over time. This data can also be queried using the perfSONAR esmond[22] client application programming interface (API). Out of band SMS notification is integrated into the system using Nagios Core network monitoring that forwards the alerts to SMS Server Tools which uses GSM network for sending SMS notifications. Figure 2 shows the network monitoring for measurement notifications.

---

[8] International Networks at Indiana University, http://internationalnetworks.iu.edu/index.html

[9] Network Startup Resource Center, https://www.nsrc.org/

[10] powstream, http://software.internet2.edu/owamp/powstream.man.html

[11] owampd, http://software.internet2.edu/owamp/owampd.man.html

[12] iperf, https://sourceforge.net/projects/iperf2/

[13] iperf3, http://software.es.net/iperf/

[14] bwctl, https://software.internet2.edu/bwctl/

[15] pScheduler, https://fasterdata.es.net/performance-testing/network-troubleshooting-tools/pscheduler/

[16] ntp, http://doc.ntp.org/4.1.0/ntpd.htm

[17] esmond: ESnet Monitoring Daemon, http://software.es.net/esmond/

[18] MaDDash, http://software.es.net/maddash/

[19] Nagios Core, https://www.nagios.org/projects/nagios-core/

[20] SMS Server Tools. http://smstools3.kekekasvi.com/

[21] KENET MaDDash - Monitoring and Debugging Dashboard, http://maddash-uon.kenet.or.ke/maddash-webui/

[22] perfSONAR Client REST Interface, http://software.es.net/esmond/perfsonar_client_rest.html

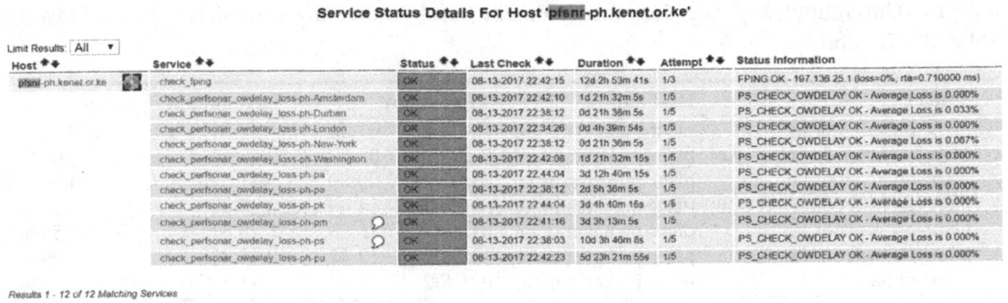

Service Status Details For Host 'pfsnr-ph.kenet.or.ke'

Limit Results: All

Host	Service	Status	Last Check	Duration	Attempt	Status Information
pfsnr-ph.kenet.or.ke	check_fping	OK	08-13-2017 22:42:15	12d 2h 53m 41s	1/3	FPING OK - 197.136.25.1 (loss=0%, rta=0.710000 ms)
	check_perfsonar_owdelay_loss-ph-Amsterdam	OK	08-13-2017 22:42:10	1d 21h 32m 5s	1/5	PS_CHECK_OWDELAY OK - Average Loss is 0.000%
	check_perfsonar_owdelay_loss-ph-Durban	OK	08-13-2017 22:38:12	0d 21h 36m 5s	1/5	PS_CHECK_OWDELAY OK - Average Loss is 0.033%
	check_perfsonar_owdelay_loss-ph-London	OK	08-13-2017 22:34:26	0d 4h 39m 54s	1/5	PS_CHECK_OWDELAY OK - Average Loss is 0.000%
	check_perfsonar_owdelay_loss-ph-New-York	OK	08-13-2017 22:38:12	0d 21h 36m 5s	1/5	PS_CHECK_OWDELAY OK - Average Loss is 0.067%
	check_perfsonar_owdelay_loss-ph-Washington	OK	08-13-2017 22:42:08	1d 21h 32m 15s	1/5	PS_CHECK_OWDELAY OK - Average Loss is 0.000%
	check_perfsonar_owdelay_loss-ph-pa	OK	08-13-2017 22:44:04	3d 12h 40m 15s	1/5	PS_CHECK_OWDELAY OK - Average Loss is 0.000%
	check_perfsonar_owdelay_loss-ph-po	OK	08-13-2017 22:38:12	2d 5h 36m 5s	1/5	PS_CHECK_OWDELAY OK - Average Loss is 0.000%
	check_perfsonar_owdelay_loss-ph-pk	OK	08-13-2017 22:44:04	3d 4h 10m 16s	1/5	PS_CHECK_OWDELAY OK - Average Loss is 0.000%
	check_perfsonar_owdelay_loss-ph-pm	OK	08-13-2017 22:41:16	3d 3h 13m 5s	1/5	PS_CHECK_OWDELAY OK - Average Loss is 0.000%
	check_perfsonar_owdelay_loss-ph-ps	OK	08-13-2017 22:38:03	10d 3h 46m 8s	1/5	PS_CHECK_OWDELAY OK - Average Loss is 0.000%
	check_perfsonar_owdelay_loss-ph-pu	OK	08-13-2017 22:42:23	5d 23h 21m 55s	1/5	PS_CHECK_OWDELAY OK - Average Loss is 0.000%

Results 1 - 12 of 12 Matching Services

Fig. 2. Integration of measurement alerts for SMS notification

4 Use Cases and Measurement Results

The perfSONAR measurement infrastructure is currently being used by different stakeholders to enhance their daily work and research. The following groups are some of the active users of the infrastructure or consumers of the data generated and archived using the perfSONAR infrastructure at KENET: NOC engineers, groups of researchers who need real-time applications or high data transfers, and global Internet measurements research community.

4.1 Supporting KENET NOC Engineers

The KENET NOC engineers are currently the most active users of the perfSONAR measurement infrastructure at KENET. KENET NOC benefits from the perfSONAR measurements by getting real-time notifications whenever the set performance measurement metrics are not meeting required thresholds. This is enhanced by integration of out-of-band SMS notifications system which has improved the resolution times for any performance degradation happening on the KENET backbone or transit networks. The second use of the measurement infrastructure at KENET is provision of network visibility. Automated visibility of the network is achieved through throughput, latency and packet loss measurements between KENET's main distribution points to the regional POPs. Table 1 shows the measurement results between two measurements nodes in Nairobi (at University of Nairobi and at United States International University) indicating packet loss and reduced network throughput because of dark fiber link degradation. Table 2 shows daily summaries of throughput measurement results between the measurement node at KENET's regional POP in Nakuru to Nairobi indicating degradation of third-party managed connection that lasted five days as highlighted in the table. In each case, the NOC engineers were alerted automatically and diagnosed the problem rapidly.

Network Performance Monitoring is the third use of the perfSONAR measurement infrastructure deployed at KENET. The measurement tools assist the KENET NOC to identify and resolve packet loss and throughput problems on the KENET backbone network arising from deteriorated fiber, loss of upstream connections or other factors

Table 1. Throughput & packet loss measurement trends indicating fiber deteroriation between UoN & USIU nodes

Source	Destination	Timestamp	Throughput	Loss (%)
pfsnr-ph.kenet.or.ke	pfsnr-pu.kenet.or.ke	01/08/2017 01:44	941.61	0.00%
pfsnr-ph.kenet.or.ke	pfsnr-pu.kenet.or.ke	01/08/2017 05:57	941.56	0.00%
pfsnr-ph.kenet.or.ke	pfsnr-pu.kenet.or.ke	01/08/2017 09:09	941.52	0.00%
pfsnr-ph.kenet.or.ke	pfsnr-pu.kenet.or.ke	01/08/2017 14:09	0.08	3.28%
pfsnr-ph.kenet.or.ke	pfsnr-pu.kenet.or.ke	01/08/2017 15:06	0.62	1.59%
pfsnr-ph.kenet.or.ke	pfsnr-pu.kenet.or.ke	01/08/2017 22:42	941.41	0.00%
pfsnr-ph.kenet.or.ke	pfsnr-pu.kenet.or.ke	02/08/2017 01:37	941.74	0.00%

Table 2. Throughput measurement trend indicating capacity constraint of managed service

Source	Destination	event_type timestamp	throughput
pfsnr-pa.kenet.or.ke	pfsnr-ph.kenet.or.ke	throughput 21/06/2017 00:00	921.78
pfsnr-pa.kenet.or.ke	pfsnr-ph.kenet.or.ke	throughput 22/06/2017 00:00	853.18
pfsnr-pa.kenet.or.ke	pfsnr-ph.kenet.or.ke	throughput 23/06/2017 00:00	394.36
pfsnr-pa.kenet.or.ke	pfsnr-ph.kenet.or.ke	throughput 24/06/2017 00:00	162.69
pfsnr-pa.kenet.or.ke	pfsnr-ph.kenet.or.ke	throughput 25/06/2017 00:00	87.15
pfsnr-pa.kenet.or.ke	pfsnr-ph.kenet.or.ke	throughput 26/06/2017 00:00	50.96
pfsnr-pa.kenet.or.ke	pfsnr-ph.kenet.or.ke	throughput 27/06/2017 00:00	550.99
pfsnr-pa.kenet.or.ke	pfsnr-ph.kenet.or.ke	throughput 28/06/2017 00:00	933.21

before they severely impact the network. Table 3 shows the scheduled end-to-end measurement results between perfSONAR probes in Nairobi, Kenya and those in Washington DC, USA. The results are used to monitor the quality of links between Kenya and the US that support collaborating researchers.

Table 3. Hourly summary measurement metrics (Nairobi, Kenya and Washington DC, USA)

Source	Destination	Timestamp	Delay(ms)	Packet loss (%)
pfsnr-ph.kenet.or.ke	wash-owamp.es.net	27/10/2017 09:00	121.25	0.00
pfsnr-ph.kenet.or.ke	wash-owamp.es.net	27/10/2017 10:00	121.52	0.00
pfsnr-ph.kenet.or.ke	wash-owamp.es.net	27/10/2017 11:00	121.65	0.00
pfsnr-ph.kenet.or.ke	wash-owamp.es.net	27/10/2017 12:00	121.68	0.00
pfsnr-ph.kenet.or.ke	wash-owamp.es.net	27/10/2017 13:00	121.66	0.00
pfsnr-ph.kenet.or.ke	wash-owamp.es.net	27/10/2017 14:00	121.45	0.00
pfsnr-ph.kenet.or.ke	wash-owamp.es.net	27/10/2017 15:00	120.38	0.00
pfsnr-ph.kenet.or.ke	wash-owamp.es.net	27/10/2017 16:00	120.60	0.00
pfsnr-ph.kenet.or.ke	wash-owamp.es.net	27/10/2017 17:00	120.38	0.00
pfsnr-ph.kenet.or.ke	wash-owamp.es.net	27/10/2017 18:00	120.39	0.00

Other notable use of the platform has been identification of un-optimized dynamic routing & route flaps due to OSPF redistribution which affect performance to selected users of the KENET network. KENET also regularly conducts on-demand performance measurement of third-party procured managed capacity as part of the network connectivity commissioning tests. This platform has been very handy in providing the appropriate measurement tools with results that are a true depiction of the implemented service by the provider.

4.2 Real-Time Applications for Research Groups

Research collaboration is very active in Kenya, with Kenyan researchers actively collaborating with their peers in Africa and other parts of the world, particularly in North America. To effectively collaborate, the researchers are supported by real-time applications such as video and web conferencing where different research groups collaborate online and hold meetings without the need to physically travel for face-to-face meetings.

For example, the deployment of a perfSONAR node at the Academic Model Providing Access to Healthcare (AMPATH) has enabled better support of real-time applications for researchers in the field of medicine and public health at Moi Teaching & Referral Hospital in Eldoret, Kenya. The researchers collaborate with their peers in North American Universities led by Indiana University. The quality of the links can be monitored not only by KENET NOC but also by network engineers at AMPATH or Indiana University. For example, KENET could extract the metrics shown in Table 4 from the archived Open Internet measurements data.

Table 4. Sample measurement metrics from measurement node in Eldoret

Source	Destination	Timestamp	Throughput	Delay (ms)	Packet metrics		
					Retrans count	Loss (%)	Duplicates
pfsnr-pe. kenet.or.ke	pfsnr-ph. kenet.or.ke	27/10/2017 09:37	699.02	1.95	40	0.00	0.00
pfsnr-pe. kenet.or.ke	pfsnr-ph. kenet.or.ke	27/10/2017 10:24	672.75	1.65	51	0.00	0.00
pfsnr-pe. kenet.or.ke	pfsnr-ph. kenet.or.ke	27/10/2017 14:15	693.35	2.06	24	0.00	0.00
pfsnr-pe. kenet.or.ke	pfsnr-ph. kenet.or.ke	27/10/2017 21:47	705.39	2.40	23	0.00	0.00
pfsnr-pe. kenet.or.ke	pfsnr-ph. kenet.or.ke	27/10/2017 23:44	680.16	2.21	27	0.00	0.00
pfsnr-pe. kenet.or.ke	pfsnr-ph. kenet.or.ke	28/10/2017 04:56	706.77	1.86	20	0.00	0.00
pfsnr-pe. kenet.or.ke	pfsnr-ph. kenet.or.ke	28/10/2017 07:10	658.32	1.91	55	0.00	0.00

4.3   Global Internet Measurements Research Community

The perfSONAR nodes deployed in Kenya by KENET are part of a global network of nodes that are open to network engineers and researchers worldwide. Engineers or researchers can use the nodes to collect Internet measurement metrics for research purposes or policy advocacy if they have access to the Internet. For example, researchers could collect measurement metrics in areas of Internet policy and research which can be used to map intra-country, inter-country and continental connectivity as depicted in Table 5. It is also possible for graduate students to conduct Internet measurements research using the open perfSONAR platform.

Internet measurements researchers can conduct on-demand measurements whenever there is a specific event, and this allows for correlation between real-life events and internet measurement metrics. The resulting data can be used to better design networks or inform policy at the global or local level.

Table 5. Analysis of delay measurements from Nairobi, Kenya to other cities in the world

	Kampala, UG	Durban, ZA	Amsterdam, NL	London, UK	Washington, US
Nairobi, KE (Outbound)	172.22	33.57	81.20	93.61	120.39
Nairobi, KE (Inbound)	9.99	79.65	71.81	92.06	129.03
Nairobi, KE (RTT)	182.21	113.22	153.01	185.67	249.42

5   Conclusion and Future Work

This paper has highlighted the perfSONAR internet measurement infrastructure at KENET, with Kenya being one of the locations in Africa where perfSONAR has been deployed and in active use. Other African countries with perfSONAR measurement nodes include Nigeria, Senegal, South Africa and Uganda. The paper has also delved into the applications that support the perfSONAR measurement infrastructure at KENET. Finally, the paper has elaborated the use cases for the infrastructure within the community in Kenya and globally where the data archived by the infrastructure can be interrogated and used in making policy or design decisions by African researchers or regulators.

Internet measurements are important in providing a benchmark for testing the quality of experience of internet connectivity services. perfSONAR is very handy in providing a platform for both scheduled and on-demand network performance measurements. These measurements can equip network engineering teams with adequate visibility of the network performance and related archives of data that can be drilled down with the aim of identifying or correlating performance problems with actual events on mutli-domain networks in partnership with other stakeholders.

Deployment of the perfSONAR measurement platform has empowered the KENET NOC with data and tools for performance monitoring. More work should be done to test a GPS clock source for use in improving the time accuracy of the measurement nodes and measure what percentage improvement is achieved by implementing a GPS clock in country. The second area that requires more work is the deployment of more perfSONAR measurement nodes in Kenya to foster more collaborative problem identification. In this regard, KENET will consider; in collaboration with partners, deployment of lower cost perfSONAR measurement nodes based on lower power consumption chipset computers like the Raspberry Pi. These will aid in having more crowdsourced data that will improve the accuracy of the measurements analyzed by researchers.

At the continental level, more perfSONAR nodes should be installed in African countries to enable measurements of network connectivity, interconnectivity and quality of experience; in addition to having reliable measurement results that will enhance future decision making.

References

1. Case, J., McCloghrie, K., Rose, M., Waldbusser, S.: Introduction to version 2 of the Internet-standard network management framework, RFC 1441 (1993). https://doi.org/10.17487/rfc1441 (1993)
2. Claise, B.: Cisco systems NetFlow services export version 9, RFC 3954 (2004). https://doi.org/10.17487/rfc3954
3. Borman, D., Braden, B., Jacobson, V., Scheffenegger, R.: TCP extensions for high performance, RFC 7323 (2014). https://doi.org/10.17487/rfc7323
4. Constantine, B., Forget, G., Geib, R., Schrage, R.: Framework for TCP throughput testing, RFC 6349 (2011). https://doi.org/10.17487/rfc6349
5. Henderson, T., Floyd, S., Gurtov, A., Nishida, Y.: The NewReno modification to TCP's fast recovery algorithm, RFC 6582 (2012). https://doi.org/10.17487/rfc6582
6. Xu, L., Harfoush, K., Rhee, I.: Binary increase congestion control (BIC) for fast long-distance networks. In: IEEE INFOCOM, pp 2514–2524, Hong Kong. IEEE Press (2004)
7. Rhee, I., Xu, L.: CUBIC: a new TCP-friendly high-speed TCP variant. In: Proceedings of the Third International Workshop on Protocols for Fast Long-Distance Networks, Conference Proceedings (2005)
8. Hanemann, A., et al.: PerfSONAR: a service oriented architecture for multi-domain network monitoring. In: Benatallah, B., Casati, F., Traverso, P. (eds.) ICSOC 2005. LNCS, vol. 3826, pp. 241–254. Springer, Heidelberg (2005). https://doi.org/10.1007/11596141_19
9. Yin, Q., Kaur, J., Smith, F.D.: Can bandwidth estimation tackle noise at ultra-high speeds? In: 2014 IEEE 22nd International Conference on Network Protocols, North Carolina, pp 107–118. IEEE Press (2014)
10. Kashorda, M., Aseda, K.: Internet measurements infrastructure at KENET. Technical Presentation, The 7th African Peering and Interconnection Forum (2016)
11. Mohan, V., Reddy, Y.R.J., Kalpana, K.: Active and passive network measurements: a survey. Int. J. Comput. Sci. Inf. Technol. 2, 1372–1385 (2012)
12. Shalunov, S., Teitelbaum, B., Karp, A., Boote, J., Zekauskas, M.: A one-way active measurement protocol (OWAMP), RFC 4656 (2006). https://doi.org/10.17487/rfc4656 (2006)
13. Nakamura, K., Tsuru, M., Oie, Y.: A perfSONAR-based integrated multi-domain network measurement platform – internet monitoring as a service. In: 2011 Third International Conference on Intelligent Networking and Collaborative Systems, pp 305–312. IEEE Press (2011)

On the African Peering Connectivity Revealable via BGP Route Collectors

Enrico Gregori, Alessandro Improta$^{(\boxtimes)}$, and Luca Sani

Institute of Informatics and Telematics,
National Research Council of Italy, Pisa, Italy
{enrico.gregori,alessandro.improta,luca.sani}@iit.cnr.it

Abstract. Internet pervasiveness in Africa has been slowly but steadily increasing since the beginning of this millennium. Thanks to several organisations which donated time and resources, it is nowadays possible to claim that the AS ecosystems of several countries in Africa are now experiencing an early stage of the peering era. In this paper, we investigate the capability of the BGP route collectors publicly available to reveal the newborn peering connectivity in African countries. By analysing BGP data available with existing techniques we found that a lot of this connectivity is missing from the dataset, mainly due to the lack of data sources in the region. In most countries, this could theoretically be solved by introducing no more than ten new ASes sharing their full routing information to route collectors.

Keywords: Internet · AS-level · BGP · Route collectors · Set coverage

1 Introduction

The Internet is composed of as a set of heterogeneous and independent networks, each of which compete and cooperate with each other by means of the Border Gateway Protocol (BGP) to build the routes that will carry the actual traffic. This ecosystem can be analysed at different levels of abstraction depending on the type of analysis that has to be carried on [1,16], e.g. Autonomous Systems (ASes) [15,22], IP/router [6,10,13], Points of Presence (PoPs) [4]. The AS-level in particular is helpful to analyse how the different players composing the Internet (i.e. ASes) interact with each other – in terms of BGP routing – without focusing too much on details concerning the inner structure of each player. The complete knowledge of the AS-level of a given region would also help network administrators in that very same region to plan their inter-domain routing in advance, therefore introducing the proper amount of redundancies in their provider choices so that possible problems of the regional Internet would have the minimum impact on the performances of their own networks.

Thanks to several heuristics and inference techniques developed in the past years, it is now possible to infer the economic agreements existing between pairs of ASes (e.g. [5,8]) and geolocate each AS to perform economic and regional

© ICST Institute for Computer Sciences, Social Informatics and Telecommunications Engineering 2018
V. Odumuyiwa et al. (Eds.): AFRICOMM 2017, LNICST 250, pp. 368–376, 2018.
https://doi.org/10.1007/978-3-319-98827-6_35

analyses [7,20]. In this paper we exploit some of these latter heuristics to analyse the Internet AS-level of the African Internet ecosystem as inferred from BGP data made publicly available by BGP route collecting projects. In particular, we focus on quantifying the completeness of the available BGP data in terms of data sources and their distribution in Africa, relying on the *p2c-distance* metric introduced in [8]. We found that the Internet ecosystem reflects the heterogeneity already shown by Africa in terms of culture and development and highlighted by recent work [2]. In the very same continent coexist countries where the ecosystem is rich in terms of ASes and Internet eXchange Points (IXPs), and countries where the Internet is at its very early stage of development [18] due to poor infrastructures and expensive transport services [24]. Most of the peering ecosystem in the area is however invisible to current route collecting infrastructure due to the overall absence of African ASes sharing their routing information, with exception of South Africa. Nevertheless, we also found that it could be theoretically possible to reveal the full peering connectivity of most countries just by adding less than ten new ASes sharing their full routing information to the current route collector infrastructure.

The rest of the paper is organised as follows. Section 2 describes the data sources exploited in our analysis and the methodologies applied to infer the AS-level. Section 3 gives a general overview of the African Internet AS-level ecosystem and Sect. 4 analyses the completeness of available BGP data. Finally, Sect. 5 concludes the paper.

2 Data Sources and Methodology

The Internet AS-level is typically represented as a graph where nodes are ASes and connections are BGP sessions established between ASes. Two ASes that decide to establish a BGP session essentially exchange a set of network reachability information which is used to route part of their Internet traffic between them. The amount and the nature of the reachability information exchanged totally depend on the economic agreements signed between the two ASes, which can typically be classified as provider-to-customer (p2c) or peer-to-peer (p2p) [5]. In the former, the provider announces to the customer the routes to reach all the Internet networks, whereas the customer announces to the provider the routes to reach its networks and its client networks (if any). In the latter, the two ASes exchange routes to reach their respective clients, typically to *keep local traffic local* and to reduce transit costs [17].

The primary data source [25] to analyse the Internet at the AS-level of abstraction is the BGP data collected and provided by organisations running route collectors, such as the Réseaux IP Européens Network Coordination Centre (RIPE NCC) with the Routing Information Service[1] (RIS), the University of Oregon with the Route Views project[2] and the Institute of Informatics and Telematics of the Italian National Research Council (IIT-CNR) with the Isolario

---

[1] http://ris.ripe.net.

[2] http://www.routeviews.org/.

project[3]. A route collector is a server running a BGP routing daemon which collects and stores routing information in Multi-Threaded Routing Toolkit (MRT) format, and does not announce any reachability information back to its BGP neighbors. Every AS is free to join and share its routing information with the public, contributing to improving the amount – and thus the quality – of BGP data available for research purposes. The fundamental piece of information found in collected BGP data to analyse the AS-level ecosystem is the AS_PATH attribute, which can be used to infer both the nodes (ASes) and the connections (AS adjacencies) of the AS-level topology.

As described in [7], it is possible to infer the AS geolocation by geolocating each of the subnets announced by the AS thanks to the availability of databases mapping IP addresses in countries. This technique allows to infer regional topologies just considering that each AS adjacency can be geolocated if both ASes are announcing (at least) one subnet in the very same country. In the end, the set of ASes geolocated in a given country/continent will contain both ASes owned by local organisations and strictly linked to the territory where they operate – hereafter *local ASes* – and ASes owned by international organisations that are operating in the very same territory for marketing purposes – hereafter *international ASes*. In this paper we will consider a given AS to be local if there is an entry in the AFRINIC registry related to that AS.

The analyses performed in the following sections are computed on BGP data collected by every route collector made available by Isolario, RIS and Route Views on August 8th, 2017. Geolocation is performed using the Maxmind Geo-Lite2 Country[4] database, while economic relationships are inferred using the algorithm described in [8].

3   A First Glance at the African AS-Level Ecosystem

Africa is an extremely heterogeneous continent in terms of language, culture, and economics, and this heterogeneity can also be recognized also in its AS-level ecosystem. In the very same continent coexist a quite large set of countries which are clearly behind the digital divide – and where the Internet is the least of their peoples' worries – with a set of progressive countries where Internet is starting to be a consolidated part of their economies. Table 1 shows details about the distribution of ASes in each country. Out of 1084 local ASes, South Africa receives the lion's share with 322 ASes, followed by Nigeria (145 ASes), Kenya (79 ASes), Tanzania (63 ASes) and Ghana (56 ASes). One of the most impressive feature that can be noticed at glance is the poor pervasiveness of IPv6 despite the efforts spent by several organisations in training sessions and IPv6 focused conferences. Every local AS announces on the Internet at least one IPv4 network while only 203 of them announce (at least) one IPv6 network. The latter set of ASes is mainly distributed among South Africa (47%), Tanzania (13%), Kenya (10%), Mauritius (9%) and Nigeria (6%). Another interesting

---

[3] https://isolario.it.

[4] https://dev.maxmind.com/geoip/geoip2/geolite2/.

Table 1. African AS-level ecosystem data (IXP list provided by AF-IX website).

Country	ASes (v4)		ASes (v6)		IXPs	Country	ASes (v4)		ASes (v6)		IXPs
	Loc	Int	Loc	Int			Loc	Int	Loc	Int	
Algeria	10	17	2	1	0	Mali	3	7	1	1	0
Angola	40	15	4	2	1	Mauritania	3	13	0	1	0
Benin	10	4	2	1	1	Mauritius	29	22	11	3	1
Botswana	18	8	2	1	1	Mayotte	1	5	0	0	0
Burkina Faso	8	8	0	1	1	Morocco	10	19	4	1	0
Burundi	9	6	0	1	0	Mozambique	19	13	1	1	1
Cameroon	17	9	1	1	0	Namibia	12	6	3	1	1
Cape Verde	3	8	1	1	0	Niger	10	10	0	1	0
Central African Rep	3	9	0	0	0	Nigeria	144	30	7	1	3
Chad	8	10	0	1	0	Rep. of Congo	11	9	1	1	1
Comore	2	7	0	1	0	Réunion	3	19	1	2	0
Cête d'Ivoire	15	5	2	1	1	Rwanda	14	6	1	1	1
Djibouti	6	6	1	2	1	São Tomé and Príncipe	2	7	0	1	0
DR Congo	23	20	0	1	1	Senegal	4	9	0	2	0
Egypt	56	30	4	2	1	Seychelles	15	36	1	4	0
Equatorial Guinea	6	8	2	1	0	Sierra Leone	10	7	0	1	0
Eritrea	1	7	0	0	0	Somalia	13	8	0	1	0
Ethiopia	1	8	0	1	0	South Africa	315	87	87	24	6
Gabon	11	19	2	1	1	South Sudan	8	5	0	1	0
Gambia	7	8	1	1	1	St. Helena	0	3	0	0	0
Ghana	56	6	4	3	1	Sudan	6	8	4	1	1
Guinea	9	8	0	1	0	Swaziland	10	8	0	1	0
Guinea-Bissau	1	6	0	1	0	Tanzania	62	19	23	1	2
Kenya	78	31	16	6	2	Togo	4	7	1	1	0
Lesotho	9	7	0	1	1	Tunisia	13	16	4	3	1
Liberia	7	11	1	1	1	Uganda	32	17	3	1	1
Libya	5	13	0	1	0	Western Sahara	2	5	0	0	0
Madagascar	5	12	1	1	1	Zambia	23	13	1	1	1
Malawi	11	9	2	1	1	Zimbabwe	17	15	4	1	0

aspect is that just 90 local ASes (about 8%) are located in more than a single country, highlighting how traffic transiting between neighboring countries is still demanded to international providers.

Similarly to the rest of the Internet ecosystem, the peering ecosystem in Africa is at a very early stage of development. Not many years ago most of local traffic was routed via Europe and North America [11], causing issues in performance due to high latencies. Things started changing during last decade, when initiatives like the African Internet Exchange System (AXIS) Project[5]

---

[5] https://au.int/en/axis.

led to a dramatic increase in the number of IXPs in the region. Nowadays in Africa, there can be found 37 active IXPs located in 34 cities in 28 countries[6] (Table 1). Scraping the websites of each IXP, it is easy to see that most of them have currently less than 20 ASes connected, with the notable exception of NAPAfrica in South Africa (273 ASes among Johannesburg, Cape Town and Durban), JINX in South Africa (82 ASes in Johannesburg), IXPN in Nigeria (54 ASes amon Lagos, Abuja and Port Harcourt), KIXP in Kenya (36 ASes between Nairobi and Mombasa), TIX in Tanzania (36 ASes between Dar es Salaam and Arusha) and UIXP in Uganda (26 ASes in Kampala). The presence of an IXP as crowded as NAPAfrica in South Africa stress even more how South Africa's Internet ecosystem is totally different from the rest of Africa, resembling the ecosystem of a European country. Finally, it must be stressed out that most IXPs interconnect ASes only at country-level [3] and it has been shown that ASes often do not peer with one another at local IXPs [11].

4   On the Completeness of African AS-Level Graph

It is well known that BGP data is far from being completely representative of the Internet AS-level ecosystem [8,19,21]. First, the number of ASes participating in any route collecting project is extremely low if compared to the whole size of ASes composing the Internet. During our analysis, only 525 ASes were sharing their routing information with Isolario, RIS and/or Route Views, while the total number of ASes routed on the Internet was 59,005. Second, route collectors are not receiving complete routing information from all of their feeders. Several collectors are placed on IXPs across the world and many feeders apply to them the very same export policies applied to other IXP participants. In other words, they announce to the route collectors only their customer cone [14], which provides an extremely limited view of the Internet. During our analysis, about half of the feeders were showing this kind of behavior, with only 257 ASes sharing an IPv4 space and 200 ASes sharing an IPv6 space close to a full routing table. The feeders announcing their full routing table to route collectors will be hereafter referred to as *full feeders*. Finally, BGP data is known to miss a large part of p2p connectivity established at IXPs and via private peering [12]. This is mostly caused by the location of full feeders in the AS graph and the presence of BGP export policies and economic relationships between ASes. Given the standard economic relationships established between ASes [5], an AS announces to the other AS its full routing information – containing routes learned from its peers, providers and customers – but only if it is a provider of the other party. As a consequence, a route collector is able to see routes established via IXPs and private peering of a given AS X only if exists a chain of transit relationships from the route collector towards X. This concept has been formalised as *p2c-distance* in [8], and it has been used to quantify the number of ASes for which it is possible to discover the full connectivity given a set of full feeders. The resulting graph incompleteness must be taken into serious consideration when

---

[6] http://af-ix.net/.

analysing the Internet at the AS-level of abstraction since it can easily lead to wrong conclusions, especially when analysing the graph properties [23]. To the best of our knowledge, this is the first work analysing the coverage of route collectors in the African region. Only Fanou et al. [2] indirectly tackled the vantage point placement issue in Africa by introducing several RIPE Atlas probes in the region.

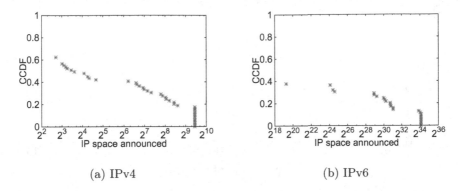

(a) IPv4   (b) IPv6

Fig. 1. CCDF of the amount of IPvX space announced by each feeder

The coverage situation in Africa is not very different from the rest of the world. Currently there are three route collectors in Africa physically deployed at KIXP in Kenya (Route Views), JINX in South Africa (Route Views) and NAPAfrica in South Africa (RIS). Those collectors receive data from 69 feeders, 63 located in South Africa, 4 in Kenya and 2 in Mauritius. An additional feeder from South Africa is connected to Isolario via multihop BGP. Figure 1 shows the Complementary Cumulative Distribution Function (CCDF) of the IPvX space announced to the route collectors by African feeders. As can be seen, the vast majority of feeders announce only a small portion of IP space, much smaller than the respective full routing table space which nowadays is composed of around 600k (v4) and 40k (v6) routes. Out of 69 feeders, only 13 can be considered v4 full feeders and only 9 v6 full feeders. All of them are located in South Africa, with the exception of one v4 and one v6 full feeders located in the island of Mauritius. Thus, it is almost straightforward to understand that the peering connectivity established at the 30 IXPs in Africa located neither in South Africa nor in Mauritius is currently completely hidden to BGP route collectors, while the small number of full feeders available in South Africa and Mauritius do not allow them to reveal much of the peering connectivity in their countries. Taking into account the p2c-distance metric, it is possible to claim that the current full feeders allow to reveal the full connectivity of 29 transit IPv4 ASes out of 129 (22.5%) and 5 out of 28 transit IPv6 ASes (17.9%) in South Africa whereas it is possible to discover the full connectivity of 6 transit IPv4 ASes out of 31 (19.4%) and no IPv6 transit ASes over 9 in Mauritius. In the rest of the African

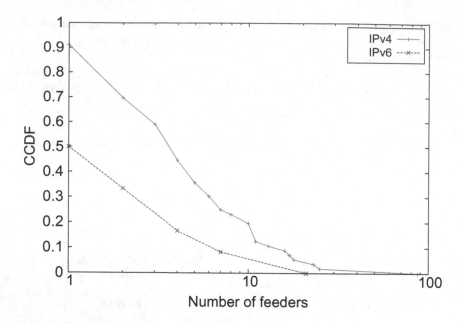

Fig. 2. CCDF of the solution cardinality of MSC problem in each African country

countries, the only ASes covered are the international ASes, which are covered from feeders outside of Africa.

To better understand how far the current BGP measurement system is from the ideal condition, where the entire p2p connectivity of each country is revealable and potentially visible, we applied the Minimum Set Cover (MSC) problem described in [9] to each regional topology gathered from BGP data. In each regional scenario every AS available is considered to be a potential feeder with its own *covering set* – i.e. the set of transit ASes having a finite p2c-distance from the AS – and the goal of the problem is to find the minimum number of ASes whose covering sets cover the whole set of transit ASes in that region. Figure 2 shows the CCDFs of the number of feeders required in each African country. Note that the v6 scenario is computed based only on 12 countries[7] where ASes were connected to each other. The scenario of South Africa is the most distinguishable in both pictures. Given the large amount of ASes in both v4 and v6 scenarios, a rather large number of feeders is required to obtain the full coverage of transit ASes. In all the other cases though, the number of feeders required is quite low, often smaller than 10 either in v4 or v6. This means that with a considerably small effort – 10 full BGP sessions to be established – it could be possible to reveal the full peering connectivity of 90% of countries in Africa.

---

[7] Angola, Botswana, Djibouti, Equatorial Guinea, Kenya, Mauritius, Morocco, Nigeria, South Africa, Sudan, Tanzania and Tunisia.

5   Conclusion

Africa shows in its AS-level ecosystem the same heterogeneity it shows terms of culture, economics and development. The most developed AS-level ecosystem can be found in South Africa, where the peering ecosystem is extremely similar to most European countries, as proved by the number of IXP available. Then, there is a small set of progressive countries (e.g. Egypt, Kenya, Nigeria and Tanzania) where Internet pervasiveness is steadily increasing and being more and more an important part of their economy. Finally, there is a large set of countries where Internet is at the very early stage of development. In this ecosystem, we found that BGP route collectors almost completely fail to reveal the peering connectivity established among ASes, thus affecting any possible graph analysis concerning the African ecosystem. Despite that, we found that theoretically it could be possible to solve this situation in most African countries by introducing just ten new full feeders.

References

1. Donnet, B., Friedman, T.: Internet topology discovery: a survey. IEEE Commun. Surv. Tutor. **9**(4), 56–69 (2007). https://hal.archives-ouvertes.fr/hal-01151820
2. Fanou, R., Francois, P., Aben, E., Mwangi, M., Goburdhan, N., Valera, F.: Four years tracking unrevealed topological changes in the african interdomain. Comput. Commun. **106**, 117–135 (2017)
3. Fanou, R., Valera, F., Francois, P., Dhamdhere, A.: Reshaping the African Internet: from scattered islands to a connected continent. Comput. Commun. **113**, 25–42 (2017)
4. Feldman, D., Shavitt, Y.: Automatic large scale generation of internet pop level maps. In: IEEE GLOBECOM 2008 - 2008 IEEE Global Telecommunications Conference, pp. 1–6 (2008)
5. Gao, L.: On inferring autonomous system relationships in the internet. IEEE/ACM Trans. Netw. **9**(6), 733–745 (2001)
6. Govindan, R., Tangmunarunkit, H.: Heuristics for internet map discovery. Proc. IEEE INFOCOM **2000**, 1371–1380 (2000)
7. Gregori, E., Improta, A., Lenzini, L., Rossi, L., Sani, L.: Discovering the geographic properties of the internet AS-level topology. Netw. Sci. **3**(1–4), 34–42 (2013)
8. Gregori, E., Improta, A., Lenzini, L., Rossi, L., Sani, L.: Improving the reliability of inter-AS economic inferences through a hygiene phase on BGP data. Comput. Netw. **62**, 197–207 (2014)
9. Gregori, E., Improta, A., Lenzini, L., Rossi, L., Sani, L.: A novel methodology to address the internet AS-level data incompleteness. IEEE/ACM Trans. Netw. **23**(4), 1314–1327 (2015)
10. Gunes, M.H., Saraç, K.: Analytical IP alias resolution. In: 2006 IEEE International Conference on Communications, vol. 1, pp. 459–464 (2006)
11. Gupta, A., Calder, M., Feamster, N., Chetty, M., Calandro, E., Katz-Bassett, E.: Peering at the internet's frontier: a first look at ISP interconnectivity in Africa. In: Faloutsos, M., Kuzmanovic, A. (eds.) PAM 2014. LNCS, vol. 8362, pp. 204–213. Springer, Cham (2014). https://doi.org/10.1007/978-3-319-04918-2_20

12. He, Y., Siganos, G., Faloutsos, M., Krishnamurthy, S.V.: Lord of the links: a framework for discovering missing links in the internet topology. IEEE/ACM Trans. Netw. **17**(2), 391–404 (2009)
13. Li, L., Alderson, D., Willinger, W., Doyle, J.: A first-principles approach to understanding the internet's router-level topology. ACM SIGCOMM Comput. Commun. Rev. **34**(4), 3–14 (2004)
14. Luckie, M., Huffaker, B., Dhamdhere, A., Giotsas, V., Claffy, K.C.: AS relationships, customer cones, and validation. In: Proceedings of the 13th ACM SIGCOMM Conference on Internet Measurement, IMC 2013, pp. 243–256 (2013)
15. Mahadevan, P., Krioukov, D., Fomenkov, M., Dimitropoulos, X., Claffy, K.C., Vahdat, A.: The Internet AS-level topology: three data sources and one definitive metric. ACM SIGCOMM Comput. Commun. Rev. **36**(1), 17–26 (2006)
16. Motamedi, R., Rejaie, R., Willinger, W.: A survey of techniques for internet topology discovery. IEEE Commun. Surv. Tutor. **17**(2), 1044–1065 (2015)
17. Norton, W.B.: The Internet Peering Playbook: Connecting to the Core of the Internet. DrPeering Press, Palo Alto (2011)
18. Nyirenda-Jere T., Biru T.: Internet development and Internet governance in Africa. https://www.internetsociety.org/doc/internet-development-and-internet-governance-africa. Accessed 06 June 2018
19. Oliveira, R., Pei, D., Willinger, W., Zhang, B., Zhang, L.: The (in)completeness of the observed internet AS-level structure. IEEE/ACM Trans. Netw. **18**(1), 109–122 (2010)
20. Rasti, A.H., Magharei, N., Rejaie, R., Willinger, W.: Eyeball ASes: from geography to connectivity. In: Proceedings of the 10th ACM SIGCOMM Conference on Internet Measurement, IMC 2010, pp. 192–198 (2010)
21. Roughan, M., Tuke, S.J., Maennel, O.: Bigfoot, Sasquatch, the Yeti and other missing links: what we don't know about the AS graph. In: Proceedings of the 8th ACM SIGCOMM Conference on Internet Measurement, IMC 2008, pp. 325–330 (2008)
22. Roughan, M., Willinger, W., Maennel, O., Perouli, D., Bush, R.: 10 lessons from 10 years of measuring and modeling the internet's autonomous systems. IEEE J. Sel. Areas Commun. **29**(9), 1810–1821 (2011)
23. Willinger, W., Alderson, D., Doyle, J.C.: Mathematics and the internet: a source of enormous confusion and great potential. Not. Am. Math. Soc. **56**(5), 586–599 (2009)
24. World Bank: World development report 2016: digital dividends. http://documents.worldbank.org/curated/en/896971468194972881/World-development-report-2016-digital-dividends. Accessed 06 June 2018
25. Zhang, B., Liu, R., Massey, D., Zhang, L.: Collecting the internet AS-level topology. ACM SIGCOMM Comput. Commun. Rev. **35**(1), 53–61 (2005)

Ego-Centered View to Overcome the Internet Measurement Challenges in West Africa

Frédéric Tounwendyam Ouédraogo[1(✉)], Tegawendé F. Bissyandé[2], Abdoulaye Séré[3], and Mesmin Djandjnou[3]

[1] Université Norbert Zongo, BP 376, Av. M. Yameogo, Koudougou, Burkina Faso
ouedraogo.tounwendyam@yahoo.fr
[2] Université Ouaga 1 Pr Joseph Ki-Zerbo, BP 7021, Av. CDG, Ouaga, Burkina Faso
tegawende.bissyande@uni.lu
[3] Université Nazi Boni, BP 1091, Bobo, Burkina Faso
abdoulayesere@gmail.com, dandjimes@yahoo.fr

Abstract. Measuring the Internet topology in West Africa is a challenge that can be overcome. We propose in this paper to perform ego-centered view measurement of the topology. We show that the obtained graph is relevant qualitatively to represent the topology. The lack of Internet Exchange points between Internet service providers in West Africa leads to high diameter in the topology, which is the result of a poor collaboration among such providers in this geographical area of the Internet. The appearance of "bogon" IP addresses in our measurements reveals a weak administration policy in this part of the Internet.

Keywords: Internet · Measurement · West Africa · Topology

1 Introduction

Many studies have been done to provide better tools and methods to measure the Internet topology [9,11,12,15,17]. Most measurement methods consist to perform traceroute-like measurement from several machines during a period of time [1]. But studying the Internet topology in West Africa remains a challenge. The instability of connection and the selective power cuts due to the insufficiency of electrical power in West Africa countries make difficult such measurement of the Internet topology.

In this paper, we present an approach of measurement in the West Africa context that consists to perform ego-centered measurement of the topology. Instead of trying to measure the entire West Africa Internet, we focus on what a single machine can see of the topology. We obtain a tree structure that is relevant to analyze in networking. We perform two-day measurement with the TRACETREE tool [11], using many sets of destinations chosen randomly among more than three million of major IP addresses blocks allocated to West Africa countries.

© ICST Institute for Computer Sciences, Social Informatics and Telecommunications Engineering 2018
V. Odumuyiwa et al. (Eds.): AFRICOMM 2017, LNICST 250, pp. 377–383, 2018.
https://doi.org/10.1007/978-3-319-98827-6_36

We obtain a graph representing the topology by the union of round measurements. We analyze this graph through some properties like the diameter, the distribution of degrees that are used to characterize complex networks. The first researchers in the field of complex networks have shown how these properties play a key role in the robustness of the Internet [4,5].

Despite the fact that our measurement is a small sample, we find a distribution of degree like that of the Internet. Among the IP addresses observed by our measurement, many of them are located outside the Africa continent. This means a weak collaboration between the Internet service providers (ISP) in West Africa. Internet exchange points (IXP) should be established between them.

The rest of the paper is organized as follows; Sect. 2 presents ego-centered view approach and the measurements; Sect. 3 gives main properties of the obtained graph. In Sect. 4, we present a discussion of our results.

2   Approach and Measurement

Most campaigns of Internet measurement are based on traceroute-like tools. It consists to perform paths measurement from computers called sources towards set of target IP addresses called destinations. The main challenges with this method are the choice of suitable sources and destinations allowing to see more the topology and the bias on the measurement due to the tool [1].

We do not aim to map the entire topology of West-Africa Internet but only on what a single machine can see of this topology [11,13]. The approach has been used to study the dynamics of the Internet in previous work and measurement tool TRACETREE has been designed for this purpose.

The TRACETREE output is a tree which is made by routes between the monitor(root) and the destinations(leaves). The obtained tree is an ego-centered view of the topology around the monitor. The recommended number of destinations must not exceed 3 000 to avoid overload the network traffic near the monitor. For more description of TRACETREE tool, see [11].

For this work, we have chosen randomly the destinations among 3 millions major IP addresses blocks allocated by AFRINIC [2] to 12 countries in West-Africa. These are Benin, Burkina Faso, Cote d'ivoire, Ghana, Guinée, Liberia, Mali, Niger, Nigeria, Sierra Leone, Sénégal and Togo.

We used three different sets of 500, 1 000 and 3 000 destinations. We make sure that the IP addresses reply to ping when chosen. For each set of destinations, we have performed 100 rounds of TRACETREE measurements with a monitor located in Ouagadougou. There is a delay of 10 min between consecutive rounds, representing two-day measurement. We finally merged the outputs of the TRACETREE measurements, which is a graph representing what the monitor may see of the topology.

3   Properties

In this section we present basic properties of ego-centered views. We analyze the Internet topology of West-Africa comparatively to the results observed with other measurements.

Figure 1 shows that the number of IP addresses observed at each round increases when the number of destination grows. Each round measurement sees the number of IP addresses nearly equal to the number of destinations used. This lower number of observed IP addresses is due to the fact that some routers do not reply to the ICMP echo-reply probe. In addition, many destinations, randomly chosen may be unreachables or belong to the same network.

Moreover, with 3 000 destinations, the number of IP addresses seen is even lower and do not reach the number of destinations used. The number of IP addresses seen during the hundred rounds is not high comparatively to usual measurements, 452 for the set1 of 500 destinations, 482 for the set2 of 1 000 destinations and 1005 for the set3 of 3 000 destinations. This observation shows a weak density of the topology of West Africa Internet. With other measurements the number of IP addresses seen at each round is three time the number of destinations used [11, 13].

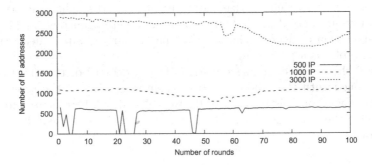

Fig. 1. Number of IP addresses observed at each round measurement for 500, 1 000 and 3 000 destinations.

We performed trial measurement with destinations without test them to ping. We observed at each round a number of IP addresses less than the half of the number of destinations. However, with the set of destinations were responding to ping before the measurement the 100 rounds of TRACETREE measurements did not allow to reach them all, see Table 1. The destinations unreached may be hidden by firewalls, the routing dynamics or they are simply out of the Internet during the measurement.

The diameter of a graph is defined as the highest distance that exists between any two vertices in the graph. The distance between two vertices is the smallest path between these vertices. The diameter is an important characteristic of the communication in a network. It characterizes the ability of two nodes to

Table 1. Basic properties of the graph of ego-centered views.

Destinations	IP addresses seen	Unreached destinations	Max degree	Diameter
set1: 500	891	61	150	28
set2: 1 000	1579	98	302	39
set3: 3 000	3341	204	837	30

communicate with each other. The smaller the diameter is, the better is the communication between them. The diameter does not grow linearly with the number of nodes. For instance the diameter of the graph of the Web with nearly one billion nodes is around 20 [3].

The diameter of the West Africa Internet topology is 30 for the measurement of the set of three thousand destinations that we consider more representative of the topology. We find this value of the diameter is relatively high comparatively to other measurements of the whole Internet at different levels of the topology [3, 6].

The degree of a node in a graph is the number of links that connect it to its nearest neighbors. The degree of a node is an indicator of its importance for the communication in the network. Obviously, more the node has a high degree, more it is important for the communication between the nodes. The distribution of degrees is used to characterize the types of networks. There are two main types of distribution of degrees, homogeneous and heterogeneous. The heterogeneous distribution of degrees characterizes particularly complex networks. The distribution follows a power-law.

Figure 2 shows the cumulative distribution of degrees of the graph of 3341 nodes obtained with the union of 100 ego-centered views of the topology. We find an heterogeneous distribution of degrees of nodes. There is around 86% of nodes having the degree less or equal than 2 whereas 1.4% of them has a degree more than 10.

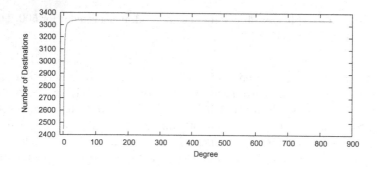

Fig. 2. Distribution of degrees of the graph obtained by the union of 100 ego-centered view measurements with 3 000 destinations.

Despite we focus on small part of the topology we find a distribution of degrees similar to those of complex networks. This result shows the relevance of our approach based on ego-centered view measurement of the topology.

4 Discussion

This work raises interesting questions on the evolution of the Internet topology in West Africa countries and the challenges to overcome regarding to topology measurement in this part of world. Many campaigns of Internet topology measurement have been made around the world but unfortunately the participation at these campaigns of Africa continent or West Africa region in particular is not enough [14–16,18]. Mostly, the campaign of Internet measurement is based on volunteers provides their computers connected to Internet to run measurement software during several weeks or months. This last condition make difficult to African volunteers to take part of these measurements. For instance, RIPE Atlas project provides measurement probes to anybody making request to participate [15]. The volunteers are free access to the measurement platform to perform their own measurement between the computers hosting the probes. Firstly, there are few volunteers in West Africa and secondly most of their computers are frequently offline, certainly due to problems of Internet connection or power cut.

We observed among the IP addresses seen by our measurement, 502 of them that are not in the major IP addresses blocks allocated by AFRINIC to twelve countries of West Africa. We made use of the Regional Internet Registry (RIR) service WHOIS to know what countries these IP addresses have been allocated. We found that most of these IP addresses belong to Countries out of Africa (Europe and USA). The presence of these IP addresses in our measurement demonstrates that some traffic have to pass by other continent before backing to the destinations located in West Africa. It appears clearly that there is not enough collaboration between the Internet service providers in West Africa countries. They have to put more Internet exchange points (IXP) in place.

Among the IP addresses that we observed in our measurement we found around ten *bogon*[1] IP addresses. Particularly, the IP addresses 10.93.187.25, 10.93.96.153 are important by their highest degrees.

A packet routed over the public Internet should never have a source address in a *bogon* list. The presence of these addresses in our measurement shows a problem of network administration that does not filter *bogon* addresses. *Team Cymru*[2] publishes a list of prefix *bogon* for this purposes.

5 Related Work

Internet measurement is among the research areas that needs more investigation in Africa. Nevertheless, there exists qualitative results showing how the state

---

[1] A *bogon* prefix is a route that should never appear in the Internet routing table.

[2] Team Cymru Research NFP is an Illinois non-profit and a US Federal organization.

and the challenges of the Internet in Africa [7,8,10]. The authors of this contribution [8] concerning the accessibility of the Web content in Africa point out clearly a poor inter-AS communication is Africa. The outcome of their work is similar to ours that shows the lack of Internet Exchange points between Internet Service Providers in West Africa.

Africa has known an emergence of IXP in the recent years but not enough solve the improve the communication between Internet Service Providers inside the continent. In previous work [7], the authors study the influence of the emergence of these IXP on AS path length. Their results show a major contribution of ISP located outside the Africa continent to the intra-continental paths.

Our work is related to this studies presented above but we emphasize however that our main track concerns the Internet mapping in Africa.

6   Conclusion and Perspectives

We presented the ego-centered view approach that we used to measure the Internet topology in West Africa. We showed that the obtained graph is relevant qualitatively to represent the topology. We analyzed the graph and found interesting results. The distribution of degrees is heterogeneous, similar to that of the Internet. But the diameter is high compared to other measures of the Internet. This high diameter is certainly due to presence of IP addresses located outside the African continent in the measurements.

This work could be considered as preliminary to an extended measure. For future work, it may be worthwhile to increase the number of sources of measure, in all the countries concerned.

References

1. Achlioptas, D., Clauset, A., Kempe, D., Moore, C.: On the bias of traceroute sampling, or: why almost every network looks like it has a power law. In: ACM Symposium on Theory of Computing (STOC 2005) (2005)
2. AFRINIC: Africa countries ip addresses allocation or assignement. ftp://ftp.afrinic.net/pub/stats/afrinic
3. Albert, R., Jeong, H., Barabási, A.L.: The diameter of the world wide web. arXiv preprint cond-mat/9907038 (1999)
4. Albert, R., Jeong, H., Barabási, A.L.: Error and attack tolerance of complex networks. arXiv preprint cond-mat/0008064 (2000)
5. Faloutsos, M., Faloutsos, P., Faloutsos, C.: On power-law relationships of the internet topology. In: Proceedings of the Conference on Applications, Technologies, Architectures, and Protocols for Computer Communication, SIGCOMM 1999, pp. 251–262. ACM, New York (1999). https://doi.org/10.1145/316188.316229
6. Faloutsos, M., Faloutsos, P., Faloutsos, C.: On power-law relationships of the internet topology. SIGCOMM Comput. Commun. Rev. 29(4), 251–262 (1999). https://doi.org/10.1145/316194.316229
7. Fanou, R., Francois, P., Aben, E.: On the diversity of interdomain routing in Africa. In: Mirkovic, J., Liu, Y. (eds.) PAM 2015. LNCS, vol. 8995, pp. 41–54. Springer, Cham (2015). https://doi.org/10.1007/978-3-319-15509-8_4

8. Fanou, R., Tyson, G., Francois, P., Sathiaseelan, A.: Pushing the frontier: exploring the African web ecosystem. In: Proceedings of the 25th International Conference on World Wide Web, WWW 2016, pp. 435–445 (2016). https://doi.org/10.1145/2872427.2882997. International World Wide Web Conferences Steering Committee, Republic and Canton of Geneva, Switzerland
9. Govindan, R., Tangmunarunkit, H.: Heuristics for internet map discovery. In: IEEE INFOCOM 2000, Tel Aviv, pp. 1371–1380 (2000)
10. Johnson, D.L., Pejovic, V., Belding, E.M., van Stam, G.: Traffic characterization and internet usage in rural Africa. In: Proceedings of the 20th International Conference Companion on World Wide Web, WWW 2011, pp. 493–502. ACM, New York (2011). https://doi.org/10.1145/1963192.1963363
11. Latapy, M., Magnien, C., Ouédraogo, F.: A radar for the internet. In: Workshops Proceedings of the 8th IEEE International Conference on Data Mining (ICDM 2008), 15–19 December 2008, Pisa, Italy, pp. 901–908. IEEE Computer Society (2008). https://doi.org/10.1109/ICDMW.2008.121
12. Latapy, M., Rotenberg, E., Crespelle, C., Tarissan, F.: Rigorous measurement of the internet degree distribution. Complex Syst. 26(1) (2017)
13. Magnien, C., Ouedraogo, F., Valadon, G., Latapy, M.: Fast dynamics in internet topology: observations and first explanations. In: Proceedings of the 2009 Fourth International Conference on Internet Monitoring and Protection, ICIMP 2009, pp. 137–142. IEEE Computer Society, Washington, DC (2009). https://doi.org/10.1109/ICIMP.2009.29
14. Internet maps from mercator. http://www.isi.edu/div7/scan/mercator/maps.html
15. Ripe network coordination centre: Ripe atlas. https://atlas.ripe.net/
16. PLANETLAB: Planetlab. https://www.planet-lab.org/
17. Shavitt, Y., Shir, E.: Dimes: let the internet measure itself. SIGCOMM Comput. Commun. Rev. 35(5), 71–74 (2005). https://doi.org/10.1145/1096536.1096546
18. Caida - skitter project. http://www.caida.org/tools/measurement/skitter/

Author Index

Printed in the United States
By Bookmasters